Map Legend

▭▭▭	Freeway
▭ ▭ ▭ ▭	Freeway (under construction)
═══	Dual Carriageway
═══	Main Road
═══	Secondary Road
═══	Minor road
───	Track
▬▬▬	Regional Boundary
─ ─ ─ ─	Province Boundary
▬▬▬	World Heritage Area
─ ▪ ─	National Park/Reserve
─ ─ ─ ─	Ferry Route
✈ ✈	Airport
✝ ✝	Church (ruins)
✝	Monastery
∴	Archaeological Site
∩	Cave
★	Place of Interest
⌂	Mansion/Stately Home
✳	Viewpoint
⚑	Beach
═══	Freeway
───	Highway
─── }	Main Roads
─── }	Minor Roads
───	Footpath
▭	Pedestrian Area
▬	Important Building
▭	Park
❶	Numbered Sight
🚌	Bus Station
❶	Tourist Information
✉	Post Office
✝	Cathedral/Church
☪	Mosque
✡	Synagogue
⚑	Statue/Monument
▯	Tower
⚓	Lighthouse

INSIGHT GUIDES
New SOUTH WaLES

APA PUBLICATIONS
Part of the Langenscheidt Publishing Group

ABERDEENSHIRE LIBRARY AND

INFORMATION SERVICES

New South Wales
[1 book, 1 map]

HJ   489414

919.44   99

2550269   PORP

919.
44

INSIGHT GUIDE
New SOUTH Wales

Editor
Jerry Dennis
Managing Editor
Tom Le Bas
Art Director
Klaus Geisler
Picture Editor
Hilary Genin
Production
Kenneth Chan
Cartography Editor
Zoë Goodwin

Distribution

Australia
Universal Publishers
1 Waterloo Road
Macquarie Park, NSW 2113
Fax: (61) 2 9888 9074

New Zealand
Hema Maps New Zealand Ltd (HNZ)
Unit D, 24 Ra ORA Drive
East Tamaki, Auckland
Fax: (64) 9 273 6479

UK & Ireland
GeoCenter International Ltd
Meridian House, Churchill Way West
Basingstoke, Hampshire RG21 6YR
Fax: (44) 1256-817988

United States
Langenscheidt Publishers, Inc.
36–36 33rd Street, 4th Floor
Long Island City, NY 11106
Fax: (1) 718 784-0640

Worldwide
Apa Publications GmbH & Co.
Verlag KG (Singapore branch)
38 Joo Koon Road, Singapore 628990
Tel: (65) 6865-1600. Fax: (65) 6861-6438

Printing

Insight Print Services (Pte) Ltd
38 Joo Koon Road, Singapore 628990
Tel: (65) 6865-1600. Fax: (65) 6861-6438

©2006 Apa Publications GmbH & Co.
Verlag KG (Singapore branch)
All Rights Reserved

First Edition 2006

ABOUT THIS BOOK

The first Insight Guide pioneered the use of creative full-colour photography in guidebooks in 1970. Since then, we have expanded our range to cater for our readers' need not only for reliable information about their chosen destination but also for a real understanding of that destination. Now, when the internet can supply inexhaustible (but not always reliable) facts, our books marry text and pictures to provide that much more elusive quality: knowledge. To achieve this, they rely heavily on the authority of locally based writers and photographers.

How to use this book

The book is structured to convey an understanding of New South Wales and the Australian Capital Territory:
◆ To understand the region today, you need to know something of its past. The first section covers its people, history and culture in lively essays written by specialists.
◆ The main Places section provides a full run-down of all the attractions worth seeing. The main places of interest are coordinated by number with full-colour maps. Margin notes provide background information and tips on how to save time and money.
◆ Photographic features illuminate the state's sports, wines, festivals, Canberra's two parliaments, and the local penchant for "big things".
◆ Photographs are chosen not only to illustrate landscapes and buildings but also to convey the life of the people of New South Wales.
◆ The Travel Tips listings section provides information on getting around, hotels, activities, etc. Information may be located quickly by using the index printed on the back cover flap.

of fascination. His work appears in *The Australian*, *Good Medicine*, and a number of in-flight publications.

The features on People, Coastal Living and the Arts were written by **Storry Walton**, whose long career has seen him fulfil the roles of producer, director, writer and manager in TV, film and the visual and performing arts, with *My Brother Jack* and *The Stranger* (for ABC television) amongst his credits. He also spent seven years working in the Outback for the Royal Flying Doctor Service. He is a writer on rural issues for *RM Williams Outback Magazine* and *Frontier News*.

Other contributors include **Zora Simic**, author of the History feature, who teaches Australian history at the University of Melbourne and is a contributor to *The Monthly* magazine; and **Michael Shafran**, who wrote the food and wine feature. The former chief sub-editor of *Delicious* magazine and a leading food and travel writer in Australia, he is a regular contributor to *Vogue Entertaining and Travel*, *Delicious* and *GQ Australia*.

The Travel Tips section was researched by **Christine Long**, a journalist of several years' experience, with *The Age*, *Sydney Morning Herald* and *Travel and Leisure Australia* on her CV.

At Insight's editorial office in London, Managing Editor **Tom Le Bas** kept the book on track, steering it through the editing process with the help of **Lesley Gordon** and **Alexia Georgiou**. **Neil Titman** proofread the text and **Isobel Mclean** compiled the index.

The contributors

This new *Insight Guide: New South Wales* has been put together by Commissioning Editor **Jerry Dennis**, who also took the bulk of the photographs. Based in Melbourne, he has laboured on countless Insight Guides, primarily as a photographer, and his work has appeared in travel publications and other media for many years.

Jerry enlisted the skills of several writers and researchers with specialist knowledge of the state, chief among whom was **Michael Gebicki**, who wrote the Places section. Michael is a Sydney-based writer who has spent much of the past two decades with a camera in one hand and a notebook in the other, tools which have brought a sense of purpose to his impulsive wanderings. Although he is often far from home, New South Wales remains a source

CONTACTING THE EDITORS

We would appreciate it if readers would alert us to errors or outdated information by writing to:

Insight Guides, P.O. Box 7910, London SE1 1WE, England. Fax: (44) 20 7403-0290. insight@apaguide.co.uk

NO part of this book may be reproduced, stored in a retrieval system or transmitted in any form or means electronic, mechanical, photocopying, recording or otherwise, without prior written permission of *Apa Publications*. Brief text quotations with use of photographs are exempted for book review purposes only. Information has been obtained from sources believed to be reliable, but its accuracy and completeness, and the opinions based thereon, are not guaranteed.

www.insightguides.com
In North America:
www.insighttravelguides.com

Contents

LEFT: Sydney's Luna
Park funfair.

Travel Tips

THE BEST OF NEW SOUTH WALES

Fabulous beaches, activities for children, galleries and museums, shopping and gourmet delights… Here, at a glance, are our top recommendations for a visit

MAJOR HIGHLIGHTS

- **Sydney Harbour**
  The best-known sight in the state and, with its balance of scenic beauty and human ingenuity, there is no better advertisement for the country. *See pages 67–103.*
- **The Outback**
  It's impossible to understand Australia without venturing into the Outback. There are many opportunities to do so in New South Wales. *See pages 167–94.*
- **The Beaches**
  From Bondi to all points north and south, beaches colour the lifestyle and character of the people. *See pages 96–97.*

- **Snowy Mountains**
  A must for skiers in the winter and a favourite destination for hikers during the. rest of the year. *See pages 153–7.*
- **Wine**
  The Hunter Valley *is* wine tourism and tempts visitors with luxurious accommodation and gourmet food. Other areas are on the case though. *See pages 204–7.*
- **Byron Bay**
  The northern coastal beauty spot where hedonists, rich and poor, congregate to make the most of the beaches, festivals and alternative lifestyle. *See pages 243–5.*

ABOVE: Sydney Harbour at sunset.
BELOW: koala cuddling is an option at Sydney's Taronga Zoo.

FOR FAMILIES

- **Sydney Powerhouse Museum**
  Kids can't keep their hands off the exhibits in this dynamic museum. Fortunately that's the point. *See page 86.*

- **Mogo Zoo**
  Visit the only white lions in the country along with a selection of other rare and endangered animals. *See page 128.*
- **Luna Park**
  A 1930s-style amusement park pitched just under Sydney Harbour Bridge. *See page 68.*
- **Questacon, Canberra**
  Fascinating hands-on fun with science and technology on the shores of Lake Burley Griffin. *See page 141.*

ART GALLERIES AND MUSEUMS

- **National Gallery, Canberra**
Repository of many of the finest artworks in the country, including the quirky Sidney Nolan series of Ned Kelly paintings. *See page 140.*
- **Museum of Sydney**
Sophisticated displays interpret the harbour city's history and character. *See page 76.*
- **Wollongong City Gallery**
This sizeable gallery specialises in 20th-century and Aboriginal art. *See page 118.*
- **Norman Lindsay Gallery, Blue Mountains** Magic Pudding mixed with pneumatic nudes at the artist's home. *See page 110.*

- **Sculpture symposium, Broken Hill**
Sandstone carvings planted in a gorgeous hilltop setting in the Outback just outside the character-filled historic mining town. *See page 176.*
- **New England Regional Art Museum, Armidale**
Exemplary collection of Australian art including almost all of the big names, put together by one man. *See page 222.*
- **Bradman Museum**
Learn about "the Don" in this museum in Bowral, his home territory, and get to grips with the history of cricket in Australia. *See page 120.*

WILDLIFE SPOTTING

- **Pebbly Beach**
Nothing beats that first glimpse of a fore-shore crowded with frolicking kangaroos. There are often rosellas on your car too. *See page 127.*
- **Whale Watching off Port Stephens**
Off Nelson Bay during the season you're almost guaranteed a sighting of these awe-inspiring mammals. *See page 234.*

- **Western Plains Zoo, Dubbo**
See a selection of Australian animals and international visitors in this open-range zoo. *See page 188.*
- **Dolphin Watching at Jervis Bay**
Take a boat trip to find and follow a pod of dolphins and come away with the distinct impression that they're playing with you. *See page 125.*

ABOVE RIGHT: a kangaroo preparing to frolic at Pebbly Beach.
BELOW: stained glass in the Bradman Museum in Bowral.
BELOW RIGHT: the Telstra Tower in Canberra.

STRUCTURES AND QUIRKY STUFF

- **Parkes Radio Telescope**
See more of the cosmos through the star of the film *The Dish*. *See page 187.*
- **The Big Banana**
Australia's first "big thing" lurks just outside Coffs Harbour. *See pages 250–1.*
- **Byron Bay Lighthouse**
Historic structure in a beautiful setting at the easternmost point of the Australian mainland. *See page 243.*

- **Telstra Tower**
Take the lift up to the viewing platform for panoramic views over Canberra and the ACT. *See page 145.*

EATING (TYPES OF FOOD)

- **Fish**
  New South Wales has one long coastline so there's a huge amount of fresh fish landed daily. There's also freshwater fish farming inland.
- **Fruit**
  Big bananas around Coffs Harbour, oranges down at Wentworth, cherries at Young – the list could take you state wide.
- **Oysters**
  Something of a staple. *The Oyster Farmer* has brought fame to the Hawkesbury beds but there are many other areas.
- **Pork**
  Bangalow pork is some of the most tender you will ever eat.

ABOVE RIGHT: a plate of fish and make it snapper. **BELOW:** eucalypts in Mutawintji National Park. **RIGHT:** Gundagai Post Office. **BELOW RIGHT:** Royal NP's coastal track is one of many in NSW.

COLONIAL STREETSCAPES

- **Broken Hill**
  Prosperity from mining brought grand civic buildings and a surfeit of drinking establishments. *See pages 174–6.*
- **Bathurst**
  Streets of preserved Victoriana culminate in the splendid Italianate courthouse. *See pages 184–5.*
- **Bellingen**
  Lovely weatherboard cottages, and a shopping strip featuring an unspoiled original department store. *See pages 237–8.*
- **Central Tilba**
  A picturesque village on the slopes of Mount Dromedary just inland from the south coast, it appears entirely unmodernised. *See page 129.*
- **Gundagai**
  A well-preserved railway station, immaculate post office and a hill setting for its high street all suggest a visit. *See page 157.*

NATIONAL PARKS

- **Kosciuszko**
  Dramatic alpine scenery that takes in the heart of the Snowy Mountains and includes the ski fields. *See pages 154–6.*
- **Sturt**
  Dramatic "jump-ups" or mesas in the top inland corner of the state. *See page 178.*
- **Barrington Tops**
  A high plateau with cliffs, waterfalls, rainforest and strands of beech woods. Good hiking country. *See pages 209–11.*
- **Mutawintji**
  Stark, red Outback country pocked with tree-filled gorges. *See pages 177–8.*
- **Royal**
  Sydney's vast back yard with its famed coastal tracks. *See pages 98–9.*
- **Bald Rock**
  Vast granite outcrop on the far northern border. *See page 228.*
- **Blue Mountains**
  A string of hill towns give access to another of the state's wonders. *See pages 109–14.*

SHOPPING IN SYDNEY

- **Queen Victoria Building**
Many exclusive boutiques, including several international brand outlets, have made their home in this sumptuously renovated block. *See page 82.*
- **Paddington Market**
Every Saturday in the

grounds of St John's Church, this is the place for hand-crafted jewellery and other hand-crafted artefacts. *See page 94.*
- **Strand Arcade**
Stunningly preserved two story arcade in the heart of the city with an array of small shops selling upmarket wares to the discerning. *See page 83.*
- **Paddy's Market**
The city's oldest market features a complete hotch potch of goods from fruit and vegetables through to the tackiest of tourist souvenirs. *See page 86.*
- **The Rocks**
With every visitor to the city passing through at some stage, this area is packed with opportu-

nities for the serious souvenir hunter. Pick up a didgeridoo, a Ken Done print or an Opera House mug. A craft and antiques market takes over the

streets at the weekend. *See pages 69–70.*
- **Pitt Street Mall**
The place for big city stores and large branches of chains. *See page 83.*

ABOVE: flower flourisher. **LEFT:** the Strand Arcade. **BELOW:** Australia was the first country to introduce polymer bank notes.

MONEY-SAVING TIPS

BYO There are restaurants and cafes across New South Wales which do not have licenses to sell alcohol but are happy for you to bring your own (advertised as BYO), for which they add a small corkage charge to the bill. This not only allows wine buffs to drink exactly what they want with their meal but also seriously reduces the cost of dining out. Even some establishments that do have licenses will allow BYO wine but the corkage tends to be set a bit higher and you need to look at the marginal benefits.

Reciprocal benefits Your interstate or overseas motoring organisation or National Trust membership cards may well give you reciprocal rights in New South Wales.

Tipping Many visitors from overseas are surprised that there is not the same culture of tipping in Australia as there is elsewhere. You will not be expected to tip taxi drivers or hairdressers and even in restaurants you only tip if you are genuinely pleased with the service, and then it's more a case of rounding up the bill than working out a percentage.

Incidentally, most taxis are equipped to take credit cards, which can make that first trip from the airport a lot easier.

Halftix If you are in Sydney and looking for some last-minute entertainment then see what's on offer at a Halftix outlet. It is a clearance house for unsold tickets to theatre, concerts, sporting and other events and offers inexpensive tickets – often half price – on the day of performance. You have a better chance of bargains on quieter nights (usually earlier in the week) and if you are flexible in your choices. Some theatre companies also sell unsold tickets cheaply around a half hour before the performance starts, direct from the venue.

QUITE A STATE

Few can deny that Sydney is the iconic city of Australia.
But besides that, New South Wales has attractions
galore, and it's about time they shared
in some of its limelight

For so many visitors, the first place they see in New South Wales is Sydney. Indeed, for travellers from overseas it is often the first place they see in all of Australia. It certainly makes one big impression: the harbour, the bridge, the opera house and little secondary features such as Bondi or Darling Harbour. So relish it, wallow in it, and pack away those first memories that will last a lifetime. But don't forget there's a whole state out there offering an immeasurably wider and richer experience. And that's before we get to Canberra.

Outside Sydney the scale of things changes. The country seems wider, the sky bigger and, as soon as you start travelling between towns or regions, you begin to appreciate what a vast state this is. However, in human terms everything is so much smaller. There are no other population centres remotely approaching the size of Sydney, and its cosmopolitan, sophisticated take on life is rarely encountered elsewhere. For the most part, people are entirely happy with that.

This is a land of country towns founded on agriculture or mining, and of coastal communities increasingly given over to service industries and tourism. A shade over 200 years since the foundation of the colony, and it's all quite settled. The extremes of climate, like the cyclones that batter Queensland and other northern states, don't ruffle this part of the country, and it's only in the far western Outback that you get a sense of communities clinging onto an inhospitable continent by their fingertips.

Decide what you want to get out of the place. If you are adventurous and want to immerse yourself in the stark remoteness of the Outback, then head west in a four-wheel drive. If that's too ambitious, but you still want to experience the natural environment, then look to the Snowy Mountains, Barrington Tops or one of the many other national parks scattered across the landscape. If country comforts are your thing head to the Blue Mountains, Southern Highlands, Hunter Valley or up around Byron Bay. And if none of these appeal? Well, you're either a politician in Canberra or you're at the beach already and will probably get round to reading the rest of this book *mañana*. ❑

PRECEDING PAGES: Pacific swells make the New South Wales coast a fantastic place for surfing; outback scenery at the opposite end of the state. **LEFT:** heading into the Warrambungles National Park.

NEW SOUTH WALES – THE FIRST STATE

Most of the people shipped to Australia in the 18th and 19th centuries chose to stay in this land of opportunity. Among them were the talented and hard-working people who founded the first state

Australia was "born" in New South Wales, and, not surprisingly, the state has a confident history and character, nowhere more obvious than in Sydney, its capital city. Sydney is simultaneously metropolis and seaside paradise, attracting more visitors than any other Australian capital and laying claim to a wealth of heritage. These enticing qualities have sometimes had the effect of eclipsing the rest of the state, in much the same way NSW has occasionally subsumed the whole of Australian history within its borders. Yet from the old mining town of Broken Hill in the west to Byron Bay on the lush north coast and the Blue Mountains outside Sydney, NSW is rich in iconoclastic cities, towns and stories.

Power and influence

If geographical and historical diversity were not enough, NSW has other persuasive claims to its premier status. It is pre-eminent in resources, people and international recognition. At its foundation it encompassed two-thirds of the continent. From NSW, four other colonies were carved – Tasmania in 1825, South Australia in 1836, Victoria in 1851 and Queensland in 1859. Of Australia's two territories, the first, the Northern Territory, was separated from NSW in 1869. The second, the Australian Capital Territory, was created within its borders in 1911 as a solution to the Sydney–Melbourne rivalry over the nation's appropriate capital. Melbourne did once have

LEFT: Sydney Cove soon after settlement.
RIGHT: the First Fleet in Sydney Cove in 1788.

legitimate claims to the role, but in contemporary Australia it is Sydney that functions as a *de facto* centre of political and financial power. Long-serving prime minister John Howard, a native Sydneysider, even took the decision to reside in the Victorian Gothic grandeur of Kirribilli House on the foreshores of Sydney's harbour rather than the Lodge in Canberra.

Meanwhile, the nation's most popular armchair sport, real-estate speculation, is most exuberant in New South Wales. And if Sydney lags behind Melbourne in attracting world-class sporting events, it can afford to bask in the afterglow of the successful 2000 Olympic Games for some time yet. New South Wales isn't immune from state rivalries, but as the state by which all others are judged, it's not required to take them seriously.

First contact

Sydney Harbour is the gateway to the city, the state, the country. Yet when the first people arrived in what is now Sydney the harbour did not exist; it was a dry valley about 10 km (6 miles) inland. This was more than 40,000 years ago, when northern Aboriginal people arrived to begin a life on the land that would sustain them for thousands of years. In 1987, stone tools dating back 45,000 years were discovered near the town of Richmond,

gate the east coast properly and the first to proclaim British sovereignty when he declared the east coast from Bass Strait to Cape York "New South Wales" in 1770. He was also the first maritime explorer to record contact with the Eora people of the "fine meadow" he would name Botany Bay. Cook commented: "All they seem'd to want is for us to be gone." Cook's *Endeavour* would spend only a week in Botany Bay, but the seeds of destruction for Sydney's Aboriginal people had been sown.

Within 20 years, the British would return, freshly interested in the Great South Land after the American War of Independence ended the flow of British convicts to southern

40 km (25 miles) from Sydney. Ice ages came and went, until the seas reached their present levels about 6,000 years ago, long before the arrival of the first Europeans.

At the time of the First Fleet's voyage to Australia in 1788, there were some 3,000 Aboriginal people residing in the wider Sydney area, with three broad languages between them – Kuring-gai was the language of the north shore, Dhurawal was spoken along the coast south of Botany Bay, and Dhurag and its dialects throughout the plains and mountains.

Captain James Cook was not the first European to sail the southern seas and skim the island-continent, but he was the first to navi-

US plantations. The *Endeavour's* botanist Joseph Banks had proposed that Botany Bay should receive a fleet of convicts. In August 1786, Home Secretary Lord Sydney approved, and the penal colony was established.

Voyage and settlement

On 13 May 1787, a fleet of 11 ships sailed from Portsmouth in England, bound for Botany Bay. Most of the 1,066 men, women and children on board were fitting occupants for the "colony of thieves", but they nonetheless proved themselves rather heroic in enduring a marathon voyage of just over eight months; 31 died along the way.

Led by Arthur Phillip, commodore and the first governor of NSW, the survivors reached the north shore of Botany Bay on 18 January 1788, but finding it unsatisfactory continued on to Port Jackson. Cook had noted and named the port, but it was Phillip who declared it to be "the finest harbour in the world". The whole colony settled by a small creek on Sydney Cove on Saturday, 26 January 1788, where Phillip declared British possession for the second time that month.

The first days of the colony were tough for the new arrivals, who struggled with the weather, poor resources and a reluctant convict labour force. The latter lived in tents

hateful as only to merit execration and curses". Only the arrival of supplies on the *Lady Juliana* saved the settlement from foundering. The arrival of the Second Fleet in the mid-1790s was a mixed blessing it brought fresh supplies, but a quarter of its prisoners perished on the voyage, more died on arrival and the survivors were incapable of work.

Gradually the settlers established themselves. By the end of 1792, when Phillip returned to England, there were 600 hectares (1,500 acres) under crop, and thriving fruit and vegetable gardens. There were fish in the harbour and pasture on the Cumberland Plain. The subsidiary town of Newcastle was estab-

before building their own houses, while the Aboriginal people kept their distance. Governor Phillip proposed a neatly planned settlement, but most settlers opted for convenience, establishing the haphazard routes that plague contemporary Sydney.

By April 1790 the settlers' weekly ration consisted of 1 kg (2 lb) of crumbling salt pork, 1 kg (2 lb) of weevil-ridden rice and 1.5 kg (3 lb) of old flour. The colonial surgeon wrote of "a country and place so forbidding and so

FAR LEFT: an attack on Captain Cook's camp, Cooktown. **LEFT:** convicts in chains c.1800.
ABOVE: working on a chain gang in 1848.

lished in 1797. The wool industry, the colony's first major export industry, was developed by John Macarthur and other enterprising settlers.

Still, survival was never assured, and Phillip and his successors (Governors Hunter, King and Bligh, who arrived some years after his crew staged a mutiny against him on the *Bounty*) faced convict rebellion. In 1804, Irish prisoners at Castle Hill Reserve rose against the government, and some 200 convicts set out to capture Parramatta, then tried to seize the ships in Sydney Harbour. Troops swiftly quelled what became known as the Battle of Vinegar Hill. Nine of the ringleaders were hanged and another nine men received 200 to

500 lashes. Four years later, Bligh was overthrown, not by convicts, but by his own officers of the New South Wales Corps in the Rum Rebellion. His authoritarianism was not appreciated in a colony where rum was currency.

From colony to community

Bligh was replaced by Governor Lachlan Macquarie, a builder, planner and reformer, who would leave an enduring mark on the colony during his 12-year term. Macquarie transformed the colony physically and socially. He established a bank, introduced currency and embarked on a programme of major public works, including a hospital sub-

stantial enough to serve still as a house of parliament. Even now Sydney bears the indelible stamp of Macquarie and his principal architect, Francis Greenaway, a forger, convict and architectural genius. Under the patronage of Macquarie, Greenaway designed some 40 buildings, including St James's Church in the City and the Hyde Park Barracks, for which achievement Macquarie granted him a pardon.

A benevolent despot, Macquarie regarded New South Wales as a place for "the reformation, as well as the punishment, of convicts". Greenaway was not the only talented and hard-working convict Macquarie would encourage and liberate. Other notables included the surgeon William Redfern and Michael Robinson, who became poet laureate. The promotion and entertainment of such men at the governor's table scandalised the free settlers and initially amused those back in London. Observing the prosperity of the colony, a British Treasury official asked in 1820: "Is there no way to get to New South Wales but by stealing?"

Eventually, Commissioner John Bigge was dispatched to NSW to enquire into its prospects as both colony and gaol, with a focus on the latter. It was emphasised that transportation should be "a real object of terror". Accordingly, the three reports presented in 1822–3 did not validate Macquarie's style. The Bigge Commission effectively ended the Macquarie period, as the dividing line between the free and the imprisoned was re-inscribed with particular force.

Yet Macquarie's achievements and legacy cannot be diminished. On his watch, NSW's population and borders expanded considerably. He facilitated the crossing of the Blue Mountains, the push to Bathurst and beyond and the flourishing townships of Richmond and Windsor. Inspired by Matthew Flinders's navigation of Australia, Macquarie echoed his championing of the name "Australia" and established 26 January as Anniversary Day.

Convicts and free men

In 1840, transportation to NSW ceased. By this time a total of 83,000 convicts had been sent to the colony. Men outnumbered women, opportunists rivalled recidivists and few chose to return home. For all the social conflict

"A NEW AND SPLENDID COUNTRY"

Charles Darwin visited Sydney in 1836 as part of his famous voyage on HMS *Beagle*, at a time when emancipationist feeling in both England and New South Wales was at its height. Darwin observed: "As a real system of reform it has failed, as perhaps every other plan; but as a means of making men outwardly honest – of converting vagabonds most useless in one hemisphere into active citizens in another, and thus giving birth to a new and splendid country – a grand centre of civilisation – it has succeeded to a degree perhaps unparalleled in history." Just four years later, New South Wales received its final convict ship.

between the "exclusivists" (free settlers) and "emancipists" (free convicts) during the Macquarie era, the lines between the free and gaoled had been blurring since the early days of the colony. First Fleeter James Ruse grew the first wheat crop of the colony and was rewarded with the first grant of land. Mary Reiby, who arrived in 1792, married a free man and turned the wine business she inherited on his death into a thriving empire. The "ticket of leave" system of parole meant that most had begun making a home in the colony before their sentences expired, and had little reason to go back. It was the children of convicts, "currency lads and lasses" such as William Charles Wentworth, who championed much of the social and political change in the decades immediately before and after the end of transportation. Such "bunyip aristocracy" influence was both feared and ridiculed. (A bunyip was local slang for a fake or impostor.)

Expansion

By 1840, NSW had become a colony of choice. From 1831, the British government began subsiding the passage of a new class of "free migrants" seeking a fresh start, and by 1839 NSW was competing with the US as a migrant destination. A further 80,000 free settlers landed in NSW during the 1840s. Sale of land was now open to the free market as the arbitrary nature of colonial rule weakened. Previously a typical squatter was an ex-convict eking a living on land nobody else wanted. By 1844, when the government fruitlessly tried to enforce an obligation to purchase, the "squattocracy" defined a privileged class of large landholders seemingly unrestrained in their pastoralist ambitions. "As well might it be attempted to confine the Arabs of the Desert… as to confine the Graziers or Woolgrowers of New South Wales within any bounds," lamented one powerless governor.

Such expansion came at a price for the Aboriginal inhabitants of wider NSW as the settlers moved beyond their southeastern corner. The names of sites of violent dispossession are telling: "Slaughterhouse Creek", on the Gwydir River of northern NSW, where 60

or 70 were "shot like crows in the trees" in 1838, was soon matched by "Mount Dispersion", "Convincing Ground", "Murdering Island" and "Skull Camp". The rapid expansion of pastoralism represented a new phase in black–white relations – from possible coexistence to sudden, traumatic encounters.

Some ex-convicts were not so keen on the harshness of rural life and resisted government attempts to move them up-country, preferring the familiar urban rowdiness of the Rocks. With the water supply sorted out, the City of Sydney was finally declared in July 1842. Meanwhile, the religiously minded, including Caroline Chisholm, founder of a female immi-

grants' home in 1841, directed their energies to instituting the family as a bedrock of the emancipated colony. Another facilitator was self-government. In 1842 the NSW Legislative Council was made partly elective through the agitation of democrats like William Charles Wentworth. Yet it would take the gold rushes and the separation of Victoria and Queensland from NSW for the colony to emerge as a truly distinct political and economic entity.

The gold rushes

Gold discoveries, according to William Wentworth, "precipitated Australia into nationhood". E.H. Hargraves, the first prospector

---

LEFT: portrait of Governor Lachlan Macquarie.
RIGHT: miners on their way to work, Newcastle c.1910.

who is recorded to have struck gold (in 1851 near Bathurst, to the west of the Blue Mountains) declared: "Here it is. This is a memorable day in the history of New South Wales. I shall be a baronet, and you will be knighted, and my old horse will be stuffed, put in a glass case, and sent to the British Museum!" He died in Sydney in 1891 without such honours, but gold did indeed transform NSW and even more so Victoria, henceforth its rival.

Word of Hargraves's discovery led to the increase of Sydney's population from 54,000 in 1851 to 96,000 in 1861. After gold fever shifted to the mineral-rich Victorian goldfields, NSW was without a proper discovery

until 1883, when rich lodes of silver and lead were found by Charles Rasp, a German boundary rider on a pastoral station in far western NSW, which became the mining town of Broken Hill.

In the wake of the gold rushes, Victoria became a bastion for protectionists and free-thinkers. NSW, not so lucky in the gold rushes, was still dominated politically by the conservative squatter class and its allies in the Sydney business community. Henry Parkes, five times NSW premier between 1872 and 1889, remained fervently committed to free trade both in principle and as a restraining measure against the more populous and richer Victoria.

Federation

In 1889, Henry Parkes delivered a landmark speech, later known as the 'Tenterfield Oration', which sparked the movement for Federation. Yet this was hardly the first sign of federalist or republican sentiment. Radical nationalism found expression in the rise of the union movement and the birth of the periodical *The Bulletin*, the home of Henry Lawson and "Banjo" Paterson, poets who located Australia's national identity in the bush.

The failure of the general strikes that swept both urban and rural Australia, in the context of crippling depression, merely slowed the rise of the labour movement and the Labor Party. In the meantime, free traders and protectionists took centre stage in discussions about what Federation would look like. Activists from the border regions of NSW, victims of trade tariffs imposed by neighbouring Victoria and Queensland, were vocal in their support of Federation (and by extension a National Tariff). By the close of the 19th century they had revived the federal movement.

On 1 January 1901 NSW the "indissoluble Federal Commonwealth" of Australia was inaugurated. Thousands gathered in Centennial Park in Sydney to watch the swearing-in of Australia's first Governor-General, Lord Hopeton, who read messages of support from Queen Victoria and others. Edmund Barton, a member of the Liberal Protectionist Party, was sworn in as prime minister. Yet national government would sit in Melbourne, even after Canberra was designated the site of the nation's future capital in 1911. But the fears of the free traders proved justified, as trade tariffs were soon imposed by the new federal government. Largely dependent on farming (mostly sheep) as well as mining (coal, lead and zinc), the economy of NSW suffered a blow.

However, by World War I, NSW was overtaking Victoria as an industrial centre. Working-class cities such as Wollongong and Newcastle, where a steelworks had opened in 1915, gave the Labor Party a mandate. In 1910, the first Labor premier, James McGowen, was elected.

War and depression

Australia was founded as a white nation; as the masthead of *The Bulletin* declared, "Australia for the White Man". This insistence on a white Australia was motivated both by British ties and geographical isolation. More than anything, Australia feared invasion from its Asian neighbours. It enthusiastically championed and participated in wars on behalf of the "Mother Country". At the beginning of World War I, Andrew Fisher, the Labor prime minister, pledged "our last man and shilling" and dispatched a force of 20,000 troops. During the next four years, 60,000 of the 330,000 Australians who served overseas were killed. War correspondent C.W. Bean mythologised the Anzac (Australia and New Zealand Army Corps) soldier above all. The nation divided

economic measures, set up the Country Party in 1919. Class divisions were amplified considerably during the Great Depression when demagogic Labor premier Jack Lang threatened to default on British loans – to the delight of his working-class supporters and the horror of the more affluent, some of whom formed a private army, the New Guard, to combat Lang and his allies. Before Lang could cut the ribbon of the freshly completed Sydney Harbour Bridge in 1932, Captain de Groot of the parliamentary New Guard rode up and slashed the ribbon with his sword, declaring the bridge open on behalf of "the decent and loyal citizens of NSW". But it was the Labor

over conscription, in two close referendums. If World War I was the first real test of the nation, Australia passed admirably and suffered immeasurably – as the proliferation of memorials in the post-war period attested.

Between the wars

Sydney continued to boom in the post-war period, with the population passing the million mark in 1922 and the underground railway opening in 1926. Farmers in NSW, however, disgruntled by lingering wartime

LEFT: a World War I poster encourages Australians to enlist. ABOVE: Sydney Harbour Bridge opens in 1932.

Party that eventually rid NSW of Lang, as they developed into the pragmatic party of today.

Sydney staged a re-enactment of Governor Phillip's landing on 26 January 1938 to commemorate the 150th anniversary of European occupation. Meanwhile, the Aborigines' Progressive Association observed a day of mourning for the "white man's seizure of our country". The following year, Australia entered World War II automatically, though not as enthusiastically, as it had entered the earlier conflict. It would take the spread of the war to the Pacific, marked locally by three Japanese midget submarines torpedoing a ferry in Sydney Harbour, to bring the war home. American servicemen flooded Sydney and other cities, and designated "enemy aliens" were interned throughout NSW.

Post-war immigration

"Populate or perish" was the mantra of the ruling Labor government in the wake of World War II. The immigration minister, Arthur Calwell, embarked upon one of the most spectacular migration programmes of the 20th century. Half of the assisted migrants were to be British, but the other half could come from anywhere – as long as they were white. More than 2 million migrants arrived between 1945 and 1965, and Australia's population leapt from 7 to 11 million. In later years, the policy

was modified slowly, with successive governments welcoming people of all races, until it was formally abolished in 1973.

The effect of this mass immigration was to be far-reaching. In 1945 Australia had been a conformist, predominantly Anglo-Saxon country in which 98 percent of inhabitants had a British background. Suddenly it was confronted with massive contingents of Italians, Greeks, Germans, Dutch and Yugoslavs who could hardly speak English and who set up their own communities, shops and newspapers, entered the workforce and schools. It all happened with surprisingly little friction, although with undeniably great hardship on

the part of the so-called "New Australians". They were the workforce behind much of the intense development of the 1950s and 1960s, providing manual labour in steelworks, mines, factories and on the roads. Initially, Melbourne attracted more migrants, but from the late 1970s, after the arrival of the first Vietnamese boat people, Sydney became the leading destination.

Sydney – city of the world

In 1965, energetic Liberal leader Robert Askin was elected NSW premier, ending 10 years of increasingly complacent Labor leadership and initiating Sydney's transformation into a world-class city. It was during the 1960s that it became a city of skyscrapers, but it was the architecturally innovative Sydney Opera House on the harbour that symbolised Sydney's ascent as a cultural capital.

The emergence of new industries in the 1970s, together with an increasingly multiethnic population, consolidated Sydney's reputation as Australia's international city. Much of this change was championed by Sydney politician Gough Whitlam, whose Labor government ruled the country, controversially, from 1973 until 1975 when it was dramatically dismissed by the Queen's representative, Governor General Sir John Kerr.

At the same time as Sydney was growing in importance, the rest of New South Wales was declining. This was partly because Australia lost key export markets (particularly in Britain after the mother country joined the EEC in 1973), and partly because industries such as shipbuilding and mining simply became less important in the modern world. This economic slide has been redressed, in coastal areas at least, by the rapid development of tourism.

Sydney's own attractions as a tourist destination have enjoyed much publicity, famously in the United States during the 1980s when local hero Paul Hogan implored Yanks to "throw another shrimp on the barbie". In the same decade, Sydney was home to many 1988 bicentenary celebrations, including the reenactment of the First Fleet sailing into Sydney Harbour. As with the Olympic Games, held in the city in 2000, the official celebrations highlighted the indigenous past and the multicultural present. Unofficial events and protests, meanwhile, reminded the world that for many local people the cultural disregard that had characterised Australia for the last 200 years had not completely disappeared.

Into the 21st century

Following what one-time federal treasurer and eventual prime minister Paul Keating labelled the "recession we had to have", Sydney emerged from a property slump as the most expensive address in the country. In 1993, it was announced, to the jubilation of many thousands gathered around the harbour in the middle of the night, that Sydney was to be the home of the 2000 Olympic Games. The state

"seachangers" move out of the most expensive city in the country.

The fortunes of regional New South Wales are less assured, as the decline in traditional industries and, to a lesser extent, agriculture, coupled with a drought that threatens never to end, close down small towns for ever as their populations are absorbed into regional centres.

For most of the past few years, the prime ministers of Australia have hailed from NSW – first Labor's Paul Keating, and from 1996 Liberal Coalition leader John Howard. Their divergent characters and styles testify to NSW's rich and complex history. Keating, a "battler" who never finished high school, famously

government immediately began committing public money, $A3.2 billion in total, to the main Olympic venues. The games were an unequivocal success, both as a mark of Australia's sporting prowess and as the ultimate high-profile evidence of Sydney's abundant beauty.

Sydney was home to over 4 million people in 2005. Not surprisingly, many, including long-serving Labor premier Bob Carr, argue that the city cannot sustain more growth. Analysts predict growth will shift to the coastal areas of New South Wales, as

looked to Asia for Australia's future, enthusiastically promoting multiculturalism and reconciliation. Howard, a lawyer by training, is a more cautious and conservative politician, championing a "relaxed and comfortable" Australia in coalition with traditional allies, the United Kingdom and the United States. Not surprisingly, both leaders chose to reside in two of Sydney's more prestigious addresses.

Sydney's attractions remain, to the sometimes smug satisfaction of local people, rather self-evident. State politicians, therefore, face the stimulating challenge of balancing Sydney's particular interests with the needs of wider New South Wales. ❑

LEFT: new arrivals, 1949.
ABOVE: the construction of Sydney's Opera House.

Decisive Dates

50,000 BC The first Australians arrive, overland from New Guinea (some authorities place it earlier).

AD 150 Geographer Ptolemy decides there must be an unknown southern land (*terra australis incognita*).

1606 Dutchman Willem Jansz, sailing east from Java, lands on the western side of Cape York Peninsula – the first verifiable European landing.

1642 Abel Tasman sees the west coast of Tasmania, names it Van Diemen's Land. *Terra Aus-*

tralis Incognita becomes *Hollandia Nova* (New Holland) on maps.

1688 English buccaneer William Dampier lands on the northwest coast.

1770 Captain Cook lands at Botany Bay, then sails north, charting 4,000 km (2,500 miles) of the east coast, claiming it for the British Crown.

1788 Arthur Philip, the first Governor of New South Wales arrives in Sydney Cove with the First Fleet bringing over 1,000 convicts.

1790 Second Fleet arrives.

1793 First free immigrants arrive in Australia.

1797 The city of Newcastle is founded. Merino sheep brought from Cape of Good Hope. The wool industry rapidly becomes the economic mainstay of the colony.

1803 Publication of *Sydney Gazette and New South Wales Advertiser*, Australia's first newspaper.

1801–3 Matthew Flinders circumnavigates Australia, proving it is a single island.

1808 Lachlan Macquarie takes over from William Bligh as Governor.

1811 Reverend Samuel Marsden exports the first commercial cargo of wool to England.

1813 Australia's own currency is established. First crossing of the Blue Mountains.

1817 The name Australia is adopted (instead of New Holland). First bank is established in Sydney.

1820–30s Numbers of free settlers begins to increase; first significant development of white settlements around rural New South Wales.

1825 Founding of Australia's first legislative body, the New South Wales Legislative Council. Van Diemen's Land, which had been part of the colony of New South Wales, becomes a colony in its own right.

1831 Publication of *Quintus Servinton,* the first Australian novel, by Henry Savery, a former convict.

1834 John Batman sails from Tasmania to Port Phillip in Victoria: he and his associates found the city of Melbourne in 1837 (still part of New South Wales).

1836 Visiting Sydney on the *Beagle*, Charles Darwin is captivated by the Australian fauna and flora, and predicts a grand future for the colony.

1840 Partly due to pressure from free settlers, the transportation of convicts to New South Wales is abolished (it continues to Van Diemen's Land until 1853).

1842 City of Sydney officially founded.

1847 Marcus Clarke's *For the Term of his Natural Life* published, the great epic of the penal system.

1842 New South Wales becomes a self-governing colony. Copper discovered in South Australia.

1850 The southern part of New South Wales becomes a separate colony called Victoria.

1851 Gold is discovered near Bathurst, starting Australia's first gold rush and bringing a wave of settlers.

1855 The Constitution Act establishes two houses of Parliament (upper and lower) for the colony. By the end of the decade there is increasing political stability and democracy.

1859 The northern part of New South Wales becomes a separate colony, Queensland. European rabbits are introduced into Australia, with disastrous later consequences.

1860: First south–north crossing of the continent (from Melbourne to Gulf of Carpentaria) by the Burke and Wills Expedition.

1872 Leading free-trade advocate Henry Parkes begins his first term as Premier in the New South Wales government.

1880 Bushranger Ned Kelly is captured and hanged.

1882 Australian cricketers beat England for the first time.

1883 Silver discovered at Broken Hill.

1891 Delegates from the six colonies meet in Sydney to draft a constitution for Australia.

1895 Banjo Paterson writes *Waltzing Matilda*.

1896 Athlete Edwin Flack (unofficially) represents Australia at the first modern Olympic Games, in Athens.

1901 The Commonwealth of Australia is proclaimed, a federation of the six colonies with a population of 3,370,000. The new capital is Melbourne, at least until a new governmental seat is established between it and Sydney (eventually at Canberra some 26 years later).

1902 Women win the right to vote in New South Wales.

1914–18 330,000 Australians serve in World War I; 60,000 are killed, 165,000 wounded.

1915 Australian troops take a major part in the Gallipoli siege in Ottoman Turkey; more than 8,000 are killed.

1922 Sydney's population reaches 1 million.

1927 Parliament House opens in Canberra and the federal parliament moves there from Melbourne.

1930 The Great Depression; 25 percent of the Australian workforce is unemployed, with New South Wales' rural and urban industrial workforce badly hit.

1939 Australians enlist to fight in Europe during World War II. Australian Air Force is active in Britain, navy operates in the Mediterranean, Australian troops fight in North Africa.

1941 Australia declares war on Japan.

1942 15,000 Australians captured when Singapore falls to Japan.

1950 Immigration peaks at 150,000 new arrivals. Sydney expands, with large numbers of immigrants arriving from southern and eastern Europe through the post-war years.

1954 Queen Elizabeth II is the first reigning monarch to visit.

1959 Danish architect Joern Utzon wins the competition to design Sydney Opera House. Population of Australia reaches 10 million.

1965 Conscription re-introduced.

1967 Aborigines granted Australian citizenship and the right to vote.

1973 Sydney Opera House is completed.

1988 In Australia's Bicentennial year, the new Parliament House opens in Canberra.

1995 Australians protest strongly over French nuclear testing in the South Pacific.

1999 Australians vote against becoming a republic.

2000 Olympic Games are held in Sydney and IOC President Juan Samaranch declares the Games "the best Olympics ever".

2002 The Bali bombing kills 88 Australians.

2005 Racially-motivated youth violence hits Sydney.

2006 PM John Howard marks 10 years in office. Australian troops land in East Timor on a peacekeeping role. ❑

LEFT: A gold rush, 1850s.
RIGHT: Loading coal in Newcastle, 1910.

PEOPLE

The population of New South Wales is amorphous, constantly in flux as migration patterns change and new cultures become assimilated. However, many of the Aboriginal people, with the oldest culture of them all, still see themselves as marginalised

Of all the people of Australia, the citizens of New South Wales seem to be the least interested in their identity. They don't even have an established state nickname. West Australians are cheerfully called Sandgropers, Queenslanders are Banana Benders, South Australians are Crow Eaters. The literal alternative – to be known as New South Welshers – doesn't sound good. Victorians focus their historic rivalry with their northern neighbours on Sydney, which they call Glitter City to indicate their perception of the place as hedonistic, sunny and uncultured. The New South Welsh (let's call them that) do not seem to care. Perhaps it is to do with being in the unrivalled position of the first colony, or with being the most populous state, or perhaps because Sydney, as the largest, richest and most globally oriented city in Australia, tends to look outwards rather than inwards.

Or maybe it's because the streets and offices of the cities, especially Sydney, are full of people who were not born here and whose tribal loyalties may lie elsewhere. Sydney teems with people from other Australian states and territories who have been promoted to their head offices, as well as business people from overseas, and thousands who are drawn to the opportunities that big cities offer. It's a place that is constantly being remade as people come and go – too restless, perhaps, to have a single archetypal identity. Nonetheless, the

latent New South Welsh self-identity comes to life when regional rivalry is organised and promoted professionally – notably, of course, in sport, where locals rally round their teams in state competitions.

A diverse population

The population of New South Wales is the most diverse in Australia. Immediately after the end of World War II Australia accepted more migrants from more countries than any other nation in the world except Israel. To date, 6 million have come. Large numbers from Britain and Europe (ironically, scarcely any from Wales) arrived to live in the three big

PRECEDING PAGES: on the beach at Bondi. **LEFT:** at the Royal Easter Show, Olympic Park. **RIGHT:** Vietnamese and Sikh – both bus drivers, both Australians.

cities of the New South Wales coast (Sydney, Newcastle and Wollongong), swelled in more recent years by immigrants from Asia. Even today, about 23 percent of Australians are overseas-born – and many of them live in NSW. By contrast, only 15 percent of Canadians and 9 percent of the population of the USA are overseas-born. Between a third and a quarter of the population now do not have Anglo-Celtic backgrounds. You notice this most in Sydney, where people from more than 100 countries live side by side, and where one of the two government-funded television stations, SBS Television, broadcasts programmes in more than 30 languages.

dian communities. One of the great Sydney festivals, attended by thousands from all over the city, is the Vietnamese Moon Festival, held in Cabramatta at the equinox each September.

Wherever you go, you will see and hear cheerful evidence of this ethnic mix. You will find it in schoolyards at break time, in the huge variety of café and restaurant cuisines, in theatre and music, in sports teams, and in the varied accents and languages of the streets.

Aboriginal people

Nowhere in the annals of British colonisation was the nature of a new land so deeply misunderstood, and the cultural gap so wide

Post-war immigration has constituted one of the biggest social revolutions in Australia. It has been strikingly harmonious and enriching, and the rate of assimilation in just 50 years has been quite extraordinary. For instance, 80 percent of marriages of second-generation people of European origin during this period have been to someone from a different background, and 70 percent of Sydneysiders are a mixture of more than two national backgrounds.

In Sydney, some ethnic concentrations have emerged in recent years. Auburn, for instance, is noticeably Lebanese and Turkish, Leichhardt has a strong Italian culture, Cabramatta and Fairfield have vibrant Vietnamese and Cambo-

between the settlers and the indigenous peoples, as it was when the British first came to Australia. Settlers found no built cities or permanent settlements, no signs of agriculture, no evident social organisation and, most perplexing, no formal and recognisable forms of warfare. Beyond the colonists' comprehension for generations were two things – a deep and spiritual bond between the land and its people of complex abstraction and symbolism; and clever ways of living harmoniously with a tough land – all evolved through more than 30,000 years of occupation. (The 200 years of European settlement today represent about 0.6 percent of that time.)

There are only about 135,000 Aboriginal people remaining in New South Wales, the majority of whom have been displaced from their own lands. Some live in separate communities, and many live in dire circumstances. Others work in rural industries, tourism, sciences, universities – and public services (a statistically inescapable fate, since about one in three of the Australian workforce is a public servant). In nearly every shire along the coast today you will find museums staffed and tours guided by Aboriginal people, often taking visitors to secluded places, offering precious glimpses of the ancestral dreamings and totemic meaning of the land around them.

ever, although 4 million people – about 80 percent of the state population – do something sporty every year, NSW people are the least active in Australia. They like to watch.

The rules of cricket were codified by the MCC in England in the year the colony was founded (1788), so you could say that Australia was destined to play the game. Australian irreverence for tradition also saw the invention of one-day cricket – a faster, less somnolent version. Played in bright colours instead of staid white flannels, the locals promptly called it pyjama cricket. Like the other big sport, rugby football, most NSW people watch from grandstands or armchairs –

Attitudes are changing at the grass roots. On a winter day in 2000, some 350,000 citizens marched across Sydney Harbour Bridge in support of a formal act of reconciliation with Aboriginal peoples. It took five-and-a-half hours to pass, and brought the city to a standstill.

Recreation

Any picture taken from space on a weekend would showpractically every playing field and beach alive with recreational activity. How-

not many actually play. But swimming, golf, tennis and bush-walking attract thousands – and one in every 15 people owns a boat – 444,000 of them. For all this exercise, you cannot help noticing that many people are on the plump side. In fact, over half of adults and a quarter of children in NSW defy the stereotypical image of the lanky Australian, and are overweight or obese – so there's a fair chance that the lean laconic local you took a photo of at Manly was a Swede.

Australians have always been big beer drinkers. Drinking was how you were measured as a man and a mate. Pubs were men's places, and the ritual of "shouting" a round,

LEFT: swimmers enjoying the water at Ulladulla.
ABOVE: a giant tuna at the Sydney Fish Market.

where each man in turn bought drinks for all his mates, was a sacred bonding ritual. It is still the done thing. But over the last 40 years the macho image of the hard drinker has taken some big knocks. Australians now lag way behind the populations of France, Germany, Italy, New Zealand and the USA as beer drinkers. They have taken avidly to drinking their local wines, and they do it both at home and as part of the vibrant café and restaurant life of towns and cities. It is a lifestyle change that has drawn a new generation of men away from the pubs and included women in the social circle. The wine is good, and bottle shops display hundreds of local labels, most at reasonable prices. NSW is a

major wine exporter, and the industry employs a lot of people. The wine-growers of the Hunter Valley, just north of Sydney, make some of Australia's finest wines, especially bold, rich reds. Down at Yenda in the Riverina there's a winery that bottles wine in world-record volumes that would make a beer brewer weep – over a million bottles a week. Most of it is exported to the USA.

Sydney or the bush

One key generalisation about the people of NSW is that those from the city and those from the bush are of different cultures and character. It is more marked in NSW than elsewhere because so many live in towns and so few live in rural locations. The rueful old saying – it's Sydney or the bush – means the choice of two extremes, and those extremes are more noticeable today than ever.

As recently as a generation ago, city life and bush life were more closely entwined. Most people in town had a relation on the land. Every year, an Uncle Jack or Grandma Jenny would come to town for the Royal Agricultural Show. In school holidays city kids would go up to the farm. Through familial contact, city folk at least knew what was going on in the bush. Not now. Today, scarcely anyone in town has a relation on the land. As the rural sector declined over the last 20 years, thousands of families left the bush. Migrants did not take their place: they settled in Sydney and other cities, and their families have no cultural connections with the bush. The country beyond the Great Dividing Range is another land. When a tourist party from overseas is marvelling at the wonders, say, of Mutawintji Gorge in far western NSW, it is possible that the Australian couple from Sydney is having a similarly exotic experience of the bush.

Sydney people

Sydney's 4.5 million people are mainly suburban. Their city sprawls untidily and inefficiently for 60 km (37 miles) north by south and east by west, across the once fertile and heavily wooded coastal plains. The spread reflects the colonists' realisation that, unlike their tenemented towns in Britain, land here seemed to be without limits, and a quarter-acre quickly became the accepted size of a residential block. Home ownership became the egalitarian goal of every citizen, and the suburbs stretched out to accommodate the phenomenon. Today, well over two-thirds of NSW people own their own homes, but they are a restless mob, and many of them yearn for bigger houses in better neighbourhoods. Politicians seductively call these people aspirational voters. It is a deeply embedded idea, this expectation to keep rising above your current material status. It means that many young and upwardly mobile earners in Sydney move out of snug inner suburbs, where their work is close to shops and services, to live in outer suburbs, where they build big houses for their small families on new estates that repeat the traditional sprawls. Then they join Sydney's spectacular, clogged commuter crawl back to the city each day to the same jobs.

Bush people

Isolation in large spaces means that rural people treasure the qualities and rituals of human contact and survival – family contact, lifelong, dependable friendships, the long drives to the footy matches, race meetings, reunions, the casual Saturday morning spent shopping and chatting in the main street of the township. For many people, this reassuring social behaviour masks very tough times in rural NSW.

miles) from the river she has successfully established legume and vegetable crops – and done it by piping one-tenth of the water she previously drew from the struggling river. Such innovations go on everywhere.

It is striking how much of the rejuvenating force of the bush is – appropriately – youthful. The well-educated rangers and scientists of the National Parks and Wildlife Service (NPWS) brim with energy and optimism. Anyone interested in the outback will find a visit to their offices rewarding – particularly if you can arrange a guided tour in the more remote areas.

They work alongside another youthful phenomenon of the bush. For young rural women

The market vagaries associated with globalisation, falling commodity prices, sustained drought, farm debt, degradation of the land, salination and the pressure on family farming have plunged many regions into deep distress. But bush people are stoics. Many communities are embracing new, sustainable ways of living on the land. Out west on the Darling River, Jan McClure, owner of Kallara Station property, has hugely reduced the number of sheep on her vast desert property to help it regenerate. To compensate, on a plain 7 km (4

who, like their brothers, want to live their lives in the bush, the best way to avoid finishing up in the cities is to get a tertiary education – especially in agricultural sciences, management or finance.

Many are doing it, and bringing back to their communities radical sustainable and managerial strategies for struggling rural industries. It is not uncommon to encounter a 28-year-old woman managing the affairs of her uncles and brothers – a subtle gender reversal in a rural and remote culture that their grandfathers would not have been able to foresee. It simply shows the adaptability and resilience of the people. ❑

LEFT: Broken Hill painter and bushman, Jack Absalom. **ABOVE:** fireman in Mount Victoria.

EATING AND DRINKING

Sydney has gained an international reputation as one of the world's gourmet cities, but the rest of the state can offer a wide range of cooking styles, an abundance of fresh produce, and excellent wine to go with it

With so much culinary interest focused on Sydney's renowned and innovative dining scene, it's sometimes hard to remember that there's a quality food culture in New South Wales that extends well beyond the limits of the shiny capital city. Truth to tell, NSW is a state with varying climates, altitudes and regions, which makes for an abundance of excellent food and its welcome habit of popping up in surprising places.

The cities

Of course, Sydney is the king of cuisine in these parts, and only Melbourne contends with it for the title of the country's gourmet capital – and as far as atmosphere is concerned, Sydney has the edge, thanks to the stunning water views of many harbourside and seaside eateries. It also helps that Sydney is home to what is arguably Australia's finest restaurant, French-Japanese superstar Tetsuya's, which has steamrolled to international prestige and is mentioned as one of the top 10 restaurants in the world. In addition to uber-chef Tetsuya Wakuda, there are a host of other internationally recognised food stars in the city, including celebrity lifestyle chef Bill Granger and his growing stable of Bills Cafés; trailblazing Rockpool chef Neil Perry, who seems to have trained a large portion of the city's best cooking talent; Luke Mangan of the Hilton's grand Glass Brasserie, whose fame includes cooking for Denmark's Australian crown princess Mary Donaldson's wedding festivities; and UK seafood maestro Rick Stein, who has made Sydney his second home.

While Sydney may be one city on the map, it's composed of endless suburbs that often seem worlds apart. The hot spot for foodies is Surry Hills, which is chock-a-block with creative and stylish fine diners, some of the city's best coffee houses and casual eateries aplenty, including a notable Indian row. Visitors to Sydney will usually stick to this and other trendy Eastern Suburbs districts such as Darlinghurst, Woolloomooloo Wharf and Paddington, as well the city centre (CBD) – there are particularly good restaurant clusters around Circular Quay and in the Overseas Passenger Terminal – and the beachside districts of Manly and Bondi, where the cliff top

Icebergs Dining Room serves up one of the best ocean views anywhere. The more adventurous will be richly rewarded by heading west and south to the city's ethnic neighbourhoods, which revel in Asian, Middle Eastern and European cuisines and are as authentic as they are cheap. The Vietnamese-Chinese community of Cabramatta is particularly notable, with a vibrant shopping and eating district that could be straight out of Southeast Asia.

There are, of course, other cities in NSW worth mentioning, albeit the largest, Canberra, belongs to its own state-within-a-state, the ACT. Still, it's easy, geographically, to lump the nation's capital together with NSW restaurants, just as it's easy to stop there for a bite while driving to the Snowy Mountains. The

There's similar optimism surrounding NSW's second-largest city, Newcastle, which is quickly shedding its image as a steel town, and now has a new waterfront redevelopment that's attracting scores of upmarket restaurants, bars and cafés. Newcastle also has a reliable restaurant row on Derby Street, favoured by students and other local people.

Once you're out of the cities, the coast is the most populous part of the state, especially to the north. There are gourmet treats in tropical Byron Bay (including seafood specialist Fins, one of the state's top regional restaurants) and its upmarket neighbour Bangalow, and in Tweed Coast hot spot Kingscliffe with

most notable restaurants, such as the lauded Water's Edge, are epicentres for power-broking among the city's endless stream of politicos and bureaucrats. As a food destination for non-residents, Canberra may arouse about as much excitement as a federal budget debate, but the burgeoning Canberra District wine region in the outlying ACT is serving as a welcome catalyst that is drawing gourmets to the city.

its relaxed escapes from Queensland's teeming Gold Coast, as well as a plethora of family eateries along the Central Coast and Coffs Harbour. Inland, the best eating is typically in wine regions (see overleaf), and upland regions like the Blue Mountains of the Southern Highlands. At the same time, some of the most rewarding finds are those towns that have just a good eatery or two, whether you're in tropical Bellingen, rural Cowra or quiet coastal Eden. Then there's the dry interior, where the variety of food and skill of the cooks may be diminished, but the opportunity to meet interesting characters at the next table will drastically improve.

LEFT: Sydney's world-famous rock oysters.
ABOVE: tucking into tucker at the Tibooburra Hotel.

Wine country

Just a hop from Newcastle is the Hunter Valley, the state's best-known wine region and worth the trip for its chart-topping Semillon, excellent Shiraz and Chardonnay, and for an accessible grape-growing lifestyle that's just two hours north of Sydney. Pokolbin is where you'll find the heart of the Hunter action, with a large array of mod-Oz and French-influenced restaurants offering hearty, rustic dishes – duck seems to be a particular staple – and, of course, plenty of local wines to match. Providores (specialised food providers) are a particular treat, from olive growers to cheese makers and even a fish farm.

one of the country's highest wine-growing regions and home to three of the state's best regional restaurants: Selkirks, Lolli Redini and Tonic. In contrast to the Mudgee's country airs, Orange has a more cosmopolitan vibe, though still set amid pristine mountains. Further afield is Cowra, with its old Chardonnay vines and its knack for non-traditional wine varietals, asparagus fields and lamb paddocks.

The largest of all the regions – even when the others are combined – is the remote Riverina, which feeds off the Murray River at the south end of the state to produce huge volumes of wine. Much of it is known for quantity rather than quality, but it does include the

It's both a good thing and a pity that the Hunter overshadows so many other worthy wine regions across the state: good in that it keeps many of the throngs and tour buses away from the others and so preserves their country idyll; a pity in that many visitors never experience the wine and food excellence that lies elsewhere. To the west, for example, is the Mudgee, a warm-climate laid-back region studded with boutique wineries turning out impressive Cabernet Sauvignon, Shiraz, Sangiovese, Chardonnay and even Zinfandel, and home to some notable organic wineries. True gourmands will want to visit the Mudgee's cool-climate counterpart to the south, Orange,

country's most famous dessert wine, DeBortoli's Noble One, and has a growing number of smaller prestige labels like Pirommet. For dining, Griffith is the most interesting of the Riverina's towns, thanks to a proliferation of authentic Italian places that have their roots in the large-scale Italian immigration here after both world wars, which helped refine the wine-growing culture. Finally, there are plenty of other exciting wine regions, where hard-to-find boutique wines and unusual characteristics provide a pay-off in lieu of fully developed tourism facilities. Among the burgeoning wine regions are Tumbarumba, Hilltops, Canberra District and New England.

Cuisine

New South Wales isn't just the most populous state in Australia, it's also the most diverse. That shows in the cuisine, which is often affected by the immigrant populations (or in more remote areas, the lack thereof) and by its proximity to Asia. In the cosmopolitan regions, fusion food is prepared with zeal and creative abandon, and is the main reason why Australia has become such a global food darling. Of course, fusion has long been a dirty word, harking back to overdone 1980s experiments, so most of the time, you'll see the word "modern" in its place, but the principle is intact. East-meets-West cuisines are rampant, most prevalent in modern Australian – mod-Oz – food, a term that is increasingly tricky to define, but in many cases means Asian meets European techniques and ingredients, possibly combined with old-school Australian or English staples. Alas, even modern may have had its day, with some journalists renaming the latest home-grown influx of fusion cooking as "contemporary Australian".

Then there are the newer-wave "mod" rages that are often Asian at their core, especially modern Asian, which mixes various Southeast Asian cuisines, possibly along with Chinese influences, and incorporates higher-quality ingredients, whether they be authentically Asian or not. You'll also find plenty of other subtly tweaked cuisines, from mod-Chinese to mod-Vietnamese, mod-Japanese, mod-Italian, mod-Greek and mod-Lebanese, among others. At the same time, with so much fusion having infiltrated Australia, there's now another movement towards skilful simplicity, with a tide of upstart Italian restaurants leading the charge. Rather than purist temples, there has been a push to innovate with mature restraint while maintaining clear flavours and a focused style.

When it comes to day-to-day eating, Thai food is king, having long overtaken Chinese as the mainstay on virtually every block of every town. Generally, Thai restaurants are excellent at what they do – great standards that are a bit sweeter and less fishy, to suit Western tastes. At the same time, Sydney is home to a couple of the world's top Thai chefs, namely Longrain's Martin Boetz and Sailor's Thai's David Thompson, even if Thompson is now based at his newer London restaurant. The only threat to Thai popularity is the next round of in-fashion Southeast Asian cuisines: Vietnamese and, to a lesser extent, Malaysian and Singaporean.

LEFT: welcome to Tempus Two Winery, Hunter Valley.
ABOVE: good local food and wine in Orange.
ABOVE RIGHT: fresh produce is the pride of NSW.

Another ever-present element is pub food. If there are two buildings in a town, one is certain to be a pub and it's likely to serve an edible scotch fillet. You can have an amazing meal in a pub, or you can have a dated experience – when in doubt, just order the steak and chips and you can't go wrong, More often than not, pubs are about simplicity and value, making up in comfort what they lack in innovation. And then there are the gastropubs, which take the whole experience to creative heights.

At its most basic, pub dining can be meat-and-two-veg land, where beef and lamb are de rigueur, with roast chicken, schnitzel, fish and chips, and barbecued prawns as frequent addi-

a well-brewed latte, flat white and mocha just about anywhere, it's equally common to find instant coffee as a staple in people's homes. Drip and percolated coffee in comparison are almost non-existent, although French-pressed coffee does appear every now and again, especially in homes or offices.

Fresh produce

Talking about produce in NSW is like discussing plant specimens in the Amazon – there's so much of it, you could write a dissertation. This is a state that relies heavily on agriculture, which naturally makes fresh foods abundant: fish, fruit, vegetables, meat, poultry,

tions. Fresh seafood can also be an option, as long as you're not far from the ocean and fairly sure of the kitchen's ability to source fresh produce. As with any cuisine, quality varies, so you can find yourself eating anything from a reheated meat pie to chermoula-encrusted John Dory with Asian-style greens.

Coffee culture in NSW is interesting. You'll be able to find a quality cup of coffee just about anywhere in the cities and regional hot spots. There are many quality coffee producers in the state, among the more notable being high-end boutique brands Single Origin in Surry Hills and the organic Byron Bay Coffee from the tropical seaside. While you can find

you name it. Such farmer-to-foodie proximity has made for a thriving market culture, where weekly growers' markets are found at every turn, the dry interior being the only exception.

In the country, farm-gate sales are another way to get your hands on the freshest produce possible, and there are popular food trails set up by the regional tourism authorities, with the Southern Highlands being among the newest, and the Hawkesbury and Hunter Valley two of the most accessible from Sydney. Throughout the state, you'll find plenty of specialities: Young's famous cherries, Windsor and Oberon's mushrooms, Hunter pecans, Bathurst cauliflower, Orange stonefruit, Bilpin apples,

Coffs Harbour bananas, Northern River coffee and Murray rice.

To Western visitors, one of the most apparent differences might be the ready availability of Asian ingredients at even stock-standard supermarkets, from lemon grass to Chinese broccoli, fresh kaffir lime leaves, custard apples and more. It's just another lasting legacy of Australia's skip and a jump from Asia. As would be expected, the more cosmopolitan areas have the greatest diversity.

Fish varieties are another eye-opener, from Balmain bugs, which look like lobster's ugly stepchildren but whose flesh is impressively sweet and tasty; the exotic-sounding barra-

whose shores are colder, less populous and more pristine than the northern waters. To get the best overview of the state's bounty, you can't beat the Sydney Fish Market in Pyrmont.

Most people realise that beef and lamb are Australian specialities. What they may not know is that NSW is also famous for its pigs, particularly Bangalow pork in the tropical north, and goat is increasing in popularity. Kangaroo meat is super-lean, tasty and not nearly as gamey as you might think. But many Aussies don't eat it, seeing roo as either vermin or fodder for tourist-trap restaurants. Seeking it out in a quality restaurant is worthwhile; like most lean game meats, it should be

mundi, a native fish that produces moderate-flavoured fillets; the infamous rock lobster (crayfish), with its large tail and lack of large claws; and freshwater yabbies, a minuscule crustacean that's the Aussie equivalent of New Orleans crawfish. Blue-eye, red snapper and bream are also common; prawns, oysters, squid and cuttlefish are staples. Inland, there are fish farms that dot the state, stocking trout, perch and other species. About 80 percent of Sydney's fish comes from the South Coast,

cooked no more than medium rare. Emu, wallaby (the kangaroo's smaller cousin) and camel meat are also available, but mostly as novelties, and are hard to find prepared by skilled chefs. The same goes for bush tucker, from lemon myrtle to bush tomatoes, although it's worth trying, especially if you want to get the complete Outback experience, and you'll find that even city restaurants will throw in a bush ingredient every now and again.

There are terrific eating options in NSW, and there's no excuse for having a bad meal. If you don't find yourself near a place that looks like a great food experience, keep driving and another one is sure to be just around the next bend. ❑

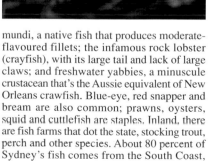

LEFT: serving varieties of yum cha in Chinatown.
ABOVE: citrus orchards are a familiar sight in NSW.
ABOVE RIGHT: catch of the day – oysters, Jervis Bay.

COASTAL LIVING

The coast of the eastern seaboard is a long narrow strip, and it is on this sliver of land, rich in fertile forests and golden beaches lapped by warm waters, that most people choose to live

The Great Dividing Range runs the 4,000-km (2,485-mile) length of Australia's eastern seaboard, from the tropical tip of Cape York in Queensland's north to the snowy alps of Victoria in the south. It divides the country into two absurdly unequal parts. On its eastern side lies a green and watered strip so narrow that its low mountains can be seen from the sea all along the 1,500 km (932 miles) of the New South Wales coast. On its western side lies all the rest of Australia, where the arid range lands and deserts of Australian mythology roll on from horizon to horizon for 3,500 km (2,175 miles) to the Indian Ocean. On the eastern side, in New South Wales, nowhere wider than 50 km (32 miles), is the largest, most densely centralised, most industrialised and most diverse population in Australia. On the western side, across thousands of kilometres, is scattered the sparse minority of the Australian people – all of those who live outside its large capital cities and regional towns.

Fabulous beaches

This Great Dividing Range, which forms the western border of coastal NSW, is really a series of rugged plateaux, immense gorges and primeval rainforests. Trade winds from the Pacific Ocean – southerly busters as Sydneysiders call their late-afternoon summer gales – bring reliable rain, and the fertile coastal plain is intersected by more than 20

LEFT: life-saver mural on Bondi Pavilion.
RIGHT: beach life at Nelson Bay.

short, fast-flowing rivers. Twelve of them are noble and navigable streams. The coast itself is deeply indented with hundreds of bays, inlets, estuaries and lakes, and it is ribboned with lovely beaches. On most of them you will rarely see a soul.

The climate is temperate – mostly. Easterly sea breezes from the ocean make it balmy, but occasionally each year, westerlies roar in across the Great Divide from the inland plains and deserts, and remind coastal dwellers of their harsh netherland. In summer, these winds are, in the words of old timers, as hot as the hobs of hell, and in winter as cold as charity. Generally speaking, the further north you go from Sydney, the more subtropical it gets. As you go south, it gets pretty nippy in the winter, with daily lows around freezing point. That is why you won't see on this coast those familiar postcard scenes of cattle and sheep grazing on arid and extended plains. It is too wet and humid. People here are occupied instead with sappy and watery things like forestry, sugar cane, fish, beef and dairy farming. In the Hunter Valley there's a rather exotic mixture of coal, horses and wine.

There are five ports, including Sydney. The largest aggregations of heavy industry in Australia are concentrated around Newcastle, the busiest coal-exporting port in the world, and

English and Irish, arrived in Sydney from their huddled cities in 1788, they were both exhilarated and appalled by their new 7,000,000-sq. km (2,703,000-sq. mile) backyard. There was limitless space, yet nearly all of it seemed harsh and unforgiving. The truth is that most Australians have never found the inland region of their country hospitable.

Today 85 percent of them live within 50 km (32 miles) of the sea on 1 percent of the land – and the people of the NSW coast best epitomise this. When you drive the 1,500 km (932 miles) from Tweed Heads in the north to Eden in the south, you will discover that no fewer than 4.3 million of the state's 6.7 million peo-

around Wollongong, which is dominated by its steel mills and aluminium smelter.

Wonderfully, with all this human and industrial activity, there are scores of state-owned forests, and some 130 National Parks, including World Heritage areas and marine parks, which run the length of the coast and the bordering ranges. Many are wild and remote wildernesses. All are beautiful and, happily, all are accessible.

The most typical Australians

Of all the Australian paradoxes, the relationship of space and people is one of the most intriguing. When the first settlers, mainly

ple live in Sydney alone. You will also find that another million live in the two industrial cities of Newcastle and Wollongong. And fewer than half a million of the remainder live on the rest of the coast.

These seaboard people, especially those of the cities, are the most diverse in Australia. Six million migrants have come to Australia since World War II *(see page 31)*, and many of them settled on this coastal strip. So while New South Wales is hardly new, undeniably south, and not very Welsh, the overwhelming majority of people who live on its coast are the most typically Australian Australians – coastal, urban and ethnically diverse.

Hope and reality

The Great Dividing Range was not just a physical barrier, it was also a poignant boundary between hope and reality. For 28 years after settlement in 1788 no way could be found across the rugged Blue Mountains behind Sydney, despite repeated forays. If you stand today at sunset on the vantage point of Observatory Hill above The Rocks in Sydney where the colony began and face the blue silhouette of the mountains, it is not hard to imagine how a belief grew up among uneducated convicts and soldiers that over the mountains lay China. With this dream came the flicker of hope that if you could only

at the very heart of the harsh land a temperate and bountiful oasis that would nurture the spirit of the new colonies. But there was no sea. The long westward rivers which rose hopefully in the Dividing Range petered out into sand or swamps. So it was on the green sliver of the coast that most Australians were destined to live.

A big backyard

For most coastal people, however, the land signifies a kind of physical freedom. Watch suntanned Sydney children frolicking in the harbour bays that meander among the suburbs, while on the foreshores, under the shade of

escape across them, you might find your way home by the trade routes and empires of the known world.

The Range was also a kind of metaphysical barrier. At the centre of nearly every other land in which the British had established colonies, there were great lakes or river systems, their discovery the stuff of epic exploration. Here, the long search for an inland sea was sustained not just by an economic urge for pastoral prosperity, but also in the hope there would exist

large Port Jackson fig trees, their parents get together with friends to enjoy a picnic with good food and local wine.

In Sydney Harbour alone there are nearly 250 km (155 miles) of foreshore, and little bays just 6 km (4 miles) from the central business district (CBD) where you can anchor a boat, or reach on foot from the suburban streets, where the old angophora forest still comes down to the water's edge, and where there is no sign of rooftops and you cannot hear the low roar of the city. It all seems just as it was 200 years ago.

Nowhere on the coast is further than a two-hour drive to mountains or beaches. And while

LEFT: schoolgirls on the way home by ferry.
ABOVE: Augustus Earle's painting of the Bathurst Plains, *circa* 1826, showing convicts breaking stones.

Sydney is one of the most expensive cities in the world, you don't have to be rich to enjoy it all. Australians revel in a sense of in-your-face egalitarianism. Citizens simply treat their coastland and bush parkland as their backyard – which, of course, it is.

Grey ghosts

Notions of backyards and space are changing. When the first settlers came to Sydney Cove they built rows of terrace houses and lived cheek by jowl as they had done in their English towns, as if to protect themselves against the alien sights and sounds of their new land. But soon, as the realisation hit them

At the same time there is a steady migration outwards to the once sleepy coastal regions, especially to the north, of people who work in the burgeoning tourist and service industries – and especially of retirees, or grey ghosts as the local people call them. Their new (and economically welcome) housing demands are putting the same old developmental pressures on the land that Sydney endured for genera-tions. You will be struck by the number of relatively new estates put down among cleared hectares of beautiful forests and coastal heathlands – many of them repeating the boxy architecture of the cities and often lacking even the protection and relaxation of

that the space around them was almost limitless, they built their homes on spacious quarter-acre suburban blocks (the entire suburb of Haberfield in Sydney has been protected by heritage regulations to preserve this phenomenon). As a result, cities sprawled out across the countryside, in the case of Sydney to its present size of 60 km by 60 km (37 miles by 37 miles).

Now two things are happening. In the cities, people are consolidating, moving inwards, to live in large towers of residential units, creating large working communities – and bringing the streets to life with shops, restaur-ants, cafés and nightlife.

sheltering verandas. But whatever criticisms there may be of style and beauty, and the legitimate ecological fears that the northern coast may become a long degraded suburban strip, life is good for the newer residents.

The primal pull of the watery ooze is extremely hard to resist. The Pacific zephyrs soothe the skin, the sun warms the limbs, there are beaches to walk along, and there's always a club near by where you can have beer, a bet and a good cheap meal. Where Americans sought the pursuit of happiness as an ideal and a constitutional right, Australians settled for comfort, which proved to be a realistically attainable wish.

Equal under the sun

But the beach represents more than comfort and relaxation. It has also had a strong influence on the nature of the people.

It was hard for people in the early days to obey accepted Victorian values of modesty, covering their bodies from neck to ankle, and keeping their faces in the shade when they could feel the wind in their hair, and the sun on their backs and the surf was so sensuous – and that went for men and women alike. Even so, sea bathing, strictly segregated at first and allowed only at night, didn't begin officially until late in the 19th century. Women embraced it readily.

champion swimmer Dawn Fraser, who is adored for her cheerful and defiant irreverence for authority.

The beach is a symbol for this kind of independence of spirit. It is hedonistic, liberating and wickedly egalitarian. Socialites, politicians and wharfies are all equal under the sun in bikinis and togs. Serious observers think the beach probably helped to underpin egalitarian ideals in the Australian polity.

Conservation matters

Away from the iconic beaches and estuaries, people are never far from issues of the viability and sustainability of their jobs. Conservation

As early as 1902, young Sydneysider Annette Kellerman won the state 90-metre (100-yd) and the 1,500-m (1-mile) swimming championships, and in short order sent the watchers into a spin with her own body-hugging one-piece swimsuits. She then went on to swim the Thames, the Seine and the Danube, and as "The Million Dollar Mermaid", became a Hollywood film star.

Her mantle was taken up in recent times (as a swimmer, not as a movie star) by another child of the harbour, three times Olympic

LEFT: an Aboriginal cultural centre is declared open.
ABOVE: aerial view looking south over Coogee, Sydney.

DAWN FRASER

Dawn Fraser, born into a working-class family in Balmain, NSW, in 1936, is a feisty, strong-willed woman who, many believe, typifies the coastal character. She won her first Olympic gold medal when she was 19 and is the only woman ever to receive three gold medals in the 100-m/yd race in three consecutive Olympics. Despite a turbulent relationship with the Australian Swimming Union, she was named Australian of the Year in 1964 and voted Australia's greatest female athlete in 1988. Dawn was also chosen as an Olympic torchbearer for the opening ceremony at the 2000 Sydney Olympic Games.

of the huge forests contends with employment for wood chippers, degradation of the waterways interferes with the nine great fisheries, coal-mining interests on the Illawarra and the Hunter run into arguments about continuing reliance on fossil fuels and global warming, wine industries cope with dearth and glut, and the whole coast is confronted for the first time in its history with prolonged drought, climate change and the serious prospect of long-term water shortages. Most industries struggle with the invisible and fateful forces of the global markets in which they now compete. You will run into these issues wherever you go.

THE DUCK-BILLED PLATYPUS

The duck-billed platypus *(Ornithorhynchus anatinus)* is a strange creature, resembling a beaver onto which a flat, blue-grey beak has been affixed. It is a semi-aquatic egg-laying mammal with webbed feet. Its body length ranges from 30–40 cm (11–16 inches), the male being larger than the female. The male also has a secret weapon: the ability to shoot poison from a spur on its ankle. This venom causes terrible pain to humans who come into contact with it, and can kill small mammals. The name comes from the Greek platys = flat and pous = foot. Aboriginal people have several names for the platypus, including mallangong and boondaburra.

Sylvan silence

In the glorious rainforests of the coast you can put aside these concerns for a while. The forests are never more than an hour or two away, and few people go there – residents and tourists alike are drawn magnetically to the iconic beaches. Eighty percent of the Eurobadalla and Eden Shires in the south, for example, are forest, and the Hastings Shire in the north has three World Heritage-listed National Parks.

These are the working territories of forestry workers, rangers and scientists. In these cool forests, some of them vast, among majestic stands of trees, you can experience what these people treasure – a sense of primal silence. Australia has 84 percent of the world's mammals, 45 percent of its birds and 85 percent of its flowering plants. In these ranges you may hear the calls of the kookaburra, bell bird and the whip bird, and encounter some of the rare creatures – wallabies, wombats and, if you approach with care, the egg-laying, young-suckling, duck-billed platypus (*see box below*). The echidna, also known as the spiny anteater, also lays eggs and suckles its young, but it is a solitary creature and rarely seen.

Experience the Ag

If you want to get a good picture of life on the coast in just one day, go to the Ag – the local Annual Agricultural Show – in any small town. Here, past traditions and present living converge, and people from all walks of life attend – foresters from the mountains, farmers from the plains, fishing folk from the coast, coal miners, sugar-cane farmers, shearers, horse-breeders, wine-producers, the boys with their "beaut utes", and retirees from the coastal estates.

At some small shows there are more than 500 categories of prizes – cattle-dog trials, ring events, wood-chopping, livestock, shearing, and displays of preserves and other crafts handed down from mother to daughter. Remember to initiate conversations. Honest curiosity is all that is needed to unlock the natural courtesy and friendliness of the coastal people of NSW. ❑

LEFT: the lush palm forest in Nightcap National Forest.
RIGHT: cattle graze on farmland near Hunter Valley.

THE ARTS

Culture was not the first thing on the minds of the colonists when they arrived in New South Wales, but over the years a lively arts scene has grown and flourished on waves of public enthusiasm

When the soldiers and convicts of the First Fleet disembarked in Sydney Cove and founded the colony of New South Wales, the artistic culture of Britain and Europe did not accompany them. It was 1788, the year in which Mozart composed his three great symphonies – the E-flat, the G-Minor and the *Jupiter*, but it was a long time before there were either audiences or players to connect the most isolated colonists in the world with their Western artistic roots 19,000 km (12,000 miles) away. It was ironic, too, that, without knowing it, the settlers had set foot in a land with the oldest continuous artistic culture in the world.

The early years

Aboriginal peoples had migrated to Australia some 40,000 years earlier and developed art forms of complex abstraction and symbolism, yet they were little understood. The British were perplexed by the land and its people and the Antipodean contradictions. The discovery of Australia – understanding its fragile physical ecology, and exploring how best to express the "Australianness" of the country artistically – has evolved over the succeeding 200 years. In the case of Aboriginal art, it is only in the last 50 or so years that it has been widely understood and appreciated.

Physical survival dominated the lives of the colonists in the early years, and there was no

place for refinements. The first music to be heard among the gumtrees and kangaroos was *"God Save the King"*, played by a ragged band of marines to accompany Governor Phillip's proclamation of the colony. It occurred on the morning after disembarkation following a night of wild debauchery and drunkenness. There is no written record of the quality of the performance.

Despite the severities of life, the first play performed in the colony – *The Recruiting Officer* by John Farquhar – was presented by convicts just a year after arrival, in 1789. (An event that forms the backbone of a play from 1988: *Our Country's Good*, by Timberlake

LEFT: Aboriginal artwork.
RIGHT: *Flower Sellers* by Tom Roberts shows Sydney's King Street in the 1890s.

Wertenbaker.) And artists, some of them convicts, began to depict the early settlement in
sketches and panoramas.

On the walls of the Art Gallery of New
South Wales (AGNSW) today, you can see how,
in the first hundred years of settlement, artists
responded to the hard, clear light and an-
gularities of the bush, by rendering it at first in
the soft hues and academic styles of their ver-
dant homeland, as if willing the bush to wear
a gentle and familiar face. But very quickly,
new generations of native-born and migrant
artists began to see the land with local eyes.
Supported by a new sense of strident nationalism ("Australia for the Australians," cried *The*

Bulletin magazine in Sydney), and calls to
paint "the real Australia", artists steadily developed naturalistic styles during the mid-19th
century. The languid summers were ideal for
painting outdoors, and as *plein air* painting
took hold through the 1860s, the ambition to
find a distinctive Australian style was realised.

It culminated in the 1880s and 1890s, when
a group of bright young painters set up their
easels in the bush around Melbourne and
established the Heidelberg Group. Some of
the group painted in studios and camps around
Sydney, including Tom Roberts and Arthur
Streeton. Their lively work is well represented
at the AGNSW.

Prosperity and migration

While the early challenges to express
Australian identity in art are most easily seen
in painting, they were a consistent theme of
all the visual and performing arts. But, over-
whelmingly, what visitors experience of the
arts in NSW today is a manifestation of the
galloping activity that followed the end of
World War II in 1945. Only 44 years a nation,
wounded by Depression, bloodied by two
world wars, still suspicious of art and ideas,
the population was nevertheless big enough,
and soon prosperous enough, to feel it was
safe to give the arts a try.

At the same time Australian artistic life was
changed irrevocably by an extraordinary post-
war migration programme. No other country
in the world except Israel has welcomed so
many people, in such a short time and of so
many nationalities – 6 million to date from
more than 150 countries and speaking more
than 60 languages.

The arts quickly became a volatile mix of
native confidence and exotic culture.
Migration enriched the arts, broadened their
British traditions, made them lively and
unpredictable, and helped immeasurably to
break down the old entrenched philistinism.

Participation

All arts flourished, as new national and state
companies and academies in opera, music,
dance, visual arts and cinema were founded.
Arts festivals – such as the annual Sydney Arts
Festival – competitions and international
touring were quickly set in the arts calendar.

Australians have landed on the international
stage in large numbers since the 1950s – artists
Sidney Nolan and Brett Whiteley, divas Dame
Joan Sutherland and Yvonne Kenny,
conductor Simone Young, writers Patrick
White and Peter Carey, film directors Peter
Weir and Phillip Noyce, actors Mel Gibson
and Cate Blanchett, to name just a few.

For those who remember the days when art
was at the nerdy periphery of life, it is extraordinary today to see the degree to which so
much arts activity outstrips its viability. While
there is generous corporate sponsorship, the
arts could not survive at their current lively
level without buckets of help from taxpayers.
In NSW the state government provides more

than A$450 million each year, and the Commonwealth government adds more.

There is a genuine sense of democracy here. People can honestly say when they attend an event, "This is my theatre, my orchestra, my gig." And so deeply embedded is the expectation of government support that when commentator Phillip Adams described a government minister who was being particularly obstructive about funding as "a pain in the arts", Australians cheered in agreement.

People in NSW participate in the arts with relish. About 17 people out of 20 attend a cultural event each year – about 1.7 million in a population of 6 million. Around 940,000

Sydney Opera House, as is the Sydney Symphony Orchestra. The Australian Chamber Orchestra, recognised as one of the best in the world, and the Brandenburg Orchestra are notable for their musical scholarship, experiment and verve.

Music in NSW is strikingly youthful; the state is home to several youth orchestras, among them the Australian Youth Orchestra, the Sydney Youth Orchestra and the SBS Youth Radio and Television Orchestra. Together, the companies train more than 300 talented musicians, commission new works, premiere music from overseas and tour internationally.

The acclaimed Australian Ballet has a large

people work in the arts and leisure sector. Most schools have music at the heart of their activities. An enterprising teacher at a boys' high school made it a condition of playing rugby that the boys must sing in the school choirs. They did, and they did well.

The performing arts

Opera Australia, claimed to be the busiest company on the planet, stages more than 200 performances each year. It is based at the

---

LEFT: Pro Hart misinterpreted the term "paint roller".
ABOVE: the Bangarra Dance Theatre combine Aboriginal and Western traditions.

SYDNEY WRITERS' FESTIVAL

The Sydney Writers' Festival, held for one week each May in sparkling winter sunshine around the wharves of Walsh Bay in the harbour, brings together round about 70 internationally prominent writers to mix it with top local writers and the public. One of the best times to visit New South Wales is during this festival, which has an air that combines intellectual excitement with sunny Sydney informality – and, best of all, most of the events are free of charge. Australians are voracious readers, so it is not surprising that this event has grown rapidly in popularity, so that it now extends to 10 suburban and rural centres.

repertoire, and produces more than 200 performances a year. The company has made numerous overseas tours since 1965. Also popular abroad is Graeme Murphy's contemporary Sydney Dance Theatre, which has made 25 foreign tours. Its headquarters are on the harbour in Walsh Bay close to the home of the Bangarra Aboriginal Dance Company. The two companies frequently collaborate.

The Sydney Theatre Company at the Wharf, and Belvoir B, which is a leading commissioner of new works, are both energetic forces on Sydney's arts scene. Tucked away over the water in tiny Careening Bay is the Ensemble, a wonderfully enterprising small theatre. Among many others is Legs on the Wall, a physical theatre group that has taken its politically and socially edgy performances all over the world. The emphasis, of course, is on Sydney, but NSW residents can enjoy regional theatre companies in 25 of the larger rural centres as well. Wagga Wagga *(see page 160)*, a town of 56,000 inhabitants, has two theatres that stage performances year-round.

Around 700 km (435 miles) south of Sydney on the Murray River at Albury is another international success story – the Flying Fruit Fly Circus, which, in an educational environment, trains 80 young people aged from 8 to 18 years in circus and physical theatre craft.

FROM ENGINEER TO PATRON OF ART

Franco Belgiorno-Nettis epitomises the influence of post-World War II migration to Australia. Born in southern Italy in 1915, the son of a train driver, he became an officer in Mussolini's army in World War II. In 1951 he arrived in NSW to build power lines in the Snowy Mountains Hydroelectric Scheme in the south of the state and, with a partner, Carlo Salteri, went on to found Transfield, the largest construction company in Australia.

Belgiorno-Nettis became one of the most generous patrons of contemporary art and sculpture in the country. His passionate love of art as an inseparable and central part of life initially confounded many of his Australian-born colleagues who kept art at a distance. He fondly cited Michelangelo as an example of unlimited versatility as a scientist and artist, who represented the continuum of art, design, engineering and construction. Speaking as an engineer himself, he said: "In all aspects of human creativity the artist is the greatest wellspring. Therefore we should give artists the maximum chance and latitude to express their ideas."

Belgiorno-Nettis founded the Transfield Prize for Art, the Transfield Trust, and the Sydney Biennale *(see opposite)*, of which he is the founding governor. He is also a life governor of the Art Gallery of NSW.

Visual arts

Twenty-five rural and remote towns and cities in the state have government-supported art galleries, and they are all worth a visit, both to see the work of local artists and for their many touring exhibitions. There are also hundreds of private art and craft galleries.

In Sydney, the Art Gallery of New South Wales has the most comprehensive collection of Australian art, including work by indigenous artists in its superb Yirribana Gallery. The Museum of Contemporary Art at Circular Quay is a major exhibitor of new work.

The Biennale of Sydney, the city's prestigious festival of contemporary art (the third-oldest in the world), has been host to more than 1,200 international artists from over 60 countries since 1973. The event is one of the most exciting in the New South Wales art calendar.

The annual Archibald Prize for portraiture is a serious business, especially as it is worth A$35,000. It is one of Australia's best-known arts awards, first awarded in 1921. But Sydneysiders also like a good joke; the winners of the People's Prize and of the Packers Prize (voted for by the backroom packing staff) are as eagerly awaited as the main prize. So, too, is the prize in the Bald Archy competition, a much-loved parody of the Archibald, in which some 40 portraits and caricatures of well-known Australians are exhibited and "judged" by Maude, a sulphur-crested cockatoo.

Sculpture by the Sea attracts 300,000 viewers to the world's biggest open-air sculpture exhibition every year. It uses 2 km (1 mile) of walks and rugged cliffs above the Pacific Ocean between Bondi and Tamarama as its gallery space. And, like so many other art events in Sydney, it is free.

Poignant memorials

At the furthest extremes of the state, sculptors have provided two poignant and unexpected responses to Australian life. In Sydney, the lovely art-deco Anzac War Memorial *(see page 81)* in Hyde Park is the location of Rayner Hoff's beautiful statue, *Sacrifice*. The towering caryatid comprises the naked body

of a young soldier born aloft on a shield by the figures of his mother, his sister and his wife. Considering the Australian machismo of war, it is a surprising and movingly feminine tribute. There should have been another Hoff sculpture here, too: the *Crucifixion of Civilisation*, which he created in 1930, showed a naked woman on a cross, above a pile of corpses. The Catholic Church was so horrified that the sculpture was withdrawn.

On a hill above the tough desert mining town of Broken Hill *(see page 174)*, 900 km (560 miles) west of Sydney, is a circle of monumental sculptures. Known as the *Broken Hill Sculpture Symposium*, it is located in the

Living Desert Reserve. Hewn from sandstone, the artworks were created in 1993 at the invitation of the townspeople as a tribute to the memory of surgeon Fred Hollows, who spent years performing free eye operations among the poorest people in the world. Local miners, families and 12 sculptors from Australia and from countries where Hollows had worked collaborated on the project. The miners provided the rocks, while families from the district supplied the artists with food and accommodation. The resulting 12 individual works of art are a graceful tribute to the human spirit, born of a close and unaffected interaction between citizens and artists. ❑

LEFT: Franco Belgiorno-Nettis admires his portrait by Australian artist Danelle Bergstrom.
RIGHT: part of the Broken Hill Sculpture Symposium.

PLACES

A detailed guide to New South Wales with the
principal sites clearly cross-referenced by
number to the maps

L ook at a map of New South Wales, and you will find it is relatively
easy to break the state down into its component parts. The coastal
areas are busy and populous; the Great Dividing Range, running
from top to bottom, provides the natural barrier to the inland country;
the plains to the west of the range catch the water as it runs off and have
developed into rich farming country. Further west still, everything dries
out and there is unmitigated Outback where, apart from a few cattle stations, the main interest is mining. Head "back of Bourke" and there's
virtually nothing: you can travel 100 km (60 miles) or more without
seeing a soul and sights are few, which is why the relevant chapter in
this book encompasses an area equal to that of an average-sized European nation.

Few travellers venture this far. This is a pity, because for overseas visitors it's likely to offer the most profound contrast to home, while for Australia's predominantly urban and coastal-dwelling population it can be a
rewarding departure from its comfort zone.

Moving back towards the coast you come to a band of vibrant country
towns, also uncelebrated: Tamworth, Dubbo, Orange, Wagga Wagga (to
pick some at random) are all interesting in their own way and provide an
insight into another facet of Australian life. Canberra looms up next in its
anomalous way: a territory-within-a-state which happens to have many
of the country's finest museums and galleries. And then you're heading
back towards the coast, perhaps cutting through the Great Dividing Range
via one of the major tourist attractions: the Blue Mountains, the Snowy
Mountains or the Hunter Valley.

Back on the seaboard the people and the visitor centres welcome you
with open arms. There are literally hundreds of kilometres of beaches to
tempt you, and the resorts to go with them – buzzing and modern to the
north, slightly more sleepy to the south. In the hinterland, lovely colonial-
era villages over-indulge their guests. And right in the middle of the coast
there's Sydney, about which you could write a whole book. ❑

PRECEDING PAGES: Sydney Harbour Bridge; Outback mailboxes. **LEFT:** quintessential
New South Wales coast.

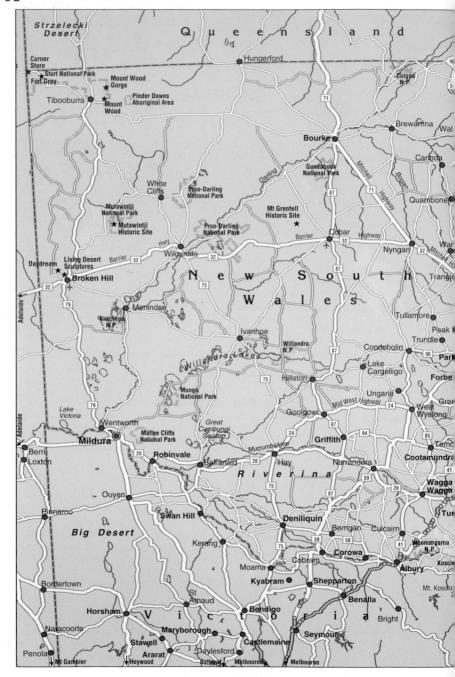

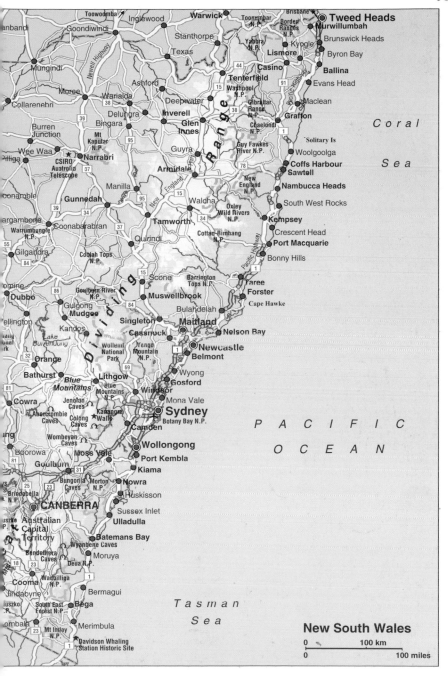

New South Wales

0   100 km

0   100 miles

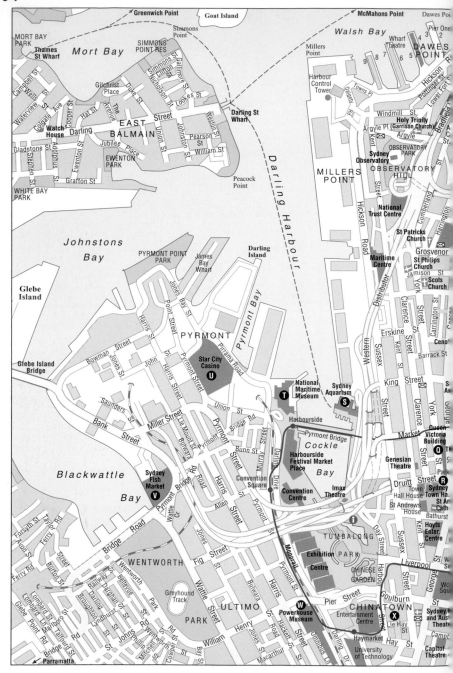

Greenwich Point

Goat Island

McMahons Point

Dawes Poi

Walsh Bay

MORT BAY
PARK

Thames
St Wharf

Mort Bay

SIMMONS
POINT RES

Simmons
Point

Millers
Point

Wharf
Theatre

Pier One

**DAWES
POINT**

Harbour
Control
Tower

Windmill St.

Holy Trinity
(Garrison Church)

Gilchrist
Place

Campbell St

Wells St

Waterview St

Colgate Ave

Hat St

Clifton St

Nicholson St

Gallimore St

Lookes St

Weston St

Dove St

The Avenue

**EAST
BALMAIN**

Street

Johnston St

Pearson
St

William St

Darling St
Wharf

Argyle Pl

Kent

Argyle

**Sydney
Observatory**

OBSERVATORY
PARK

OBSERVATORY

Watch
House

Darling

Cooper St

Adolphus

Jubilee
Place

Union St

**OBSERVATORY
HILL**

Gladstone St

Stephen St

Eventon St

EWENTON
PARK

Grafton St

Peacock
Point

Darling Harbour

**MILLERS
POINT**

Hickson

National
Trust Centre

St Patricks
Church

WHITE BAY
PARK

Cumberland St

Harrington St

Grosvenor

*Johnstons
Bay*

PYRMONT POINT
PARK

James
Bay
Wharf

**Darling
Island**

St Phillips
Church

Jamison

Scots
Church

Cenc

**Glebe
Island**

Pyrmont Bay

Road

Clarence

York

Street

Erskine St

Sussex

Carrington St

Barrack De

Glebe Island
Bridge

Jones Street

Point Street

Harris St

Pirrama Road

PYRMONT

Bowman St

John

Jones St

**Star City
Casino**

U

King Street

Kent St

Clarence

Sa

York

George

Saunders St

Union St

National
Maritime
Museum

Sydney
Aquarium

S

Market

St

Queen
Victoria
Building

Q

Bank

Street

Miller Street

Le Mount St

Harris St

Bulwara Rd

Pyrmont Bridge Rd

Pyrmont Street

Murray St

Darling Drive

Bridge Rd

T

Harbourside

Pyrmont Bridge

Cockle

Genesian
Theatre

Druitt Street

Town
Hall House

Sydney
Town Ha

St Ar
Cath

R

Blackwattle

Allen St

Bunn St

Harbourside
Festival Market
Place

Bay

**Sydney
Fish
Market**

V

Wattle Cr

Convention
Square

Convention
Centre

Imax Theatre

St Andrews
House

Bathurst

i

Hoyts
Enter.
Centre

Bay

Taylor Rd

Ferry Rd

Avon St

Bridge

Road

Jones

Street

Fig St

WENTWORTH

Railway

Wentworth

Bellevue St

Pyrmont St

Harris

TUMBALONG

PARK

Exhibition
Centre

Day Street

Sussex

Kent St

Liverpool

Wc
Squ

Forsyth St

Burton St

Lombard St

Ferry Rd

Broughton St

Darghan St

Lyndhurst

Wattle

Street

ULTIMO

PARK

Greyhound
Track

William

Henry

Jones St

Bulwara

Harris

Pier Street

Street

**CHINESE
GARDEN**

Monorail

Harbour

Goulburn

George

Sydney
and Aus
Theat

Lombard St

Glebe Point Rd

Marlboro St

Talfourd St

Bridge

Johns

Wentworth

Rd

Mitchell

Macarthur

William St

Hackett St

Darling

Drive

Omnibus Ln

**Powerhouse
Museum**

W

Entertainment
Centre

CHINATOWN

Le Hay St

Haymarket

Hay St

X

Capitol
Theatre

University
of Technology

Parramatta

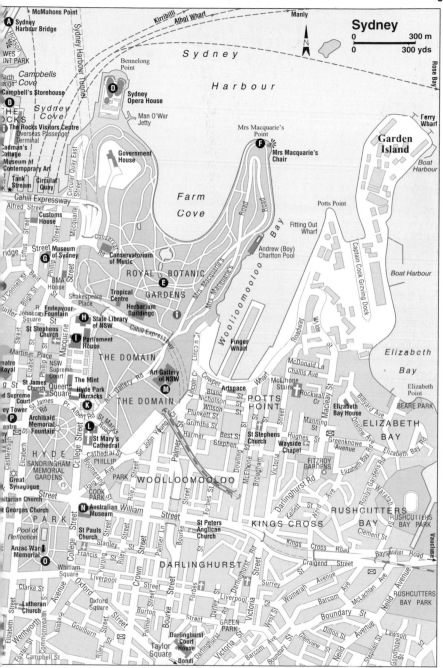

Sydney

0   **300 m**
0   **300 yds**

McMahons Point

A Sydney
Harbour Bridge

Kirribilli   Athol Wharf   Manly

S y d n e y

WES
INT PARK

Hudson

arth
ange

*Campbells
Cove*

Campbell's Storehouse

*S y d n e y
C o v e*

THE
OCKS

The Rocks Visitors Centre

Overseas Passenger
Terminal

adman's
ottage

Museum of
Contemprary Art

B

Tank
Stream

Circular
Quay

Cahill Expressway

Alfred Street

Customs
House

ridge

Street

Loftus

Young

Macquarie

Phillip

Museum
of Sydney

BMA
House

Shakespeare
Place

R. Endeavour
Fountain

St Stephens
Church

Martin Place

NSW
Supreme
Court

St James
Church

Queens
Square

d Supreme
Court

ey Tower

P

entre

ey

Castlereagh

Elizabeth

Archibald
Memorial
Fountain

Phillip St

Circular Quay East

Macquarie St

Conservatorium
Rd

Bennelong
Point

D

Sydney
Opera House

Man O'War
Jetty

H a r b o u r

Mrs Macquarie's
Point

F

Mrs Macquarie's
Chair

Government
House

*Farm
Cove*

Conservatorium
of Music

ROYAL BOTANIC

E

Tropical
Centre

GARDENS

Herbarium
Buildings

i

Cahill Expressway

Mrs Macquaries

Mrs Macquaries Rd

Rd

Road

Woolloomooloo Bay

Fitting Out
Wharf

Andrew (Boy)
Charlton Pool

Potts Point

Captain Cook Graving Dock

**Garden
Island**

Boat
Harbour

Boat Harbour

*Elizabeth
Bay*

Elizabeth
Point

Ferry
Wharf

Rose Bay

G

O'Connell St

Bligh

Bligh St

Hunter

Johnson
Square

St

Phillip St

Bent

H State Library
of NSW

I Parliament
House

THE DOMAIN

heatre
loyal

St James
Rd

Art Gallery Rd

K

Hyde Park
Barracks

The Mint

THE DOMAIN

L

St Mary's
Cathedral

Prince Albert Rd

Cathedral St

St Mary's Rd

Lincoln Cr

Lincoln Cr

Cowper Wharf

Blanc

Nicholson St

Witson

Plunkett St

Griffiths St

Best St

Harmer

Stephen

Finger
Wharf

Artspace

McDonald Ln

Challis Ave

McElhone
Stairs

**POTTS
POINT**

St Stephens
Church

Wayside
Chapel

Hughes St

Manning
St

Rockwall
Cr

Wylde

Broadway

McElhone St

Victoria St

Dowling

Brougham St

Palmer St

**FITZROY
GARDENS**

Elizabeth
Bay House

Greenknowe
Avenue

Billyard Ave

Onslow Ave

Macleay St

Elizabeth Bay Rd

Roslyn Gardens

**ELIZABETH
BAY**

BEARE PARK

Elizabeth Bay Rd

Waratah

HYDE

**SANDRINGHAM
MEMORIAL
GARDENS**

Great
Synagogue

Street

aitarian Church

t Georges Church

PARK

College Street

Pool of
Reflection

Anzac War
Memorial

O

Whitlam
Square

Clarke St

Lutheran
Church

Oxford
Square

Wentworth

Commonwealth

Elizabeth

Campbell St

Goulburn

Brisbane

Riley

Oxford

Street

Crown

Street

Bourke

Street

Burton

Street

N Australian
Museum

St Pauls
Church

Stanley

Francis

Liverpool

Yurong

Palmer Ln

Palmer

WOOLLOOMOOLOO

William

Street

Forbes

DARLINGHURST

Darlinghurst Court
House

Bondi

Street

St Peters
Anglican
Church

Forbes

**GREEN
PARK**

Darley

Liverpool

Victoria

Surrey

Darlinghurst Rd

Bourke

**COOK
PARK**

**HAIG
PARK**

Dowling

Forbes

KINGS CROSS

Kings

Craigend

Cross

Road

Street

Barcom

Womerah

Avenue

Kellett

Ward

Avenue

Bayswater

Glenview

Road

Boundary St

Dillon St

**RUSHCUTTERS
BAY**

Clement St

Neild

Avenue

Lawson

Goodhope

Stephen La

**RUSHCUTTERS
BAY PARK**

**RUSHCUTTERS
BAY PARK**

Neild Avenue

McLachlan Ave

Vaucluse

C Circular
Quay

Tank
Stream

Alfred Street

Taylor
Square

Taylor

Cook St

Shakespeare
Place

**Art Gallery
of NSW**

M

Man O'War
Jetty

SYDNEY

The largest city in Australia and gateway to the country for most overseas visitors, Sydney is a laid-back international metropolis. It also has some fine beaches, along with world-class dining

ustralia's oldest city – as well as its most expansive, most expensive and most populous – Sydney deals in superlatives. Sydney has the tallest buildings of any city in Australia, the most celebrated beaches, the priciest real estate, the naughtiest nightlife and world-class traffic congestion. Its harbour alone has made it a front-runner in any urban beauty contest. If this is your first stop in Australia and the flight path of your aircraft takes you in a loop west of the city, with the Opera House and the Harbour Bridge cast in miniature against the harbour, chances are you'll be smitten.

The end of penal rule

The city didn't have a happy beginning. Sydney was conceived as a penal colony, an open prison for the refuse of British society flushed from the prisons of late 18th-century England and consigned to the ends of the Earth. Early Sydney was nasty, brutish and controlled by a corrupt soldiery whose main business gave them the name "The Rum Corps".

However, in 1810, more than two decades after the colony was founded, luck delivered Lachlan Macquarie, an inspired governor who charted a new course for the place as a society of free men and

women. It was Macquarie who was mainly responsible for several of the fine old buildings that you'll see as you tour the city, and who is remembered in its most illustrious boulevard, Macquarie Street.

During the Victorian era Sydney boomed, when gold and agriculture created a solid economic base. Many of the city's most elegant public buildings date from this period. By the time the Commonwealth of Australia came into being in 1901, its population was close to half a million.

Map on pages 64–5

LEFT: a ferry sails away from Circular Quay.
BELOW: time for a coldie.

Luna Park sits on the water under the northern end of the Harbour Bridge. Built in 1935, it is modelled on the similarly named amusement park at New York's Coney Island. There is another example in St Kilda, Melbourne.

BELOW: the Harbour Bridge from the south, with yachts moored by McMahon's Point.

Transformation

Over the second half of the 20th century, Sydney's character was transformed from a predominantly Anglo-Irish population to one of the world's most ethnically diverse. In the post-war years, Australia opened its doors to waves of immigrants from Italy, Greece, Turkey, Lebanon, Thailand, China, Malaysia, Indonesia, Vietnam and Cambodia, and for many of these groups Sydney has been their first choice.

As you tour the city you'll notice this cultural intermingling, particularly in the cafés and restaurants, and taxi drivers who speak English as a first language are rare.

Your inbound flight will confirm another fact. This is a sprawling giant of a city. Measuring 65 km (40 miles) from north to south, and 50 km (30 miles) across – Sydney is twice the size of Greater London, which has a population of over 7 million, compared with just over 4 million in Sydney. Part of the reason for this is topographical. Sydney's coastline is deeply indented by several large sea inlets, of which Sydney Harbour is

only one. Despite its size, most visitors will find that the major areas of interest are the city centre and a few outlying pockets.

The central Sydney area stretches from the harbour foreshores to Chinatown in the south and from Darling Harbour in the west to the Royal Botanic Gardens in the east. This is a relatively compact area that can be easily covered on foot. Within these boundaries is a rich repertoire of outdoor and indoor pleasures – including views, noble buildings, a few good walks and some essential museums and galleries that will provide reference points for wider explorations of Sydney and New South Wales.

Spectacular city views

A favourite icon of the city it spans, the **Sydney Harbour Bridge** Ⓐ flexes its muscular grey biceps high above the waters of the harbour.

As early as 1815 Macquarie's principal architect, the forger, convict and architectural genius Francis Greenway, had proposed a bridge to connect the two sides of the harbour,

yet it was not until 1924 that work began, and it was not completed until 1932. By this time Sydney badly needed the forested, undulating hills north of the harbour to house its burgeoning population. Until then, ferries provided the only transport service between the two halves of the city. Nowadays the bridge has eight traffic lanes and two railway lines. It is the latticework of steel that does the work; despite their solid appearance, the four stone pylons are purely decorative.

The walkway on the eastern side of the bridge overlooks the city centre and the Opera House. Access is via the Argyle Stairs, located at the lower end of The Cut in Argyle Street. At the top of this staircase, turn left, cross Cumberland Street and take the steps signposted "Cahill Walk". A high fence obstructs the spectacular view from the walkway here, but there are two ways to overcome this.

Located inside the southeast pylon, the **Pylon Lookout** (daily 10am–5pm; admission charge) has three levels of exhibits dedicated to the bridge and the engineers, masons and steelworkers who built it. The lookout is on the top storey, and the view is certainly worth the 200 steps it takes to get there.

Another high-altitude view is available from **BridgeClimb** (5 Cumberland Street, The Rocks; tel: 8274 7777; admission charge; www.bridgeclimb.com). Wearing a special Bridgesuit, harness and communication equipment, climbers hook on to a cable and ascend the arch of the bridge to a height of 134 metres (440 ft) above sea level. By comparison, the top deck of the Pylon Lookout is 89 metres (290 ft) above sea level. As well as the additional cost there is another important difference between the BridgeClimb and the pylon – for safety reasons, cameras are forbidden on BridgeClimb, but not on the pylon.

The Rocks mark the spot

The stubby peninsula that extends a blunt thumb into the harbour, **The Rocks ❸** is the crucible of modern Australia. Not many nations can date their foundation to an exact

Map on pages 64–5

This chapter covers the centre of Sydney, from Pyrmont in the west to Potts Point in the east, and from the Harbour Bridge (and places around Milsons Point at its northern end) south to Haymarket, Chinatown and Surry Hills. For Kings Cross, Darlinghurst and other inner (and all outer) suburbs, see the Sydney Suburbs chapter (pages 90–105).

BELOW: under the bridge. The view from Milson's Point looking south towards the Opera House.

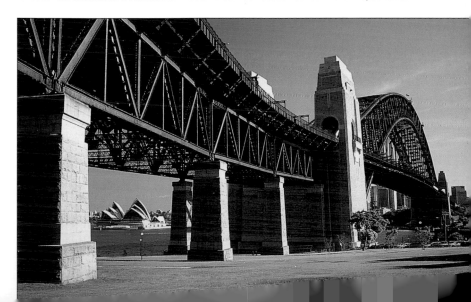

Ken Done (pronounced as in "bone") is a popular local artist and designer who has a gallery in The Rocks exhibiting his paintings. A shop sells clothes, ceramics and other items featuring his work.

BELOW: taking a stroll by The Rocks warehouses.

time and place, but it was here on 26 January 1788 that Europeans landed and scraped the first settlement on Australian soil from the harsh, rocky bushland. In The Rocks, you will find tangible evidence of that settlement – an open book of modern Australian history.

The site for Australia's first European settlement was determined by a mundane fact: the availability of fresh water. Originally, the site intended for the penal colony was Botany Bay, a few kilometres to the south, but the lack of fresh water there made it unsuitable. Charged with the responsibility for establishing the settlement, Governor Arthur Phillip sailed north out of Botany Bay and after a short distance turned west into Port Jackson, as Sydney Harbour was known at the time. At once, Phillip recognised the superior anchorage that this wide, branching waterway offered, and on the southern shore he found a stream and the fresh water he was searching for. Although this stream, the Tank Stream, now trickles underground, it still enters the harbour at

one end of the ferry terminal at Sydney Cove, diagonally opposite the Opera House.

Phillip named this small bay Sydney Cove, in honour of Lord Sydney, the British home secretary who was responsible for the plan to settle convicts at Botany Bay. The date when the ships of the First Fleet dropped anchor is now celebrated as Australia Day.

Open-air museum

The peninsula to the west of the stream was christened The Rocks, and here the first crude shelters were erected, to be followed by sandstone buildings as the colony tottered to its feet. Almost immediately, Sydney Cove became the colony's main port. Warehouses grew up along the waterfront, backed by the merchants' shops, offices, hotels, banks, bars and brothels that went with the seafaring trade of the 19th century. Behind them, gradually ascending Observatory Hill, was a tangle of alleys lined with the cottages of wharf labourers and boatmen. At the northern end of the peninsula, a few streets of patrician terrace houses were home to successful merchants and ships' officers, but respectability eluded The Rocks. By the beginning of the 20th century the area had become a tough, squalid part of the city, infested with criminal gangs and rats, which caused an outbreak of bubonic plague in 1900.

By the 1960s The Rocks had long outlived its original mercantile function. The area was ripe for redevelopment, and the state government was anxious to capitalise on this chunk of prime real estate. The entire precinct nearly fell to the wrecking ball, but a series of courageous and far-sighted industrial actions by the conservationists and the powerful Builders Labourers Federation forced the state government to retreat.

Today, The Rocks is virtually an open-air museum, where you can absorb Australia's early history with a leisurely stroll – although the entire area is now unashamedly devoted to tourism.

National Park

The Rocks begins where George Street passes beneath the railway line and the Cahill Expressway at the intersection of Alfred Street, and stretches north toward the Harbour Bridge. The oldest building in the area is **Cadman's Cottage**, built in 1816 to house the caretaker of government boats, on what was once the shoreline.

Only a small number of buildings remain from the first half of the 19th century. Many more date from the Victorian era, when cargoes of wool, wheat and gold provided a rich source of income that allowed the architectural flourishes of the period to blossom. The contrast between these ornate buildings and the simple, unembellished stonework of the Georgian era is striking. Cadman's Cottage houses the

Sydney Harbour National Park Information Centre (tel: 9247 5033; Mon–Fri 9.30am–4.30pm, Sat–Sun 10am–4.30pm). Covering less than 400 hectares (950 acres), **Sydney Harbour National Park** may be small, but this is some of Sydney's dazzling best, knitting together beaches, parks, islands, convict buildings, stretches of wild bushland and sandstone caves where rocks rubbed smooth by spear points bear witness to the presence of Sydney's Aboriginal people. You can book tours of the National Park in the information centre.

Continue along George Street, then turn left into Argyle Street, where The Cut carves a deep trench through the sandstone. At the top, the **Holy Trinity Anglican Church** is also known as the **Garrison Church** since it once ministered to the spiritual needs of the soldiers at Dawes Point Battery, which stood on the grassy knoll beneath the Sydney Harbour Bridge. The church maintains its links with the military, and the walls are lined with commemorative plaques and military

Map on pages 64–5

Bunting flutters on the old warehouses at The Rocks to celebrate Australia Day on 26 January.

BELOW: Circular Quay and the city from the terrace of the Opera House.

insignia from many branches of the armed services. The green apron at the front of the church is Argyle Place, which closely resembles an English village green, with houses along one side and a pub and a church at opposite ends.

Sails and stars

If you feel like stretching your legs, climb to the top of **Observatory Hill** for a fine view across The Rocks and a shady seat beneath the Moreton Bay figs. This was once known as Windmill Hill, since it was the site of Australia's first wind-mill, built in 1796 to grind grain into flour, but it wasn't a success. Almost as soon as it began turning, the can-vas sails were pilfered and a storm wrecked the machinery, and within a decade, the mill was defunct.

Although a fort was built on the hilltop in 1803, the oldest building still standing on the site is the **Signal Station**, which was built in 1848. In 1855 the hill became the site for the **Sydney Observatory** (tel: 9241 3767; daily 10am–5pm; www.sydney observatory.com.au), which began as

a time-keeping device. Every day at precisely 1pm, the yellow ball would drop from the mast of the square time-ball tower, enabling the captains of ships anchored in the harbour to set their chronometers, crucial for calculating longitude on long Antipodean voyages. And although ships no longer rely on chronometers, the ball still drops at the appointed hour, as it has since the tower was completed in 1858.

Later in the century the role of the tower was expanded and it became a fully-fledged astronomical ob-servatory, but, because of the ever-brightening lights of the city and technological changes in the sci-ence, it was superseded by far more sophisticated telescopes in remote locations. Since 1982, Sydney Observatory has been a museum of astronomy, with an imaginative **3-D Space Theatre** (daily 10am–5pm; admission charge; tour bookings are essential) that takes you on a guided tour of the universe. At night, you can still view stars, galaxies and planets through a telescope with one of the Observatory's astronomers.

TIP

If you want to arrange a rendezvous, meeting on the Town Hall steps (see page 83) under the clock is a Sydney tradition.

BELOW: Sydney Observatory.

Times of the tour vary according to sunset times.

On the waterfront

From Observatory Hill you can climb to the heights of the Harbour Bridge or follow Lower Fort Street, which runs from the Garrison Church toward the base of the bridge. Some of the most ornate terrace houses in The Rocks survive along this street, as well as Sydney's second-oldest pub, the **Hero of Waterloo**, which served its first pint in 1844. At the end of Lower Fort Street, **Dawes Point Park** has a sweeping view over the harbour. Five cannons remain from the original Dawes Point Battery, built to protect the infant colony, but these days they're trained on nothing more fearsome than the Sydney Opera House. Against the backdrop of the Opera House, the palm trees along the waterfront make a classic photograph, particularly in warm evening light.

As you turn from the bridge along Hickson Road, just beyond the Park Hyatt Hotel is **Campbell's Storehouse**, the oldest surviving example of a Sydney warehouse. Robert Campbell was a Scottish merchant who arrived in Sydney in 1798. He leased the land on the western side of Sydney Cove and built a flourishing trading enterprise based on the export of whale and seal products and imports from India.

The stone warehouse was built in 1838, by which time Campbell had created a mercantile empire that included significant landholdings, earning him the subtitle "the father of Australian commerce". To compensate Campbell for the loss of his ship, the *Sydney*, which had been chartered on official business, the government granted Campbell 4,000 acres (1,600 acres) of land and 710 ewes on the limestone plains southwest of Sydney.

Campbell called this property Duntroon, after his ancestral home in Scotland, but it became better known as Canberra, the site of the national capital. Today, the warehouses have become part of a complex of waterfront restaurants, while the masts at the front recall the merchant ships that once carried Campbell's cargoes.

Despite its portly, bunker-like appearance, the **Museum of Contemporary Art ❻** (140 George Street; tel: 9245 2400; daily 10am–5pm; www.mca.com.au) stands at culture's cutting edge. Formerly the home of the Maritime Services Board, this is the country's only museum devoted exclusively to contemporary art in all its myriad forms – performance, sculpture, photography and video as well as painting. To anyone unfamiliar with the muddy syntax that is contemporary art, its speciality is bafflement. Those who might be inflamed by the idea of a video showing football star David Beckham asleep in a Madrid hotel room as a work of art should probably keep their distance.

Map on pages 64–5

The Museum of Contemporary Art is always worth a look, if only to gain access to a café table on the terrace overlooking the harbour.

BELOW: bear-faced line. Colourful display outside the Museum of Contemporary Art.

Sydney Opera House one-hour guided tours run every half-hour 9am–5pm (tel: 9250 7250). Tours are organised by the Guided Tours Booking Office on the Lower Concourse, close to the water's edge.

BELOW: Jørn Utzon designed one of the iconic buildings of the 20th century.

Continuing along the waterfront you come to Circular Quay, the terminus for most of the famous Sydney Harbour ferries and a place you're likely to pass through several times on your excursions.

Architectural landmark

Almost single-handedly, **Sydney Opera House** ❶ (Bennelong Point; tel: 9250 7111; guided one-hour tours for a fee every half-hour 9am–5pm; www.sydneyoperahouse.com) validates Sydney's status as a world-class city. The Opera House had its inception in the 1950s, when the state government ran an international competition for a performing arts centre to stand on what was formerly a tram depot on Bennelong Point, the promontory at the eastern end of Sydney Cove. The winner was a young Danish architect, Jørn Utzon, whose brilliant design captured the imagination of some of the more visionary judges. But from the beginning the building faced formidable obstacles. The technology to cast the soaring sails and to join enormous sheets of glass into

vast, seamless walls did not exist at the time. The building was supposed to take four years to construct and cost A$7 million. However, it took 15 years and cost over A$100 million – yet it was financed entirely by the Opera House Lottery, without any contribution from the public purse. Utzon faced constant interference from unions and from the state government. In 1966 he abandoned the project in disgust, and never returned to see his design completed. The Opera House finally opened in 1973, with a firework display that lit up the harbour.

Today, the Opera House is urban Australia's most potent icon, and a much-loved symbol for the city of Sydney. This is the city's premier venue for the performing arts, home of the Australian Ballet, the Sydney Dance Company and the Australian Opera Company. Its various theatres host symphony concerts, dance, films, plays and, of course, opera. With high demand for tickets to performances, particularly in the Opera House and Concert Hall, you'll need to book well in advance.

Government House

Close to the city, the chimneys that rise from the trees just behind the Opera House belong to an impressive building, **Government House** (tel: 9931 5222; daily 10am–4pm; guided tours every half-hour Fri Sun 10.30am–3pm), formerly the official residence of the governor of New South Wales until it was handed back to the people in 1996. Built between 1837 and 1845 in Gothic Revival style, some of Australia's best-known painters, including Tom Roberts, Arthur Streeton and Russell Drysdale, are represented on the walls inside the house.

Botanic Gardens

Unfurling to the east of the city centre, the **Royal Botanic Gardens ⑤** (Mrs Macquarie's Road; tel: 9231 8111; winter 7am–5pm, summer 7am–8pm; www.rbgsyd.nsw.gov.au) is Sydney's serene, green wonderland, a treasury of tropical and temperate flora, green lawns, ponds, shady trees and some of Sydney's finest views. It was here that Australia took its first faltering steps towards self-sufficiency. As soon as the First Fleet arrived it was crucial to establish gardens to feed the 1,373 convicts, soldiers and administrators, and the spot chosen was Farm Cove, the horseshoe-shaped bay that lies to the east of the Opera House.

The first attempts were a dismal failure because few of the convicts or their guards had any agricultural experience, and the crops withered in the sandy soil. By contrast, the Aboriginal people of the region lived healthy lives on a diet provided by the sea and the bushland, although they were relatively few in number and dispersed in small hunter-gatherer groups. For the first couple of years, the settlers teetered on the brink of starvation, and it was not until farms were established on the rich alluvial soil to the west that the colony's future was assured.

Today, the gardens incorporate palm groves, rose gardens, classical statuary, a succulent garden and glasshouses. A café/restaurant is located near the ponds, set back among the palm trees. This is a lovely spot for a drink or a meal, but

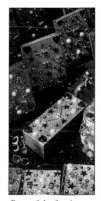

Part of the fun in Sydney is to happen upon a craft stall selling hand-crafted jewellery.

BELOW: Government House.

beware if you decide to picnic on the lawns – the strutting, long-beaked ibis are notorious lunch burglars.

Mrs Macquarie's Point

At the end of the peninsula that forms the eastern arm of Farm Cove, **Mrs Macquarie's Point** ❻ (Royal Botanic Gardens, Mrs Macquarie's Road) looks west across the water to the Opera House, Fort Denison, the Harbour Bridge and the city office towers. This is one of Sydney's finest views, especially at sunrise, when the Opera House glows in the early light. It's also a favourite spot for wedding pictures for the Japanese couples who visit specifically for a white wedding.

Mrs Macquarie, wife of the governor who presided over the colony 1810–21, requested a road be built on the ridge that runs along the spine of this peninsula. Carved from the sandstone at the tip is **Mrs Macquarie's Chair**, the bench where she would sit to admire the view, if legend is to be believed. Above the seat is a stone inscription marking the completion of the scenic road.

TIP

Tours of Fort Denison, which is just off Mrs Macquarie's Point, can be booked from the National Parks Information Centre in Cadman's Cottage *(see page 71)*. Tours also begin here.

BELOW: stone poses. An exchange of views in the Royal Botanic Gardens.

Walk around the curve of the peninsula for a glimpse of **Garden Island**, Sydney's Royal Australian Navy dockyard. Visiting ships from foreign navies also berth here. In the bay between here and the dockyard, the **Finger Wharf** is one of Sydney's most glamorous addresses. Actor Russell Crowe has a condominium at the top of the building, front of house, as you might expect. At lunchtime, the path that winds along Farm Cove from the Opera House to Mrs Macquarie's Chair is Sydney's favourite corporate jogging track.

Around the city

The city centre combines a startling mix of architectural styles, from old colonial buildings to sleek modern commercial blocks.

At the northern end of Phillip Street is the **Museum of Sydney** ❼ (37 Phillip Street; tel: 9251 5988; daily 9.30am–5pm; admission charge), built on the site of the original Government House. It contains subtle, provocative displays that document the city's history from the pre-contact era of the Eora Aboriginal

people to the present. Artefacts, pictures, and audio and digital technologies tell the story of Sydney's evolution from wilderness populated by hunter-gatherers to penal settlement to cosmopolitan metropolis. When you visit, please bear in mind that the museum doesn't believe in spelling it out; the lack of interpretative material invites an intelligent response.

The site of the first Government House lay undiscovered for years until the foundations were unearthed by accident in 1983, remnants of which can now be seen inside the museum.

Macquarie Street

Almost opposite the top of the Botanic Gardens is one of the city's most impressive buildings, the **State Library of New South Wales** ❻ (Macquarie Street; tel: 9273 1414; Mon–Thur 9am–7pm, Fri 9am 6pm, Sat 11am–5pm; www.sl.nsw.gov.au). It consists of several different collections, including the holdings of the Mitchell and Dixson Libraries, which contain some of the most important archives of Australiana, such as early botanical drawings, historic documents, photographs and maps.

Other than for academics, the library will probably have limited interest, but look inside the foyer behind the classical façade. Inlaid in marble on the floor is a reproduction of Abel Tasman's 17th-century map of Australia, the first of its kind.

In the modern extension of the complex, around the corner in Macquarie Street, the shop on the ground level of the General Reference Library has an excellent book section and some unusual souvenirs.

Set back slightly from Macquarie Street behind steel railings, the **Parliament House** ❶ (Macquarie Street; tel: 9230 2319 or 9230 2111 [to book a place in the public gallery]; Mon–Fri 9am–5pm) is the seat of the New South Wales state government. The building has an intriguing history.

This was originally the north wing of the General Hospital and Dispensary, built 1811–16 during Governor Lachlan Macquarie's time. The British government had

Pillar talk. An installation at the Museum of Sydney symbolises links between Aboriginal and European cultures.

BELOW: the inscription above Mrs Macquarie's Chair.

Map on pages 64–5

The Sydney Gay and Lesbian Mardi Gras

You only have to stroll along Darling-hurst's Oxford Street any night of the week to realise that Sydney is a very gay city indeed. In fact it prides itself on a status as one of the leading lights of the gay and les-bian world, a position reaffirmed each year when it hosts the Gay and Lesbian Mardi Gras.

Held annually since 1978, the Mardi Gras is a celebration of gay and lesbian arts, sport, culture and pride that encompasses more than 100 individual events spread over a four-week period. Among the highlights is Fair Day, a day of music, food and live enter-tainment held at Camperdown's Victoria Park, on the western fringe of the city. There's also a Mardi Gras Film Festival, literature events, theatre and music, cabaret and other nightly entertainment at the Mardi Gras Festival Bar.

Focus of the action is the inner suburb of Darlinghurst, long the home of the city's premier gay clubs and bars, but the festival casts a wide net to include other areas of the city with a prominent gay population.

The festival climaxes with the Gay and Lesbian Mardi Gras Parade, which features more than 6,000 gays, lesbians and sup-port groups who strut, prance, skip and shimmy along the streets of Darlinghurst, to an appreciative and raucous audience who line the streets. This is the world's biggest celebration of gay and lesbian culture, attracting a live audience of close to half a million, and a television audience many times larger. The pre-parade entertainment – known as Foreplay – begins at 5.30pm, followed by the parade itself at 7.15pm, led by the hot chrome and thunder brigades of Dykes on Bikes and Boys on Bikes – motorcycle aficionados dressed to thrill in their finest leather and studs. From the inter-section of Elizabeth Street and Liverpool Street near Hyde Park, the parade sashays up Oxford Street, then turns right at Taylor Square into Flinders Street, to end at the corner of Moore Park Road and Anzac Parade. Combining pure entertainment with political statement, the parade lampoons politicians and outspoken anti-gays in par-ticular, harking back to the origins of the event which began as a protest march for gay civil rights.

Costumes vary enormously, from next-to-nothing to fabulous feathered concoctions that turn the wearer into a human flamingo. The dancing, the music, the atmosphere and the choreography add up to a razzle-dazzle evening even if you don't score a front-rank position. Some surprising sections of the community organise floats for the event, including gays and lesbians from the police force, the army and the Jewish community. The parade takes place on the Saturday night following Ash Wednesday, and the best van-tage points are along Flinders Street – although spectators must be in place by mid-afternoon if they're to have a hope of a clear view. At the end of the parade, the action con-tinues with an all-night party at the Hordern Pavilion in Fox Studios. Up to 20,000 crowd into themed venues the size of aircraft hangars for the world's biggest queer rave party. The last survivors won't stagger home-wards until mid-morning the next day.

For information visit the festival website at www.mardigras.org.au. ❏

LEFT: Dykes on Bikes.

refused to provide Macquarie with the funds he needed to build the hospital, so he granted the builders the right to import 60,000 gallons of rum. Since rum was a precious commodity in thirsty Sydney, the city got a free hospital, which rightly became known as the Rum Hospital. After 1829, the Legislative Council, set up to advise the governor, began meeting in the Chief Surgeon's Quarters. With the increase in democratic and self-governing powers later in the century, the state parliament eventually occupied the entire north wing.

The parliament consists of a lower house, the Legislative Assembly, and an upper house, the Legislative Council. The colours in the chambers follow the British tradition – green for the lower house, red for the upper. Members of the public can watch the action when parliament is sitting, generally between mid-February and the end of May, and again mid-September to late November. On sitting days, it is advisable to book in advance if you want to visit the Legislative Assembly during question time, which is when the opposition grills the government and debate is at its liveliest. On non-sitting days, visitors may inspect both chambers.

Southwest of Parliament House and overshadowed by office blocks and banks, **Martin Place** ❶ (between Macquarie and George streets) is the heart of the central business district (CBD). The pedestrian plaza is flanked by several notable buildings, the most striking of which is the Renaissance-style **General Post Office**, now the façade of the Westin Hotel. At the lower end, close to George Street, the **Cenotaph** commemorates Australians who died in the service of their country in World War I. The Anzac Day march on 25 April, when Australians remember those who died in war, begins here every year

following a dawn service. On weekdays from 12.30pm the amphitheatre at the upper end of Martin Place is the venue for concerts, which are usually well attended by workers from the surrounding offices.

The Barracks

Returning to Macquarie Street and a short distance to the right is **Hyde Park Barracks** ❷ (Queens Square, on Macquarie Street; tel: 8239 2311; daily 9.30am–5pm; admission charge). This was Sydney's original lock-up, built to accommodate male convicts employed on government projects. Before it was completed in 1819, most convicts were free to wander the streets, which made Sydney a dangerous place to be after dark. The building, which was designed by the architect Francis Greenway, is remarkable for its simplicity and symmetry, the hallmarks of the Georgian style.

Greenway, who had been convicted of forgery and sentenced to 14 years in New South Wales, was commissioned by Governor Lachlan Macquarie, who was determined

Map
on pages
64–5

The Anzac War Memorial in Hyde Park was completed in 1934 after public donations begun during World War I had totalled $60,000.

BELOW: Martin Place.

After it ceased to be used for male convicts in 1848, Hyde Park Barracks became a depot for single female immigrants seeking work and a female asylum. From 1887 it housed law courts and government offices, and it is now a museum.

BELOW: the Art Gallery of New South Wales with Henry Moore's *Reclining Figure.*

to create a society of free men and women rather than an open gaol, and who embarked on an ambitious programme of public buildings. Macquarie recognised Greenway's architectural talents and conscripted him to design many of these buildings, some of which still stand along Macquarie Street.

Now a museum, the Barracks uses artefacts as well as the building itself to provide some social history and create a vivid picture of convict life in the early days of the colony.

Macquarie eventually fell foul of his overlords in London when a report commissioned by the British government criticised his excessive spending, on public works in particular, and forced his resignation. Deprived of his patron, Greenway lost his position as civil architect and spent his remaining years living in poverty in a hut with dirt floors.

St Mary's Cathedral

Towering above Hyde Park at the eastern boundary of the city proper, **St Mary's Cathedral** ❶ (College Street and St Mary's Road; tel: 9220

0400; Sun–Fri 6.30am–9.30pm, Sat 8am–6.30pm) is the city's largest church, the cathedral church of Sydney's Catholic archdiocese. From the date of its foundation the city had a large Catholic population, due to the high number of Irish among the convict population. However, it was not until 1820 – 42 years after settlement – that the first official Catholic chaplains arrived.

A year later the foundation stone of the first St Mary's Chapel was laid by Macquarie. The original building was destroyed by fire in 1865 and construction began of a much grander church in Gothic Revival style, built from sandstone that was quarried at Pyrmont, just over a kilometre to the west. The northern section of the cathedral opened in 1882, but it was not until 1928 that the building was completed – almost. The spires were not added until 2000, but since the sandstone for their facings came from a different quarry from the rest of the cathedral, they were artificially stained; the match is not quite perfect.

Inside, notable features include

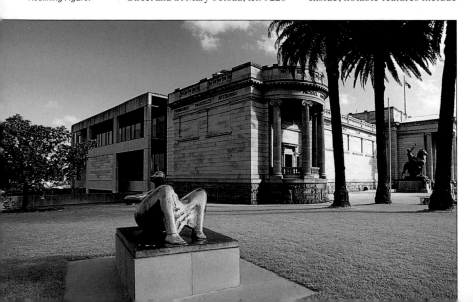

the fine mosaic floor in the crypt and the stained-glass windows.

The Domain

A large public garden known as **The Domain** stretches north from St Mary's Cathedral and is bordered on its western side by colonial buildings such as the State Library and Parliament House. To the east, at the end of an avenue of Moreton Bay fig trees is the **Art Gallery of New South Wales** (Art Gallery Road, The Domain; tel: 9225 1744; daily 10am–5pm, Wed until 9pm; www.art gallery.nsw.gov.au), a stout block of a building devoted to Australian art. Established in 1874, the gallery has been overhauled several times. A 1971 extension almost doubled the exhibition space, and the Cook Bicentenary Wing was added in 1988.

The prestigious collections include work by all major Australian artists and reveal the development of a distinctly Australian approach, to the depiction of landscapes in particular. The gallery has the largest permanent collection of Aboriginal art in the world and also has a notable Asian collection, which includes many fine works from Japan, China and Southeast Asia. There is usually a headline exhibition, which might be the work of a major French Impressionist or a retrospective by one of Australia's leading contemporary Aboriginal artists. This is also the venue for the annual Archibald Prize, Australia's pre-eminent and often controversial portraiture prize.

Historical highlights

South of The Domain on the corner of William Street, the **Australian Museum** (6 College Street; tel: 9320 6000; daily 9.30am–5pm; free; www.austmus.gov.au) is the country's foremost museum of natural history, a vast, imposing assembly of the creatures that crawl, hop, burrow and swim across Australia's lands

and seas. Early naturalists were fascinated by the weird life forms they found, such as the platypus, an egg-laying mammal, and this museum – the country's first, established in 1827 – was set up to catalogue the continent's biota.

As well as its vast collection of 14.5 million insects, molluscs, fishes and rocks, the museum also has a significant sampling of artefacts from Aboriginal and Pacific Islands cultures in its anthropological and archaeological collections. Many of these were acquired during the first contact period, when these cultures were being exposed to the rest of the world for the first time.

Only a fraction of its collections are displayed, but the museum mounts ever-changing exhibitions designed to captivate young minds.

Across College Street, in the southern section of Hyde Park, the art-deco **Anzac War Memorial** commemorates the Australian servicemen who fought in World War I. The acronym "Anzac" comes from the Australian and New Zealand Army Corps, formed during World War I.

Map on pages 64–5

TIP

The Sydney Visitors' Centre Darling Harbour (33 Wheat Road, tel: 9286 0111) is located behind the Imax Theatre, under the expressway. It is open 9.30am–5.30pm for general advice and information about tickets for a variety of city attractions.

BELOW: bone idol. A young boy is enraptured by the dinosaurs at the Australian Museum.

The Brett Whiteley Studio is the workplace of one of the greats of 20th century Australian art. It has been kept much as he left it when he died in 1992, complete with unfinished pictures, and there are changing exhibitions of his work. (2 Raper St, Surry Hills; tel: 9225 1740; www.brettwhiteley. org/thestudio.html; Sat–Sun 10am–4pm; admission charge.)

BELOW: stained glass at the Queen Victoria Building.

Over 416,000 Australians served in the country's armed services during World War I, about 10 percent of the total population, all volunteers. The conflict redefined Australia's notion of its place in the world. In particular, the memory of the disastrous landing at Anzac Cove, where Australian troops were deployed as part of a combined British imperial force to open a front in southern Turkey, still resonates even among Australians three generations removed from the conflict.

The central motif of the building is *Sacrifice*, a bronze sculpture set below floor level depicting a young warrior lying naked on his shield, which is supported by his mother, wife and sister. At the front of the memorial, the poplar trees bordering the Pool of Reflections denote the battlefields of France.

A panoramic view

Sydney Tower (100 Market Street; tel: 9333 9222; Sun–Fri 9am–10.30pm, Sat 9am–11.30pm; admission charge) is instantly recognisable, a golden minaret rising head and shoulders above every other building in the city – or possibly a lightly singed marshmallow at the end of a very long toasting stick.

At 250 metres (820 ft) high, the view from the observation deck is Sydney's finest, covering the entire metropolitan area as far as the Blue Mountains in the west on a smog-free day. Sign up for the Skywalk tour and you can admire the view from outside the enclosed deck. Wearing a one-piece blue-and-yellow "sky suit" (definitely not a jumpsuit, as your guide will tell you) and tethered to the railing, skywalkers ascend another 10 metres (33ft) above the observation deck and outside onto a glass-floored walkway with a heart-stopping view below.

Victorian elegance

The **Queen Victoria Building** (George Street, between Market and Druitt streets; tel: 9265 6855; Mon–Sat 9am–6pm, Thur until 9pm, Sun 11am–5pm), QVB for short, is one of the city's Victorian-era masterworks. The ornate shopping arcade was built in Romanesque style and designed by George McRae, who was one of the final architects for the neighbouring Town Hall.

Occupying an entire city block, the QVB has performed various functions since it opened as a produce market in 1898, housing a concert hall, coffee shops, offices, showrooms, warehouses and various traders. In the 1930s the interior was remodelled in art-deco style, but in subsequent years it was partitioned into a warren of offices and low-rent shops.

A resurgence of civic pride saved the building from demolition, and it was restored to its original splendour in the 1980s, following a multimillion-dollar refurbishment. The stained-glass windows, sweeping staircases and balustrades and tessellated floors bear witness to the vision of its architect and the artistry of its builders.

Inside, the most notable features are the glass central dome and the huge hanging clock. Above the clock face, a model of an Aborigine with a spear parades in a circuit past dioramas depicting various scenes from Australia's history, including the forced separation of Aboriginal children and their families – a sad fact of Australian life until the 1960s.

Tiered galleries of upmarket stores elevate shopping to new levels of opulence. For the most part, the ground floor is devoted to well-known international brands, but the upper two levels have several small, distinctive speciality shops.

A short distance away, another historic shopping thoroughfare, the **Strand Arcade**, runs between Pitt Street and George Street Mall.

Meeting place

Still on George Street, opposite the Queen Victoria Building is **Sydney Town Hall** ® (483 George Street; tel: 9265 9333; Mon–Fri 9am–5pm), an outstanding example of Victorian architecture. Constructed from sandstone between 1873 and 1888, it was designed by a succession of architects, several of whom had a tumultuous relationship with the city's aldermen.

The façade reflects a kaleidoscope of influences, from Greco-Roman to Flemish to Italianate. It also reflects an emerging sense of Australian pride. This was one of the first buildings to use native flora and fauna as decorative motifs. Within the triangular pediment above the entrance, Sydney's coat of arms is surrounded by waratahs, the state flower. Inside, etched glass windows are inscribed with native ferns, cabbage tree palms, lyrebirds and cockatoos, while the stair railings are decorated with waratahs and flannel flowers.

The vestibule is open to the public, but the Centennial Hall, immediately beyond, is only open for functions. Dominating the front of the hall, the Grand Organ ranks among the world's largest, with close to 9,000 pipes. Free organ recitals (tel: 9265 9007 for information) are held at various times throughout the year.

ABOVE: Sydney Tower.
BELOW: Aboriginal dancers take it to the streets.

The Olympic Legacy

A s you travel around Sydney, from time to time you might happen to notice a blue line painted on the road. This is no ordinary line. It weaves across streets from one side to the other in a permanent state of anarchy, in total defiance of lane markings, seemingly a law unto itself. In fact, when they glance down and notice this line, some Sydneysiders feel a warm glow of satisfaction.

It was this line that marked the route of the marathon during the Sydney 2000 Olympic and Paralympic Games, leading the world's greatest distance runners from one side of the city to the other, through the grey canyons at its heart, through parklands and suburban streets, as it threaded its way over the 42-km (26-mile) course. And although parts of the line have been painted out, most of it still remains, a tangible, everyday reminder of Sydney's 17 days in the world's sporting spotlight.

The most spectacular residue of those days can be found at Homebush Bay, the focus of the Sydney 2000 Olympic and Paralympic Games. Once an industrial wasteland, the 640-hectare (1,600-acre)

site west of the city along the Parramatta River was transformed into a dazzling sporting complex. Stadium Australia, the magnificent centrepiece of the Games, was renamed the Telstra Stadium, a venue for rock concerts as well as for championship rugby, AFL and cricket games.

The Aquatic Centre is used daily by thousands of people, while the Superdome, the indoor arena for gymnastics events, has become the home of the Sydney Kings basketball team. As a result of the Games, Sydney also has tennis, hockey, equestrian and cycling centres. At Penrith, to the west of the Homebush Olympics site, Sydney has a white-water run as well as a superb rowing course that is used regularly for school and club races.

The city also acquired a suburb, Newington, the world's largest solar-powered residential development, a 90-hectare (220-acre) complex with houses, shops, a business park, wetlands and a nature reserve – all constructed as part of the Olympic Athletes Village, and afterwards sold for private use.

The Games also left Sydney with a spiritual legacy. Ask anyone who was there and they'll tell you it was a magical time to be in the city. Schools were closed for a week longer than the standard two-week holiday and most people took time off work. The entire city had a holiday air. Even the weather cooperated, bringing warmer-than-usual spring days and blue skies that left visitors marvelling. Trains ran on time and, what's more, they were free. Complete strangers talked to one another, and the Homebush sporting complex worked like a dream.

All this in spite of those detractors who said it couldn't be done or that it shouldn't be done; the stadiums wouldn't be finished in time; ticket sales would be a disaster; the money could be better spent elsewhere; despite the political shenanigans that went on behind the scenes, the Sydney Olympic Games were an outstanding success, and remain one of the city's proudest memories. ❏

LEFT: The Sydney 2000 opening ceremony.

Darling Harbour

The redevelopment of Darling Harbour revitalised a 54-hectare (133-acre) area that had become an unsightly industrial wasteland and created a new tourist precinct.

Extending from the city side of Darling Harbour, the **Sydney Aquarium** ❺ (Aquarium Pier, Darling Harbour; tel: 8251 7800; daily 9am–10pm; admission charge; www.sydneyaquarium.com.au) is the best place to see Australia's extraordinary aquatic life at close quarters without getting wet or eaten.

As well as crocodiles and tanks full of multicoloured tropical fish, the aquarium has transparent tunnels that take you underwater for a spectacular, fish-eye journey through various habitats teeming with sea creatures – the Great Barrier Reef, a Seal Sanctuary and the Open Oceanarium – where sharks, sea turtles and stingrays glide alongside. You can save 10 percent on the admission price when you book online.

Australia has a long association with the sea, and the **National Maritime Museum** ❼ (2 Murray Street, Darling Harbour; tel: 9298 3777; daily 9.30am–5pm; www. anmm.gov.au) chronicles that relationship with a riveting display of artefacts, paintings and boats of all descriptions. Included are a number of significant Aboriginal works, some fine examples of mariners' craftwork and the *Spirit of Australia*, a jet-powered hydrofoil which has held the world speed record of 511 km/h (317 mph) since 1978. Moored at the front of the museum in Darling Harbour, a floating exhibit includes an unmanned lightship, an Indonesian trading perahu, a boat that carried Vietnamese refugees to Australia, a submarine and a destroyer.

After decades of trying to curb illegal gambling, the state government allowed a giant casino to be built, despite some local opposition.

Star City Casino ⓤ (80 Pyrmont Street, Pyrmont; tel: 9777 9000; 24 hours; www.starcity.com.au) brings a touch of Las Vegas to Sydney's waterfront. The décor inside the huge main gaming room is a chaotic blend of fake palm trees and chunky rocks, enhanced by fountains and lots of neon. Its appeal is blunted slightly since gambling is a feature at pubs and clubs throughout the city, but Australians are enthusiastic gamblers, and for those who want 24-hour action and 200 gaming tables with blackjack, roulette, slot machines, Caribbean stud poker and pontoon, this is the place.

From market to museum

On the far side of Pyrmont from Darling Harbour, the **Sydney Fish Market** ⓥ (Bank Street, Pyrmont; tel: 9004 1100; daily 7am–4pm approx) claims to be the second-largest, in terms of variety, after Tokyo's equivalent, although it doesn't cover a particularly large area. This bustling market is open until mid-afternoon, and, as well as buying fresh fish here, many

Map on pages 64–5

Red-light area. The Carpentaria is an unmanned lightship, built in 1917, now moored in front of the National Maritime Museum.

BELOW: semaphore display above the entrance to the Maritime Museum.

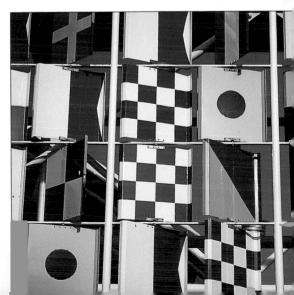

Map
on pages
64–5

*Under pressure.
Control systems
aboard a submarine
at the National
Maritime Museum.*

BELOW: the
Powerhouse Museum.

Sydneysiders come to sample a plate of seafood – which might be anything from sashimi to grilled prawns to fresh oysters or a traditional plate of fish and chips – at one of the market's indoor or outdoor cafés.

Prices are keen, and the squawking seagulls and the boats of the Sydney fishing fleet in the background contribute to the atmosphere. As well as the cafés and fish stalls, the market has a bakery, fruiterer, wine shop and delicatessen.

Southeast of the market is one of the gems of the development, the **Powerhouse Museum** Ⓦ (500 Harris Street, Ultimo; tel: 9217 0111; daily 10am–5pm; admission charge; www.powerhousemuseum.com) takes the hammer, spanner and screwdriver to dissect the technology of the industrial era, and the result is fascinating.

Housed inside the building that once provided electricity for Sydney's trams, various principles of steam power, electricity, magnetism and chemistry are illustrated through a series of thoughtful exhibits, working models and hands-on displays.

The emphasis is on learning through observation and participation, which makes this a special source of delight for children, although not all of the exhibits that whirr, beep, flash and ignite at the press of a button are in working order. Highlights include chuffing steam engines, the Strasburg Clock and aeronautical exhibits.

Chinatown

Away from the museum and the harbour area towards the city centre lies **Chinatown** Ⓧ, a compact section from Harris Street to Castlereagh Street, which was once the home of Chinese traders and fruit-and-vegetable vendors who worked at the adjacent Central Markets, now better known as Paddy's Market. Today, the main activity of the area is gastronomy – everything from Peking duck to Mongolian lamb, Japanese teppanyaki to spicy Malay soups and Indonesian stir-fries.

At the heart of Chinatown, Dixon Street is a pedestrian plaza guarded by lion gates, where restaurant tables spill out across the pavement and aromatic scents fill the air. ❑

RESTAURANTS, CAFÉS, BARS & PUBS

Restaurants

Across the Harbour Bridge

Aqua Dining
Corner Paul & Northcliff Streets, Milsons Point
Tel: 9964 9998
www.aquadining.com.au
Open: L & D daily. **$$$**
With a blinder of a position above the Olympic swimming pool by the Harbour Bridge, Aqua could probably get away with serving any old rubbish. But this is ambitious modern cooking with a high success rate. Pricey wine though.

Milsons
17 Willoughby Street, Kirribilli
Tel: 9955 7075
www.milsonsrestaurant.com.au
Open: L Mon-Fri, D Mon-Sat.
$$$
Up by the northern end of the Bridge sits this reliable purveyor of modern Australian cooking.

Chinatown & Haymarket

Dragon Star Seafood
Level 3, Market City, 9-13 Hay Street, Haymarket
Tel: 9211 8988
L & D daily. **$**
Sydney's biggest Chinese restaurant and dim sum venue. Go for brunch on Sunday and watch the waiters

communicate by walkie-talkie as they serve some 800 patrons. BYO.

Golden Century
393-399 Sussex Street, Haymarket
Tel: 9212 3901
www.goldencentury.com.au
L & D daily. **$**
Chinese-style seafood at its best, and with all the hustle and bustle of a Hong Kong dim sum restaurant.

Circular Quay to Bennelong Point

Aria
1 Macquarie Street, East Circular Quay
Tel: 9252 2555
www.ariarestaurant.com
Open: L Mon-Fri, D daily.
$$$$
Contemporary cooking with a healthy French influence scores a lot of points in this smart restaurant right on Circular Quay and with outstanding views.

Café Sydney
Level 5, Customs House, 31 Alfred Street, Circular Quay
Tel: 9251 8683
www.cafesydney.com
Open: L Sun-Fri, D Mon-Sat.
$$$
A sublime setting with all the vistas of Circular Quay. It has a graceful historic interior and a great terrace for balmy summer dining. The food,

whilst OK, has yet to catch up with the setting.

Guillaume at Bennelong
Sydney Opera House, Bennelong Point
Tel: 9241 1999
www.guillaumeatbennelong.com.au
Open: L Thur-Fri, D Mon-Sat. **$$$**
This award-winning restaurant offers modern French cuisine from Guillaume Brahimi. For food and setting it can't be beaten. Must book.

Downtown Sydney

Bilson's
Radisson Plaza Hotel, 27 O'Connell Street
Tel: 8214 0496
www.bilsons.com.au
Open: L Mon-Fri, D Mon-Sat.
$$$$

The extravagant classic French-based cuisine from Tony Bilson is absolutely scrumptious. And there's a wine list to match.

Botanic Gardens Restaurant
Royal Botanic Gardens, Mrs Macquarie's Road
Tel: 9241 2419
Open: L daily. **$$**
Another lovely setting, this time in the Botanic Gardens. Serves

PRICE CATEGORIES

Prices for three-course dinner per person with a half-bottle of house wine:
**$** = under A$ 50
**$$** = A$ 50–80
**$$$** = A$ 80–120
**$$$$** = over A$ 120

RIGHT: a full plate of ocean goodies.

accomplished fusion cooking, but patience may be needed.

The Summit
Level 47, Australia Square, 264 George Street
Tel: 9247 9777
www.summitrestaurant.com.au
Open: L Sun-Fri, D daily. $$$
Revolving restaurant with amazing views, decorated in space-age style. You wouldn't even notice if the food was poor, but it isn't.

Hyde Park to Surry Hills

Beppi's
Yurong Street (corner Stanley Street), East Sydney
Tel: 9360 4558
www.beppis.com.au
Open: L Mon-Fri, D Mon-Sat. $$
This traditional restaurant, popular with the media, is the finest in Sydney's Little Italy. Opened in 1956 by Beppi Polese and family-run to this day.

Billy Kwong
3/355 Crown Street, Surry Hills
Tel: 9332 3300
D daily. $$
There's not much room and you can't book ahead, but wait for a

PRICE CATEGORIES

Prices for three-course dinner per person with a half-bottle of house wine:
$ = under A$ 50
$$ = A$ 50–80
$$$ = A$ 80–120
$$$$ = over A$ 120

table and you'lll be rewarded with Kylie Kwong's imaginative Chinese cooking. BYO.

Diethnes
336 Pitt Street, Hyde Park
Tel: 9267 8956
www.diethnes.com.au
Open: L & D Mon-Sat. $
One of Sydney's oldest Greek restaurants. Old favourites like moussaka, lamb casserole, and cabbage rolls, complemented by Greek coffee and baklava. Busy but friendly.

Longrain
85 Commonwealth Street, Surry Hills
Tel: 9280 2888
www.longrain.com
Open: L Mon-Fri, D Mon-Sat. $$$
Spacious 100-year-old warehouse with chic ambience and some terrific food; a fusion of Thai and Chinese.

Marque
355 Crown Street, Surry Hills
Tel: 9332 2225
www.marquerestaurant.com.au
Open: D Mon-Sat. $$$
Elegant French cuisine from master chef Mark Best. For sophisticated food with imagination, there's nowhere better.

Millers Point, Darling Harbour & Wynyard

Machiavelli
123 Clarence Street
Tel: 9299 3748
www.machiavelli.com.au
Open: L & D Mon-Fri. $$$
Big, loud Italian restau-

rant. The massive antipasto dishes are the city's best.

The Malaya
39 Lime Street, King Street Wharf, Darling Harbour
Tel: 9279 1170
www.themalaya.com.au
Open: L Mon-Sat, D daily. $$$
Authentic Malaysian cuisine – reputedly the best laksa in town. Dine by the water, or inside in an open-plan setting.

Tetsuya's
529 Kent Street
Tel: 9267 2900
www.tetsuyas.com
Open: L Sat, D Tues-Sat. $$$$
Held in awe by locals, Tetsuya Wakuda combines French and Japanese cooking techniques with the freshest of Australian seafood and other ingredients to produce Sydney's most exciting food. Book way ahead.

The Wharf
Pier 4, Hickson Road, Walsh Bay
Tel: 9250 1761
www.wharfrestaurant.com.au
Open: L & D Mon-Sat. $$
Interestingly eclectic food in a casual industrial space propped out over the water.

Zaaffran
Level 2, Harbourside Shopping Centre, Darling Harbour
Tel: 9211 8900
www.zaaffran.com.au
Open: L & D daily. $$
Australia's only 5-star Indian restaurant. Tradi-

tional, home-style Indian cooking, presented with a contemporary flair.

Potts Point

Arun Thai
28 Macleay Street, Potts Point
Tel: 9326 9132
www.arunthai.com.au
Open: L Thur-Sun, D daily. $$
The unusual décor – in the style of an 18th-century Thai nobleman's house – supports the quiet and relaxed atmosphere, and complements the traditional Thai food. Excellent wine list.

Pyrmont

Flying Fish
Jones Bay Wharf, 19-21 Pirrama Road, Pyrmont
Tel: 9518 6677
www.flyingfish.com.au
Open: L Tues-Fri & Sun, D Tues-Sat. $$$
Lots of timber in this old wharf building, offset by theatrical lighting. Fish prepared with flair.

The Rocks

Bel Mondo
Gloucester Walk (up Argyle Stairs from Argyle Street), The Rocks
Tel: 9241 3700
www.belmondo.com.au
Open: D Mon-Sat. $$$
Once you've found it, watch the chef preside over the preparation of Italian-style food in an open kitchen on a raised dais. The wine list is extensive and exotic.

est.
Establishment Hotel, 252 George Street

Tel: 9240 3010
www.merivale.com/
establishment/est
Open: L Mon-Fri, D Mon-Sat.
$$$$
Enjoy Peter Doyle's
brilliantly accomplished
modern cuisine in classy
surroundings, with an
adjoining sushi restau-
rant, cigar bar and an ele-
gantly retro downstairs
bar. Top marks.

Quay
Overseas Passenger
Terminal, The Rocks
Tel: 9251 5600
www.quay.com.au
Open: L Tues-Fri, D daily.
$$$$
Inspired cuisine with an
unmistakable French
influence.

Rockpool
107 George Street,
The Rocks
Tel: 9252 1888
www.rockpool.com
Open: D Tues-Sat. **$$$$**
Choose between the 5-
course and 8-course
degustation menus.

Sailors Thai
106 George Street,
The Rocks
Tel: 9251 2466
Open: L Mon-Fri, D Mon-Sat.
$$$
Beautifully crafted Thai
street food. There's a
cheaper option in the
downstairs canteen.

Yoshii
115 Harrington Street,
The Rocks
Tel: 9247 2566

www.yoshii.com.au
Open: L Tues-Fri, D Mon-Sat.
$$$$
Simplicity and experi-
mentation are the two
key ingredients at this
award-winning Japanese
restaurant in The Rocks.

Cafés, bars & pubs

Downtown Sydney
Art Gallery Restaurant
Art Gallery of NSW,
1 Art Gallery Road
Tel: 9225 1819
Open: L daily. **$$**
A comfy restaurant
upstairs and a deli-café
for gallery visitors and
passers-by. Both get
busy at weekends.

**Hyde Park Barracks
Café**
Queen Square,
Macquarie Street
Tel: 9222 1815
Open: L daily. **$$**
Over the road from
Hyde Park, this large
café has a historic,
colonial feel thanks to
the architecture and
surroundings. Modern
Australian cuisine.
Fully licensed.

Haymarket/Hyde Park
Century Tavern
Liverpool Street, corner
George Street
Tel: 9264 3157
Open: L & D daily. **$**
An upstairs bar, tucked
away overlooking
George Street. Dark,
low-key décor. Attracts a
mixed crowd.

Civic Hotel
388 Pitt Street (corner
Goulburn Street)
Tel: 8080 7000
www.civichotel.com.au
This 1940s pub with an
attractive, retro style
hosts live music, club
sessions and jazz.

Three Wise Monkeys
555 George Street (corner
Liverpool Street)
Tel: 9283 5855
www.3wisemonkeys.com.au
A pub in the thick of
things on one of
Sydney's busiest inter-
sections. Attracts young
locals and fashion-
conscious international
backpackers.

Millers Point
**Lord Nelson Brewery
Hotel**
Corner Kent & Argyle streets
Tel: 9251 4044
www.lordnelson.com.au
Competes with the Hero

of Waterloo for title of
Sydney's oldest pub.
Several beers are
brewed in-house.

The Rocks
Hero of Waterloo
81 Lower Fort Street
Tel: 9252 4553
A truly historic Rocks pub
and a local landmark. If
you want to experience a
true-blue Australian
hotel, this much-loved
and historic watering
hole is a prime choice.

MCA Café
140 George Street
Tel: 9241 4253
www.mca.com.au
Open: L daily. **$$**
Part of the Museum of
Contemporary Art on
Circular Quay West, this
is more like a restaurant
than a café, but one
with a relaxed feel. Enjoy
the great views of the
Opera House.

RIGHT: Chinatown is packed with restaurants.

SYDNEY'S SUBURBS

Sydney 's development has been shaped by the snaking course of its harbour. Close to the centre it's a water city, with the ferry system linking the harbour suburbs. Further out you'll need road or rail to transport you to some of the sights that most visitors miss

A visit that took in nothing more than the city centre itself would leave you with a lop-sided view of Sydney. In fact there are plenty of good reasons to venture beyond the immediate confines of the city – including glamorous beaches, fine historic houses, lively inner suburbs and the vast sporting complex that was built for the 2000 Olympic Games *(see page 84)*.

Further afield you'll find pockets of colonial history, rivers that have carved broad waterways from sandstone plateaux and National Parks teeming with the sights, sounds and smells of wild Australia.

The northside

On a bush-clad hillside overlooking the harbour, **Taronga Zoo** ❶ (Bradleys Head Road, Mosman; tel: 9969 2777; daily 9am–5pm; admission charge) has been a popular destination for daytrips since it opened in 1916. The zoo has a spectacular array of creatures – lions, snow leopard, rhino, red pandas, seals and primates – in sensitive surroundings that recreate, as far as possible, the animals' natural habitats.

There's also a comprehensive range of Australian wildlife with an especially fine collection of reptiles, as well as kangaroos, wombats and koalas. Intelligent use of space and

water helps the animal enclosures blend with the surroundings, while the views over the harbour are among Sydney's best. (*Taronga* is an Aboriginal word for "water view".)

The zoo also has a few unusual tours, such as "Roar and Snore", an evening supper followed by a nocturnal safari and a night in a tent – while the animals roar, bellow and chatter to the stars.

Although it can be reached by car, it's easier to buy a ZooPass at the terminal at Circular Quay and catch

Map on page 93

LEFT: Bondi Beach.
BELOW: Taronga Zoo, with the city skyline beyond.

The grand entrance to Taronga Zoo.

BELOW: an inner suburb terraced house.

a ferry, which departs twice each hour, across the harbour to the zoo. Then take the cable car to the upper entrance and zigzag down the hill past the various enclosures on your way back to the terminal. The ZooPass covers most activities.

Manly

Take the ferry further round to the northeast where, on a spur that ends at the cliffs of North Head, you'll find **Manly ❷**, one of Sydney's summer favourites, with a choice of beaches and a lively atmosphere. Manly was named by Captain Arthur Phillip, commander of the First Fleet, who landed here in January 1788 and, according to legend, was so impressed by the confident and manly behaviour of the Cannalgal and Kayimai people who waded out to his boat that he gave it the name Manly Cove. He might have reconsidered two years later, when he was speared through the shoulder by those same people on the beach here, but to his credit, Phillip saw it as a misunderstanding, and refused to allow any punitive action.

Before the Harbour Bridge was completed, Manly was a popular holiday spot for many Sydneysiders, and in fact this is the only Sydney suburb with both harbour and ocean beaches. The ferry, water taxi and fast catamaran connections with Circular Quay are excellent so it's a good choice if you feel like a day at the beach without a long road trip.

Running along the curve of Manly Cove, where the ferry comes in, **Manly Esplanade** is a busy thoroughfare with many cafés and restaurants. At the end of the Esplanade furthest from Manly Wharf, **Oceanworld Manly** (West Esplanade; tel: 8251 7877; daily 10am–5.30pm; admission charge) is a historic aquarium with transparent underwater tunnels that transport you into the realm of sharks, giant stingrays, turtles and seals. For the brave (or foolhardy) there is Shark Dive Xtreme – a scuba session with sharks – suitable even for novices.

The mainly pedestrianised shopping plaza, **The Corso**, runs between the Esplanade and **Manly Beach**. It

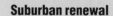

Suburban renewal

For years many of Sydney's inner suburbs languished as slums, ignored in favour of new developments with larger plots of land and often easy access to, or views over, the harbour. This began to change in the latter half of the 20th century when areas such as Paddington began to attract a younger, cashed-up clientele prepared to embrace urban living. Minimal backyards and tricky parking conditions weren't a problem if your priority was easy access to the CBD by day and a buzzing local café, bar and club scene at night. Today terrace houses in Paddington cost a fortune, and there's always a buyer.

is a busy place where people come to browse the souvenir shops with their 1930s facades, or stop off at one of the cafés for an inexpensive snack.

Manly Beach is one of Sydney's finest – a broad, golden sweep of sand backed by cafés. This is a more family-friendly beach than Bondi, and the shade of the Norfolk Island pine trees is a welcome relief, although it doesn't have the same gloss as its more famous neighbour – nor the same exhibitionist appeal.

Protected by North Head, **Shelley Beach** is a small delight with calmer waves than Manly Beach.

The inner suburbs

Close to the Central Business District (CBD) are some of the most sought-after properties in Sydney, even though they're not on the harbour – this in a city that appears to value its waterside suburbs above all else.

Most of the inner suburbs have emerged from neglect to become fashionable districts inhabited by the urban elite. The innermost suburb of **Kings Cross**, however, doesn't quite fit into this pattern. For many, this is the epicentre of edgy, vibrant nightlife; to others, it's the city's grubby, sordid underbelly,

Map below

TIP

Manly Scenic Walkway begins behind the town's and museum. The 10-km (6-mile) trail has two stretches, each less than 2 km (1 mile), accessible to wheelchair users.

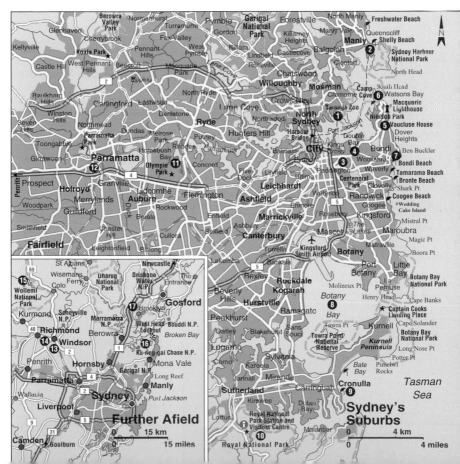

where tricks are turned and substances abused. All this can be found, but for many visitors it's simply the bustling suburb where their hotel is located and where they might go out for a reasonably priced meal. On the whole, it's relaxed, friendly and worth a wander.

Most of **Paddington ❸**, south of Kings Cross, was built during the Victorian era, and the suburb derives its appeal from the integrity of its streetscapes. The undulating rows of terrace houses wrapped in filigreed iron balconies have inspired the name "Paddington lace".

Oxford Street, Paddington's main thoroughfare, is Sydney's fashion catwalk, a 1-km (½-mile) boulevard of boutiques, cafés, galleries and homeware shops. The suburb also has Sydney's favourite, fashion-conscious market, Paddington Village Bazaar, also known as **Paddington Market** (St John's Church, Oxford Street; Sat 10am– 4pm). This is the place to go for didgeridoos, tribal silver, massages, slinky t-shirts or eye-catching one-offs from up-and-coming clothes designers.

The original owner of Vaucluse House, William Charles Wentworth, was born in 1790. The son of a convict, he took part in the first successful inland exploration across the Blue Mountains and co-founded the colony's first independent newspaper, The Australian, *in 1824.*

BELOW: Paddington pair. A couple contemplate jewellery at the Sunday market.

Pick up something to eat from the market and stroll up Oxford Street to **Centennial Park**, where most of Sydney comes to cycle, rollerblade, ride a horse, walk the dog or fling a frisbee amid 360 hectares (900 acres) of palm-lined avenues, fig groves and paperbark-fringed lakes.

The interior harbour

East of the CBD there are sunny parks, beaches, bays, and spectacular cliffside views over the harbour or the Pacific. It is a superb setting for the mansions of the wealthy who compete for prime sites and push up residential property prices.

Glossy and glamorous, **Double Bay ❹** is synonymous with chic boutiques crammed with expensive European labels, gourmet delicatessens and pavement cafés. This handsome harbourside suburb is one of Sydney's most desirable addresses, but unless you're shopping, the main reason to come here is people-watching. Park yourself at an outdoor café and watch the action – and the Mercedes endlessly cruising as they search for that most elusive of all Double Bay commodities, a parking space.

Vaucluse House

Follow the South Head Road east from Double Bay to reach **Vaucluse House ❺** (Wentworth Road, Vaucluse; tel: 9388 7922; Tues–Sun 10am–4.30pm; admission charge). Built in the Gothic Revival style, it is one of the few surviving examples of the grand 19th-century "marine villas" that once dotted Sydney Harbour's southern shores. It was the residence of William Wentworth, an explorer, publisher and politician who lived here almost continuously between 1827 and 1862, with his wife and their 10 children. Two of these children were born out of wedlock, which was one of the reasons why the

Wentworths were not readily accepted in polite society.

The house includes all the apparatus of a patrician home of the colonial era, such as stables, lavish entertaining rooms, large kitchens and storage areas and quarters for the servants, some of whom were convicts. Now operated by the Historic Houses Trust, the house interior includes many original pieces that would have been in daily use by the Wentworth family.

At one time the Vaucluse estate covered more than 200 hectares (515 acres), and even though it has since been whittled down to a mere 10 hectares (25 acres), it still occupies a sizeable chunk of the suburb to which it gives its name. The grounds are magnificent, a rambling parkland of lawns, palm groves, fountains, waterfalls, creeks and stone bridges, laid out and planted as they would have been in the Wentworths' day Adjacent to the house, the Vaucluse House Tearooms, a gracious, Edwardian-style conservatory, is just the place for a spot of tea and cake.

The South Head peninsula

As you head further east, easy enjoyment is to be found in the coastal walks, beaches and parks. **Watsons Bay** ❻, which at one time was a fishing village with a naval station occupying the natural defensive position afforded by the high sandstone cliffs of the South Head peninsula. **Robertson Park**, which lies just beside the local pub, is a lovely place for a picnic, and you can buy takeaway seafood from the kiosk near the wharf.

Climb the cliffs on the ocean side of Watsons Bay for a dramatic view of **The Gap**, where the Pacific rollers explode against the cliffs. There's a fine walk from here up through Gap Park, which follows the cliffs toward the **Macquarie Lighthouse**. This was Australia's

first lighthouse, constructed in the time of Governor Macquarie, and the simple, satisfying lines bear witness to the skills of his convict-architect, Francis Greenway.

Follow the one-way system along Military Road and then Cove Street to discover **Camp Cove**. This is one of Sydney's prettiest small beaches, a favourite with the glamorous eastern-suburbs set, but don't come on a hot day and expect to park close by. A marker on the grassy hillside at the end commemorates the landing of Captain Phillip, commander of the First Fleet, who gave the cove its name.

Although some of the houses here hark back to the time when this was still a fishing village, even the smallest cottage would set you back several million today. A walking track along the cliffs leads to **Lady Jane Beach**, one of Sydney's few – and best-known – nudist beaches.

The southside

The southern suburbs include several industrial areas, places of natural beauty, such as the Georges

Map on page 93

The Macquarie Lighthouse was built in 1818 and has been operating ever since.

BELOW: the edge of the continent – South Head at Watsons Bay.

TIP

Sydney's convoluted geography, set around the harbour, the winding Parramatta River and other large inlets, makes it one of the world's most beautiful cities, but means that getting around can be rather time consuming. Where possible, it's usually best to take a ferry.

BELOW: gently down the stream. Or through the waves.

River recreation area, a historic landing spot and, as important as any of these, more beaches.

Most overseas visitors get their first glimpse of Australia here, at Kingsford Smith Airport. The airport and its related industries take up a large chunk of the area; the runway even extends into Botany Bay to accommodate large jets bringing the ever-growing number of tourists.

Bondi Beach

Big and beautiful, **Bondi Beach ❼** is where Sydney comes to shed its clothes and most of its inhibitions. Bondi (pronounced Bon-die) is Australia's most celebrated beach. The 1-km (½-mile) stretch of sand extends between two rearing headlands, where nobody is ever too tanned, too muscular and no bathing suit too flimsy.

This is also a popular meeting place for international backpackers, many of whom take up temporary residence in the backpacker hostels set back from the beach. Families prefer the more sheltered, northern end of the beach, where there is a

toddlers' pool. At the centre of the beach, **Bondi Pavilion** has changing rooms and a Community Cultural Centre, which incorporates a 230-seat theatre, a gallery, a ballroom, studios, workshops and recreation rooms.

In general the southern part of the beach, populated by teenage and twentysomething fun-seekers, tends to be livelier than the north. The demographics change again at the Bondi Baths, at the far southern end. This belongs to the Bondi Icebergs, a league of mostly elderly folk well-known for their mid-winter dips – with ice added to the water for extra shivers.

From this spot the Scenic Walkway winds south, a two-hour trek that passes sea-sculpted sandstone cliffs to **Tamarama Beach** and beyond, as far as **Coogee Beach** – with plenty of cafés and sparkling views along the way.

Idyllic as it might appear, Bondi's surf has a number of dangerous rips which can sweep you out to sea faster than you can swim back in – a particular hazard for unsuspecting

visitors. Swim between the flags, in the patrolled area. If you get into difficulty, try to stay calm, and raise one arm above your head to signal the lifeguards.

Botany Bay

Continuing south, the road terminates at La Perouse and the northern headland of a historic area. From here take the Foreshore Road eastwards past Port Botany and underneath Kingsford Smith Airport's north–south runway reaching into the bay.

Botany Bay ❽ is one of the four large waterways that indent the coast of Sydney, and it occupies an important place in Australia's history. It was here in April 1770 that Lt James Cook, commander of the *Endeavour*, became the first European to set foot on Australia's east coast. Cook originally named the bay the Stingray Harbour, until Joseph Banks, the botanist on board the *Endeavour*, persuaded him to change it to Botany Bay, so impressed was he by the number of new species that he found in the area. Many of these belonged to the *banksia* genus that bears his name. Banks later proposed the place as the site for a penal colony in 1788. However, when Captain Phillip arrived 18 years later he found poor soil, a lack of water and no sheltered anchorages. Within days he had abandoned the bay in favour of somewhere with better water supplies – Sydney Harbour, which he named Port Jackson.

Despite its historical significance, time has not been kind to Botany Bay. The northern end of the bay has been taken over by a major shipping container wharf, with Sydney's Kingsford-Smith Airport in the background. The Grand Parade, a busy road, follows the inside curve of the bay, backed by unlovely suburbs, and on the peninsula at the southern end of the bay, the suburb of Kurnell is home to a large oil refinery.

Follow Captain Cook Drive through Kurnell to the southern section of **Botany Bay National Park**, where a monument at **Inscription Point** commemorates Captain Cook's landing place. In the same

Map on page 93

When Captain Arthur Phillip and the 1,034 men, women and children of the First Fleet landed at Botany Bay, they had been travelling for over eight months.

BELOW: Bondi Beach from the air.

The 26-km (16-mile) Coastal Walk runs the entire length of the Royal National Park.

BELOW: Royal National Park rainforest.

area, the Banks-Solander Track has many of the plant species that Banks collected in 1770.

Cronulla

Cross the Captain Cook Bridge on the way to **Cronulla ❾**, home of Sydney's most southerly beach and also its biggest – a whopping 10 km (6 miles) from end to end, with room to spare even on the hottest day. Most people stick to the southern end of the beach, which has easy parking, sea pools, a grassy park with shade, shops near by and surf patrols. Cronulla is the only Sydney beach that you can get to by train, but it's a long trip from the city.

The Royal National Park

On the southern edge of Sydney, some 32 km (20 miles) from the CBD, the **Royal National Park ❿** (Farnell Avenue, Audley Heights; tel: 9542 0648; daily 7.30am– 8.30pm; admission charge) is 150 sq. km (60 sq. miles) of beaches, sandstone cliffs, wild-flower heaths, rainforest gullies, swamps and rugged bushland. The outstanding

natural beauty of this region was recognised as early as 1879, when it was declared a national park, the second anywhere in the world (Yellowstone in the USA was the first).

Originally known simply as the National Park, the area was set aside for the enjoyment and recreation of Sydneysiders – but the concept of a national park did not have the same conservation status as it does today. At various times, the park has been logged for its native trees, planted with lawns and imported ornamental shrubs, had deer, rabbits and foxes introduced for sport, and been used by the military as a training ground during World War II.

The park has a number of walking tracks of varying levels of difficulty. The short and easy **Forest Path** gives a taste of the park's rainforests, the 5-km (3-mile) **Karloo Track** takes in a popular swimming and picnic area, while the more arduous **Werrong Beach Track** will take you to the park's only authorised nude-bathing area.

Royal National Park is at its most photogenic in spring, when the

Map on page 93

wild-flowers are in bloom, although each season brings its own rewards, from the cool swimming holes that make summer walks a delight to the winter views of migrating whales from the clifftops. More than 200 bird species have been recorded.

There is access to the park by ferry from Cronulla and by train via the stations at Engadine, Loftus Heathcote, Otford and Waterfall on the Cronulla–Illawarra railway line. However, it is the road access via the Princes Highway (which skirts the park boundary) that gives by far the best range of options within the park. Turn off the highway at either Farnell Avenue, just south of Loftus, which takes you to the **visitor centre** (tel: 9542 0648; 9.30am– 4.30pm, from 8.30am at weekends and school holidays), where you can pick up detailed maps and information.

Homebush Bay

The western suburbs of Sydney are where you will find the majority of the city's population as well as industrialised areas of minimal aesthetic appeal. Nonetheless, there is also a good supply of open spaces and plenty for the visitor to do.

For evidence of how large-scale urban renewal can transform an area, visit **Homebush Bay ⑪**, which is synonymous with the Sydney 2000 Olympic Games. For many years, the 640-hectare (1,600-acre) site along the Parramatta River was a sadly neglected part of the city, a largely redundant industrial zone with abandoned factories and pits that had been contaminated with toxic wastes. When Sydney was awarded the rights to stage the 2000 Olympics, the area was speedily transformed into a glittering, soaring complex of stadiums, arenas, tracks, parks and residential complexes. Centrepiece of **Olympic Park** is the 85,000-seat, A$665-million **Telstra**

Stadium, venue for the opening and closing ceremonies and track-and-field events. And, unlike some of its Olympic predecessors in other cities around the world, it remains an active part of city life, the place where Sydney's major swimming, rugby, track, tennis and Australian Rules events are staged.

Olympic Park is also an important recreational facility for Sydneysiders. Visitors can use the picnic and barbecue facilities at **Lake Belvedere**, play some golf, swim in the aquatic centre, walk or jog the scenic pathways, or explore the wetland boardwalks. A number of tours operate around the various facilities within the park, commencing from the **Sydney Olympic Park Visitor Centre** (tel: 9714 7888; daily 9am–5pm) at the corner of Showground Road and Murray Rose Avenue.

The park is accessible by train, ferry or road from the city. By far the most relaxing and scenic option is the RiverCat ferry (Sydney Ferries, tel: 131 500), which departs from Circular Quay at roughly hourly intervals throughout the day.

In 1994 the Royal National Park was devastated by a fire that affected 90 percent of its terrain and resulted in the evacuation of thousands of residents living near by.

BELOW: Telstra Stadium – built for the 2000 Olympics – has since hosted other major events, such as the final of the 2003 Rugby World Cup.

The rainbow lorikeet is found all along Australia's east coast in woodland, forest and heath habitats.

BELOW: Church Street in Parramatta.

A bus service also operates between Sydney Olympic Park Wharf and the visitor centre.

Parramatta

About an hour west of the city is **Parramatta ⑫**, Australia's second-oldest European settlement. Although the suburb is accessible by road, rail and ferry, the best option is to take a RiverCat ferry from Circular Quay. The town is set on the banks of the Parramatta River, which this far inland has shrunk to a modest size.

The name Parramatta is derived from the Aboriginal *Burramatta*, which means "eel creek". It is also applied to a local clan of the Dharug people, who, along with the Dharawal and Gandangara tribes, occupied the land before it was secured by Europeans.

Early attempts at agriculture close to Sydney Cove were a disaster, but the fertile land upstream held far greater promise. As early as 1789, one year after the foundation of the colony, Parramatta's agricultural produce was helping to feed the settlement at Sydney Cove. The colony's first orchard, vineyard, tannery and legal brewery were also established here.

Today, despite its importance as a commercial and retail centre, Parramatta is also known as "Sydney's Living Museum", with outstanding examples of colonial architecture, especially related to agriculture.

Historic buildings

Bordering the Parramatta River, **Parramatta Park** (main entrance off O'Connell Street) incorporates woodlands, water features and several important historic buildings, including Australia's first **Observatory**, completed in 1822, and **Old Government House** (tel: 9635 8149; Tues–Fri 10am–4pm, Sat–Sun 11am–4pm; admission charge), run by the National Trust. The two-storey Georgian building houses an important collection of Australian colonial furniture.

Another significant historic building within the park, **Dairy Cottage** is a modest farmworker's dwelling dating from 1798. It has remained almost intact, making it an outstanding example of early colonial architecture. It became the Government Dairy in 1815.

Close to the railway station at the heart of Parramatta, **Linden House** (2 Smith Street; tel: 9635 7822; Sun 10am–4pm; admission charge) is a classic example of early Australian architecture, built in 1828 as a School of Industry, teaching domestic arts. It's now a regimental museum and centrepiece of the **Lancer Barracks**, the oldest surviving military establishment in Australia, with memorabilia ranging from the 19th century to World War II.

A 10-minute walk from Linden House, **Experiment Farm Cottage** (9 Ruse Street, Harris Park; tel: 9635 5655; Tues–Fri 10.30am–3.30pm, Sat–Sun 11am–3.30pm;

admission charge) was built on farmland granted to the convict-settlers James and Elizabeth Ruse, who grew the first crops for the colony – the "experiment" that proved Sydney could support itself. The couple were given pardons in 1789 as a reward. John Harris, a doctor, eventually bought the land and built the cottage in 1834. The building underlines the strength and simplicity of colonial domestic architecture and furnishings.

Another short (10-minute) stroll from the cottage will take you to **Elizabeth Farm** (70 Alice Street, Rosehill; tel: 9635 9488; daily 10am–5pm; admission charge), a simple but elegant house built in 1793 by John Macarthur, often referred to as the father of Australia's wool industry. Many historians, however, contend that it was his wife, Elizabeth, who did the pioneering work with the merino sheep that they imported from the Cape of Good Hope – pointing out that John was exiled from the colony for more than eight years. Merinos thrived in the warm, dry climate

and became the economic backbone of rural Australia. Elizabeth Farm contains part of Australia's oldest surviving European building, and the broad verandas and low roof became a prototype for the Australian homestead.

Northwest of Sydney

About 50 km (30 miles) northwest of Sydney is the fertile region of the Upper Hawkesbury River. When the visionary governor Lachlan Macquarie arrived in 1810 he laid out plans for a series of towns to be established on high ground because of the Hawkesbury River's propensity to flood the land. The result was what became known as "Macquarie's Five Towns": Windsor, Richmond, Pitt Town, Wilberforce and Castlereagh.

The historic riverside town of **Windsor** ⓑ, 30 km (20 miles) from Sydney, is at the centre of the five towns. It has handsome colonial Georgian architecture, and although the town has been less than sensitive to its architectural riches, it bears witness to Macquarie's enlightened

Map on page 93

BELOW: an aerial view of Sydney's sprawling suburbs.

governorship, and to the talents of his architect, Francis Greenway.

Begin a tour at the **Hawkesbury Historical Museum** (7 Thompson Square; tel: 4577 2310; daily 10am–4pm; admission charge). Originally a house, it was later expanded to become an inn. The museum is also an information centre. The well-presented displays include Aboriginal artefacts and chronicles from early settlers.

Built by convict labour between 1817 and 1820, **St Matthew's Anglican Church** (Moses Street) is regarded as one of the finest of Greenway's works, and certainly one of the best-preserved. The head-stones in the graveyard beside the church testify to some remarkable lives, notably that of Andrew Thompson, a convict sent to the colony aged just 17. He so distinguished himself that he was made chief magistrate of the district before his death at the age of 37.

Windsor Court House, at the corner of Court and Pitt streets, is another fine example of an early 19th-century Greenway building,

while **John Tebbutt's House** and **Observatory** (Palmer Street; tel: 4577 2485; by appointment only; admission charge) celebrates the work of a remarkable astronomer, who had the comet he discovered in 1861 named after him. The house was built by Tebbutt's father in 1845 and it remains in the family.

Richmond ⓮ is another Macquarie town, 7 km (4½ miles) from Windsor. Its historic appeal is confined to the 19th-century architecture on its main thoroughfare, Windsor Street, and the two parallel streets on either side, March and Francis. These have fine examples of houses built in the period between 1820 and 1850.

Wollemi National Park

Measuring approximately 5,000 sq. km (2,000 sq. miles), **Wollemi National Park** ⓯ is the largest wilderness area in the state, part of the Greater Blue Mountains World Heritage Area. It's also incredibly rugged, an impenetrable maze of canyons, cliffs and dense forest. The plant equivalent of a living dinosaur,

BELOW: yachts on the Hawkesbury River at Brooklyn.

the Wollemi pine, was discovered here in 1994 in a small gorge within the park (it's exact location is a closely guarded secret). It grows to a height of 38 metres (125 ft) in its native habitat – less than 100 km (60 miles) from the heart of Sydney.

On the eastern side, the park is accessible only from an unpaved road, Bob Turners Track, which runs off the Windsor–Singleton Road into a scenic gorge. Its demanding terrain makes the park suitable for experienced bush-walkers and canoeists.

Ku-ring-gai Chase National Park

Overlooking the Hawkesbury River 30 km (20 miles) from Sydney's northern outskirts, **Ku-ring-gai Chase National Park ⑯** (Bobbin Head Road; daily 7.30am–5.30pm, to 8pm during daylight saving; admission charge) frames the shores of Pittwater and Broken Bay with sandstone cliffs, eucalypt forests and rainforest. There is abundant and colourful bird life, and a rich legacy of rock art by the Aboriginal Guringai people, after whom the park is named.

West Head Lookout has a panoramic view over the estuary of the Hawkesbury River and Pittwater, while the picnic ground is popular at weekends, especially with kookaburras, which exploit the bounty of the picnic tables by swooping down and plucking sandwiches straight from visitors' hands.

The park has a number of walking tracks of varying degrees of difficulty. In the warmer months, the **Basin Track** is popular since it ends at a sheltered beach. You'll receive a map as you pass through the park gates, but more detailed information is available from the information centre at the **Bobbin Inn** (Bobbin Head Road, Mount Colah; tel: 9472 8949; daily 10am–4pm).

The sleepy village of **Brooklyn ⑰** is the main town along the Hawkesbury River, and the starting point for adventures along this attractive waterway. From here it's possible to rent a houseboat, a small aluminium fishing boat or take a cruise along the river. In particular, the trip with the *Riverboat Postman* (Ferry Wharf, Dangar Road; tel: 9985 7566; Mon–Fri 9.30am–1.15pm; charge), the vessel that delivers mail and supplies to the isolated communities upriver, provides a fascinating glimpse into the life of the castaways who live there.

An alternative is the short ferry trip to **Dangar Island**, a small community of about 50 houses, many of them owned by high-profile Sydneysiders who value the island's casual, barefoot style, its strong sense of community and freedom from traffic and noise. The Island Store at the ferry wharf serves light meals and drinks.

Brooklyn itself has several waterfront cafés and restaurants, with views of bobbing boats and pelicans, and seafood a speciality. ❑

Map on page 93

There are plenty of surf beaches in Sydney's northern suburbs.

BELOW: a great Sydney tradition – the picnic on the beach.

RESTAURANTS, CAFÉS, BARS & PUBS

Restaurants

Inner suburbs (Kings Cross, Darlinghurst)

Balkan Seafood
215 Oxford Street
Darlinghurst
Tel: 9331 7670
Open: D Tues-Sun. **$$**
Some of the best and cheapest seafood in town, cooked in the Croatian way. BYO.

Bayswater Brasserie
32 Bayswater Road,
Kings Cross
Tel: 9357 2177
Open: daily 7am–midnight. **$**
A long-established eatery, serving good quality modern Australian cuisine.

Buon Ricordo
108 Boundary Street,
Paddington
Tel: 9360 6729
Open: L Fri-Sat, D Tues-Sat.
$$$
Fine Italian food, friendly atmosphere and good Italian wine list.

Café Sel et Poivre
263 Victoria St, Darlinghurst

Tel: 9361 6530
Open: B, L & D daily. **$**
Good-value French cuisine, served with gusto. Opens daily at 7am for breakfast.

Oh, Calcutta!
251 Victoria Street,
Darlinghurst
Tel: 9360 3650
Open: L Fri, D daily. **$$**
Bistro-style restaurant at the heart of the tourist district, serving subtle modern Indian food with an Australian twist (like stir-fried kangaroo with sesame seeds). BYO.

Una's
338-340 Victoria Street,
Darlinghurst
Tel: 9360 6885
Open: Mon-Sat 6.30am–11pm, Sun 8am-11pm. **$**
An old, economical Kings Cross favourite serving hearty German and Austrian food at low prices, from breakfast to supper. BYO. No reservations, no credit cards.

Glebe

Boathouse on Blackwattle Bay
End of Ferry Road, Glebe
Tel: 9518 9011
Open: L & D, Tues.–Sun. **$$$**
Some of Sydney's best seafood in a converted boathouse on the edge of the harbour.

Mixing Pot
178 St John's Road, Glebe
Tel: 9660 7449

Open: L Mon-Fri,
D Mon-Sat. **$$**
Italian seafood cuisine and outdoor dining amidst the relaxed chic of inner-city Glebe.

Eastern suburbs

Art e Cucina Café
2 Short Street, Double Bay
Tel: 9328 0880
Open: L & D Mon-Sat. **$$**
Much more than a café, despite its name, serving fine modern Australian and Italian cuisine.

Bistro Moncur
Woollahra Hotel, 116 Queen Street, Woollahra
Tel: 9363 2519
Open: L & D Tues-Sun. **$$$**
Classic French bistro cuisine in a stylish Eastern Suburbs restaurant. No reservations.

Pier
594 New South Head Road,
Rose Bay
Tel: 9327 6561
Open: L & D daily. **$$$**
Consistently voted Sydney's best seafood restaurant, this beautifully sleek outfit hovers over the harbour waters.

Northside

Bathers Pavilion
4 The Esplanade,
Balmoral Beach
Tel: 9969 5050
Open: B Sun, L & D daily. **$$$**
Understated elegance in decor and carefully selected produce characterise this upmarket

beachside eatery. Good ocean views, occasionally indifferent service.

Chequers
Mandarin Centre, 65 Albert Avenue, Chatswood
Tel: 9904 8388
Open: L & D daily. **$$**
A popular Chinese *yum cha* and seafood eatery with a core of devoted regulars. Above average decor and service for a Chinese restaurant. BYO.

Jonah's
69 Bynya Road, Palm Beach
Tel: 9974 5599
Open: B Sat-Sun, L & D daily.
$$$
Popular, long-established restaurant in a romantic setting with outdoor dining and water views. Modern Australian and seafood cuisine. Not cheap, but good value.

Minato
47 East Esplanade, Manly
Tel: 9977 0580
Open: D daily. **$**
A very economical Japanese dining experience in beach-y surroundings. Attentive service and above average decor for a low-cost eatery. BYO.

Southside

Mint Restaurant
43 Gerrale Street, Cronulla
Tel: 9523-9381
Open: L Thur-Sun,
D Tues-Sun. **$$**
A Mediterranean and seafood restaurant with

PRICE CATEGORIES

Prices for three-course dinner per person with a half-bottle of house wine:
**$** = under A$ 50
**$$** = A$ 50–80
**$$$** = A$ 80–120
**$$$$** = over A$ 120

water views. Relaxed and intimate, with attentive service.

The Pool Caffe
94 Marine Parade, Maroubra
Tel: 9314 0364
Open: B Sun, L & D daily. $
A large restaurant with outdoor seating and an economical modern Australian and seafood menu.

Sean's Panorama
270 Campbell Parade, Bondi Beach
Tel: 9365 4924
Open: B, L Sat-Sun, D Mon-Sat. $$
An eccentric little place at the north end of Bondi Beach. The modern Australian menu is very good and the weekend breakfasts are legendary. BYO.

Treehorn
19 Havelock Avenue, Coogee
Tel: 9664 4005
Open: L & D daily. $
Vegetarian eatery offering lots of healthy, fresh food and tasty desserts. Laidback but efficient staff. Live music at weekends.

Western Suburbs
Pho Minh
42 Arthur Street, Cabramatta
Tel: 9726 5195
Open: L & D daily. $
One of the many Vietnamese noodle eateries in Cabramatta, basic but spacious, with very economical prices. Also has a seafood menu, and simple, no-fuss service.

RIGHT: lunch beside the seaside.

River Canyon
96 Philip Street, Parramatta
Tel: 9689 2288
Open: L & D daily. $$$
Modern Australian cuisine and steakhouse in historic, colonial Parramatta. Has live music, outdoor dining and bar.

Cafés, bars & pubs
Inner Suburbs (Kings Cross, Darlinghurst)
Bar Coluzzi
322 Victoria Street, Darlinghurst
Open: daily until late, including breakfast
A local landmark. The outdoor seating on the wide Victoria Street footpath makes this tiny coffee shop a lot larger.

Dov Café
252 Forbes Street, Darlinghurst
A sparse, colonial feel characterises this hip inner city hangout, situated in an old sandstone building opposite the East Sydney Art School.

Kitty O'Shea's
384 Oxford Street, Paddington
A crowded and sociable Irish-themed pub in the centre of Paddington. Big crowds at weekends.

Piccolo Bar
6 Roslyn Street, Kings Cross
Open: early morning to late at night
A tiny place in the thick of Kings Cross street activity, and something

of an institution. Neapolitan owner Vittorio Bianchi has been brewing coffee for the local Bohemians for 40 years.

Eastern suburbs
Royal Hotel
Five Ways, Paddington
Situated in the pleasant, villagey Five Ways. Ornate Victorian architecture and affordable pub food.

Woollahra Hotel
116 Queen Street, Woollahra
Two bars (one refined, one hip), live jazz on Sundays, pool tables, 2-for-1 cocktails on Thursdays.

Northside
Bhaji on the Beach
315a Barrenjoey Road, Newport
Tel: 9979-6680
Open: D Tues-Sun. $
An economical Indian diner in an attractive

beach setting. Popular after a day on the beach.

Newport Arms Hotel
2 Kalinya Street, Newport
A long-time favourite pub with the northern suburbs' surf culture, young and old. The beer garden ($) also serves up basic, standard pub fare. Deck shoes and a sun-tan are de rigeur.

Southside
Bondi Icebergs
1 Knotts Avenue, South Bondi
Enjoy a beer while soaking up one of the best views in Sydney. Live music at weekends.

Hotel Bondi
178 Campbell Parade, Bondi Beach
This is the real Bondi – loud, friendly, sun-and-sea soaked, despite its yuppification.

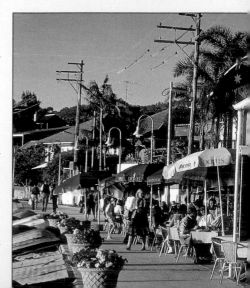

SPORTS

Like so many clichés, there's a lot of truth behind the image of the sports-mad Aussie. In New South Wales there's plenty of evidence to back it up

Whatever the time of year, there will be at least one sporting event gripping the public imagination. It may be the bread and butter of teams jostling in their local or national leagues in any one of a myriad different sporting codes, or it may be an annual event like the Sydney-Hobart yacht race or the Bathurst 1000. Occasionally it's a marquee occasion such as the Olympics or the Rugby World Cup. Whichever it is, views will be cogently and forcefully expressed and, as likely as not, the pundit involved will have something riding on the result, whether it's a bet or just a point in the office tipping competition. And every office has a tipping competition, either for the rugby – union or league – or Australian Rules football; sometimes all three.

If NSW has a favourite sport, it's rugby union, but tastes fluctuate. Interest in soccer is growing rapidly on the back of Sydney FC's success in the fledgling national A League and the inspired achievements of the national team – the Socceroos – in the 2006 World Cup. Aussie Rules too is on a high. Whatever you favour, try to have a taste.

LEFT: Union may be the preferred rugby code but in June all eyes are on league for the traditional State of Origin competition against Queensland. In the best-of-three series local support is passionately behind the blues over the dreaded maroons, or "banana benders" as the Queenslanders are sometimes known.

ABOVE: V8 Supercars – essentially over-pumped versions of the local Fords and Holdens – race in the iconic Bathurst 1000 around Mount Panorama every October.

RIGHT: Sydney Swans' victory in the September 2005 Grand Final gave a great boost to Aussie Rules in the state.

THE TROTS

Harness racing, or the "Trots", doesn't arouse particular interest in itself; arcane and tightly enforced regulations on trotting rather than galloping, and the faintly absurd looking "sulkies" in which the competitor sits, all mitigate against widespread popular interest. However, it's not really about the sport. The trots, unlike other horse racing, can run at night and that means more betting time.

People in New South Wales are the biggest gamblers in Australia. In the early days, gambling reflected the bust and boom nature of life – the cycles of gold rush and failure, of droughts and plenty. To have a bet was a fatalistic gesture to match the spirit of land itself and it is still said that an Australian will bet on anything that moves.

People from all walks of life go to the great horse racing events in Sydney, held at beautiful courses such as Randwick and Rose Hill, but only 12 percent of betting money goes on the horses. Over 70 percent goes in the slots of poker machines in clubs and pubs statewide. It is part of the culture.

ABOVE: one of Australia's sporting megastars is New South Welshman Ian Thorpe. The "Thorpedo" is the country's most successful swimmer ever, having won five Olympic gold medals and 13 world championship titles.

RIGHT: cricket has always been popular in Australia and with the ongoing success of the national side – apart from the odd blip against England – it shows no sign of losing its appeal. The big event is the New Year's test match at the SCG (Sydney Cricket Ground) against whichever side is touring that year. Every four years it will be an Ashes game when passions are really roused. The state team has been consistently successful over the years and currently includes fast-bowling pin-up Brett Lee (pictured) in its line-up.

BELOW: one of the biggest events in the yachting calendar is the Sydney-Hobart Race which sees the Sydney Harbour foreshore packed every Boxing Day as spectators see off the contestants. The stormy Bass Strait usually leads to a high attrition rate.

THE BLUE MOUNTAINS

Eucalyptus forests, waterfalls, lush valleys and dizzying
cliffs characterise the spectacular Blue Mountains
region, home to the famous Three Sisters rock
formation and the Jenolan Caves, a limestone labyrinth

Sydney

Bordering Sydney to the west,
the Blue Mountains is the
name given to a densely
forested sandstone plateau, etched
by rivers into trough-like valleys
with sheer-sided sandstone walls.
Although the "mountains" label
might seem like overstatement for
hills barely 1,000 metres (3,300 ft)
high, these hills presented a formidable barrier to early exploration.
Initial attempts to push west were
foiled when explorers found themselves facing vertical cliffs – a problem you'll understand when you
look down from Echo Point into the
depths of the Jamison Valley. It was
not until 1813, a quarter of a century after European settlement, that
explorers finally blazed a trail
across the area.

Settlement in the Blue Mountains was shaped by the railway,
which inched west in the second
half of the 19th century. Villages
grew up along the railway line, and
for many years the area was a
favourite weekend escape for Sydneysiders, especially during the
sticky heat of summer. Numerous
walking trails took shape during
this time, and hiking is one of the
best reasons to visit the mountains.
The region is also famous for its
cool-climate gardens, at their best
in spring and autumn.

A hazy shade of blue

The name "Blue Mountains" relates
to the scattering of blue light as it
comes into contact with dust par-
ticles. This phenomenon is known
as "Rayleigh Scattering", after Lord
Rayleigh, the physicist who
described it. It is also possible that
the evaporation of oil from the eucalyptus forests enhances this coloura-
tion: some locals say that during the
summer months – when evaporation
rates are higher – the Blue Mountains appear even bluer.

Map
on page
110

LEFT: The Jamison
Valley from Katoomba.
BELOW: retired railman
David Johnston
convinces as the Fat
Controller at Mount
Victoria station.

TIP

Glenbrook is the starting point for a three-hour return walking track to Red Hand Cave, where the rock face displays some extraordinary early Aboriginal hand stencils.

An accessible wilderness

Although its eastern ridges have been tamed by suburbia, the Blue Mountains is still a wild and majestic place. You only have to amble slightly off the trail to get lost for days – as many weekend walkers still do. When the creeks rise they turn into raging monsters that can sweep you away like a twig, and if the weather is hot and dry there's the risk of forest fires. Luckily, there are many layers to the Blue Mountains experience, and you can just as easily spend your weekend curled up in front of a fire in a cosy guesthouse as dangling off the edge of a canyon with a hundred metres of nothing between you and terra firma.

Thanks to Sydney's ever-improving road network, the mountains are close by, even if you've only a day to spare. Just 90 minutes after leaving central Sydney, you can be standing on the brink of the Jamison Valley at Wentworth Falls, or settling down to scones and tea in a Leura café. The natural beauty of the region was confirmed in 2000, when it was added to UNESCO's World Heritage List.

Glenbrook and higher

The Blue Mountains region begins just west of Penrith, on Sydney's outskirts, where the M4 Motorway becomes the Great Western Highway, changes into forested hills at Lapstone and enters the town of **Glenbrook ❶**. Immediately on your left, the Blue Mountains Visitor Information Centre (Great Western Highway, Glenbrook; tel: 1300-653 408; Mon–Fri 9am–5pm, Sat–Sun 8.30am–4.40pm) is an invaluable source of information if you're planning an overnight stay.

If you haven't seen kangaroos in the wild, the **Euroka Campground** (daily 8.30am–6pm, to 7pm during daylight saving) is something you won't want to miss. At Ross Street, the first street on your left past the visitor centre, turn left. At the end of Ross Street, just before the railway station, turn left into Bruce Road and follow as it snakes across the railway bridge. Continue as the road enters the Blue Mountains National Park, crossing the causeway at Glenbrook Creek. The campground is located 4 km (2 miles) after the park gates. The eastern grey kangaroos that graze here have become so used to humans that you can usually approach them to within a few metres. Look for the females with young joeys in their pouches.

A little higher up the mountains, **Springwood ❷** is the second-biggest town in the Blue Mountains, and the first taste of the weatherboard architecture and cool-climate gardens that typify the region. On the border between Springwood and Faulconbridge, the next town along the highway, a sign points down Grose Road to the **Norman Lindsay Gallery** (14 Norman Lindsay Cresent, Faulconbridge; tel: 4751

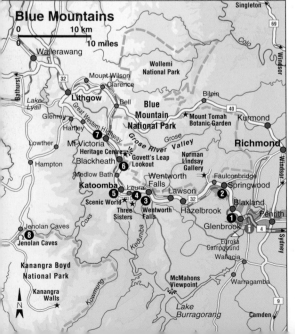

1067; www.hermes.net.au/nlg; daily 10am–4pm; admission charge). Voluptuous nudes and children's literature are an odd mix, yet Norman Lindsay juggled both. He also built model boats, sculpted, wrote poetry and sketched, but most consenting adults remember him almost exclusively for his celebration of the female form. Until his death in 1969, Lindsay lived for 57 years in this house, which is now a museum crammed with his drawings, paintings and sculptures. Lindsay is also remembered as the author of *The Magic Pudding*, a classic of Australian children's literature. Purely in the interests of art, Elle MacPherson bared all in the 17-hectare (42-acre) bushland surrounding the house for the film *Sirens*, which was partly inspired by Lindsay's own life.

Spectacular views

The Blue Mountains shift into high gear at the village of **Wentworth Falls ❸**. Just above the village, turn into Falls Road. At the end of this road, follow the one-way street that takes you in a circuit around the large,

shady picnic ground to the parking area. A short walk from here will take you to a number of lookouts with astonishing views across the yawning chasm of the Jamison Valley.

The view becomes even more staggering if you follow the signs to Wentworth Falls, where Jamison Creek topples from the lip of the cliff in a drift of spray and disappears into the forest below *(see below)*. The finest walk in this area is the **National Pass**, zigzagging down the cliffs to your left. The walk cuts across the base of the falls, following a narrow ledge to the cascading **Empress Falls**. From here the trail follows the Valley of the Waters back to the top of the cliffs, where you can recover with a snack at the Conservation Hut before returning along paved roads to the parking lot above Wentworth Falls. Allow about three hours for the circuit, and take water.

The gardens of Leura

Turn off the Great Western Highway to visit **Leura ❹**, which has the prettiest main street of any village in the Blue Mountains. This is **The Mall**, a

Map on page 110

Nymph maniac. A satyr gets fresh in one of several sculptures featuring voluptuous nudes in the grounds of the Norman Lindsay Gallery.

BELOW: the Jamison Valley from Wentworth Falls.

In Darwin's footsteps

In January 1836, a young English naturalist stood at the spot where Jamison Creek hurls itself into the void and described the scene at his feet. The naturalist was Charles Darwin, and he was at the mid-point of his voyage around the world aboard HMS *Beagle* – a voyage that would eventually lead to the publication of *On the Origin of Species by Means of Natural Selection*, in which he challenged the biblical account of creation.

The walk alongside the creek from the village of Wentworth Falls to the falls themselves now bears his name, and is but one of the many wonderful walks in this area.

A peaceful spot at the edge of the Cherry Terrace at Everglades gardens. Everglades is run by the National Trust, so take your membership card if you have one.

BELOW: Leura Post Office now houses a restaurant. **BELOW RIGHT:** genteel graffiti.

concise and upmarket strip of cafés and restaurants, antique shops and gourmet food stores, all of it classified by the National Trust. This is a fine place to stop for lunch or afternoon tea, although it's crowded on weekends.

Leura is a popular spot for weekend refugees from Sydney and well-heeled retirees, and the gardens around the town testify to their green-fingered expertise. Among the most distinguished of the local gardens, **Everglades** (37 Everglades Avenue; tel: 4784 1938; www.everglades gardens.info; daily 10am–5pm, autumn–winter until 4pm; admission charge), 20 minutes' walk from the town centre, is the work of visionary Paul Sorensen. Sorensen was schooled in the great traditions of European landscape gardening, yet his distinguishing genius was his appreciation of Australia's native flora – a source of conflict with Henri Van de Velde, the owner of Everglades, who particularly disliked banksias. The successful integration of gum trees, gnarled banksias and white-trunked birches is confirmation

of Sorensen's capabilities. The garden delights as much for its drystone walls, art-deco wrought-iron panel in the courtyard wall and wisteria-covered pergola that frames the Jamison Valley views as for its cherry terrace. Now under the stewardship of the National Trust, the garden is recovering from a long period of neglect, yet its structural strength – it is anchored by its mature trees – gives the place its intrinsic appeal.

The Three Sisters

At the lower end of The Mall, turn right into Gordon Road, which quickly becomes Cliff Drive and sets off on a looping, swooping, roller-coaster ride along the rim of the Jamison and Megalong Valleys, with barely a dull moment in all its 20 km (12 miles). The drive takes in several famous attractions, the first of which is the **Three Sisters** (Echo Point, Katoomba). While the surrounding sandstone has been eroded, these three pillars of more resilient rock have remained almost intact. Australia's geological history is spelled out in these walls. The horizontal

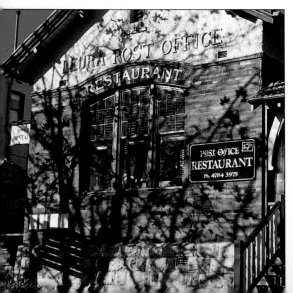

line of dark mudstone separates the finer, paler sandstone – laid down when Australia was joined to Antarctica as part of the supercontinent Gondwanaland – from the more recent, rust-coloured stone that followed after the continents drifted apart. This whole area was once a sea bed that was uplifted and then eroded over many millions of years, leaving the deep valleys that imbue this landscape with drama.

Another branch of the Blue Mountains Visitor Information Centre (tel: 1300-653 408; Mon–Fri 9am–5pm, Sat–Sun 8.30am–4.40pm) is located at Echo Point.

Along Cliff Drive

The next stop along Cliff Drive is **Scenic World** (corner Violet Street and Cliff Drive, Katoomba; tel: 4782 2699; www.scenicworld.com.au; daily 9am–5pm; admission charge), where the Skyway, a cable car, makes a dizzying journey into the centre of a giant chasm, 270 metres (880 ft) above the waterfall leaping from the cliff's edge. The cable car's glass floor enhances the vertigo factor.

On the other side of the Scenic World complex, the Scenic Railway glides 415 metres (1,350 ft) down through rainforest to the foot of the cliffs, along a railway line that was originally constructed to haul coal and shale out from the valley. Cliff Drive continues its swerving journey along the edge of the cliffs, rejoining the Great Western Highway just outside Katoomba.

Katoomba

The largest town in the region, **Katoomba 5** was once the epicentre of tourism in the Blue Mountains, and the town has many guesthouses and hotels left over from those days. Only pockets of historic character remain however. **The Paragon** (65 Katoomba Street; tel: 4782 2928; daily 9am–6pm) is a celebrated art-deco café and a traditional favourite for afternoon tea; but if you decide to sit down, remember that you're here for the ambience – the food and the service are nothing special.

Perched on the summit of the Blue Mountains, **Blackheath 6** is

Map on page 110

The NPWS oversees the Blue Mountains National Park, which attracts over 3 million visitors each year. Their office is in Blackheath (Govetts Leap Road; daily 9am–4.30pm).

BELOW LEFT: the Skyway cable car. **BELOW:** check off the Three Sisters – a must-do for every visitor to the Blue Mountains.

Map on page 110

YULEFEST SEASON
✿✿ June & July ✿✿
LUNCHEONS & DINNERS
Traditional CHRISTMAS Fare

Christmas in June and July is celebrated in Mount Victoria and other locations where the winter is particularly cold. It's a nostalgia trip for immigrants from the northern hemisphere, entailing rich feasts of turkey and plum pudding, and a liberal amount of festive imbibing.

BELOW: Mount Victoria's Victoria and Albert Guesthouse.

a rambling village of stone and weatherboard houses, and the starting point for some of the most spectacular of the area's bush-walking trails. At the end of Govett's Leap Road a number of trails descend into the **Grose River Valley**, varying in duration from a couple of hours to several days. All involve steep descents and climbs that will have your leg muscles protesting. The view from Govett's Leap Lookout will give you a hint of what to expect. Govett was a government surveyor who mapped the region in the 1830s, but despite the name, he never leapt.

Close to the lookout, the **Heritage Centre**, operated by the National Parks and Wildlife Service (tel: 4787 8877; daily 9am–4.30pm) functions as a valuable source of information on local Aboriginal and European historic sites, as well as local bush-walks.

Mount Victoria ❼ is the most westerly village in the Blue Mountains and the highest, despite what the elevation signs along the highway say. These signs measure the

height of the local railway station, and while Blackheath has a loftier station, Mount Victoria is the higher town. A sleepy, ramshackle township that has been classified by the National Trust, Mount Victoria has a number of historic buildings and hotels that date from the late 19th century, when this was a popular retreat for Sydneysiders. A stroll along Station Street, which runs off the highway beside the Hotel Imperial, will take you past the bank building (1885), the Mount Victoria Police Station (1887), the library (1875) and the gracious Victoria and Albert Guest House (1914).

The Jenolan Caves

Continue along the highway to just past the next town, Hartley, and turn off to **Jenolan Caves ❽** (tel: 6359 3307; www.jenolancaves.org.au; 9am–8pm during school holidays, 9.45am–5.30pm at other times; admission charge). One of the highlights of the Blue Mountains, Jenolan Caves is a labyrinth of stalactite-lined limestone chasms carved by underground rivers. Nine of the 300 caves are open for public viewing, some of which can be explored without a guide, but the best formations are within the caves that require a guided tour. Allow one hour to drive from Mount Victoria to the caves, and note that the last section of the road into the Jenolan Valley is one-way in the direction of the caves from 11.45am to 1.45pm daily.

From Mount Victoria, there is an alternative route back to Sydney via Bell's Line of Road. For keen gardeners, the village of **Mount Wilson** and the **Mount Tomah Botanic Garden** (www.rbgsyd.nsw.gov.au) make this an essential detour, especially in spring and autumn. Otherwise, the drive is still a scenic one, but will add an extra 90 minutes to your journey time back to Sydney. ❑

RESTAURANTS, CAFÉS, BARS & PUBS

Restaurants

Blackheath

Ashcrofts
18 Govetts Leap Road
Tel: 4787 8297
Open: D Wed-Sun, L Sun.
$$$
One of the best restaurants in the Blue Mountains, with modern Australian-style offerings. BYO & licensed.

Vulcans
33 Govetts Leap Road
Tel: 4787 6899
Open L & D Fri-Sun. **$$$**
Fantastic food and great service at this fine-dining institution. BYO.

Katoomba

Arjuna
16 Valley Road
Tel: 4782 4662
Open: D Mon-Thurs. **$**
Locals and visitors rub shoulders at this great-value Indian eatery. In summer, ask for a table on the balcony – the views are wonderful. BYO.

Avalon
18 Katoomba Street
Tel: 4782 5532
Open L Wed-Sun, D daily.
$$-$$$
Delicious modern cuisine using fresh local produce. Retro atmosphere (the restaurant occupies an old cinema), pleasantly informal and relaxed. BYO & licensed.

Chork Dee
216 Katoomba Street
Tel: 4782 1913
Open: D daily. **$**
Good Thai fare in central Katoomba keeps the locals coming back for more. BYO.

Darley's
Lilianfells Avenue
Tel: 4780 1200
Open: L Sun, D Tues-Sat.
$$$
Superb dining overlooking the Jamison Valley in the swish Lilianfells Resort and Spa. Dishes include Murray cod with mussels and roasted pheasant.

Loura

Silk's Brasserie
128 The Mall
Tel: 4784 2534
Open: L & D daily. **$$$**
This highly rated restaurant has an eclectic, ever-changing menu and extensive wine list.

Solitary
90 Cliff Drive
Tel: 4782 1164
Open: L daily, D Wed-Sun.
$$$
Outstanding modern Australian cuisine matches the spectacular views of the Jamison Valley and Mount Solitary.

Wentworth Falls

Il Postino's
13 Station Street
Tel: 4757 1615

Open L & D daily. **$**
A cheerful, good-value place in the old post office. BYO.

Cafés, bars & pubs

Blackheath

Gardner's Inn Hotel
255 Great Western Highway
Tel: 4787 8347
Open L & D daily. **$**
A cosy place for a post-bush-walk drink and pub grub.

Katoomba

Hatter's Café
197 Katoomba Street
Tel: 4782 4212
Open: B & L daily, D Fri-Sat. **$**
Whether it's breakfast, lunch, dinner or afternoon tea, the food is consistently good. BYO & licensed.

The Paragon
65 Katoomba Street
Tel: 4782 2928.
Open 9am-6pm daily. $-$$
Stylish and historic café, slightly let down by the food.

Leura

Alexandra Hotel
62 Great Western Highway,
Leura. Tel: 4782 4422
Open: L & D daily. **$**
A friendly, easy-going place for a drink, light lunch or main meal.

PRICE CATEGORIES

Prices for a three-course dinner per person with a half-bottle of house wine:
$ = under A$50
$$ = A$50-A$75
$$$ = over A$75
L = lunch, D = dinner, BYO = bring your own alcohol.

RIGHT: soup-supping time at Katoomba's Paragon café.

SOUTH COAST

From the rolling meadows and quaint 19th-century villages of the Southern Highlands to the glorious natural attractions of Jervis Bay and Montague Island, the South Coast's summer refuges embody relaxed living

Sydney
Canberra

Stretching south from Sydney to the Victorian border, the South Coast, or at least the part of it where population is concentrated, is the strip of undulating country between the sea and the coastal escarpment, varying in width from no more than a couple of metres to about 25 km (15 miles).

European settlement began in the region in the 1820s, early on in Australia's colonial history due to the large number of coastal inlets and rivers which provided relatively easy access from the sea. Timber cutters were followed by fishermen and farmers searching for pastures, and the dairy industry still plays an important role along many parts of the coast. More recently, tourism has created a new economic mainstay for the region.

Natural beauty

The South Coast is particularly popular with those who prefer a relaxed atmosphere, since it lacks the big resorts that are a feature of some towns along the state's north coast. However, it's still busy duringholiday periods, and best avoided in the summer school holidays, between Christmas and the end of January. The area's main assets are its natural attributes – beaches, national parks, forests and wildlife – with a handful of country towns providing historic interest.

The thread running through the South Coast is **Highway One**, also known as the Princes Highway, which continues to Melbourne. However, the highway rarely shows the best that the region has to offer, with only the occasional glimpse of the coast. To make the most of it, you'll need to get off the highway and explore. For anyone travelling between Sydney and Melbourne, the Princes Highway is a more

Map on page 118

BELOW: there's no shortage of good seafood along the south coast.
BELOW: Central Tilba, beneath the slopes of Mount Dromedary.

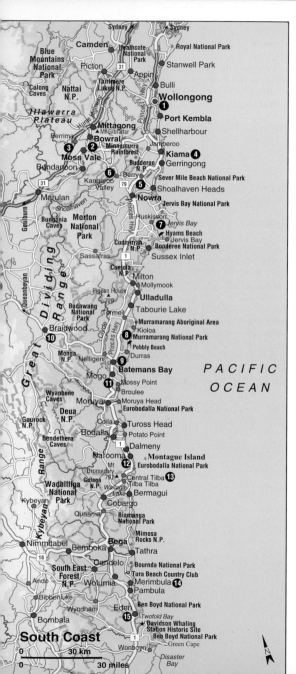

PACIFIC
OCEAN

South Coast

0   30 km

0   30 miles

attractive alternative to the inland route along the Hume Highway – although it also requires more time.

Travelling south along the Princes Highway from Sydney, the road skirts the rim of the **Illawarra Plateau**. Stop off before Wollongong at the Panorama House Italian Restaurant (www.panoramahouse.com.au), located on the left, shortly after the speed limit on the Sydney–Wollongong F6 Freeway changes from 110 to 80 kph (68 to 50 mph). The view over Wollongong is sensational.

Wollongong

The third-largest city in the state, **Wollongong ❶**, is home to the country's biggest steel mill, whose furnaces are kept burning by the coal mines along the Illawarra Escarpment, just north of the city. Although most travellers flash by along the Princes Highway – from where the view of tall chimneys and industrial plants does little to encourage further exploration – "the gong" is a vibrant, cosmopolitan city thanks to its large populations of immigrants and tertiary students. Set on the strip of land where the green hills of the coastal escarpment press close against the sea, the city sprawls along the coast.

Originally settled in 1816, the town grew up around the horseshoe-shaped scoop of Wollongong Harbour, which is also known as **Belmore Basin**. It is a fine backdrop for a stroll, with its nautical array of lighthouses and fishing boats.

The harbour's earliest **lighthouse**, which still stands, was constructed from cast iron and riveted boiler plates in 1871, after several ships had foundered on reefs. **Wollongong City Gallery** (Kembla and Burelli Streets; tel: 4228 7500; www.wollongongcitygallery.com; Tues–Fri 10am–5pm, Sat–Sun noon–4pm) is one of the largest regional art museums in Australia, with an outstanding collection of 20th-century Australian painting and sculpture, Aboriginal art and colonial-era views of the Illawarra.

Good restaurants and a pleasant shopping district complete the picture. The town's beaches are rated highly and are good for surfing, but while they are undeniably lovely, they are not exceptional for this part of the world. If the pleasures of surf and sand between the toes come high on your travel wish list, there are beaches just as fine – and less crowded – to the north and south.

On the Princes Highway just south of the city, easily identifiable by its sweeping orange roofs, the magnificent **Nan Tien Temple** (Berkeley Road, Berkeley; tel: 4272 0600; www.nantien.org.au; Tues–Sun 9am–5pm) welcomes anyone who wants to learn about Fo Guang Shan - Buddhism. The name Nan Tien means "Paradise of the South". The temple complex consists of a pagoda, extensive rose gardens and a dining hall serving vegetarian food.

The Southern Highlands

Sydneysiders and coastal dwellers often weekend in the Southern Highlands. From Wollongong it's a matter of taking the Illawara Highway; while from Sydney, you follow the **Hume Highway**, the main inland route from Sydney to Melbourne, and pass **Mount Gibraltar**, a denuded volcanic plug known locally as "The Gib" which marks the gateway to the Southern Highlands.

Nestling beneath Mount Gibraltar, to the west of Wollongong, is Mittagong, home of Australia's first iron smelter at Fitzroy Ironworks (1848–80).

Bowral

Five km (3 miles) from Mittagong, cradled between Mount Gibraltar and the Wingecarribee River in the cool, moist heights of the Highlands, **Bowral ②** is the aristocrat of the district. Along with its superb setting, the city has benefited from enlightened intervention: in the 1880s, Bowral began a tree-planting programme, and today its avenues of deciduous trees and magnificent public and private gardens give the town a calm and gracious air.

Map on page 118

The hamlet of Mount Kembla, on the west side of Wollongong, was the site of one of Australia's worst mining disasters. In 1902 an explosion deep in a coal mine split the mountain and buried 95 men.

BELOW: the gateway to Nan Tien Temple.

An annual tulip festival has been held in Bowral at the end of September/beginning of October since 1958.

BELOW: "the Don's" statue at the Bradman Museum.

At a height of 660 metres (2,150 ft), Bowral is cooler and less humid than the coast, and has long been a summer escape for wealthy Sydneysiders. Towards the end of the 19th century many of the small towns of the Southern Highlands became popular summer refuges, and several monied families carved out large estates and built grand country houses on the undulating slopes surrounding the town.

A century later, the town boomed again when the great-grandchildren of the original city-dwellers rediscovered the delights of Bowral. The house prices spread wings – and a fresh sense of style came to the town. Bowral is one country town where you can count on an urban-strength espresso, or shop for expensive European antiques.

The Bowral experience begins with the view from the 863-metre (2,800-ft) summit of Mount Gibraltar. On the road into Bowral from Mittagong, turn left into Oxley Drive, which will take you to the scenic lookouts and a bird's-eye view of Bowral, Wingecarribee Dam, Moss Vale and the Cuckbundoon Range near Goulburn.

Sir Donald Bradman, Australia's cricketing hero, played cricket in Bowral as a boy, and the town has adopted him as its favourite son. Next to the Bradman Oval and opposite Sir Don Bradman's former Bowral home, the **Bradman Museum** (St Jude Street; tel: 4862 1247; www.bradman.org.au; daily 10am–5pm; admission charge) celebrates the game as well as the sportsman. Historic photos, film footage, interactive displays and the equipment he used recreate the days when "the Don", as he was known, captained an all-conquering Australian side. His final tour with the national team was in 1948.

Flora and fauna

Bowral is a gardener's paradise. The town prides itself on its parks and gardens, revelling in the cool-climate species that bring a splash of English colour to the place and reach their full glory in the spring. The town puts its best foot forward for the **Bowral Tulip Time Festival**, which takes place over a two-week period at the

Sir Donald Bradman

Australia's finest cricketer and batsman, Donald George Bradman, affectionately known as "the Don", was born in Bowral in the Southern Highlands in 1908. He attracted attention at an early age, batting golf balls against a local water tank with only a thin strip of wood. He made his Test cricket debut in 1928, at the relatively early age of 20. Two years later, he scored a record 334 not out in a Test against England and, in a match against Queensland, the highest first-class innings ever achieved (452 not out) – a record he would continue to hold until 1959.

His international career spanned 20 years, during which he played in 52 Tests and captained Australia for over a decade. His unequalled reputation stems from his unique batting average of 99.94 runs per innings – he made more than 35,000 runs throughout his career. Sadly, in his final Test, he famously needed only a further four runs to reach an average of 100, but was dismissed for a "duck" on the second ball. Bradman retired from the game in 1948 and died in 2001, aged 92. But his name continues to grace cricket halls of fame, both in Australia and the world over.

end of September and the beginning of October. The centrepiece of the event is **Corbett Gardens** in Bendooley Street, Bowral's public park, its lawns, paths and flower beds surrounding the ornamental ponds ablaze with 100,000 tulips.

Several of the town's more distinguished private gardens also throw open their front gate at this time of the year. Among the perennial favourites are Red Cow Farm, Buskers End and Redlands.

On the banks of the Wingecarribee River, just south of Bowral on the road to the market town of **Moss Vale**, is the **Cecil Hoskins Nature Reserve** (Moss Vale–Bowral Road, Moss Vale; tel: 4887 7270). It is a haven for waterfowl and a great spot for summer picnics. Pelicans, black swans and swamp hens are just some of the 90 species that frequent the area. Kangaroos and wallabies can be found grazing on the grasslands at the western boundary of the reserve, and, in the early morning or late afternoon, the stealthy visitor might even be rewarded by a glimpse of a platypus.

Berrima

In the fertile valley of the Wingecarribee River, 8 km (5 miles) west of Bowral, is one of the gems of the Southern Highlands. **Berrima ❸** is an outstanding example of a Georgian colonial town, with the patina of age spelled out on its honey-coloured sandstone walls. Even the local gaol looks benign.

Founded in the 1830s as a commercial and administrative centre, the town quickly acquired a number of handsome stone buildings. But Berrima never attracted a population of more than 250 and lapsed into a coma when the settlement was bypassed by the railway. It was eclipsed by the far larger and more prosperous towns that lay on the railway route through the Southern Highlands, such as Bowral, Mittagong and Moss Vale.

However, it was poverty and neglect that preserved Berrima from modern-day improvements. Today, wide awake in an age with a taste for the past, it has become the high-quality, albeit rose-tinted version of colonial Australia.

Map on page 118

BELOW: The Old Bakery Cottage at Berrima.

In the Southern Highlands cottage gardens echo the homelands of the earliest settlers.

BELOW: Kiama's Blowhole.

The best way to absorb the atmosphere is with a stroll along the main street. Begin at the **Berrima Court House** (corner Wilshire and Argyle Streets; tel: 4877 1505; www.berrima-courthouse.org.au; daily 10am–4pm), which also includes a museum and information centre. Built between 1835 and 1838, this is a fine example of the craftsmanship of the period. The museum has an audiovisual presentation, which provides insight into the European history of the region from the time of earliest exploration, and details some of the more grisly trials heard within the court. The jury room continues the theme of crime and punishment with an exhibition of devices used to administer 19th-century justice corporally and letters from condemned prisoners.

Just below the court house, **Berrima Gaol** is Australia's oldest surviving prison. Built in the 1830s by chained convicts, the gaol was used as an internment camp in World War I. Today, the building lives on as a women's prison.

Below the governor's house, the **Surveyor General Inn** is the country's oldest continuous licensed hotel – a proud claim in thirsty Australia. A little lower down on Market Street, the handsome two-storey sandstone building, the **White Horse Inn** (www.whitehorseinn.com.au), was built in the 1830s as Oldbury's Inn. It has a two-room cellar where convicts used to be locked up for the night.

At the top of Market Street on the left is the **Holy Trinity Anglican Church**, possibly the first church designed by Edmund Blacket, who was appointed Colonial Architect in 1849 and designed several Sydney churches in the same Gothic Revival style. Sandstone for the church was quarried from the banks of the Wingecarribee River at the rear of the building. From here, there are several cafés on your stroll back towards the court house.

Around Kiama Bay

East of Berrima and south from Sydney along the Princes Highway, the town of **Kiama** ❹, on a peninsula rising up from the sweeping curve of Bombo Beach, comes as a breath of fresh air. To most Australians, Kiama is synonymous with its blowhole, which was discovered by explorer George Bass in 1797 as he charted the southern coastline. On the cliffs at **Blowhole Point**, waves surging into an underground cavity are compressed and forced upwards, exploding high into the air with a loud "oomph". The strength of the eruption varies according to wind, waves and tides, and the blowhole is not as vigorous as it once was (since waves have eroded the underground chamber), but it still draws a crowd. The area is fenced, but beware, visitors have been swept to their deaths off these rocks.

Next to the visitor centre at Blowhole Point, the **Pilot's Cottage Museum** (tel: 4232 1001; Fri–Mon 11am–3pm; admission charge) reveals the story of Kiama's colour-

ful past since its foundation in the 1830s, from the time when cedar-cutting, basalt quarries and dairy farming were the town's mainstay.

Just inland from Kiama at the foot of the Great Dividing Range, **Minnamurra Rainforest** (Minnamurra Falls Road, Jamberoo; tel: 4236 0469; daily 9am–5pm; admission charge) offers a small but sensational taste of the wilderness that once stood along the coastal escarpment. From the Minnamurra Rainforest Centre, a 1.6-km (1-mile) elevated boardwalk winds towards the escarpment and across Minnamurra Creek, providing easy access to the 400-hectare (1000-acre) rainforest with its cabbage tree palms, red cedar, staghorn ferns and spectacular Illawarra fig trees. For a more energetic excursion, the return walk to Minnamurra Falls can take up to two hours.

The route from Kiama to Minnamurra passes through **Jamberoo**, a delightful little village surrounded by emerald-green farms with the palisades of the escarpment rearing in the background. The township was established around 1820, originally to exploit the rich cedar forests that built much of colonial Sydney. Take a short stroll around the town to explore its historic churches and poke around in Fredericks General Store.

The Town of Trees

South from Kiama, the Princes Highway slopes through a rolling sea of rich dairy meadows dotted with red-roofed farmhouses, rising to a crest at the rugged peaks of the coastal escarpment before it slinks into **Berry ❺**. Strung out along the highway, Berry subtitles itself "The Town of Trees", a reference to the oak, elm and beech trees that were planted extensively in the late 19th century. This is another country town in idyllic surroundings that's been "discovered" by Sydneysiders, to the astonishment of long-time residents who have seen real-estate prices soar.

The main street is dominated by the day-to-day commerce that the highway brings, but the National Bank and the court house stand out as examples of Classical Revival

TIP

The Jamberoo Pub stirs from its rustic slumber on Sundays, when bush bands perform live.

BELOW: the lush Minnamurra Rainforest.

One of the finest vistas in Australia is to be had from Cambewarra Lookout in Morton National Park, just past the village of Kangaroo Valley, where a sweeping landscape of escarpment rainforest interspersed with tracts of dairy farmland greets the eye.

BELOW: crenellated bridge to Kangaroo Valley.

architecture of the Victorian era. The **Berry Museum** (135 Queen Street; tel: 4464 3097; Sat and school holidays 11am–2pm, Sun 11am–3pm) tells the story of the district's history. Formerly a bank, the building was designed in the Gothic style known as Scottish Baronial by William Wardell, who also designed some significant public buildings along Sydney's Bridge Street.

If time allows, take the Kangaroo Valley Road, which leaves Berry on its southern outskirts and spirals into the hills behind the town. Tourist trap it may be, but the rambling, historic village of **Kangaroo Valley ❻** is surrounded by majestic scenery, set against the dark curtain of the escarpment. There are 23 walking trails in the region, from genteel strolls to rugged hikes through **Morton National Park**.

South of Berry, the landscape along the Shoalhaven River had a powerful effect on Arthur Boyd (1920–99), one of Australia's most celebrated painters. For many years he lived along its banks at **Bundanon** (170 Riversdale Road, Cambewarra

West; tel: 4423 0433; www.bundanon.com.au; Sun 10.30am–4pm; admission charge) – not to be confused with Bundanoon – just inland from Nowra, which is 162 km (100 miles) south of Sydney.

It was here that Boyd painted some of his most provocative landscapes. The artist bequeathed his home to the National Estate, and on Sunday, the house and grounds, Boyd's studio and a collection of his work are open to a reverent public. It is a popular attraction so book well in advance.

To reach Bundanon, follow the Princes Highway south from Berry toward Nowra and turn right along Illaroo Road at the set of lights before the Shoalhaven River bridge at Nowra. Continue along Illaroo Road for 13½ km (8 miles), then turn left at the dirt road signposted "Bundanon".

Jervis Bay

Just south of Nowra, a left turn off the Princes Highway toward Huskisson takes you to **Jervis Bay ❼**. Instantly you're in another world, looping through a green tunnel of paper-

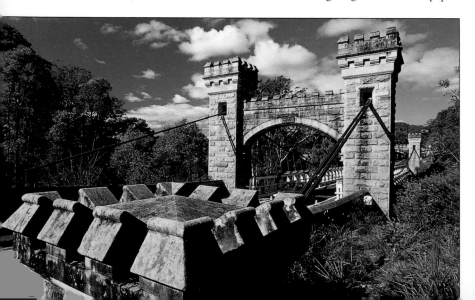

Map on page 118

barks, banksias and grevilleas with lorikeets arrowing through the branches. As Jervis Bay Road heads towards Booderee National Park at the southern arm of the bay you may spot a few eastern grey kangaroos, and pelicans wheeling overhead.

A huge bite in the state's east coast, Jervis Bay measures about 15 km (9 miles) from north to south and about 10 km (6 miles) across. The main town is **Huskisson**, from where dolphin-watching cruises and fishing trips depart and there are boats for hire; but it's the natural credentials of the area that seduce. The bay's beaches are glorious, a series of scalloped coves bracketed by knuckles of rock and backed by blackbutt, ti tree and mahogany forest.

Hyams Beach

The best-known of all the beaches is **Hyams**, on the southern shores of the bay, which has the whitest sand in the world according to the *Guinness Book of Records*. This is also Jervis Bay's style capital, and the mood is evident from the houses that you pass as you meander down the hill through the town.

Instead of the standard South Coast brick-veneer contemporary plonked down on a clear-felled block, these houses are hung with big balconies that exploit the views. They are also fitted with rippling, wave-like roofs and snuggle into the native vegetation in a way that suggests an expensive architect. Over the past few years, Hyams Beach has become a salty holiday haven for well-heeled urbanites who have imported their own sensibilities, most notably in the Beach Store, where the menu might easily grace a smart inner-Sydney brasserie.

The bay's sparkling waters, its underwater topography of arches, caves and rock stacks, and a marine population that includes groupers, wrasses, sharks, cuttlefish and sea dragons, also make this one of the finest dive sites in the state. Most of the dive sites are located on the seaward faces of the northern and southern headlands that guard the approaches to the bay. Shore diving is possible from Hyams Beach and Green Patch, but the best sites require a boat. Dive operators in Huskisson can supply all the gear, as well as providing regular boat trips.

At its southern end, Jervis Bay is enclosed by **Booderee National Park** (www.deh.gov.au/parks/booderee), shaped like a broadaxe blade, a pristine coastal wilderness that has defied plans to build a refinery, a major naval base and a nuclear reactor. Cupped within the inside curve of the bay, the national park is strung with beaches – Green Patch, Hole in the Wall, Bristol Point – all the way to glorious **Murrays Beach**, in the shelter of Bowen Island which guards the bay's southern headland. From Wreck Bay village on Summercloud Bay, in the park's south, a walking trail circles the peninsula to St Georges Head, passing a succession of quiet beaches, cliffs and forests.

First sighted and named by Captain James Cook in 1770, Jervis Bay once rivalled Sydney Harbour (Port Jackson) in importance as a colonial port, with its surrounding headlands providing shelter.

BELOW: the dolphin-watching boat at the jetty in Huskisson.

Three towns

Ulladulla is one of the few places where the Princes Highway passes the sea, swooping down past its pretty enclosed harbour with fishing trawlers tied up along the far side of the quay. The grassy hillside overlooking the harbour is a pleasant place to stretch your legs, but the town itself has little that demands a stop. Ulladulla is one of a trio of towns that have grown and blended together over the years, yet distinct differences remain.

Milton, the most northerly town of the three and the only one without a seafront, is a lively place that still has a rustic flavour to its weatherboard architecture. Milton has a better choice of cafés and shops than Ulladulla, and some excellent craft shops in the **Cultural Centre**.

The first land grant in the area was made to the Revd Thomas Kendall in 1827. His grandson, Henry Kendall, who was born on the estate in 1839, became one of Australia's most distinguished poets. It was the people of the district who helped launch his literary career when they contributed towards the publication of his first book, *Poems and Songs*, in 1862.

Separated from Milton by a deep, green valley, **Mollymook**, the third town, has a beautiful beach which is patrolled at the southern end by the local surf club. There are shady picnic tables in the adjacent park, and a shop and cafés near by.

To the west of Ulladulla, Pigeon House Mountain is a local landmark at the southeast corner of **Morton National Park**, one of the state's largest. It is possible to climb to the top of the 720-metre (2,350-ft) peak, but it's a tough scramble that involves ladders as you approach the summit. For experienced bushwalkers, Morton National Park has some tough but rewarding walks over its deeply dissected sandstone plateaux.

Murramarang Park

Stretching for 44 km (25 miles) along the coast south of Ulladulla is **Murramarang National Park** ❽. Due to the large number of creeks and inlets, no roads run parallel to the coast; as you head south from Ulladullla, the

TIP

The best access to the summit of Pigeon House Mountain is via Wheelbarrow Road, which turns inland from the Princes Highway 5 km (3 miles) south of Ulladulla.

BELOW: the bay at Ulladulla.

most convenient access to Murramararang is from the Princes Highway via Pebbly Beach Road.

The park is known for its beaches, rock fishing and coastal bush-walks, but best of all for its kangaroos. At **Pebbly Beach**, eastern grey kangaroos eagerly await visitors in anticipation of treats. Over time, these animals have lost their natural fear of humans – so much so that some of them have become quite aggressive as they plunder the picnic baskets of visitors. Eventually, the over-zealous kangaroos must be relocated by the park's rangers, so even though they are hard to resist, it's better not to encourage dependency by feeding them. Sometimes the kangaroos enter the surf, although they've yet to take up surfing.

At the northern end of the park, **Murramarang Aboriginal Area** is a headland midden mound with shells and other artefacts of importance to local Aboriginal people. This is the largest known Aboriginal midden in the state, indicating a long history of human habitation around the site. Access to the midden is via Murramarang Road, which leaves the Princes Highway at Termeil. Roads within the park are unsealed but are generally in reasonable condition.

Land of fish

The next stop is just a few kilometres south of the National Park. Spread out along the estuary of the Clyde River, **Batemans Bay ❾** was named by James Cook as he sailed past on the *Endeavour* in 1770 – although he noted that the bay was too exposed to be a safe harbour.

Originally settled by timber cutters and fishermen, the town has been transformed by tourism and by the seaside villages that have sprung up along the coast to the south. These villages are especially popu-

lar with visitors from Canberra, since this is the closest spot on the coast to the capital city.

The river is navigable for 30 km (20 miles) from the town, and the journey aboard one of the small cruisers that operate as far as Nelligen, 11 km (7 miles) upriver, makes for a relaxing half-day.

Gold-rush towns

For the next stop you need to travel 61 km (38 miles) inland along the Kings Highway. The adjective "historic" attaches itself naturally to **Braidwood ❿**, a town which emerged as the centre of an agricultural district in the 1820s. It boomed suddenly when gold was discovered in the area mid-century and for a few years was flushed with money and miners. This was a spirited period in the town's history, with Braidwood plagued by bushrangers who preyed on the gold consignments leaving the town. The most notorious of these were the Clarke family, outlaws led by Tom Clarke. Their nefarious deeds culminated in the murder of four special consta-

Map on page 118

Kangaroos fed with foods not usually part of their diet can develop the fatal "lumpy jaw" bacterial infection.

BELOW: boomer time at Pebbly Beach.

The three white lions at Mogo Zoo are the only ones to be found in Australia.

BELOW: cabin at Old Mogo Town.

bles before the Clarkes were eventually captured, tried and hanged at Sydney's Darlinghurst Gaol.

Almost as soon as it had begun, the rush was over, but Braidwood continued to prosper modestly and a number of impressive banks, hotels and public buildings were erected during the second half of the 19th century. That streetscape altered little during the following century and today the entire township is classified by the National Trust. Its historic credentials now provide Braidwood with its bread and butter, and the town is well supplied with cafés, quilt shops, a wood-fired pizzeria and a delicatessen selling boutique olive oils.

Start at the high end of Wallace Street, the main street, with the **Braidwood Historical Society Museum** (186 Wallace Street; tel: 4842 2310; Mon–Fri 10am–4pm; admission charge), which reveals the town's history in words, illustrations and artefacts. Continue down Wallace Street, where most of the town's historic buildings, churches, banks and hotels are located. At the lower end of

the street, Braidwood cemetery has a monument to the four men murdered by the notorious Clarke gang.

Return to Batemans Bay and, rather than continuing south along the Princes Highway, turn off at the road signposted "Batehaven, Malua Bay". This route takes you past the town centre and along the estuary of the Clyde River, past marinas and then south along the coast. The Clyde is the only major river on the east coast of Australia that is not dammed. This is a great fishing spot, as the number of pelicans testifies. The town's streetlights are a favourite perch for these giant fish-eaters – to the peril of pedestrians who must pass underneath.

The road dawdles along the coast, past a string of villages and beaches – Sunshine Cove, Lilli Pilli, Malua Bay and Guerilla Bay – tiny sweeps of sand cradled by headlands where the waves leave a frosting of foam across splintered fingers of shale. The village of **Mogo** ⓫ lies 28 km (17 miles) south of Batemans Bay by the coast road or 10 km (6 miles) on the Highway. It is a one-time tumbledown gold-mining settlement that has been given the kiss of life by the art galleries, craft shops and cafés that have taken root there.

The discovery of a single nugget here in 1857 sparked a gold rush that saw the town grow from nothing to a population of 10,000 virtually overnight. **Old Mogo Town** (Annett Lane and James Street; tel: 4474 2123; www.oldmogotown.com.au; daily 9am–5pm; admission charge) is a re-creation of the 19th-century gold-rush village that existed here, complete with mining equipment, historic shops and houses and a walk-through mine. Visitors can even try gold panning near the giant waterwheel.

Mogo Zoo (222 Tomakin Road; tel: 4474 4930; (www.mogozoo.com.au); daily 9am–5pm; admission

charge) is a major attraction in itself. Dedicated to the preservation of endangered exotic species, the zoo houses red pandas, golden lion tamarind monkeys, otters, ring-tailed lemurs, Syrian brown bears, lions and Bengal tigers.

Around Narooma

Further south along the Princes Highway, the small coastal resort of **Narooma** ⑫ is another popular holiday town, especially with fishermen who come here for big-game fishing. The town is well endowed with beaches, and the **Narooma Golf Club** (Ballingalla Street; tel: 4476 2522; www.naroomagolf.com.au; daily 6.30am–6pm; admission charge) is rated among the country's best. Six holes of this spectacular 18-hole course are perched on the cliffs high above the ocean.

The waters around **Montague Island**, 8 km (5 miles) off Narooma's coast, teem with fish, a fact which once made the island a haven for seabirds and seals, and a hunting ground for the local Wallaga and Djiringanj Aboriginal people.

The island's wildlife has been devastated since the arrival of Europeans but the National Parks and Wildlife Service is gradually restoring it to its natural state. Today, Montague Island has the state's only known colony of Australian fur seals, as well as sea eagles, fairy penguins, mutton birds, hawks, crested terns, silver gulls, harriers and peregrine falcons.

Charter operators in Narooma run guided tours of the island, bookable through the local National Parks and Wildlife Service office (30 Princes Highway; tel: 4476 2881; Mon–Fri 8.30am–4.30pm; admission charge).

Tilba

A modest assortment of weatherboard buildings set on a rippling green ridge against the towering peak of Mount Dromedary, **Central**

Tilba ⑬ is the postcard incarnation of a country town. Some 29 km (18 miles) southwest of Narooma, the town was established around the cheese factory that was built here in 1891. The ABC Cheese Factory is open (daily 9am–5pm) for cheese tasting, and the old equipment is on display in the souvenir shop.

All but one of Tilba's buildings were erected in the same decade, and all from timber that was milled in this region. This gives the town its distinctive sense of unity, although the arrangement of the buildings themselves was dictated more by convenience and practicality than by aesthetic considerations. These days Central Tilba devotes itself ardently to tourism, and a number of shops in the town have been taken over by craft workers.

You can saunter from one end of the town to the other in five minutes, but you could easily spend a couple of hours here, too.

Central Tilba grew at the side of **Mount Dromedary** (797 metres/ 2,615 ft) in the 1870s, when gold was discovered. There are fine views from

Map on page 118

Named after Paul Hogan who once filmed a commercial here, Hogan's Hole, at the Narooma Golf Club, is a par-3 with an ocean carry from clifftop to green.

BELOW: one of the beaches at Narooma.

Since 1992 Mrs Jamieson has been hand-making Mrs Jamieson's Tilba Fudge *at Bates Emporium in Central Tilba. Most visitors will find at least one of the 117 varieties to their taste.*

BELOW: a path from Tilba Tilba leads up to Mount Dromedary.

the mountain, which the local Aboriginal people knew as Gulaga. It is the highest point on this part of the coast, christened by that profligate name-giver, Lt James Cook. The summit has some strangely shaped granite outcrops, making this a sacred site for the Yuin people.

Rainforest species thrive in several places on the upper tiers of the mountain. A walking track to the top begins at Pam's General Store in the centre of nearby Tilba Tilba. Allow half a day, and take plenty of water. If you're looking for somewhere to stop for the night, there are several atmospheric B&Bs in this area, oozing with rustic character.

South of Central Tilba, just before it rejoins the highway, **Tilba Tilba**. The village is cast from the same mould as Central Tilba, although on a smaller scale. The main attraction here is **Foxglove Spires** (Corkhill Drive; tel: 4473 7375; daily 9am–5pm), a luscious woodland garden arranged around a farm cottage. The gardens are amply planted with wisteria, lavender, clivea and arum lilies, but

their most arresting feature is a 55-metre (165-ft) arbour of espaliered Manchurian pears, which is enough to inspire strong men to poetry.

The Sapphire Coast

Surfing, boating and fishing are the main attractions along the so-called "Sapphire Coast", stretching from Wallaga Lake in the north to beyond Eden in the far south of the state.

Merimbula ⑭ is a popular holiday town, spread out on forested hills around the broad mouth of the Merimbula River, which arcs to form Merimbula Lake at the back of the town. For the overwhelming majority of visitors, it's the town's watersports that attract, and Merimbula has several majestic beaches. Main Beach is 5 km (3 miles) long, while Short Point and Tura Beach are backed by ti trees and banksia trees set among coastal heaths.

Merimbula is often twinned with the historic village of **Pambula**, just a few kilometres to the south. This region is known for its golf, and the most illustrious of its courses is **Tura Beach Country Club** (The Fairway,

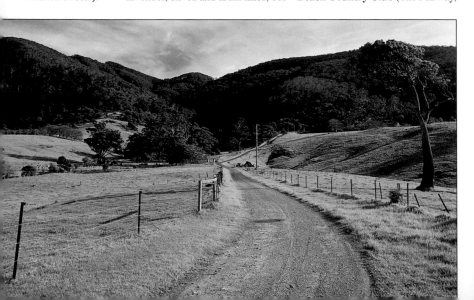

Tura Beach; tel: 6495 9756; www.tura club.com.au; admission charge). A coastal 18-hole course designed by Peter Thomson, it has a mixture of links-style terrain and hills, with six par-5s that demand real muscle.

The whales of Eden

Tucked into the jaws of Twofold Bay, **Eden** ⑮ is the last town of any size on the state's south coast before you cross the Victoria state border. Eden still makes its living largely from fishing and timber, as it has since the earliest days of European settlement.

This is the site of Australia's first mainland whaling station. The whales' annual migration took them past Twofold Bay, heading north from Antarctic waters in May and back again in November. In the 1920s, Eden became famous for its killer whales. Led by a whale known as Old Tom, the pod would alert local whalers of other whales in the vicinity, and whalers and killer whales would unite to herd their victims into the shallow waters of Twofold Bay. For their efforts, the killer whales would feed on the lips and tongue of the dead whales, leaving the blubber and whalebone for the whalers.

The **Killer Whale Museum** (Imlay and Cocora Streets; tel: 6496 209; www.killerwhalemuseum.com.au; Mon–Sat 9.15am–3.45pm, Sun 11.15am–3.45pm; admission charge) is Eden's essential attraction, a fascinating display of boats, whaling gear, photographs and brassy nautical apparatus. The most intriguing exhibit is the skeleton of Old Tom, found dead in his former hunting ground in 1930, which coincides with the end of Eden's whaling days.

Whales can still be found cruising past Eden on their annual migration, but these days they're hunted with cameras instead of harpoons. Whale-watching cruises operate between late September and late November.

At other times of the year, cruises take in the bottlenose dolphins, seals and penguins found around the bay. Whales are increasing in numbers with each passing year, and when a whale enters Twofold Bay, a siren sounds from the museum.

Extending north and south of Eden, **Ben Boyd National Park** is a sensational tract of wild coast, beaches, wild-flower meadows and eucalypt woodland, named after the founder of Boydtown. Banker-adventurer Ben Boyd established the settlement in 1842.

The coast, where the shales and conglomerates have been gnawed by the sea into fantastic arches, cliffs and caves, is particularly dramatic. The most striking man-made feature of the park is **Boyd's Tower**, located at the extreme end of the promontory in the south of Twofold Bay. Built from Pyrmont sandstone quarried in Sydney, it was used as a whaling lookout. The tower was designed by Oswald Brierly, an English artist and student of naval architecture, who was later appointed official Marine Painter to Queen Victoria and knighted. ❏

Map on page 118

EST

EDEN KILLER WHALE
MUSEUM
HOME OF 'OLD TOM' THE KILLER WHALE

OPEN DAILY

ADULTS $4ea   CHILDREN $2ea

The skeleton of killer whale Old Tom, who used to help whalers in their hunt, is now on display in Eden.

BELOW: ahoy there.

RESTAURANTS, CAFÉS & PUBS

Restaurants

Batemans Bay

On the Pier
Old Punt Road
Tel: 4472 6405
www.onthepier.com.au
Open: L daily, D Mon-Sat. **$$**
Simple but stylish cooking in this restaurant that sits, as you might expect, right over the water.

Berrima

The Journeyman
Old Hume Highway, 3km north of Berrima
Tel: 4877 1911
Open: L & D Wed-Sun. **$$**
Interesting and well-executed modern Australian dishes at this pleasant venue in the heart of Berrima. BYO.

Surveyor General Inn
Old Hume Highway
Tel: 4877 1226
Open: L & D daily. **$$**
Situated in spacious rural grounds, the convict-built Surveyor General has traded since 1834 and is Australia's oldest continuously licensed inn. Hearty, country-style fare is on offer: cook your own steak on the barbecue or sample the à la carte menu at the Bushranger Bistro.

Seagulls
Esplanade Motor Inn, 23 Beach Road
Tel: 4472 0253
www.bayinfo.com.au/seagulls
Open: D Wed-Mon. **$$**
Good quality ingredients sometimes get lost under the sauces but the waterfront views more than compensate. BYO.

Berry

The Silos
B640 Princes Highway,
Jaspers Brush
(6km south of Berry)
Tel: 4448 6160
www.silos.com.au
Open: L Wed-Sun, D Wed-Sat. **$$$**
There's some interesting and adventurous food on offer in this rustic country setting. BYO.

Bowral

Bistro Mont
250 Bong Bong Street
Tel: 4862 2677
Open: L Tues-Fri & Sun, D Tues-Sun. **$$**
Good hearty meals go with the effervescent atmosphere in this busy place. The lack of subtlety in the field doesn't seem to matter. BYO.

Hordern's
Milton Park Country House Hotel, Hordern's Road
Tel: 4861 1522
www.milton-park.com.au
Open: L & D daily. **$$**
A licensed restaurant in the former mansion of the local Hordern family with elegant country-style décor. Uses delicious local produce.

Eden

Wheelhouse
253 Imlay Street
Tel: 6496 3392,
Open: L & D daily (closed Mon May-Aug). **$$**
Down at the wharf where the fleet comes in, the Wheelhouse is well set

to grab the best of the local fish. It does so and then, with minimal fuss, creates mouth-watering platters.

Jervis Bay

The Gunyah
Paperbark Camp, 571 Woollamia Road, Huskisson
Phone: 4441 7299
www.paperbarkcamp.com.au
Open: D daily. **$$**
Dinner, bed and breakfast is a sensible choice at this eco resort. Dinner in the elevated dining room is a successful mix of contemporary cooking with indigenous bush flavours. BYO.

Kiama

55 on Collins
Shop 1, 55 Collins Street
Tel: 4232 2811
Open: B & L daily, D Mon-Tues, Thur-Sat. **$$**
Effortlessly retaining the mantle of best restaurant in Kiama, 55 employs good local produce in innovative and satisfying combinations. Allow room for one of the fabulous deserts. BYO.

Merimbula

Donna's Cantina
56 Market Street
Tel: 6495 1085
Open: L & D Mon-Sat. **$$**
The Latin influence is in evidence and there are tapas to be had, but closer inspection reveals a menu with input from a much broader spectrum including southeast Asia and the Middle East.

RIGHT: coffee stop at Kiama.

Mollymook

Bannister's
191 Mitchell Parade
Tel: 4455 3044
www.bannisterspointlodge.com.au
Open: L Sun only (summer) & D Tues-Sun (summer), Tues-Sat rest of the year. **$$**
This is the place for crispy zucchini flowers filled with chilli jam scallops with mint, lime and yoghurt and other such adventurous fare that makes it stand out, all served ina stylish, light-filled dining room.

Narooma

Lynch's Restaurant
135 Wagonga Street
Tel: 4476 3002
Open: L & D daily. **$$**
Slightly old-fashioned feel to this small restaurant but the food is never less than interesting and sometimes inspired.

The Quarterdeck
Riverside Drive
Tel: 4476 2723
www.quarterdeckcafe.com.au
Open: L & D daily. **$$**
Good, straightforward seafood to be enjoyed on the deck over the water. Doubles as a music venue as well.

Ulladulla

Elizans
39 Burrill Street
Tel: 4455 1796
www.guesthouse.com.au/restaurant
Open: D Mon, Thur-Sat **$$**
Make a booking at this restaurant in the 5-star Ulladulla Guest House

even if you're not staying there, for a fine combination of local produce and the best local wines.

Wollongong

Caveau
122-124 Keira Street
Tel: 4226 4855
www.caveau.com.au
Open: D Tues-Sat. **$$**
Sophisticated French dining with a modern Australian twist that reveals real flair in the kitchen. Try the braised ox tongue with celeriac remoulade and truffle dressing.

Lorenzo's Diner
119 Keira Street
Tel: 4229 5633
Open: L Fri , D Mon-Sat. **$$$**
Italian but wiith Asian and Middle Eastern accents makes for vibrant dining. BYO.

Cafés and bars

Berrima

Cafe Fraiche
2/9 Old Hume Highway
Tel: 4877 1342
Open: B & L daily. **$**
Good ingredients and lots of them make this a favourite spot to refuel in Berrima.

Berry

Berry Wood-Fired Sourdough Bakery
23 Prince Alfred Street
Tel: 4464 1617
www.sourdough.com.au
Open: B & L Wed-Sun. **$**
Produce from the bakery is sensational and there's a fine deck to enjoy it on. BYO.

Braidwood

Café Altenburg
102 Wallace Street
Tel: 4842 2077
Open: L daily. **$**
Some delicious homemade cakes and snacks keep people coming back to this simple café.

Central Tilba

Dromedary Hotel
Bate St, Central Tilba
Tel: 4473 7223
Open: L & D daily. **$**
The food's not the highpoint but this is an atmospheric and cosy old weatherboard pub.

Jervis Bay

Fresh at the Bay
64 Owen Street, Huskisson
Tel: 4441 5245
Open: L daily. **$**
Good pastries and coffee along with the usual rolls and wraps.

Wollongong

Diggies Beach Café
1 Cliff Road, North Beach, North Wollongong
Tel: 4226 2688
Open: L daily. D daily in summer. **$**
Find a spot in this lovely old listed building, grab a coffee and a well crafted snack, and just hang out and watch the beach life.

PRICE CATEGORIES
Prices for a three-course dinner per person with a half-bottle of house wine:
$ = under A$50
$$ = A$50–A$75
$$$ = over A$75
L = lunch, D = dinner, BYO = bring your own alcohol.

CANBERRA AND THE AUSTRALIAN CAPITAL TERRITORY

Planned down to its last detail, pristine Canberra was born inland from a need for a capital. But a sense of spaciousness and serenity, and leisurely proximity to the bush, give this city the advantages of country-town living

anberra, the national capital, is unlike any other place in Australia. The city projects order, spaciousness and an almost unearthly sense of calm. Even geography sets it apart: of all Australia's capital cities, it's the only one not on the coast.

Canberra exists purely as a political entity, no commercial or strategic imperative underlies its foundation. The sheep pastures that were originally carved from the plains along the Molonglo River scarcely merited a parliament, nor any of the other institutions of nationhood, yet it was nationhood itself that required Canberra's existence.

Towards Federation

Before Federation, every one of the six Australian colonies was a self-governing entity, each with its own parliament, passing laws that often seemed to fly in the face of reason. Each state had a different railway gauge, for example, so that passengers, goods and livestock had to unload from one train and join another at every state border. Even though political union has brought agreement on a broad range of national issues, the states remain doggedly determined to pursue their own regional interests – with bizarre results. In summer, when some states switch to daylight-saving time – but

on different dates – Australia has up to five different time zones.

The movement towards Federation was instigated by some of the more far-sighted politicians and gathered pace in the 1890s. On 1 January 1900, Federation became fact and the Commonwealth of Australia was born. A primary need was for a capital, to be located between Sydney and Melbourne, Australia's two largest cities, neither of which would ever have allowed the other to monopolise the national agenda. For

Map on page 136

LEFT: the Carillon on the shore of Lake Burley Griffin.
BELOW: the view from Black Mountain.

The pathway around Lake Burley Griffin is a popular spot for joggers and cyclists, who are guaranteed one stunning view after another. This one is of the Old Parliament with the New behind.

reasons of defence, an inland site was preferred, but it was not until 1906 that one was finally chosen from more than 60 candidates.

Even the naming of the capital was a contentious issue. Among the options were "Cookaburra", "Kangaremu" and "Wheatwoolgold", as well as wild agglutinations along the lines of "Sydmelperadbrisho". Political cynics suggested "Swindleville" and "Gonebroke". No doubt a collective sigh of relief was breathed when in 1913 Lady Denman, wife of the governor general, mounted a crimson-draped platform and declared, "I name the capital of Australia, Canberra".

The city takes its name from "Canberry", the sheep station that was established at the foot of Black Mountain by Joshua Moore in 1824, roughly where the National Museum of Australia stands today. The name comes from a local Aboriginal word which probably means "meeting place", a reference either to the junction of the Molonglo and Queanbeyan Rivers, or to the Aborigines who came here for the autumn feast of migrating bogong moths.

The building of a capital

Initially, progress was slow. Not until 1926 did federal parliament move from Melbourne to Canberra, and the Great Depression and World War II stalled the city's growth. By 1945, its population stood at only 13,000. During the 1950s and 1960s growth accelerated as the government increased its efforts to shift the public service from Melbourne. In the 1960s the Molonglo River was dammed to create Lake Burley Griffin, the defence complex was built on Russell Hill and work began on satellite town centres. The 1980s saw the completion of most of Canberra's significant buildings, including the Parliament, the National Gallery, the High Court and the

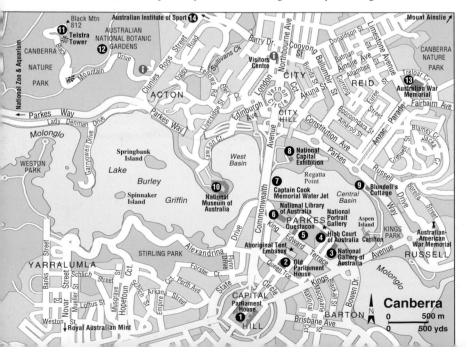

National Science and Technology Centre. Today the city has a population of more than 300,000, making it Australia's largest inland city.

From the time the first sod was turned, Canberra was a totally planned city. Faced with almost unlimited space, and working in a now automotive era that took personal mobility for granted, Canberra's designers chose an expansive mode. The city sprawls over a vast area, and many of the horrors that afflict other cities have been banished. Unsightly billboard advertising is non-existent, and car yards and industry are tucked away backstage.

To many Australians, the planning rules that govern Canberra intrude into private life to a ludicrous extent. Citizens may not erect a fence around their front garden, for example; nor may they walk to the corner shop for a litre of milk, since corner shops don't exist. The overall effect is of a slightly bland, homogeneous city that lacks extremes both in its architecture and in its population – no ugly high-rises disfigure the Canberra skyline, but then neither are there any architectural masterpieces.

Conversely, those who live here value its lack of pollution, its well-endowed galleries and museums, its freedom from traffic congestion and its easy access to the great outdoors. Leave it in droves every weekend they may, but they will hasten to assure you that life in Canberra is far from dull: evidence has shown that Canberra has the liveliest adult products trade in all of Australia, and is the only place in the country where fireworks are sold legally – although only to residents of the city, and only for a short period of the year.

Getting your bearings

Surrounding Canberra, the **Australian Capital Territory** (ACT) covers an area of 2,400 sq. km (900 sq. miles), most of it bushland.

Although there are some captivating parts to this region – such as **Namadgi National Park** which covers about 40 percent of the ACT – for most visitors it is the city itself that is of prime interest.

Exploring is easy thanks to Canberra's excellent road system, and with most of the capital's major attractions clustered in a relatively small area, in close proximity to **Lake Burley Griffin**. It's most likely that you'll approach Canberra from the north, and your first stop should be the **Canberra Visitors Centre** at 330 Northbourne Avenue, signposted on your left (tel: 6205 0044; Mon–Fri 9am–5.30pm, Sat–Sun 9am–4pm). The centre has information on current events, and staff will assist you in reserving a hotel room if you haven't already.

Continue along Northbourne Avenue, around the grassy top of City Hill and down towards the lake. Just before crossing Common-

Map on page 136

A tour of the Old Parliament brings you within inches of the ceremonial mace.

BELOW: power boat, Canberra-style.

Free guided tours of Parliament House take about 45 minutes and include both Houses, the Great Hall and the roof.

BELOW: the gallery above the Members Hall.

wealth Avenue Bridge, turn left where the sign indicates the National Capital Exhibition. From here you can get a sense of the city's layout and plan your visit.

Parliament House

Return to the bridge, cross over the lake and ahead you will see a hill surmounted by a huge flagpole. **Parliament House ❶** (Capital Hill; tel: 6277 7111; www.aph.gov.au; daily 9am–5pm; free) is the beating heart of the nation's capital: the reason for Canberra's existence and a potent national symbol, as well as a showcase for Australian materials, design, craftsmanship and aspirations. Completed in time for Australia's 1988 bicentennial celebrations, Parliament House cost more than A$1 billion (making it Australia's costliest building ever), yet much of it is buried underground. A domed, grassed roof covers the building, designed to blend with the contours of Capital Hill. At a distance, its most striking feature is the four-legged, 81-metre (265-ft) high flagstaff that hovers over the building. The flag at the top measures 12.8 by 6.4 metres (40 by 20 ft) – about the size of 20 king-size beds.

The enormous mosaic in the courtyard is *Meeting Place*, designed by Aboriginal artist Nelson Tjakamarra. Inside the foyer, 48 grey-green marble columns represent a eucalypt forest, while the timber panels depict some of Australia's native plants. Beyond the Great Hall, near the gallery that runs above the Members Hall, one of only four extant originals of Magna Carta is on permanent display. This ink-on-vellum document, which was written in 1297, is known as the Inspeximus issue. Signed by King John in 1215, the Magna Carta curbed the absolute powers of the British monarch and is regarded as the first step on what was to be the long road to constitutional law.

The main chambers are the **House of Representatives**, decorated in green along the lines of the British Parliament, and the **Senate**, in red. These colour schemes are more muted than in their British counterparts to reflect the dusky pastels of the Australian bush. The

A design for the people

The design for the new Parliament was chosen by an international competition that attracted over 300 entries. The winning design was the work of a New York-based Italian architect, Romaldo Giurgola, whose concept was a circular building that "would nest into the hill". He envisaged a people's Parliament, a building that matched the country's character and would allow anyone to roam freely over the grass-covered roof as a symbol of the supremacy of the people over the politicians they elect. Heightened security concerns have largely put an end to such unsupervised wandering across the roof.

parliament building has a significant collection of Australian art, much of it displayed in the public areas. On the upper floor, the terrace has a view over the lake towards the Australian War Memorial, and the café next door has tables both inside and out. The best view though is from the section of roof that is still accessible to the public, one storey up.

Free guided tours of the building depart every half-hour when parliament is not in session. At other times, talks on the building are held in the Great Hall. At all times, visitors are welcome to wander around the public areas. When parliament is sitting, anyone can watch Australian parliamentary democracy in action from the Public Galleries. The livelier of the two chambers is the House of Representatives, and the best time to be there is Question Time, when the opposition takes a blowtorch to the belly of the government. Question Time is generally held at 2pm, for which you'll need to book by calling the Sergeant-at-Arms' office on 6277 4889 by 12.30pm of the day required.

Old Parliament House

From the front of Parliament House. walk down Federation Mall ahead. Surrounded by lawns and reflective ponds sloping down to the lake, **Old Parliament House ❷** (King George Terrace, Parkes; tel: 6270 8222; www.oph.gov.au; daily 9am–5pm; admission charge) is a stately, sprawling, colonial-style building that was completed in 1927. Although this was only intended as a temporary home for the country's politicians, more than 60 years passed before it was finally replaced by the present parliamentary building. When the politicians moved out, the building underwent a major renovation that revealed some surprises, such as the peephole between the prime minister's office and the office of his private secretary. The official explanation for this peephole – to allow the private secretary to see whether the prime minister had guests – strains credibility.

These days, this gracious old building serves as a museum of Australian political history. The House of Representatives Chamber, the

In the gallery above the Members Hall in Parliament House there are portraits of past prime ministers, including this one of Gough Whitlam by Clifton Pugh.

BELOW: Old Parliament House across the lake.

The Sculpture Garden at the National Gallery of Australia is freely accessible from the path around Lake Burley Griffin.

BELOW: Cones by Bert Flugelman in the Sculpture Garden.

Senate Chamber and the Prime Minister's Suite are open to view, and guided tours lift the lid on some of the lesser-known foibles of Australian political life.

Arranged on the walls of King's Hall, just beyond the building's main entrance, the official portraits of Australia's prime ministers reveal some interesting facets to those who have served in that position. Bob Hawke, the Labor prime minister of the 1980s who was famed for his silver locks, looks like he's been caught in a hairdryer. By contrast, Prime Minister John Howard looks relaxed and comfortable, standing with his wife in a waterside location that is obviously Sydney, the address he prefers above the official prime ministerial residence in Canberra.

Old Parliament House is the temporary home of the **National Portrait Gallery**, which celebrates some of Australia's headline makers, often with a surprising twist. Past exhibitions have been dedicated to Kylie Minogue, Australian sporting heroes, some of the greats of Australian portraiture and even *Fuzzy Prime*

Ministers of Australia – the complete line-up of prime ministers, captured for posterity in hooked-wool rugs.

Australia's artistic bunker

On either side of the glass-like pond at the front of the building is the **Aboriginal Tent Embassy**, first set up here in the 1970s to focus attention on the Aboriginal land-rights campaign and a permanent fixture since 1992. Depending on your point of view, it's either an icon or an eyesore; but it does serve to remind visitors of how many Aboriginal people feel that they do not share equally in the fruits of modern Australia.

The most easterly of the major public buildings on the lake's southern shore, the **National Gallery of Australia** ❸ (Parkes Place, Parkes; tel: 6240 6502; www.nga.gov.au; daily 10am–5pm; admission charge) is the country's leading showcase for Australian and international art, and includes a smattering from the megastars: Rubens, Warhol, Picasso, Matisse, Monet, and Rembrandt.

However it is in the collections hailing from Australia and Asia, and

in particular in its Aboriginal and Torres Strait Islander collections, that the National's credentials as a world-class gallery lie. The gallery documents the history of Aboriginal art through exhibits covering some of the earliest collectable works to the most recent, with the renaissance of Aboriginal art since the 1970s as its focus.

Other major disciplines within the building include Decorative Arts and Design, Photography and Indonesian Textiles. The gallery also hosts a varied artistic programme of lectures, film, dance, music and children's events, and features a sculpture garden.

To the west of the gallery, the **High Court of Australia** ❹ (Parkes Place, Parkes; tel: 6270 6811; www.hcourt. gov.au; Mon–Fri 9.45am–4.30pm; free) is the highest court in Australia's judicial system, the final court of appeal and the referee on matters of constitutional law. The court is made up of six justices and a chief justice. Since 1903, when it was established, there have been 11 chief justices and 39 justices – all but one of them men.

The concrete-and-glass building was opened in 1980. The approach to the court is via a long ramp which rises alongside a tiered water feature. An expansive Public Hall has a series of murals depicting the history and functions of the court. Sittings are open to the public – but don't expect fireworks; this is the legal system at its most ponderous, and the argument is usually creaking and obscure. Decisions are rarely made at the end of a hearing but reserved, in other words delivered after suitable reflection by the justices.

Making science fun

Next along, **Questacon** ❺ (King Edward Terrace, Parkes; tel: 6270 2800; www.questacon.edu.au; daily 9am–5pm; admission charge), although aimed unashamedly at children, is the light-relief chapter in the

Parliamentary Triangle. Subtitled the National Science and Technology Centre, Questacon is a hands-on museum that uses earthquake simulators, zero-gravity simulators, robotic dinosaurs and computers, not to mention devices as simple as pendulums and balances, to stimulate and challenge young minds. Earth sciences, meteorology, human perception and physics are all plumbed in a series of interactive exhibits designed to transform the study of science into a painless experience, and there are plenty of staff on hand to answer the questions that baffle parents. If you're travelling with children, plan to spend a couple of hours here at least. But a warning: Questacon is a victim of its own success. On weekends and during school holidays, arrive around opening time to beat the crowds.

National Library

The **National Library of Australia** ❻ (Parkes Place, Parkes; tel: 6262 1111; www.nla.gov.au; daily 9am–5pm; free) is the country's largest reference library, with a vast collection of over

Map on page 136

Australia's Aboriginal art dates back over 50,000 years, making it by far the longest continuous chain of creative expression to be found anywhere on the planet.

BELOW: Cato cutout. One of a series of sculptures by Ken Cato outside Questacon.

5 million items. These include maps charted by early explorers, election posters, recordings of Dame Nellie Melba, and Captain Cook's *Endeavour* journal. Although its main focus is on Australian items, the library also has a significant quantity of material from the wider Asia-Pacific region.

This was the first of the major institutional buildings to be completed along the southern lakeshore of the parliamentary triangle. The building takes its architectural cues from the temples of classical Greece, with prominent columns on all four sides supporting a flat roof. University students and specialist researchers make up most of the earnest heads bent over books in the library's reading rooms; but the changing exhibitions, delving deep into different aspects of Australian culture, are often riveting to all. As you might expect, the bookshop in the foyer has a fine collection of books on Australia.

Across the lake, Canberra's gushing wonder, the **Captain Cook Memorial Jet** ❼ (Regatta Point, Lake Burley Griffin) is one of the tallest components of the city's skyline – and one of the world's highest fountains. The jet of water was first unleashed on 25 April 1970 when Queen Elizabeth II flicked the switch to commemorate the bicentenary of Captain James Cook's discovery of the east coast of Australia. Lake water is sucked through a 50-metre (160-ft) intake tunnel to the underground pump house, where two pumps force the water through twin nozzles. These nozzles can drive the water to a height of 147 metres (480 ft), but the jet shuts down progressively according to wind speed, and closes off altogether in high wind to prevent an accidental car wash on Commonwealth Avenue Bridge. Normal hours of operation are between 11am and 2pm, later during the summer holidays.

Making sense of Canberra

On the opposite shore from the Library at Regatta Point, just by the bridge, is the **National Capital Exhibition** ❽ (Regatta Point, Commonwealth Park; tel: 6257 1068; www.nationalcapital.gov.au; daily 9am–5pm; free) – essential if you want to make sense of the layout of Canberra and the plan that drives it. The exhibition offers fine views of the city, from the buildings of the parliamentary triangle on the opposite side of the lake to the white spire of the **Carillon** on Aspen Island, the defence complex on Russell Hill and the brown plains to the east. Inside, exhibits document the gradual transformation from raw bushland to the seat of the nation.

The plan for Canberra had its roots in 1911, when the commonwealth government announced the Capital Competition, an international design competition for a new federal capital. A number of Australian architects were unhappy with the fact that the final judge of the competition would be a flamboyant

Previous exhibitions at the National Library have included the bullet-puckered helmet of outlaw Ned Kelly; the notebook kept by William Bligh after he was cast adrift by the Bounty *mutineers; and a diary kept on a toilet roll by an Australian soldier captured during World War II.*

BELOW: the Cook Memorial shows the routes taken by his various expeditions.

politician, King O'Malley, the minister for home affairs, rather than architects and town planners. A total of 1,537 entries were received, some of which are included in the exhibition, showing grandiose cities that drew their inspiration from classical Greece and Rome.

In 1912, O'Malley announced that the winning entry was by Walter Burley Griffin, who had worked for the celebrated Chicago architect Frank Lloyd Wright. Rather than grafting on an alien townscape derived from another epoch and continent, Griffin's plan merged with the natural contours of the land, the surrounding hills and the floodplain of the Molonglo River. The centrepiece of the design was an artificial lake that would be created by damming the Molonglo River, with the principal buildings on the southern lakeshore within a parliamentary triangle. At the high point of the triangle furthest from the lake, Griffin located his capitol building – "a structure for popular assembly and festivity more than for deliberation and counsel – a place for the people". The northern

lake foreshores were to be devoted to public gardens and recreation.

Transferring Griffin's plans from paper to soil proved a difficult process, and after 1920, Griffin's contract was not renewed. He embarked on a number of other projects in Australia, particularly in Sydney, where he is best remembered as the architect of many houses in the suburb of Castlecrag, whose character he indelibly shaped. Although many of the details have been blurred, the spirit of Griffin's vision for Canberra has been honoured. As you stand in front of the National Capital Exhibition, what you see is largely a realisation of Griffin's vision.

Blundell's Cottage

A few hundred metres along the shore to the east, **Blundell's Cottage** ❾ (Wendouree Drive, Russell; tel: 6273 2667; www.act.nationaltrust.org.au; daily 11am–4pm; admission charge) is an unembellished stone building that recalls the hard times of Canberra's pioneering past – and serves as a reminder that this area was not a

Map on page 136

The model of Canberra at the National Capital Exhibition can easily be compared with the real thing through the picture windows.

BELOW: National Capital Exhibition.

Hills of many colours

As well as documenting the story of Canberra's genesis, the National Capital Exhibition contains some curious sidelights on the shaping of the capital. According to the original plan, the surrounding hills were to be planted with flowering shrubs in different colours: Mount Ainslie in yellow, with plantings of wattle and broom, Black Mountain in pink and white with flowering fruit trees, and Red Hill – in red, of course. The plan was never implemented with any enthusiasm, although Red Hill does live up to its name, a dazzling flash on the landscape with its springtime flush of scarlet bottlebrush and *callistemon lanceolatus*.

blank slate before the politicians arrived. Much of the land on which Canberra now stands was granted to Robert Campbell, the Sydney merchant, in 1825. Campbell established a sheep station on the property, which he named "Duntroon" after his family's ancestral castle on Loch Crinan in Argyll, Scotland. Blundell's Cottage is one of 27 cottages that were originally built on the 1,600-hectare (4,000-acre) sheep station for the station hands. Made from fieldstone in 1858, the exterior walls are about 25 cm (1 ft) thick, to provide insulation against the region's extreme temperatures.

George Blundell was a bullock driver who worked for the Campbells, moving wool and supplies between Duntroon and Sydney. Blundell occupied the house from 1874 with his wife, Flora, yet it wasn't until the Blundells' eighth child was born that they added the two rooms at the back of the house. The cottage was used as a dwelling until 1958. The interior is furnished with period objects that have been donated, and visitors are encouraged to wander freely around the rooms and inspect the furnishings and artefacts. At the back of the house, the slab hut has a splendid collection of tools and agricultural implements from the 19th century, including a huge pair of bellows used in the blacksmith's forge.

National Museum

Double back, go under the bridge, and across the water on your left is a remarkable sight. Casting its arcing steel ribbon high into the air, the **National Museum of Australia** (Lawson Crescent, Acton Peninsula; tel: 6208 5000; www.nma.gov.au; daily 9am–5pm; free) injects a note of anarchy into the Canberra skyline. It freely admits that it doesn't look like a museum, nor does it feel like one – most visitors find themselves wandering haphazardly from one exhibit to another – but it is hugely engaging. Rather than an attempt to chronicle the grand movements in Australia's history, this is a celebration of everyday Australian life, a nostalgic look at the way life used to be, and the exhibits include such

TIP

Children have their own gallery, KSpace FutureWorld, at the National Museum of Australia. Here they can use touchscreen computers to design cities and vehicles, then watch their designs come to life on a 3D theatre screen.

BELOW: the National Museum of Australia.

humble household staples as Vegemite and a can of Golden Syrup.

The museum features items that have entered Australian legend, such as the only known surviving prototype of the Holden, the first Australian-built car, which went on sale in 1949; a convict jacket from the colonial era; the heart of Phar Lap, the famous racehorse who captivated the nation with his powerful performances in the 1920s; and a shrivelled but intact thylacine, or Tasmanian tiger, which became extinct in the 1930s.

The museum also houses a significant collection of Aboriginal and Pacific Islands art, but it's not all good news. The seamier side of Australian life is documented with a series of exhibits relating to the Aboriginal rights movement. Using audiovisual displays, the museum takes the visitor on a 20,000-year journey through the rock art of Kakadu to Sydney Cove, more than two centuries ago, to await the arrival of the First Fleet.

While the museum may not please those who prefer their museums in an academic register, Australians have shown their approval by voting with their feet. It's invariably busy.

Telstra Tower

Piercing the Canberra skyline from the summit of Black Mountain, **Telstra Tower ⑪** (Black Mountain; tel: 6219 6111; daily 9am–10pm; admission charge) is the capital's most visible landmark. It's only a short drive or ride – Canberra is best traversed by bicycle. Known by irreverent locals as "the hypodermic needle", the 195-metre (640-ft) high tower has a viewing gallery with 360-degree views. This is the place to go if you want to get a comprehensive overview of the city and its surrounding environment. Otherwise, the drive to the top of the mountain is scarcely worth the trouble. The best time to visit, especially for photographers, is towards sunset.

On the lower level of the Tower's entrance foyer, *Making Connections* traces the history of Australian telecommunications from the time the first telegraph line was laid, in Victoria in 1854, to the present. The

Map on page 136

TIP

Every year during January and February the Botanic Gardens host a Summer Concert Series, on weekends starting at 6pm. Call the Gardens' Visitor Centre, tel: 6250 9540, for more information.

BELOW LEFT: tower of babble. The Telstra Tower keeps the mobile phones going.
BELOW: Blundell's Cottage.

One reason that the exhibition at the Australian War Memorial is so comprehensive is that in World War I troops were officially urged to collect souvenirs from the battles in which they fought.

BELOW: a memorial to air crew in the grounds of the War Memorial.

tower serves a practical purpose as well, providing the capital's telecommunications link and broadcasting television and radio signals.

Botanical bounty

At the foot of Black Mountain, the **Australian National Botanic Gardens** ⑫ (Clunies Ross Street, Acton; tel: 6250 9450; www.anbg.gov.au; daily 8.30am–5pm; Jan Mon–Fri to 6pm, Sat–Sun to 8pm; free) is devoted exclusively to Australia's plants. Australia has an extraordinary botanical wealth that sets it apart. Many of these species have evolved strategies for coping with the fierce fires that are a feature of much of Australia's native woodlands; for instance, some rely on fire to open their seedpods. But one of the most amazing sights of the Australian bush has to be that of the green branches of the eucalypt emerging from bare and blackened trunks after fire has swept past.

Set in 90 undulating hectares (220 acres), this is the most complete garden of Australian native flora, with more than 6,800 species from the country's rainforests,

deserts, alpine meadows and scrublands. The Main Path is an easy stroll of 1.5 km (1 mile) that takes around one hour. You can also walk to the summit of Black Mountain from here, a 90-minute return trip.

Australia at war

Set at the foot of Mount Ainslie, directly east of Black Mountain, the **Australian War Memorial** ⑬ (Treloar Crescent, Campbell; tel: 6243 4211; www.awm.gov.au; daily 10am–5pm; free) is the national monument to all who served Australia in wartime, especially the 102,000 men and women who died in the various wars. The building is also a museum which houses an outstanding collection of memorabilia and hardware from those wars.

Although Australia has only ever maintained a small, professional military force in peacetime, Australians have been quick to take up arms when the need has arisen. During World War I, more than 400,000 enlisted in the armed services, about one in ten of the total population, and all volunteers. Paradoxically, conscription was narrowly defeated when it was put to a people's vote.

Since World War II, Australia has forged a close military alliance with the USA. Along with South Korea, Australia is the only country to have contributed troops to all the major post-war conflicts in which the USA has been involved.

The idea of a national museum to commemorate the sacrifice of Australians in war has its origins in the bloody battlefields of World War I. Rather than a monument that celebrated the victory and demonised the enemy, the designers envisaged a sombre memorial. The building takes its inspiration from the Byzantine, whose influences can clearly be seen in the cruciform shape, the rather squat dimensions and the low, copper-sheathed dome. These ele-

ments were modified by the art deco style prevalent at the time it was built (between 1933 and 1941).

The memorial consists of 20 galleries, each one dedicated to a separate conflict. The entire east wing is devoted to World War I, with a major exhibition on the Gallipoli campaign, which left a permanent scar on the psyche of the Australian nation. The west wing is dedicated to World War II, with armaments and uniforms, as well as memorabilia from Australians incarcerated in Japanese prisoner-of-war camps. Other galleries are dedicated to conflicts since 1945; to the role of peacekeeping troops; and to the 96 Australian recipients of the Victoria Cross, the highest award for bravery awarded to British and Commonwealth forces in war.

At the rear of the main building, the most recent part of the memorial is a radical departure from its dominant art deco style. The **ANZAC Hall** opened in 2001. Recessed into the landscape, this fan-shaped hall houses a World War II Lancaster bomber and a trio of Messerschmitt fighters from the same era, arranged as part of a dramatic sound and light show that evokes the terror and tension of night-time bombing raids over Nazi Germany. Also on display is a Japanese midget submarine which has been recreated by joining sections from two of the three midget subs that penetrated Sydney Harbour on the night of 31 May 1942 to attack US and Australian vessels.

Anzac Parade, the broad boulevard that rises from the lake, is an intrinsic part of the memorial. The roadway is bordered by various commemorative monuments, while the red gravel symbolises the blood that Australians have shed in war.

Institute of Sport

Love of sport is one of Australia's common denominators, and the **Australian Institute of Sport** ⓮

(Leverrier Crescent, Bruce; tel: 6214 1010; www.ais.org.au; tours at 10am, 11.30am, 1pm and 2.30pm; admission charge) was set up to polish the performances of Australia's athletic elite. To get there you need to follow Northbourne Avenue to Lyneham and then head west towards Belconnen. The Institute is located to the left off Ginninderra Drive. It's the facilities that are on display here – the swimming pools, gymnasiums and workout tracks, and you'll probably see some of the young athletes going through their paces.

See how you measure up against Australia's finest with **Sportex**, an interactive facility that assesses your performance as a golfer, rower, wheelchair basketball player or skier. Or if that's likely to cause embarrassment, hop onto the Olympic dais and experience what it feels like to be a gold medallist. You can book in for a swim, an abs class, a spa or a game of tennis, but the chances of finding yourself doing the breast stroke alongside Ian Thorpe are remote. ❑

Map on page 136

TIP

The 90-minute tours at the Australian Institute of Sport are guided by the athletes who train at the institute themselves. They can give you the inside story on just what it means to perform at this level.

BELOW: winning shirt at the Australian Institute of Sport.

RESTAURANTS, CAFÉS, PUBS & BARS

Restaurants

City (Civic)

Anise
Melbourne Building,
20 West Row, City
Tel: 6257 0700
Open: L Tues-Fri,
D Tues-Sat. **$$**
There is strong emphasis on local produce and some good robust country flavouring, all overlaid with contemporary twists. Corned beef and mash is simple but done with panache.

Courgette
54 Marcus Clarke St, City
Tel: 6247 4042
www.courgette.com.au
Open: L Mon-Fri, D Mon-Sat.
$$$
Classy eatery where simple but stylish decor, discreet lighting and the gentlest murmur of voices suggests reverence for the food about to appear. Quite appropriate for some of the city's most imaginative modern cooking.

The Chairman & Yip
108 Bunda Street, City
Tel: 6248 7109

Open: L Mon-Fri,
D Mon-Sat. **$$**
Terrific food under the umbrella term "Asian" and steady service to go with it keeps people coming back for more. BYO.

Dijon
24 West Row, City
Tel: 6230 6009
www.dijon.com.au
Open: L Mon-Fri, D daily.
$$$
There are famous tasting menus of 5 and 7 courses and an à la carte option filled with irresistible combinations of flavours. BYO.

Mezzalira
Melbourne Building,
20 West Row, City
Tel: 6230 0025
www.mezzalira.com.au
Open: L Mon-Fri ,
D Mon-Sat. **$$**
Claiming "an atmosphere indistinguishable from the restaurants of Milan", the Trimboli family has matched that with some exquisite regional cooking. BYO.

Milk and Honey
Center Cinema Building, 29 Garema Place, City
Tel: 6247 7722
www.milkandhoney.net.au
Open: B & L daily,
D Mon-Sat. **$$**
There's café eating or a more formal restaurant menu in the two split-level dining

areas of this bright modern enterprise with its ironic references to 1970s styling. Good food too.

Tasuke
Sydney Building,
122 Alinga Street, City
Tel: 6257 9711
Open: L & D Mon-Sat. **$**
This tiny place looks like a sandwich bar but inside some of Canberra's finest and freshest Japanese food is lapped up by the cognoscenti. BYO.

Barton

Ottoman Cuisine
9 Broughton Street (corner Blackall Street), Barton
Tel: 6273 6111
Open: L Tues-Fri,
D Tues-Sat. **$$**
With such a huge menu of superbly executed Turkish delights, it may be prudent to put yourself in the hands of the chef and settle for one of the "banquets".

Dickson

Fekerte's
74/ 2 Cape Street, Dickson
Tel: 6262 5799
Open: L Tues-Fri,
D Tues-Sun. **$**
Effortlessly cornering the market in Ethiopian cuisine, Fekerte Tesfaye cooks up a range of wholesome meaty offerings as well as a compre-

hensive selection of excellent vegetarian options. BYO.

Parkes

The Ginger Room
Old Parliment House (enter by Queen Victoria Terrace), Parkes
Tel: 6270 8262
www.gingercatering.com.au
Open: D Tues-Sat. **$$**
Impressive, elegant Pacific rim eating in the tastefully refurbished former private dining room of Old Parliament House.

The Lobby
King George Terrace, Parkes
Tel: 6273 1563
www.thelobby.com.au
Open: L Tues-Fri,
D Tues-Sat. **$$$**
If you think politicians deserve a dish like sautéed gnocchi in truffle cream with pesto and parmesan crisps, then this is the place to come and watch them eating it.

Waters Edge
40 Parkes Place, Parkes
Tel: 6273 5066
Open: L Tues-Fri & Sun,
D Tues-Sun. **$$$**
This is one of Canberra's finest restaurants, currently at the top of its game with chef Pablo Tordesillas' inspired take on modern European cuisine.

RIGHT: fine dining in the city centre.

Kingston & Griffith

Artespresso
31 Giles Street, Kingston
Tel: 6295 8055
www.artespresso.com.au
Open: B Sat & Sun,
L Tues–Fri, D Tues–Sat. **$$**
It's café meets bistro
meets restaurant – but
the modern Australian
food is reliably good
whatever you're after.
BYO.

Aubergine
18 Barker Street, Griffith
Tel: 6260 8666
www.auberginerestaurant.com.au
Open: L Mon–Fri, D daily. **$$$**
In a pleasant setting that
the floor-to-ceiling win-
dows exploit to the full,
there are some fine
European-inspired
dishes to enjoy. BYO.

Manuka

Abell's Kopi Tiam
7 Furneaux Street, Manuka
Tel: 6293 4199

Open: L & D Tues–Sat. **$**
A lot of Malaysian
and other regional
classics produced
with aplomb in this busy
but friendly restaurant.
BYO.

Cafés, pubs & bars

City (Civic)

Benchmark Wine Bar
65 Northbourne Avenue, City
Tel: 6262 6522
www.benchmarkwinebar.com.au
Open: L Mon–Fri, D daily. **$$**
Offers not just an
outstandingly comprehen-
sive wine list but excel-
lent food to go with it.

Blue Olive Café
56 Alinga Street, City
Tel: 6230 4600
Open B, L & T Mon–Sat. **$**
In the lovely old Mel-
bourne Building, loads of
great snacks with an
emphasis on home-baked
bread and cakes. BYO.

The Café
Barrine Drive, City
Open: L & D daily. **$**
Just a really nice place to
pause by the lake with a
coffee, looking over
towards the National
Museum of Australia.

Caffe della Piazza
19 Garema Place, City
Tel: 6248 9711
Open: B Sat-Sun,
L & D daily. **$**
Sturdy Italian food and
acclaimed coffee is aug-
mented by an excep-
tional wine list. BYO.

Café Essen
Shop 5, 6 Garema
Arcade, City
Tel: 6248 9300
Open: B, L & D daily. **$**
Primarily a coffee house,
this old favourite does
great breakfasts. BYO.

Gus's Café
Shop 8, Garema Centre,

Bunda Street, City
Tel: 6248 8118
Open: B, L & D daily. **$**
A young crowd is
attracted by the good
value staples in this local
institution. BYO.

The Phoenix
23 East Row, City
Tel: 6247 1606
Open: L & D daily. **$**
Not very large, but the
Phoenix is a popular pub
with a friendly and
relaxed atmosphere.
There's occasionally live
music and usually some
local art on the walls.

Kingston

Silo Bakery
36 Giles Street, Kingston
Tel: 6260 6060
www.silobakery.com.au
Open: B & L Mon–Sat. **$**
A popular and lively café
is part of this superb
bakery. Some Mediter-
ranean leanings.

PARLIAMENTS

Canberra, specially designed and built as the seat of government, has not one parliament but two

When consideration is given to the number of working politicians per head of population, Australia is one of the most over-governed countries in the world. No surprise, then, that in the Australian Capital Territory and its city of Canberra there are two complete national parliament buildings, not to mention the ACT legislative assembly. Admittedly Old Parliament House has been pensioned off from active government, but its bulky presence in the centre of the city reinforces the feeling that this is a place where legislators rule the roost, where each facet of the city is dedicated to the smooth running of the machinery of power. Tours are available of both buildings and it's always worth securing a spot in the public gallery if either house of the new Parliament House is in session, particularly if there's a chance to witness Prime Minister's question time. The same applies in Sydney, only for the State Parliament where, again, there are two houses.

ABOVE: long-serving Prime Minister John Howard at the dais in the House of Representatives in Federal Parliament.
BELOW: the distinctly home-grown national crest.

ABOVE: the annual Canberra Balloon Fiesta each March sees the sky above the capital filled with colourful craft. A ready supply of hot air is believed to be incidental to the location.

BELOW: in an echo of the Westminster system the Senate or upper house is fitted out in red, the lower house in green.

ABOVE: the mosaic in front of Parliament House is derived from a painting by acclaimed Aboriginal artist Michael Nelson Tjakamarra of the Northern Territory's Papunya community. *Possum Wallaby Dreaming* is made up of over 90,000 pieces. The artist also has a huge painting in the foyer of Sydney Opera House.

PLACE OF PROTEST

On the afternoon of 26 January 1972 – Australia Day – a tent was set up on the lawn in front of Old Parliament House as part of an Aboriginal protest against government tardiness in dealing with issues of land rights and compensation for indigenous people. Thus was born the Aboriginal Tent Embassy, which existed on and off for many years, and has been permanently since 1992. The original protestors felt like "aliens in our own land, so like the other aliens we need an embassy". The site, despite claims that it is an eyesore, has now taken on such symbolic significance as the focus for Aboriginal struggle that its future seems assured. It would take a foolhardy politician to order its removal, especially after its listing on the National Estate by the Australian Heritage Commission in 1995.

ABOVE: a panel in the exhibition area of Parliament House celebrates the role of women in parliament since the election of the first MP, Enid Lyons from Tasmania, in August 1943. The first woman senator, Dorothy Tangney of Western Australia, took up her seat at the same time. In the 21st century one in four of the members of the lower house are women, while in the Senate the proportion is around 30 per cent. Australia is yet to have a woman prime minister.

RIGHT: in Walter Burleigh Griffin's carefully planned city a line can be drawn from the centre of Parliament House through Old Parliament House, the Australian War Memorial and on to the peak of Mount Ainslie, as can be seen from this view from the main entrance to Parliament House. Visitors can also take in the scene from the grassed-over roof of the building, but the favourite spot is the Queen's Terrace Cafe on the first floor.

SOUTHEAST AND THE RIVERINA

Rivers are the lifeblood of this largely fertile farmland, which includes the wine-producing Riverina, while to the east, the Snowy Mountains region offers alpine activities against the backdrop of Australia's highest peak

I n the east of this region, the hills of the Great Dividing Range have rucked up to become Australia's highest mountains. They are the source of some of the continent's greatest rivers, including the Murray and the Murrumbidgee, which flow west to pass through the **Riverina**. Here, vast irrigation schemes have transformed the arid plains into some of Australia's richest farmland.

The southeast and the Riverina provide a lesson in how geography has shaped the pattern of settlement in Australia. Many of the towns here sprang up where the Murrumbidgee or the Murray were shallow enough to permit a bullock team hauling a dray or a mob of sheep to wade across. Inns and stores flourished around these outposts, often followed by a police post or a gaol, since mischief stuck as closely as the drover's dog in Australia's pioneering days. By the time a bridge was built and the crossing became redundant, the town was already established.

Gateway to the mountains

Cooma ❶, on the Monaro Table-land, is the gateway to the state's alpine region and the largest town in the Snowy Mountains region. This is also the centre of the Snowy Mountains Scheme, the most ambitious civil engineering project ever

undertaken in Australia. Rivers were diverted and dams built to harness water and provide hydroelectric power and irrigation water for the Murray and Murrumbidgee Valleys. Towns were built or relocated, roads constructed. Work began in 1949 and did not end until 1972, during which time over 100,000 people from more than 30 countries worked on the scheme. As the headquarters for the enterprise, Cooma was transformed from a sleepy town to a bustling, multinational community.

Map on page 154

LEFT: monument to Strzelecki in Jindabyne.
BELOW: the Snowy Mountains Authority Information and Education Centre.

The Avenue of Flags in Cooma's Centennial Park features a series of mosaics illustrating the history, wildlife, activities and attractions of the region.

Ski country

The **Snowy Mountains Authority Information and Education Centre** (Monaro Highway; tel: 1800 623 776; www.snowyhydro.com.au; Mon–Fri 8am–5pm, Sat–Sun 9am–2pm; free) tells the story of the Snowy Mountains Scheme with photos, models and hands-on, interactive exhibits. There's also a fascinating display that pinpoints where the electricity from the scheme is being distributed to in real time.

In Cooma's **Centennial Park** (Snowy Mountains Highway), the International Avenue of Flags commemorates the 27 nationalities that worked on the Snowy Mountains Scheme during its first 10 years.

Overlooking the lake of the same name, **Jindabyne ❷** is the closest town to the state's Snowy Mountains ski resorts. The town itself is purely functional – a place to eat and bed down before heading out to the slopes and streams. During the ski season,

Jindabyne offers many budget-priced alternatives to the relatively high-priced accommodation at the ski resorts, thus attracting many younger skiers and snowboarders. It can, therefore, get boisterous after dark.

Shuttle buses make the 45-minute journey between Jindabyne, the ski resort of Thredbo, and the Skitube terminal that leads to Perisher Blue, which combines the Perisher, Smiggins and Blue Cow ski fields. The town is outside the national park, so drivers who park at Jindabyne don't need to carry chains for their vehicle. In summer, Jindabyne acts as a base for activities such as sailing, kayaking, cycling, fishing and hiking.

Kosciuszko National Park

Kosciuszko National Park ❸ is the state's largest national park as well as Australia's most extensive alpine region, incorporating glacial lakes, alpine meadows, snow gum forests and Mount Kosciuszko itself, the

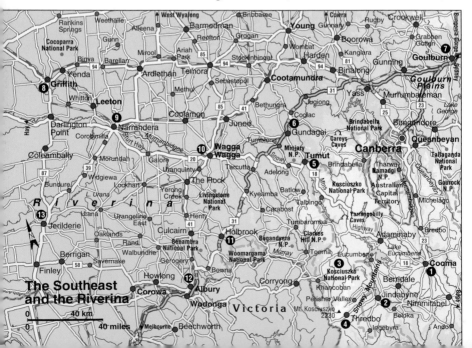

country's highest peak. This is also the state's winter playground, with its ski resorts all located within the park boundaries. Even in a good season, however, skiing in the sunburnt country is down to luck. In recent years the area has developed into a summer resort for outdoor pursuits, from hiking and mountain biking to horse-riding and kayaking.

Alpine trails

The Polish explorer Count Paul Edmund de Strzelecki was the first to climb **Mount Kosciuszko**, which he named after a compatriot. From the 1830s, stockmen used the summer pastures of the Snowy Mountains to graze their stock. Stories of these stockmen and their tough mountain ponies supplied Australia with some of its most enduring folklore, as epitomised by the ballad *The Man from Snowy River*, by "Banjo" Paterson

Grazing by hard-footed animals caused extensive damage to the soft, boggy soil and alpine grasses, and, under pressure from conservationists, cattle were banned altogether in 1967. Some wild horses still run free, but these are being progressively culled.

The alpine trails in the National Park comprise some of the state's finest summer bush-walks. During the warmer months, the granite flanks of these mountains are covered with tiny, delicate snow daisies and yellow button daisies, occasionally interspersed with patches of summer snow. The most popular walk by far is the hike to the 2,230-metre (7,316-ft) summit of Mount Kosciuszko. The easiest route is to take the Crackenback Chairlift from Thredbo, from where it's a moderate two-hour walk over a well-formed track to the top. The track passes the outcrops of the Ramshead Range, before crossing open heaths.

The trail to the summit is a ramp rather than a climb, and it's usually crowded on the roof of Australia. A

Map on page 154

"Banjo" Paterson wrote Waltzing Matilda *and is on the* A$10 *note.*

BELOW: skiing in the Snowy Mountains.

longer and far less crowded trail starts at the top of the car park above Charlotte's Pass and follows the old road for 9 km (5 miles) to the summit. Take water, some food, sun protection and insect repellent.

Thredbo

Huddled in the depths of a valley at the foot of Mount Crackenback, **Thredbo** has a European flavour that makes it unique among Australian ski resorts. It also has the longest downhill runs in the country and probably the most efficient of all the lift systems. Compared to other ski resorts within Kosciuszko National Park, its slopes are heavily timbered and the runs generally more challenging. Thredbo has also developed as a summer alpine resort, and there are several adventure sports operators in the village as well as numerous accommodation options.

Yarrangobilly Caves

On the Snowy Mountains Highway, which joins Tumut with Cooma, **Yarrangobilly Caves** (tel: 6454 9597; daily 9am–5pm; admission charge) is a group of about 60 limestone caverns with many spectacular formations. Only three are open for inspection, two of those by guided visit. However, an admission ticket is required for all of them. Tours generally take place at 11am, 1pm and 3pm. The most impressive, as well as the most easily accessible, is the **Glory Arch Cave**. There's also a thermal pool in the vicinity, filled by a spring whose water notches up a comfortable 27°C; but it's at the bottom of a steep trail, 1 km (½ mile) from the car park. Facilities at the caves are limited.

Set on a river that threads its way across the plain, greened by the poplars and willows planted by early settlers, and with the foothills of the Snowy Mountains as a backdrop, **Tumut** is one of the prettiest of all the high country towns. Its early history follows a pattern familiar to the region: an explosive growth spurt during the gold rush, followed by a long and rather sleepy stint as a services base for the pasturelands around it. More recently, Tumut has been revitalised

BELOW: Thredbo village before the snow arrives.

by the timber industry, which harvests the radiata pines planted extensively hereabouts.

The Tumut Region Visitors Centre (Gocup and Adelong Roads; tel: 6947 7025; daily 9am–5pm) has a brochure with a guide to the town's historic buildings, among them several hotels, two old banks, the court house and All Saints Church.

Dog ballad days

On the banks of the Murrumbidgee River, **Gundagai** ❻ is known to every Australian schoolboy thanks to a series of poems. *The Dog on the Tuckerbox* entered Australian folklore as a ballad sung by the bullock drivers who would drive their teams roughly along the route of the present-day Hume Highway. The *Gundagai Times* published a version of this poem under the title, *Bullocky Bill*, which told the story of a luckless bullock driver who got bogged at Five Mile Creek, broke his team's yoke, and to round off an already bad day, "The dog shat on the tuckerbox [used to store food], five miles from Gundagai". The lyric became popular and a sculpture of the dog on the tuckerbox was installed in 1932, 5 miles (8 km) north of Gundagai, beside the highway.

Set on low-lying flats close to the Murrumbidgee River, the original town was completely destroyed in 1852 when the river burst its banks, sweeping away buildings and drowning more than 80 local residents – a third of the population. Almost 50 more were rescued by Yarri, a local Aboriginal man, who paddled out to the rescue in his bark canoe.

Although the current is usually no more than a few metres across, you can get an idea of what happens when the river floods from the sheer size of the **Prince Alfred Bridge**, the original road bridge and the longest wooden bridge ever built in Australia – 921 metres (3,000 ft) from end to end.

In the Gundagai Tourist Information Centre (249 Sheridan Street; tel: 6944 1341), **Rusconi's Marble Masterpiece** is the work of an exceptional local craftsman. This multi-tiered miniature cathedral was created from 20,948 individual

Map on page 154

In the 1920s, balladeer Jack Moses came up with the alternative lyric, "The dog sat on the tuckerbox" – which may be more polite, but a lot less newsworthy.

BELOW: the old bridge at Gundagai.

Rusconi's Marble Masterpiece is one of those projects which provokes some awe and the suspicion that Gundagai can't have had much in the way of entertainment.

BELOW: St Saviour's Cathedral in Goulburn.

pieces of marble, and took 28 years to complete. Its creator was Frank Rusconi, who also sculpted the statue of the dog on the tuckerbox.

Goulburn

Goulburn is one of Australia's oldest inland cities. Early explorers recognised that the Goulburn Plains, which surround the town, offered excellent grazing, and pastoralists were quick to follow in their footsteps. Sheep grazed these pastures from as early as the 1820s, and the first buildings were erected in 1833. With the area to the west found to be more suitable for growing wheat, Goulburn became almost exclusively a sheep-farming town.

Many handsome houses were built relatively early in Goulburn's history, among them **St Clair** (318 Sloane Street; tel: 4823 4448; Fri–Sun 1pm–4pm; admission charge), now a history museum and research centre. Notable features in the 20-room house include lavish cedar architectural details and the fluted columns on the posts of the front veranda. Costumes and furnishings from Goul-

burn's past are displayed in the house.

Built in the 1840s as a coaching inn, at a spot where the Great South Road forded the Wollondilly River, **Riversdale** (Twynam Street; tel: 4821 4741; Sat–Sun 10am–4pm; admission charge) is a fine example of a simple, colonial Georgian cottage. This is the only building that survives from the "Old Township", the original settlement before Governor Bourke selected another site for Goulburn, two miles south. The house has a collection of Australian colonial furniture and decorative objects, much of it donated by the Twynam family, who occupied the house from 1875 to 1967. The gardens are notable for their espaliered apple trees and flowering shrubs.

The city has a splendid church. It also caters to the Australian affection for larger-than-life roadside attractions, with "Rambo", a 14-metre (46-ft) high concrete merino, at the **Big Merino** (Hume Highway and Lansdowne Street; tel: 4822 8013, which has a craft centre, educational centre, lookout and restaurant.

Just a short distance east of Goulburn is Bungonia State Conservation Area. Its chief feature is **Bungonia Gorge**, an extreme example of erosion, where the Shoalhaven River has gouged a huge trough from deep layers of limestone. Bungonia also has many karst landforms, created when limestone is dissolved by water. Among its many caves are the five deepest on the Australian mainland, all more than 130 metres (426 ft) deep. The rugged landscape makes it a favourite destination for cavers, canyoners and also climbers, since the sheer cliffs of the canyon constitute some of Australia's biggest walls. Bungonia is accessible from the Hume Highway, approximately 2 km (1 mile) south of Marulan.

Griffith and the MIA

It is a 296-km (184-mile) run eastwards on Route 94, through a succession of small rural towns, to **Griffith ❽**. This is the heart of the Murrumbidgee Irrigation Area (MIA), a vast scheme that has replenished what was once a sun-seared landscape of clay pans and saltbush with a green brush. The Murrumbidgee Miracle began in the 1890s when the enterprising Sir Samuel McCaughey of Yanco Station demonstrated the potential for irrigation on the flat Riverina plains. Dams were built to store water for the area, and by 1924, 48,000 hectares (120,000 acres) were under irrigation. Today, the MIA includes more than 2,350 km (1,500 miles) of supply channels that carry water from the main channel to about 2,500 farms.

At the beginning of the 20th century, fewer than 100 people earned a living from the 5,000 sq. km (2,000 sq. miles) that now lie within the Murrumbidgee Irrigation Area. Today, the population of that same area is close to 50,000. The main crop is rice, but the MIA also produces 90 percent of the state's citrus and 70 percent of all its wine grapes. Although it is not nearly as well known as the Hunter Valley wine region, the Riverina produces far more wine – about a quarter of Australia's total.

Griffith was designed by Walter Burley Griffin, the architect responsible for the original design of Canberra, and his radial street pattern is an echo of the national capital. Italians who migrated to Australia during the 1950s played a prominent role in the development of the region, and the names on the city's shops, the food in its cafés and overheard snatches of conversation all bear witness to their contribution.

The district has several wineries open for cellar-door sales, and while the region's wine producers are better known for their quantity rather than their quality, some also produce a range of premium wines that have attracted favourable reviews. De Bortoli Wines (De Bortoli Road Bilbul; tel: 6966 0111; www.debortoli. com.au; Mon–Sat 9am–5.30pm; free) has won many medals for its Noble One Botrytis Semillon; while McWilliams Hanwood Estate (Jack

Map on page 154

The combined storage capacity of Burrinjuck and Blowering Dams is 2.5 million megalitres (550 million gallons), more than five times the volume of water in Sydney Harbour.

BELOW: learning to ride in the Riverina.

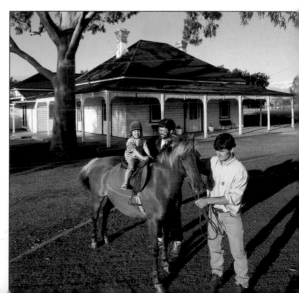

One of several historic churches in Narrandera.

BELOW: colonial-style architecture at Wagga Wagga railway station.

McWilliam Road, Hanwood; tel: 6963 0001; www.mcwilliams.com.au; Mon–Sat 9am–5pm; free) is a family-owned winery, part of a winemaking empire that stretches across three states. Its shady gardens are a lovely spot for a picnic.

One of the oldest farms in the MIA, **Catania Fruit Salad Farm** (Farm 43, Cox Rd, Hanwood; tel: 6963 0219; cataniafruitsaladfarm.com.au; tours daily at 1.30pm; admission charge) lies just to the south of Griffith. The guided tour explains the mechanics of the irrigation system and allows you to sample the wide range of fruit and nuts grown on the farm.

Narrandera

Narrandera ❾ began as a crossing on the Murrumbidgee. When gold was discovered in Victoria, the crossing suddenly became a busy place. Development was relatively slow until the railway line arrived in 1881. A number of industries were then established, in particular cypress and red-gum timber milling.

Irrigation now supports an extensive range of crops, such as rice, stone fruit and citrus groves. The **Parkside Cottage Museum** (Cadell and Twynam Strees; tel: 6959 1372; daily 2–5pm; admission charge) is a simple, weatherboard cottage with a surprising and diverse collection. It includes early Telecom equipment; a set of silver ingots commemorating 1,000 years of monarchy; seashells collected from all over the world; and the Macarthur cloak, a scarlet cloak woven from the first bale of wool sent from Australia to England – a pivotal moment in Australia's history.

Wagga Wagga

Although its name is usually shortened to "Wagga" (rhymes with "logger"), **Wagga Wagga ❿** is no pint-sized wonder. Since Canberra belongs to a separate state, Wagga, with a population of 60,000, is the largest inland city in New South Wales. Located at a convenient crossing point on the south bank of the Murrumbidgee, the town grew initially on the strength of the surrounding pastoral holdings, which were established in the 1830s. The town swelled during the post-war years,

helped along by government decentralisation, which saw many state and federal institutions located to Wagga, among them Charles Sturt University, the NSW Agricultural Research Institute and the Kapooka Military Camp, 10 km (6 miles) away. As a result, Wagga's character derives essentially from the modern era.

Spilling across 9 hectares (22 acres) on Willans Hill, the **Botanic Gardens** (tel: 6926 9621; daily winter 7.30am–4.15pm, summer 7.30am–8pm; free) are the city's pride and joy, divided into camellia, cactus, succulent and Shakespearean gardens. In fact Wagga Wagga is known as the "garden city", and this is but one of several parks and gardens that give the place a relaxed and romantic air.

Culture is well served by the **Wagga Wagga Art Gallery** (Baylis and Morrow Streets; tel: 6926 9660; www.waggaartgallery.org; Tues–Sat 10am 5pm, Sun noon– 4pm; free), which has works by some of Australia's leading 20th-century artists, such as Arthur Boyd, Lloyd Rees, Barbara Hanrahan and Pro Hart, in

relaxed surroundings. The gallery complex also has a unique and outstanding asset in the shape of the **National Art Glass Gallery**. Its collection of about 300 works, the largest of its kind in the country, was begun in 1979. Since then, the gallery has acquired some real treasures, shown to great advantage in this luminous, purpose-built exhibition space. The gallery works in concert with Charles Sturt University, the first in Australia to teach studio glassmaking.

Holbrook

From Wagga take the Sturt Highway east for 15 km (9 miles) and take a left to Kynamba, where you join the Hume Highway heading south to **Holbrook ⑪**. This town has one of Australia's most unusual roadside attractions – a retired submarine. HMAS *Otway* was one of six Oberon-class submarines operated by the Australian navy. When it was decommissioned, Holbrook acquired the 90-metre (295-ft) long superstructure and installed it beside the highway. The city's affection for submarines goes back a long way. Holbrook was

Map on page 154

Hospitable country hotels, as celebrated here on one of the Cooma mosaics, are a great feature of rural New South Wales.

Architecture

The first New South Wales settlers employed building patterns from their homeland since there was no tradition of indigenous architecture to borrow from. Only minor concessions were made to the environment, such as higher ceilings, and verandas – a necessity. Lessons were also learned from other British colonies, and similarities can be seen with buildings in India, the Caribbean and elsewhere.

Trends popular in Britain soon took root. The Georgian disciplines of proportion and balance were easy to transpose, and fine examples of the genre can be found around the country. Palladian influences can be seen too, particularly in grand public buildings. Victorian styles dominate in many towns, from rows of terraced housing in the cities right down to pockets of Gothic Revivalism. Façades count too; in some towns it's like the Wild West, with a main street of ornate frontages and deep verandas belying nondescript sheds backstage.

Where a colonial style did evolve it had much to do with the availability of materials: wattle and daub in the early days as well as local timber – countless weatherboard houses today testify to its resilience. These features combine in the classic Australian homestead.

Admiring the national art glass collection at the Wagga Wagga Art Gallery.

BELOW: Wagga Wagga Art Gallery is a regional highlight.

originally known as Germantown, but during World War I a name change became imperative. In December 1914, Lt Holbrook of the Royal Navy navigated the submarine B-11 into the hazardous Dardenelles Strait and sank a Turkish battleship. For this feat he became the first sailor to win Britain's highest military award, the Victoria Cross, in that war, and the citizens of Germantown renamed their town after the hero.

Albury

On the north bank of the Murray River, **Albury** ⑫ is usually paired with its Victorian twin, **Wodonga**, on the south side of the river, giving the hyphenated metropolis of Albury-Wodonga a combined population of 68,000. Geography alone determined that Albury would prosper. The town grew up at a crossing point on the Murray, on the main overland route between Sydney and Melbourne. River steamers could navigate the river as far as Albury and this contributed to its development from the 1850s. The railway line between Sydney and Melbourne reached the town

in 1883, spelling the end of the river-steamer trade; but since the railway gauges, different until 1962, forced passengers and freight to change trains here, Albury developed as a trans-shipment point, with the railway providing major employment.

These days Albury's business is largely government-driven: state and federal governments named the city the first Regional Growth Centre in the 1970s, and both have concentrated services here.

The **PS *Cumberoona*** (www.cumberoona.com.au) is an authentic replica of the original paddle steamer which once operated between Albury and ports downstream. Noisy but fun, the vessel chugs along the Murray River every Saturday and Sunday between October and mid-April, and daily throughout January, water levels permitting. Cruises depart from Noreuil Park at noon and at 2pm.

The **Botanic Gardens** (Dean Street and Wodonga Place; tel: 6023 8111) were established in 1877 when the first tree, an English elm, was planted, and today they radiate the benefits of a well-tended life. The

gardens' ornamental trees, water features and rotunda are all part of a free-flowing design that showcases plants from a broad array of habitats.

Albury is also home to the Flying Fruit Fly Circus (609 Hovell St; tel: 6021 7044; www.fruitflycircus.com.au), one of the world's leading youth performing arts companies. Featuring children as young as eight, the company brings a modern twist to traditional circus acts, winning applause from audiences in New York, Japan and at the opening ceremony of the 2000 Sydney Olympics.

Jerilderie

Jerilderie ⑬ is famous as the town where Australia's legendary bushranger, Ned Kelly, and his gang staged one of their most audacious robberies. On 8 February 1879, after enjoying dinner at the Woolshed Hotel, just outside town, the gang of four rode in and locked the two local policemen in their own cells. To allay suspicion, the wife of one of the constables was allowed to prepare the courthouse for Catholic mass, as she did every Sunday, a mass that was

attended by two of the Kelly gang dressed in police uniforms. The following day, the gang took hostage all the patrons in the Royal Mail Hotel, relieved the bank next door of £2,000, cut the telegraph lines to prevent word from spreading, and departed.

Just before the raid, Kelly wrote what became known as the Jerilderie Letter. Passionate and articulate, the manifesto conveys his smouldering sense of outrage at the injustice done to the Kellys at the hands of the police. The letter, which he handed to the town's bank clerk, has provided vital psychological material for those who have sought to portray Kelly as a misunderstood martyr rather than a common criminal. It survives in the State Library of Victoria.

Jerilderie strives to keep the Kelly memory alive, since this town of 870 inhabitants depends on tourism to put bread on its table. There are 16 sites connected to Kelly, including the police stables, the court house, the Royal Mail Hotel and a printing shop where Kelly tried to have the Jerilderie Letter published – only to find that the printer had escaped. ❑

The omnipresent farm windmill.

BELOW: Lake Hume, Albury.

RESTAURANTS, CAFÉS & BARS

Restaurants

Albury

The Commercial Club
618 Dean Street
Tel: 6021 1133
www.commclubalbury.com.au
Open: L & D daily. **$**
This massive social club has a choice of eating. A-la-Carte Dining Room is the silver service venue or there are the progressively cheaper Sevens Restaurant and Reflections Café.

New Albury Hotel
491 Kiewa Street
Tel: 6021 3599
www.newalburyhotel.com.au
Open: L & D daily. **$**
The Bistro in Paddy's Irish bar serves up good value counter meals or you can settle for that nutritious meal in a glass – a pint of Guinness.

Cooma

Ex Services Club
106 Vale Street
Tel: 6452 1144
www.coomaexservicesclub.com.au
Open: L & D daily. **$**
The Soldiers Club, as it's known locally, is open to

non-members who can fill up in the Cooma Town Bistro or enjoy the marginally superior Rubies Restaurant.

Goulburn

Fireside Inn
28 Market Street
Tel: 4821 2727
www.firesideinn.com.au
Open: L Tues-Fri & Sun, D Tues-Sat. **$$**
A table within comfortable range of the open fire and food denoting good traditional kitchen skills make this a local favourite – at least in winter.

Griffith

Michelin
72 Banna Avenue
Tel: 6964 9006
Open: B Sun, L Tues-Sun, D Tues-Sat, D. **$$**
Sophisticated and sleek – and that goes for both the space and the menu. Michelin would not look out of place in Sydney and could hold its own in elevated company.

L'Oasis
150 Yambil Street
Tel: 6964 5588
Open: L Mon-Sat, D Tues-Sat. **$$**
Bright and friendly, this is a good bet for generous portions of Asian-infused tucker.

Gundagai

18 Karat Restaurant
Gundagai District Services Club, 254 Sheridan Street

Tel: 6944 1719
Open: L & D daily. **$**
Chinese and Australian meals are on offer in this restaurant in the town's social club. Visitors can take out free temporary membership to gain access.

Jindabyne

Crackenback Cottage
Alpine Way, Thredbo Valley
Tel: 6456 2198/
1800 645 008
www.crackenback.com.au
Open: winter L daily, D Wed-Mon; otherwise L Thur-Sun, D Fri-Sun. **$$**
Good use is made of regional specialities in this warmly atmospheric rustic cottage.

Il Lago
19 Nuggets Crossing
Shopping Centre
Tel: 6456 1171
Open: D Wed-Mon. **$**
Pizza, pasta and a la carte options in this reliable Italian. BYO.

Lake Jindabyne Hotel
Kosciuszko Road
Tel: 6456 2203
www.lakejindabynehotel.com.au
Open: B, L and D daily. **$$**
Massive steaks and other hearty platefuls go down well after all that skiing and hiking. It's not just quantity though, the standards are more than adequate.

Sante
Shop 4, Squatters Run, Mowamba Mall
Tel: 6457 6083
Open: D Tues-Sat. **$$**
An adventurous mix of influences from around the world make for an interesting night out.

Narrandera

Historic Star Lodge
64 Whitton Street
(Newell Highway)
Tel: 69591768
www.historicstarlodge.com.au
Open: D Tues-Sat. **$$**
Reasonable standards are achieved here in a one-player market. Indian and Indonesian amongst the influences.

Thredbo

Credo
Riverside Cabins
Tel: 6457 6844
www.credo.com.au
Opening times dependent on snow and weather conditions. **$$**
This attractive chalet of timber and glass offers large helpings from a small but interesting menu. Beautiful outlook and sound cooking.

Tumut

Tumut Bowling and Recreation Club
Richmond Street
Tel: 6947 2358
Open: D daily. **$**
The Falling Leaf Bistro provides good-value,

RIGHT: Goulburn's atmospheric Paragon Café.

wholesome meals for members and visitors alike.

Wagga Wagga

Romano's Hotel
Corner Sturt & Fitzmaurice streets
Tel: 6921 2013
www.romanoshotel.com.au
Open: L & D Mon-Sat. **$$**
Creeds Restaurant specialises in fresh seafood, including live lobster and crab, along with indigenous game, such as kangaroo and crocodile.

Three Chefs
Townhouse International Motel, 70 Morgan Street
Tel: 6921 5897
www.threechefs.com.au
Open: B daily, L Mon-Fri, D Mon-Sat.
Ignore the inauspicious motel setting and enjoy a contemporary Australian feast matched with some good wines.

Cafés and bars

Cooma

Lott Food Store Bakery and Café
178 Sharp Street
Tel: 6452 1414
Open: B & L daily. **$**
Coffee, cakes and rolls featuring fresh local produce give this bright and breezy cafe the edge.

Jindabyne

The Pub Bar and Bistro
Thredbo Alpine Hotel
Tel: 6459 4200
Open: L & D daily. **$**
Relaxed bar for snacks and meals.

Wilfred's Café
Snowy Region Visitors Centre, Kosciuszko Road
Tel: 6450 5600
Open: B, L & D daily. **$**
A pleasant setting in the Visitor Centre and a good place to relax and read all the brochures.

Goulburn

Paragon Café
174 Auburn Street
Tel: 4821 3566
Open: B, L & D daily. **$$**
Wonderful old-fashioned diner and social hub where the staff know most of the clientele. The staple-packed menu probably hasn't changed much in years. BYO.

Griffith

Dolce Dolce
449 Banna Avenue
Tel: 6962 1888
Open: B & L daily. **$**
Authentic Italian pasticceria and gelateria.

Gundagai

Niagara Café
124 Sheridan Street
Tel: 6944 1109
Open: B, L & D daily. **$**
Attractive old-fashioned café with original 1930s features.

Thredbo

Altitude 1380
Thredbo Village
Tel: 6457 6190
Open: B, L & D daily. **$**
Buzzy place that will keep you warm, fed and watered for that next trip up the mountain. BYO.

Wagga Wagga

Magpie's Nest
Old Narrandera Road
Tel: 6933 1523
Open: L Wed-Sun, D Wed-Sat **$$**
Provides choice local produce in converted stables.

Premium Coffee Roasters
34 Trail Street
Tel: 6921 4155
Open: B & L Mon-Sat.
Once a butcher's, now a coffee gourmand's mecca. Has a nice line in cakes, too.

FAR WEST OUTBACK

Some remarkable communities and sensational birdlife dot these vast, sun-blistered spaces, where the endless plains of the sheep stations give way to sand dunes, and where only the sunsets can match the blood-red earth

A bout one-third of New South Wales lies "back of Bourke", as the state's Outback region is known — a vast, raw, brooding landscape where river red gums picket the creek beds and corellas crowd the waterholes in a raucous scrum at dusk. In this region, sheep stations are measured in square kilometres, the first white explorers passed through barely 150 years ago and the land, sky and even the silence exert an almost mystical force. Its extraordinary flora and fauna, its scenic grandeur, its rich Aboriginal culture and the remarkable people who live here are a constant reminder of the uniqueness of the Australian continent.

Hot, dusty and frequently fly-ridden, the experience is not for everyone. But for those with a predilection for wilderness, wildlife or wide-open spaces, this is one of the most inspiring corners of the continent.

Planning your Outback trip

Travelling in the far west requires more planning than in other parts of the state. Towns are often far apart, and the petrol stop you just passed might be 150 km (100 miles) from the next. Summer temperatures are blistering, although many prefer this dry heat to the humidity of the coast. The best time for visiting the region is the relatively cool months from March to May, and again between September and mid-November.

Driving also demands special care. Most conventional vehicles should have no problems even on unsealed Outback roads, but on these, slow down and exercise a feather touch on the brake pedal. After rain, check local conditions with police or park rangers. Carry water if you go off sealed roads. If you plan to travel in isolated areas, let someone know your route and when you expect to return. If you break down, stay with

Map on page 168

LEFT: red rock west. The Sculpture Symposium at Broken Hill. **BELOW:** rush hour in the outback.

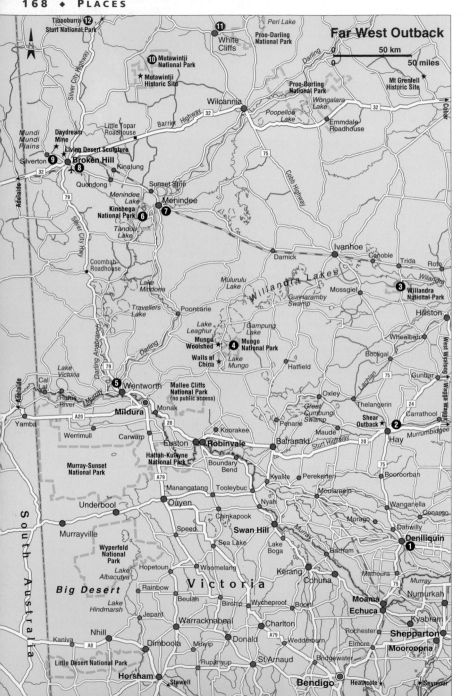

Far West Outback

0   50 km

0   50 miles

your vehicle. Hitting a kangaroo is one of the most common hazards in the Outback. This is more likely to happen towards evening, when the animals become more active. If a collision seems unavoidable, don't swerve or brake violently to try and avoid the animal – chances are you'll put yourself in a worse situation.

Deniliquin

The starting point is 250 km (155 miles) west of Wagga Wagga. **Deniliquin ❶** – Deni to the locals – is the centre of a proud and diverse agricultural region, bordered by red-gum country to the south and flat plains to the north. Surprisingly, the town is also a major rice producer, thanks to the wonders of irrigation.

Housed inside the former George Street Public School, the **Peppin Heritage Centre** (Cressy and George Streets; tel: 5881 4150; daily 9am–4pm; admission charge) celebrates the work of the Peppin family, experienced English sheep breeders who had an enormous impact on Australia's wool industry. Dissatisfied with the quality and yield of the wool they were getting from their merino flock at nearby Wanganella Station, they set about breeding a superior-quality merino sheep, and were so successful that almost 90 percent of all Australia's sheep now have Wanganella blood.

The town celebrates another vital agricultural connection in the **Deni Ute Muster** (www.deniutemuster. com.au), when more than 5,000 utilities – the staple working vehicles, multi-purpose and open-backed – congregate for a weekend of mateship, music and madness. The event takes place in late September.

Hay

Established at a ford on the Murrumbidgee, 150 km (93 miles) to the north is the spirited town of **Hay ❷**. The surrounding landscape is known

for its flatness, and a stop is highly recommended if you want to maintain sanity on what can otherwise be a long and tedious drive. The **Hay Prisoner of War and Internment Camp Interpretive Centre** (Hay Railway Station, Murray Street; tel: 6993 4045; Mon–Fri 9am–5pm; admission charge) tells the remarkable story of the town's role in World War II, when it was the site of an internment camp – not for enemy aliens but for Jews who had escaped to England from Nazi Germany and Austria. Although these victims of the war were not regarded with suspicion in Great Britain, thousands of displaced Jews were rounded up as part of the general internment of Germans and Austrians and 2,036 were sent to Australia on board the HMT *Dunera*, which gave them the name "The Dunera Boys". When they arrived in Australian in September 1940, they were reclassified as enemy aliens and sent to an internment camp in Hay – along with Italian and Japanese prisoners of war – before the government realised it had made a serious mistake and released them in 1942. During their

Map on page 168

Aboriginal guides at Mungo National Park and elsewhere explain indigenous traditions and how they relate to the landscape.

BELOW: barren land in the far west.

BELOW: the Walls of China in Mungo National Park.

time in Hay they set up a university and a symphony orchestra, and printed their own currency.

Shear Outback: The Australian Shearers' Hall of Fame (Sturt and Cobb Highways; tel: 6993 4000; www.shearoutback.com.au; daily 9am–5pm; admission charge) is a tribute to the "jumbuck barbers" who snip the wool from the country's 120 million sheep. Australia is the world's largest wool producer, and at this impressive, interactive centre, you can see a shearer at work, try throwing a fleece, shake hands with a sheep and watch sheepdogs at work.

Willandra National Park

Now it's time to go 159 km (99 miles) up the Cobb Highway. At the eastern end of the Willandra Lakes system, accessible via the Mossgeil Trunk Road which runs off the Hillston–Mossgiel Road, **Willandra National Park** ❸ covers an area of 190 sq. km (75 sq. miles) – a mere one-eighth the area of what was once the original Big Willandra Station. These days, the early 20th-century

homestead has been preserved as an example of an Outback pastoral property. The interior looks much as it would have in its heyday, with books and letters lying open on the furniture, as if the owners had just stepped out for the day. The shearers' quarters, ram shed and woolshed are all open for inspection.

The homestead is located close to Willandra Creek, where the relative abundance of water fosters a prolific bird and animal life.

Although the area once supported one of the largest Aboriginal populations in the state, little evidence remains of their occupation. With sharp eyes, however, you might happen to spot some of the stone shards from their tool-making against the fine sediment of the clay pans. The best way to explore Willandra's natural environment is a 20-km (12-mile) drive along the Merton Motor Trail, for which a four-wheel-drive vehicle is required. Contact the National Parks and Wildlife Service in Griffith (tel: 6966 8100) to check road conditions before setting out.

Mungo National Park

There are unsealed tracks across country but it's probably as easy to return to Hay and aim for Mildura 293 km (182 miles) westwards on the Sturt Highway. From Mildura take the road to Wentworth and just past the Buronga limits turn right into Arumpo Road and follow the signposts. Deep in the southwest corner of the state, **Mungo National Park ❹** is a wild, lonely moonscape of saltbush and sand dunes. Before the last Ice Age much of this area was covered by the Willandra Lakes, a series of 17 large, shallow lakes that provided a rich habitat for fish, shellfish and wallabies. Drawn by this natural abundance, Aboriginal people lived here possibly as long as 60,000 years ago. Thirty thousand years ago they evolved burial rituals, which are regarded as one of the earliest manifestations of a spiritual dimension to human existence.

The lakes dried up about 10,000 years ago, but a journey into this desiccated landscape, scalped by the wind and seared by the sun, is an evocative experience. Along the eastern sides of the dry lakes are crescent-shaped dunes called lunettes, formed from quartz sands cemented together by powdered clay. The most famous of these is the **Walls of China**, which towers 30 metres (100 ft) above the plain and runs for 30 km (20 miles). By moonlight, the Walls of China appear a stark, ghostly white.

Before it became a national park, this region was for many years a grazing property. **Mungo Woolshed**, built by Chinese workers in about 1869, is an atmospheric reminder of those hard-working times.

The 70-km (43-mile) self-drive tour through the park has 15 stops, and takes in all the main attractions. A four-wheel-drive vehicle is not essential, although it's more comfortable; be sure to fill your petrol tank before leaving Mildura.

The park has limited drinking water.

The only accommodation options are the park's campsites or Mungo Lodge (Arumpo Road, Mungo National Park; tel: 03-5029 7297; www.mungolodge.com.au), which has cottages with en suite bathrooms. The lodge is on Mildura Road, 2 km (1 mile) from the entrance to the park. Owned and operated by the local Barkindji people in the town of Wentworth, Harry Nanya Outback Tours (33 Darling Street; tel: 03-5027 2076; www.harrynanyatours.com.au) takes visitors out to Mungo National Park for one-day tours – ideal for anyone who wants an Aboriginal perspective of the landscape, plants, animals and spiritual dimension of the region.

Wentworth

At the junction of the Murray and Darling Rivers, **Wentworth ❺** is a sleepy town with several reminders of its important place in Australia's history. The first European to arrive here was the explorer Charles Sturt, who made a journey by whaleboat in 1830, following the course of the Murrumbidgee and eventually the

Map on page 168

Chain reaction. Try the manacles for size at Wentworth Gaol.

BELOW: Kinchega Woolshed.

Murray, Australia's longest river.

The first river steamer made the journey up the Murray in 1853, and a thriving river trade developed around the paddle steamers that towed barges piled with wool and crops downstream to the river ports in South Australia. Wentworth flourished on the strength of its location at the junction of the two rivers, and by the time it was declared a municipality in 1879, it was Australia's busiest inland port. The expansion of the railway network later in the century spelt the end of the town as a commercial port, a decline that intensified when Mildura, 30 km (20 miles) upstream, became the commercial centre of the region.

The **PS Ruby** (Wentworth Wharf; Tues–Wed 8.30am–3pm; admission charge) is a 205-ton, 1907 paddle steamer that was dragged from the muddy river bottom where it lay, handsomely restored by the local Rotary Club and donated to the city of Wentworth.

Junction Island, where the Darling and the Murray meet, is a nature reserve with a walking track and a viewing tower offering an elevated view of the merging of the waters.

Built in 1879–81, **Old Wentworth Gaol** (Beverley Street; tel: 03-5027 3337; daily 10am–5pm; admission charge) ceased operation in 1927, although it served as a prison of sorts when it provided extra classrooms for the Wentworth Central School until 1963. Today, it's a harmless historic relic where you can try on the prisoners' and warders' uniforms.

Along Darling River Road

Cutting a slash across western New South Wales, the Darling River Road follows the course of the Darling from Wentworth to Bourke – a journey rich with memories of a time when the paddle steamers opened up the Outback region of New South Wales. Although the intervening years have cushioned some of the hardships, the countryside is still rugged and challenging, and the journey along the Darling still potent with a sense of adventure. The total length of the trip is about 750 km (450 miles), most of it along unsealed roads. While a four-wheel-drive vehicle is virtually

At the corner of Adelaide and Adams Streets is a monument to a local hero, the Ferguson TEA20 tractor. Before it was tamed with weirs and locks, the Murray was subject to flooding. When inundation threatened in 1956, local farmers used their Fergusons to shore up levee banks, thus saving the town.

BELOW: sunset over a lake in Kinchega National Park.

a necessity for the full journey, the southern third – from Wentworth to Menindee – can be tackled in a conventional vehicle, except after heavy rainfall. It's also practical, since it links together Mungo and Kinchega national parks, with Wentworth and Broken Hill at either end. You can avoid camping if you plan overnight stops at Mungo Lodge and Menindee.

Kinchega National Park

At **Kinchega National Park ❻**, 189 km(117 miles) north on the Silver City Highway and turn right, the Darling River forms a chain of natural lakes. Irrigation dams have broadened these lakes, and the tracts of grey, lifeless river gums drowned by the rising waters give the lakeshores a starkly surreal quality, especially when silhouetted by the setting sun. For the most part, the park's landscape is bleak and flat, but the bird life here is sensational: flocks of black swans, pelicans, ducks, waterhens, egrets, ibises and even seagulls. Local operators in Menindee offer boat tours exploring the bird rookeries along the banks.

The national park was created from Kinchega Station, one of the first large pastoral holdings to be taken up in the west of the state by pioneering families. The original property covered more than 4,000 sq. km (1,500 sq. miles). In the late 1800s, steam engines were used to pump water from the Darling to flood the station's paddocks, which supported more than 100,000 sheep at its peak. **Kinchega Woolshed**, still stands, a monument in corrugated iron to the millions of sheep that were shorn here and to the stout hands that worked the blades. Remnants of the homestead, built of locally made bricks, are near by.

The only lodgings within the park are the fairly basic accommodation within the old shearers' quarters, or one of the park's campsites. The picnic area at Morton Boolka is especially good for birdwatching. Most vehicles should have no problem with the gravel roads in the park, but after rain, check local conditions with the National Parks and Wildlife Service in Broken Hill (tel: 08-8080 3200).

Menindee

The arid land surrounding **Menindee ❼** has been greened by irrigation schemes from the Darling River, providing water for groves of citrus and stone-fruit trees. Menindee was the first town to be established along the Darling River, and quickly became a port for the steamers that carried cargoes of wool downriver. Although it never grew to any great size, the town was an important outpost that made settlement viable for the sheep stations scattered across the semi-desert of western New South Wales.

Menindee is also the gateway to Kinchega National Park, and provides motel accommodation as an alternative to the park's campsites.

The **Menindee Hotel** underlines the town's long history. This is the

Map on page 168

A steward on the Indian Pacific train which runs through the heart of the continent from the Indian Ocean (Perth) to the Pacific (Sydney).

BELOW: camels are well suited to the Outback.

There's no escaping the fact that Broken Hill's a mining town. Street names were apparently drawn from a handy mineral catalogue.

BELOW: cap that.

second-oldest pub in the state still serving beer. Its most famous visitors were the explorers Robert O'Hara Burke and William John Wills, who arrived in 1860 by river steamer. After a few days here they set off to try to reach the Gulf of Carpentaria, the first attempt to cross the continent. Although they reached their goal, the expedition ended in tragedy when, on the return journey from the gulf, they ran desperately short of supplies. Only one of the party of four, John King, survived the ordeal; he was fed by the local Aborigines, who were able to find food where Europeans found only a desolate wilderness.

Most of the Menindee Hotel was destroyed in a fire in 1999 and rebuilt the following year. Although many historic artefacts were lost, the pub is still cherished for the well-chilled beer it dispenses to the thirsty Outback traveller.

Broken Hill

The capital of Outback New South Wales, **Broken Hill ❽** is known for its isolation, for its rich silver deposits and as the town which gave birth to BHP – now reincarnated as BHP Billiton, the world's largest mining company. In 1885, Charles Rasp, a boundary rider at Mount Gipps Station, found what he thought were tin deposits here. The tin turned out to be silver, and Rasp staked a mining claim of 16 hectares (40 acres) and set up a syndicate of seven to buy up all the surrounding land. The land turned out to hold the richest silver-lead-zinc concentration ever found, a continuous ore body 7 km (4 miles) long and 220 metres (700 ft) across.

Today, mining plays a less important role in the working life of Broken Hill, but its historical significance is underlined by the huge piles of crushed rock that still dominate the city. Most of the notable buildings are clustered around Argent Street, where the turreted post office and the effusive, Victorian town hall dominate the corner with Chloride Street. And during March, visitors to Broken Hill should try and attend the St Patrick's Day Races (www.stpatricks.org.au), one of the social events of the year.

Although the mines are no longer worked, at least one has become a tourist attraction. On the **Delprats Underground Mine Tour** (Federation Way; tel: 08-8088 1604; tours Mon–Fri 10.30am, Sat 2pm; admission charge), visitors don miners' boots and helmet and descend in a cage 400 metres (1,300 ft) underground for a two-hour walk through the mineshafts. Ex-miners, who paint a vivid picture of mining and the history of Broken Hill, lead the tour. From the Visitors Centre, turn right into Argent Street and right again at Iodide Street, cross the railway tracks and follow the signs.

A thriving art scene

While it prides itself on its nuggety, frontier character, the city has a softer side. These days there are more art galleries than pubs in

Broken Hill, a fact truly astonishing for an Outback city. The most illustrious of its artists are the so-called "Brushmen of the Bush" – a group of self-taught painters who draw their inspiration from Broken Hill and its desiccated surroundings. The most famous was **Pro Hart**, a Broken Hill native whose gallery (108 Wyman Street; tel: 08-8087 2441; www.prohart.com.au; Mon–Sat 9am 5pm, Sun 1.30pm–5pm; admission charge) houses a significant private collection of European masters as well as Hart's own paintings. Sadly, they cannot be seen at their best: the pictures are poorly hung, some on cramped landings which don't allow you to step back, some, unforgivably, under fluorescent strip lighting. See how it should be done at **Jack Absalom's Gallery** (638 Chapple Street; tel: 08-8087 5881; daily 9am–5pm; free), where state-of-the-art lighting and plenty of space allow his striking landscapes to breathe. You may well run into the artist, famous all around Australia for his long-running TV show.

The most unusual gallery in Broken Hill is **White's Mineral Art Gallery** (1 Allandale Street; tel: 08-8087 2878; daily 9am–5pm; admission charge), which has been made to look like a mineshaft with stout beams and rock walls. It is the creation of Kevin White, who uses ground-up minerals in his paintings.

For an overview of work by leading local artists, as well as an interesting programme of temporary exhibitions, drop by the **Broken Hill Regional Art Gallery** in the beautifully renovated Sully's Emporium (404–8 Argent Street; tel: 08-8088 687; daily 10am–5pm; free).

There's even an art pub. Located close to the heart of Broken Hill, **Mario's Palace Hotel** (227 Argent Street; tel: 08-8088 1699; daily 9am–10.30pm; free) is a rambling construction that dates from the town's mining heyday. Inspired by the city's wealth of creative talent, Mario himself painted a copy of Botticelli's *Birth of Venus* on the hotel's ceiling, and now the daubs have spread to most of the walls and ceilings.

Map on page 168

Public sculpture by Pro Hart, one of Broken Hill's favourite sons who died in 2006.

BELOW: the redundant Junction Mine.

Education in the ether

The **School of the Air** (Lane Street, behind North Public school; tel: 08-8087 3565; www.schoolair-p.schools. nsw.edu.au; admission charge) has a total enrolment of about 80 only, but its "classroom" covers an area of more than 1 million sq. km (375,000 sq. miles). Most of its students live on isolated sheep and cattle stations scattered across the Outback. They rely on computers, which are linked by satellite, to communicate with their teacher and classmates, supplementing what would otherwise be a dull educational diet. Visitors are welcome to sit in on the class, which is held from Monday to Thursday, 8.30am to 9.30am, except for school and public holidays, but you must turn up at the school by 8.15am. For bookings, contact the Broken Hill Visitor Centre (Blende and Bromide Streets; tel: 08-8088 9700; daily 9am–5pm).

About 10 km (6 miles) west of Broken Hill, in the middle of the Living Desert Reserve is Sundown Hill, site of the iconic **Living Desert Sculpture**. International artists col-

A steward on the Sculptors flew in from around the world to create the works in the Living Desert Sculpture Symposium.

BELOW: Mad Max pops into the Silverton Hotel for a quick one.

laborated to create this group of 12 sandstone sculptures in 1993. The dramatic pieces are particularly impressive at sunset.

Doing the bush mail run

One of the best ways to get a close-up look at Outback life is to take a trip with the **Bush Mail Run** (tel: 08-8087 2164; admission charge). Every Wednesday and Saturday, the bush mailman sets off from Broken Hill in his Toyota Landcruiser to deliver mail and supplies to sheep and cattle stations across a wide swathe of country south of Broken Hill – one of the world's longest mail runs. Besides its cargo the mail wagon also carries paying passengers. In a single day, passengers will travel about 550 km (350 miles), visiting about 20 different properties. For many of the people on the stations, these passengers are the only fresh faces that they will see from one week to the next. Lunch is at an 1880s homestead near the banks of the Darling River. Although the country is rugged, the air-conditioned vehicle does an excellent job of soaking up the bumps.

Silverton

About 25 km (15 miles) west of Broken Hill, **Silverton ⑨** was once a thriving mining town, but when the silver gave out at the end of the 19th century the miners moved to Broken Hill. Today it is a ghost town with a population of less than 100, but its photogenic qualities – blood-red earth, solitary stone buildings, scarlet sunsets and camels in the main street – make it a favourite with tourists and film-makers in search of "authentic" Outback scenery. Itself a prominent feature in these cinematic offerings, the Silverton Hotel has a display of stills from films shot locally. The town also has several resident artists, and there are usually studios and galleries open.

If you happen to be in Silverton in the evening, drive 5 km (3 miles) to the lookout west of town and watch the sun sink across the **Mundi Mundi Plains** – from where the land seem to stretch to eternity.

On the road between Silverton and Broken Hill, a side road leads to the **Daydream Mine** (tel: 08-8088 5682; daily 10am–3.30pm; admission charge), where the one-hour walking tour through the silver mine is an insight into the gruelling business of mining 100 years ago. Opened in 1882 and worked intermittently for almost a century, the mine employed 150 men and 20 boys at its peak, many of them Cornish miners. The narrow mine shafts meant the miners often had to work on their sides by candlelight. Sturdy footwear is essential.

Mutawintji National Park

Another 112 km (70 miles) north-east of Broken Hill, the scorched sandstone peaks of **Mutawintji National Park ⑩** rise suddenly from the plain. All around is a flat,

baked landscape but here, in the cracks and folds of the red rock of the Bynguano Range, there is water. It was the permanent water supply that made this area a virtual oasis for Outback Aboriginal people, a place where even in the worst drought they could find rock wallabies and goannas, or gather berries and fruit. And it was here that they left their totemic figures inscribed on the rock, the finest examples of which are found in the **Mutawintji Historic Site**, a restricted area that can be visited only on a guided tour with a park ranger. The tour also visits the Cultural Resource Centre, which has colourful murals depicting the Aboriginal view of creation.

Much more artwork is scattered throughout the park, in the rocky overhangs where the Aboriginal people once sheltered. In the early 1980s, the Mutawintji people blockaded the site after they became concerned that unfettered access was destroying what was to them an area of profound spiritual significance. The blockade was short, but it had an impact and as a

Map on page 168

TIP

Visitors to Mutawintji who know what they're looking for can still find Aboriginal "barbecues" – small mounds where they would cook their meat and where the accumulation of hot animal fats bonded the soil into an erosion-resistant clump.

BELOW: Mutawintji National Park.

Map on page 168

The searing heat of the summer provides the town of White Cliffs with much of its electrical power, thanks to the 14 giant parabolic multi-faceted mirrors which capture the sun's rays.

BELOW: soda time in Bell's Milk Bar in Broken Hill.

consequence, Aboriginal people were increasingly involved with the running of the park and the way it was interpreted to visitors. This process culminated in a hand-back ceremony in 1998.

Mutawintji's sun-blistered landscape of red rock, saltbush and cypress pines has made it a favourite subject for the landscape painters of Broken Hill. It can only be explored on foot and one of the finest short walks in the park is the track that leads along a creek from the original Mootwingee Homestead to Homestead Gorge, where water trickles from a fissure in the sheer red walls into a rock pool. From the gorge, the Bynguano Route makes a five-hour circuit of the ranges. In these hills you can expect to see euros, or rock wallabies, and shingleback lizards, and, around the water holes, a rich and colourful birdlife which includes corellas, ringneck parrots, nankeen kestrels and peregrine falcons. The information office for the park is located in Broken Hill (183 Argent Street; tel: 08-8080 3200).

Subterranean living

There's more to the town of **White Cliffs** ⓫ than meets the eye because most of the town lies underground. Opal mining began here in the late 1880s and peaked in the early 1900s, when as many as 4,000 miners dug for the fiery gemstone, leaving a lunar landscape pockmarked with small burrows. Fierce summer temperatures make life outside unbearable, while underground it's a constant 23 degrees. It was only logical, therefore, that when they wanted to create a home, the miners simply put a door on the front of a mine shaft and set up house.

Today most of White Cliffs lives underground. There's an underground motel and an underground bed and breakfast, both with neat, cool, all-white rooms – and you won't hear a sound all night. The sights of White Cliffs are tailormade for the collector of Outback oddities. There's an underground museum of mining and memorabilia, a golf course which hasn't a single blade of green grass, and even a "Hilton" Hotel, where you can bend an elbow with the locals.

Return to the Silver City Highway and drive north for the remotest corner of the state. Milparinka, 287 km (178 miles) north of Broken Hill, is just a handful of structures, including a historic court house. But drive another 46 km (29 miles) for a real frontier town – **Tibooburra** ⓬. There's a hotel on either side of the road, a school and a scattering of houses. Otherwise it's people passing through on impossibly long journeys. Nearest attraction is the Sturt National Park. After that you're at the border with Queensland. To go further you'll have to pass through the gate in the Dog Fence, the 5,320-km (3,300-mile) barrier that runs from Toowoomba, near Brisbane, to the coast of South Australia. ❑

RESTAURANTS & BARS

Restaurants

Broken Hill

Trinders @ The Astra
393 Argent Street
Tel: 8087 5428
www.theastra.com.au
Open: L & D daily. **$$**
This is one of the newer restaurants in town and like the rest of this hotel, it's had a lot of money spent on it in the hope of attracting up-market customers. The menu is subtly ambitious and well executed, while the service is a notch above some of the competition.

Broken Earth Cafe Restaurant
Federation Way
Tel: 8087 1318
www.tandou.com.au/cafe.html
Open: B, L & D daily. **$$$**
The futuristic building on top of the Line of Lodecan be seen dominating the skyline from all over town. Inside there's a pretty good café which transforms into an upmarket restaurant at night. The menu is ambitious and cosmopolitan, but not always successful. However, the views over town are terrific.

Barrier Social & Democratic Club
218 Argent Street
Tel: 8088 4477
Open: B, L & D daily. **$**
The "Demo" is one of several social clubs around town and the competition means that you can get sizeable bistro meals very cheaply. The Sturt Club at 321 Blende Street (08-8087 4541) is also worth a look.

Hay

Jolly Jumbuck Bistro
Riverina Hotel,
148 Lachlan Street
Tel: 6993 4718
Open: L & D daily. **$$**
Smart dining room of bare brick and polished wood where some classic bistro fare has made it the most popular eatery in town.

Menindee

Maidens Hotel
Yartla Street
Tel: 8091 4208
Open: L & D daily. **$**
The counter meals aren't particularly exciting, but there's a good atmosphere – and it's not as if there's anywhere else in town.

Silverton

Silverton Hotel
Laynard Street
Tel: 8088 5313
Open: L & D daily. **$**
Tuck in to a simple counter meal while drinking in the atmosphere Odds are you'll end up in one of the countless films or commercials filmed here.

Tibooburra

Tibooburra Hotel
Briscoe Street
Tel: 8091 3310
www.outbacknsw.com.au/tibooburra.htm
Open: L & D daily. **$**
A friendly welcome and huge meals to satisfy the most demanding of itinerant stockmen or whoever else may be passing through.

Wentworth

Wentworth Club
Darling Street
Tel: 5027 3302
www.wentworthclub.com.au
Open: L & D daily. **$**
Another giant social club with its Junction Bistro providing functional meals at keen prices. There's also a coffee shop open 11am-3pm every day and some evenings.

White Cliffs

White Cliffs Underground Motel
Smith's Hill
Tel: 8091 6677
www.undergroundmotel.com.au
Open: D daily. **$**
The Underground Restaurant provides reasonable 3-course dinners, while a bistro has a more informal menu.

Cafés and bars

Deniliquin

The Crossing Café
295 George Street
Tel: 5881 7827
www.thecrossingcafe.com.au
Open: B, L & D daily. **$$**
Round the-clock operation that ranges from snacks through to some seriously interesting dinners. Gets some good bands in as well.

Broken Hill

Bells Milk Bar
160 Patton Street
Tel: 8087 5380
www.bellsmilkbar.com.au
Open: B, L & D daily. **$**
Make an effort to seek out this wonderful 1950s throwback lurking on the quiet side of Broken Hill. It was renovated in 1956 and has not changed since. Enjoy a milkshake, soda or spider made from homemade syrups derived from 50-year-old recipes.

Tibooburra

Corner Country Store
Briscoe Street
Tel: 8091 3333
Open: B & L daily. **$**
No culinary pretensions here, despite the claims to being an "up-market cafe", just the usual fodder for working men (and the occasional woman) on long treks.

PRICE CATEGORIES

Prices for a three-course dinner per person with a half-bottle of house wine:
$ = under A$50
$$ = A$50–A$75
$$$ = over A$75
L = lunch, D = dinner, BYO = bring your own alcohol

CENTRAL NEW SOUTH WALES AND OUTBACK

On these great plains some of the country's oldest European settlements saw a gold rush, huge wealth and notorious outlaws. Nowadays there's fertile farmland, a prosperous wine region, National Parks and areas important to Aboriginal tradition

Sydney

Extending west from the slopes of the Great Dividing Range, this is where the continent begins to stretch out. Once the first explorers crossed the Blue Mountains and saw the great plains extending to the horizon, graziers were quick to follow, herding sheep and cattle across the ranges to spacious pasturelands as early as the 1830s. This movement brought the settlers into conflict with the Aboriginal inhabitants of the plains, and the "heroic" story of European westward expansion is paralleled by a very different story of tragedy and exploitation for the continent's indigenous people.

This is also the region where gold was first discovered in Australia, providing the infant nation with a sudden flush of wealth that enabled even small towns to finance the construction of stately public buildings and parks. For the most part, this region now makes its living from agriculture. Facilities for tourism are limited, yet within a day's drive of the coast, the central west and Outback region conveys a potent sense of Australia's wide open spaces, and the frontier society that provides the visitor with iconic experiences, from the opal-mining town of Lightning Ridge to the full-blooded taste of a Mudgee Cabernet Sauvignon.

Industrial beginnings

The first major town west of the Blue Mountains, **Lithgow ❶** developed as an industrial, coal-mining and agricultural centre. Its industrial heritage diverts some visitors from the Great Western Highway, which barely grazes the edge of the city.

Lithgow's most popular attraction is the **Zig Zag Railway** (tel: 6353 1795; Sat–Sun, daily during school holidays, 11am, 1pm and 3pm; www. zigzagrailway.com.au), part of the original railway line to Sydney. The

Map on page 182

LEFT: a truck raises dust on a dirt road near Forbes.
BELOW: kombi nation. Parked up in the hills above Lithgow.

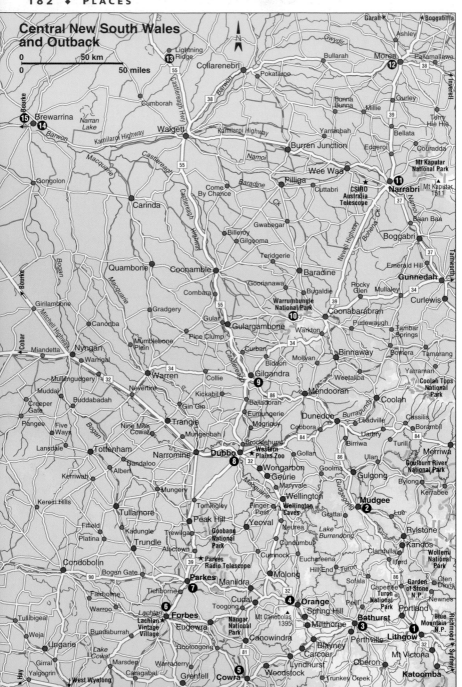

Central New South Wales and Outback

0   50 km
0   50 miles

Garah   Boggabilla
Ashley
Lightning Ridge   **13**
Collarenebri   Moree **12**   Pallamallawa
Bullarah   Gwydir   Gurley
Pokataroo   Terry Hie Hie
Cumborah   Bunna Bunna   Millie   Bellata
Bourke   **15** Brewarrina **14**   Walgett   Kamilaroi Highway   Yarranbah   Edgeroi   Couradda
Narran Lake   Banwon   Burren Junction   Mt Kaputar National Park
Gongolon   Macquarie   Namoi   Wee Waa   CSIRO Australia Telescope   Narrabri **11**   Mt Kaputar 1511
Carinda   Pilliga   Baan Baa
Come By Chance   Baradine   Cuttabri
Billeroy   Gwabegar   Boggabri
Quambone   Coonamble   Gilgooma   Emerald Hill   Gunnedah
Combara   Teridgerie   Baradine   Rocky Glen   Mullaley   Curlewis
Girilambone   Gradgery   Goorianawa   Warrumbungle National Park **10**   Purlewaugh   Tambar Springs
Gulargambone   Gulan   Pine Clump   Coonabarabran   Bowlera   Tamarang
Miandetta   Mumblebone Plain   Curban   Warkton   Yarraman
Nyngan   Warrigal   Biddon   Gilgandra **9**   Molliyan   Binnaway   Weetaliba   Coolah Tops National Park
Warren   Collie   Kickabil   Balladoran   Mendooran   Coolah
Mullengudgery   Neventire   Gin Gin   Eumungerie   Dunedoo   Leadville   Cassilis
Muddai   Buddabadah   Trangie   Mogriguy   Cobbora   Darby   Borambil
Creeper Gate   Nine Mile Cowal   Mungenbah   Brockhurst   Birriwa   Turill   Merriwa
Pangee   Five Ways   Western Plains Zoo   Gollan   Ulan   Goulburn River National Park
Lansdale   Bogan   Narromine   Dubbo **8**   Wongarbon   Goolma   Gulgong   Bylong
Kerriwah   Dandaloo   Albert   Geurie   Maryvale   Kerrabee
Tottenham   Mungery   Wellington   Grattai   Mudgee **2**   Lue
Kerein Hills   Tullamore   Tomingley   Finger Post   Wellington Caves   Neurea   Rylstone
Fifield   Peak Hill   Yeoval   Cundumbul   Lake Burrendong   Clandulla   Kandos
Platina   Kadungle   Goobang National Park   Currinock   Eucareena   Ilford   Wollemi National Park
Trundle   Albictown   Parkes Radio Telescope   Molong   Hill End   Turon   Garden of Stone N.P.   Glen Davis
Condobolin   Bogan Gate   Parkes **7**   Manildra   Sofala   Capertee   Newnes
Fairholme   Tichborne   Cudal   Orange **4**   Peel   Turon National Park   Portland
Warroo   Forbes **6**   Toogong   Spring Hill   Bathurst **3**   Blue Mountain N.P.
Tullibigeal   Lachlan Vintage Village   Eugowra   Millthorpe   Perthville   Lithgow **1**
Ungarie   Weja   Bundaburrah   Nangar National Park   Mt Canobolas 1395   Canowindra   Blayney   Mt Victoria
Hay   Girral   Lake Cowal   Gooloogong   Carcoar   Oberon   Katoomba
Yalgogrin   Marsden   Warraderry   Woodstock   Lyndhurst   Trunkey Creek
West Wyalong   Caragabal   Grenfell   Cowra **5**

dramatic views and the huff and puff of a vintage steam engine make this cliff-hugging, 16-km (10-mile) train ride a thriller, but it's also a prodigious feat of engineering.

Built in 1869, this was the main line across the Blue Mountains until 1910. The name comes from the track, which is laid in a giant "Z". The train climbs the steep incline by chugging backwards and forwards for each alternate section of the track, and thus the name. The train runs between Clarence Station and Bottom Points Station, the lower of the two. The round trip from Clarence takes about 90 minutes. Clarence is 10 km (6 miles) east of Lithgow on Chifley Road.

Another worthwhile diversion is to follow Lithgow Street past the old pottery and climb up to **Hassans Walls Lookout** for dramatic views across the surrounding valleys.

Wine and gold

North of Lithgow (122 km/76 miles) is **Mudgee ❷**, which takes its name from an Aboriginal word meaning "nest in the hills", and the surrounding rim of low hills gives the town a secluded sense of mystery. Mudgee sprang to life during the gold rush and, after Bathurst *(see page 184)*, this is the second-oldest town west of the Blue Mountains. Several of its buildings date from the 1850s and 1860s, and while they're often simple and unembellished, they give the town a real sense of character.

Complementing its historic attributes, Mudgee is tranquil, making it a delightful place for a stroll. The **Mudgee Visitor Centre** (84 Market Street; tel: 6372 1020; Mon–Fri 9am–5pm, Sat 9am–3.30pm, Sun 9am–2pm) has a "Mudgee Walks" brochure with a self-guided tour of the town's heritage buildings.

Gold proved a meteoric commodity for Mudgee, and its day was spectacular but short. The wool trade proved a far more reliable source of income, but from the earliest years of settlement, the area showed promise for wine producers. Vineyards were planted in the 1850s, and these play an ever-increasing part in the life of the region. Although they are not as well known as the Hunter Valley wineries, Mudgee's characteristic wines are robust and deeply coloured Cabernet Sauvignon and Shiraz, and concentrated Chardonnays.

The Mudgee wine region has close to 50 wineries, most of them open for tastings and cellar-door sales. Simon Gilbert, Huntington, Frog Rock, Abercorn and Robert Stein are among the region's most distinguished producers. Maps of the wineries with opening hours are available from the Mudgee Visitor Centre.

Henry Lawson, the poet and short-story writer whose writing championed the earthy language and humour of bush life, spent his youth in the village of **Eurunderee**, which lies just on the outskirts of Mudgee. Lawson lived here between the ages of about six months and 15, along the road that now bears his name, but

Map on page 182

The remarkable Zig Zag Railway was the easy way to traverse the mountains. The alternative – a tunnel – would have needed 10 million bricks.

BELOW: Edward Hargraves was credited with the first gold discovery in 1851.

The 35 bells of the Bathurst War Memorial Carillon in Kings Parade ring out daily at noon and 1pm.

BELOW: Bathurst Courthouse is the home of the Bathurst Historical Museum.

little remains of the schoolhouse, the post office, the houses and shops of the small community that Lawson would have known.

Far more evocative of Lawson's life and times is the town of **Gulgong**, virtually a living museum, which lies 30 km (20 miles) north of Mudgee. Founded in the days of the gold rush, a short stroll along Gulgong's main street – which has 130 buildings with National Trust classification – will reveal an architectural treasury. The **Pioneers Museum** (73 Herbert Street; tel: 6374 1513; daily 9am–5pm; admission charge) is probably the most complete record of 19th-century frontier life in the country, while the **Henry Lawson Centre** (148 Mayne Street; tel: 6374 1024; Mon–Fri 10am–noon, Sat–Sun 10am–3pm; admission charge) houses the largest collection of Lawson's writings and memorabilia outside Sydney's Mitchell Library.

Bathurst and beyond

South from Mudgee, branch off to the oldest inland settlement in the country, **Bathurst ❸**. It boomed when gold was discovered in the 1850s, but it was due to the agricultural riches of the surrounding district that the city prospered after the gold rush ended. Two legendary Australians were born here – the stagecoach company, Cobb & Co., and Ben Chifley, the son of a blacksmith and Australia's prime minister from 1945 to 1949.

The city is scattered with imposing reminders of its splendid past, such as the magnificent court house, one of the most impressive colonial buildings in the state. It now houses the **Bathurst Historical Museum** (Russell Street; tel: 6332 4755; Tues–Sat 10am–5pm, Sun 2pm–5pm), which has fine exhibits that add flesh and blood to the gold-mining history of the district.

The **Bathurst Regional Art Gallery** (70–78 Keppel Street; tel: 6331 6066; Tues–Sat 10am–5pm, Sun 11am–2pm) has a fine collection of work by Lloyd Rees, one of Australia's foremost landscape artists.

A 40-km (25-mile) drive north from Bathurst leads to the village of **Sofala**, a tumbledown country town

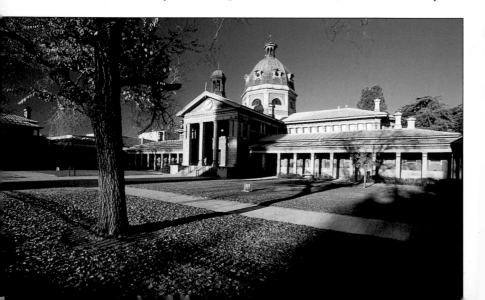

strung out along the banks of the Turon River, with a fascinating general store that also serves as the local post office, souvenir shop and café.

Near by is **Hill End**, and although it's hard to believe these days, this sleepy village was once a boomtown, where your fortune could be made if you stuck your pickaxe into the right bit of dirt. Today the town is still littered with giant boilers and rusting cogs from the gold-rush era, which lie where they were abandoned. Some of Australia's famous landscape painters found inspiration in Sofala and Hill End, including Russell Drysdale and Donald Friend, and at Hill End in particular, the rich patina of time that is spelt out on its weathered façades continues to make this a compelling source of inspiration.

Orange

Further inland, 53 km (33 miles) west of Bathurst along the Mitchell Highway, is **Orange ●**. The town takes its name from the Prince of Orange, who fought alongside the British forces against Napoleon in the Peninsular War; although the city is the centre of one of the country's biggest fruit-growing areas, it's too cold for oranges.

The city is dominated by **Mount Canobolas**, an extinct volcanic peak that has walking trails and picnic spots. Even though it's not particularly high at 1,395 metres (4,576 ft), travelling west across the continent you will not find a higher peak until the coast of Africa – as the locals like to point out. It is increasingly known as a source of high-quality rare and exotic produce. Held at the end of March, the F.O.O.D. (Food of Orange District) Week Festival showcases the varied produce of the region, such as figs, soft berry fruits, edible fungi, brook trout and wines.

For the rest of the year, Orange is a businesslike town with heritage buildings that can be seen on the Orange City Heritage Trail. Details of the walk are available from the **Visitor Information Centre** (Byng and Peisley streets; tel: 6393 8226; daily 9am–5pm).

In 1851 the first gold discovered in Australia was at **Ophir**, which lies 30 km (20 miles) northeast of

Map on page 182

The discovery of a nugget worth L35 by a Mr Austin at Ophir in 1851 triggered Australia's first gold rush. Further mayhem ensued when another discovery was made in Victoria six months later.

BELOW: gold ingots.

A large army training facility built at Cowra at the start of World War II was used as an internment camp for Japanese and Italian prisoners of war from 1942. In 1944, the Japanese prisoners staged a mass breakout. Of the 378 prisoners who escaped, most were rounded up within a few days. The furthest point reached by any escapee was about 50 km (30 miles) from the camp. A total of 231 prisoners died and another 108 were wounded, while four Australians were killed.

BELOW: the Japanese Garden at Cowra.

A symbol of reconciliation

A leisurely 104 km (65 miles) southwest of Orange, and surrounded by fertile farming country in the valley of the Lachlan River, **Cowra 5** is famous as the scene of one of the most famous episodes in Australia's wartime history *(see margin, left)*. Tragic as the event was, Cowra has become a shining example of international reconciliation. The townspeople took care of the graves of the prisoners, and in 1979 the **Japanese Garden and Cultural Centre** (Binni Creek Road; tel: 6341 2233; daily 8.30am–5pm) was opened as a symbol of friendship and peace. Created by Japanese garden designer Ken Nakajima, the 5-hectare (12-acre) garden features many of the traditional elements associated with Japanese horticulture, such as a tea pavilion, a bonsai house, a dry *kare-sansui* garden, a wisteria pergola, two *koi* ponds, waterfalls, streams spanned by arched bridges and stone

Orange, although there's nothing there today apart from a recreation reserve and abandoned mine sites.

lanterns. Over 120 species of birds have made their home here, which also has more than 100 plant species.

The Cultural Centre has three galleries of exhibits, including paintings, dolls, ceremonial kimonos and masks, model samurai and weapons, a collection of Japanese ceramics and model *torii* gates. Spring blossoms transform the gardens in early October, when it becomes the focus of *Sakura Matsuri*, Cowra's annual cherry blossom festival. The festival also features traditional Japanese foods, arts and crafts, kite flying, tea ceremonies, martial arts and *shakuhachi* flute recitals.

Bushranger territory

On the banks of the Lachlan River 92 km (57 miles) northwest of Cowra, **Forbes 6** is a blend of historic buildings, parks and gardens. Here is another town where the fortunes won on its goldfields can still be seen in many of its handsome Victorian buildings. Gold also attracted bushrangers (outlaws and highwaymen), and Forbes was close to the centre of the action for Ben Hall, one of the most professional of all Australia's bushrangers.

At **Eugowra**, east of Forbes, the biggest gold robbery in Australia's history took place in 1862, when Frank Gardiner and his gang – including Ben Hall – relieved the mail coach of £3,700 in cash and 2,719 oz of gold, worth more than A$1.3 million at today's prices. Hall's career as a bushranger ended in 1865 when he was killed in a shoot-out with police at Billabong Creek near Forbes. He was 28.

In the town's main street, the **Albion Hotel** (135 Lachlan Street; tel: 6851 1881) is a sprawling hotel floridly ornamented in the style of the Victorian era. In the basement are the remains of the tunnel system that once connected the hotel – which also served as the local Cobb & Co.

office – with the town's banks. Gold would be transported through the tunnels rather than above ground to foil the local bushrangers.

The cellar also houses the "Bushrangers Hall of Fame", which tells the tale of some of the more notorious locals who crossed to the wrong side of the law. The display is open during pub opening hours – ask the barman to let you in.

On the southern outskirts of Forbes, the **Lachlan Vintage Village** (Newell Highway; tel: 6852 2655; daily 8am–5.30pm; admission charge) is a recreated village of about 55 historic buildings, most of which have been relocated here from surrounding areas. The village is virtually an open-air museum, intended to evoke the sounds and smells as well as the sights of 19th century rural life. The complex also includes the Lachlan Diggings, built on the site of the original Forbes goldfield, where visitors can pan for gold in the creek. There's a museum of farm implements, farm animals, Ben Hall's cottage and the home of Henry Lawson *(see page 183)*.

Heavenly view

Thirty-three km (20 miles) north of Forbes is **Parkes ❼**, a former gold-mining town that is the centre of a rich agricultural district, with a few fine examples of Victorian architecture built during the brief but spectacular gold boom. The town is best known for the 64-metre (210-ft) radio telescope 25 km (15 miles) north of Parkes on the Newell Highway.

The CSIRO (Commonwealth Scientific and Industrial Research Organisation) **Parkes Radio Telescope** uses the radio energy that is emitted by distant objects such as quasars, galaxies, molecular clouds, pulsars and spacecraft to generate "images", which are reported as a graph, a map or a number sequence on a computer screen. The system amplifies weak signals more than a million million times, enabling it to investigate objects that might be millions of light years away. The telescope is also an important link in the worldwide network of tracking devices that are used to locate NASA spacecraft – a link that was the subject of the 2001 film, *The Dish*.

Map on page 182

A stroll in Forbes' distinguished town centre is as rewarding as many so-called attractions

BELOW: the Parkes Radio Telescope.

The site to the north of Parkes was chosen for the radio telescope because of its remoteness from urban areas and because of its dry atmosphere, both of which create ideal conditions for radio astronomy.

Overshadowed by the enormous dish, the **Visitors Centre** (daily 8.30am–4.15pm; www.parkes.atnf.csiro.au) has various displays and interactive exhibits that explain the workings of the radio telescope as well as principles of astronomy in general. The centre also has two film theatres, one of which has 3D films that take viewers on board spacecraft for a simulated flight.

Frontier spirit

The agricultural land continues to **Dubbo ❽**, which lies in the middle of the wheat belt 115 km (71 miles) to the north. It is a lively, thriving city of close to 40,000 that combines a sense of the frontier with an entrepreneurial spirit. The first permanent European settler was Robert Delahunty, one of Australia's wealthiest men at the time, who established a large grazing property a short distance up the Macquarie River from the present city site. Dubbo benefited from its position on the Overlanders route, the main stock route used by graziers who fattened sheep and cattle further north before driving them to markets in Victoria and South Australia.

In the later years of the 19th century, Dubbo became the major services centre for western New South Wales, the last big town before the state's Outback region. Today it's an important commercial centre for an enterprising rural area.

Among the city's banks, hotels, churches and civic buildings are some outstanding examples of 19th-century architecture, such as the **Commercial Hotel**, the **Lands Office Building** and the **Court House**. The **Tourist Information Centre** (Corner Erskine and Macquarie streets; tel: 6884 1422; daily 9am–5pm) has a Heritage Walk brochure that details the city's historic buildings. The centre also has brochures for two excellent heritage drives that explore historic areas and buildings in the city's surroundings.

Wildlife safari

Eclipsing all other attractions in Dubbo, **Western Plains Zoo** (Obley Road; tel: 6881 1400; daily 9am–5pm; admission charge; ticket valid

BELOW: fishing on the Macquarie River.

for two consecutive days; WWW.ZOO. NSW.gOV.aU) is the reason that most travellers find themselves in the city. This is Australia's leading open-range zoo, home to more than 1,100 animals from around the world, many of them endangered species. Its 300 hectares (750 acres) are divided into five geographical areas: Africa, Eurasia, North America, South America and Australia, each with enclosed habitats specially created for the animals from that region.

A 6-km (4-mile) road runs in a loop through the zoo, and visitors can either drive, walk or cycle, passing the various animal enclosures en route. Bicycles and electric carts are available for hire, and they are the best way to get around, as drivers have to park and then walk to get close to the animal enclosures.

African animals such as lion, elephant, rhino, giraffe and various antelope species make up a large part of the population, but there are also many Australian animals, such as wallabies and kangaroos. Most of the primates are on islands surrounded by lakes.

Many of the animals are at their most active at dawn, and the zoo's Early Morning Walk (from the main gate at 6.45am Wed, Fri–Sun during school holidays, Sat–Sun only outside school holidays) is a wonderful opportunity to see the animals at close quarters. Since they're often fed early, this is also a good time for photographs. The tour visits the **Black Rhinoceros Conservation Complex**, the **Giraffe Night House**, several primate species and the **South American Habitat**.

Other prime events include the Wild Africa Encounters, when keepers feed the zoo's black and white rhinos and giraffe and the Big Cat Encounters, a feeding session with lions or a Sumatran tiger. An extra charge applies for both the morning walk and the two animal encounters.

If your taste in sleeping quarters runs to hearing roaring lions in the night or perhaps a trumpeting elephant, **Zoofari Lodge** is for you. It is a complex of canvas-covered accommodation in the style of an African safari camp. Surrounded by tawny plains in the African Savannah section of zoo, each lodge sleeps four in comfort, despite the canvas walls. There is also a swimming pool and a bar and restaurant.

Town of windmills

Continue north on the Newell Highway to reach **Gilgandra ⑨**, a small town of barely 3,000, yet with a big story to tell. During World War I, the citizens of Gilgandra played a leading role in rallying support for the war effort at a time when motivation was flagging. The Australian contribution to the war effort was an all-volunteer force, and in 1915, in the aftermath of the disastrous Gallipoli campaign and heavy casualties in France, numbers were waning.

In a spontaneous outburst of imperial pride, R.G. Hitchen, the local butcher, and his brother Bill,

Map on page 182

Western Plains Zoo was set up as a sister facility to Sydney's Taronga Zoo and runs key breeding programmes.

BELOW: downtown Dubbo.

the town plumber, organised a party of volunteers to march to Sydney, enlisting recruits along the way. They assembled some locals and set out in October 1915, and these 26 men, who quickly became known as the Coo-ees for their rallying cry, had swollen to 236 by the time they reached Sydney. When they arrived, after a march of 500 km (320 miles) over rough roads, the citizens of Sydney crowded the streets to welcome these country heroes. Their action was responsible for turning the tide of recruitment numbers.

The **Coo-ee Heritage Centre** (Coo-ee Memorial Park, Newell Highway; tel: 6847 2045; daily 9am–5pm) tells the story of the march, as well as the Aboriginal and European histories of the region. The windmill at the front of the building is another historic reference. The Gilgandra townspeople lacked a water supply until 1966, and used windmills to draw water from the sub-artesian basin. As a result, Gilgandra was sometimes known as the "Town of Windmills".

The Gilgandra Visitor Centre is

Crater Bluff in the Warrumbungle National Park, one of the best places in New South Wales to get the feel of the ancient Outback.

BELOW: Gilgandra observatory.

also located within the Heritage Centre. The **Gilgandra Observatory** (Willie Street; tel: 6847 2646; winter 7–10pm; summer 8.30–10pm; admission charge; www.gilobs.com.au) is one of several in the district, but this one was built by a retired farmer, Jack Estens. Visitors can attend evening sessions for a talk by the astronomer and to view the heavens through the main telescope, which is a 31-cm (12-inch) Newtonian Reflector.

Take a walk in the park

North of Gilgandra, rearing abruptly from the flat landscape of the state's central west, the tortured trachyte spires of **Warrumbungle National Park** ❿ (admission charge) bear witness to a history of tremendous volcanic eruptions. This unique landscape of heavily timbered rock domes and bare spears has wonderful bush-walks, some of the finest rock climbs in the country and a natural paradise for birdwatchers. This is one of the few places where rainforest can be found in such arid surroundings, and this diversity of landscapes and altitudes gives the park tremendous vitality as well as an abundant bird and animal life.

Its icon is the **Breadknife**, a 100-metre (330-ft) spur of vertical rock that towers above the wooded slopes. Those who prefer more demanding walks will find inspiration in the 12-km (7-mile) Breadknife and Grand High Tops walking track, one of the most thrilling walks in the state. For something more gentle, the short Wambelong Walk unwinds from the Canyon Picnic Area through tall she-oaks along the banks of Wambelong Creek, one of the few permanent water sources in the park and a magnet for birds.

The park lies just west of **Coonabarabran**, at the junction of the Newell and Oxley Highways.

The park is at its most spectacular in spring, when wild flowers spread a blush of colour across the hillsides. **Warrambungle National Park Visitor Centre** (30 Timor Street, Coonabarabran; tel: 6842 1311; daily 9am–4pm) has maps and information on camping and park trails.

Cotton country

Park and farmland stretch north to **Narrabri ⓫**, which is at the centre of the country's largest cotton-farming district, and one of the success stories of modern Australian agriculture. On the banks of the Namoi River, the **Australian Cotton Centre** (Newell Highway; tel: 6792 6443; daily 8.30am–4.30pm; admission charge) is the showcase for the cotton industry. From the massive Case IH Express cotton picker to the 3D theatre, the centre uses modern wizardry to tell the story of cotton.

To the east of Narrabri, **Mount Kaputar National Park** is the remnant of volcanoes that erupted around 20 million years ago, weathered over the aeons into a dramatic range of sharp-edged peaks. One-tenth of New South Wales is visible from the 1,511-metre (4,957-ft) eyrie of **Mount Kaputar Lookout**. Most distinctive of the park's formations is **Sawn Rocks**, a conglomeration of basalt columns that resembles titanic organ pipes.

Moree

Much further north (357 km/222 miles) and situated on the Gwydir River, **Moree ⓬** is at the heart of a rich agricultural area. Wheat, pecans and olives are among the crops grown here, and the area is notable as a major cotton producer.

The **Moree Hot Mineral Baths** (Anne Street; tel: 6757 3450; Mon–Fri 6am–8.30pm, Sat–Sun 7am–7pm; admission charge) consists of two artesian pools fed by water at 41.6°C (107°F), although one is cooled slightly during summer. There's also an Olympic pool and two children's pools, and the complex is surrounded by lawns. The popular waters are reputed to relieve rheumatic and arthritic

Map on page 182

At the Australian Cotton Centre, an interactive element encourages visitors to grade cotton, become a genetic engineer, and maximise yield while minimising pesticide use.

BELOW: view of Mount Belougery from the road, Warrambungles National Park.

Moree proudly wears the title "Artesian Spa Capital of Australia". It was already well established in 1895, when farmers searching for underground water for irrigation sunk a bore to a depth of 850 metres (2,800 ft) into the Great Artesian Basin, the water-bearing layer that underlies much of Australia. The water that gushed to the surface had a high mineral content unsuitable for irrigation, but was highly prized for its rejuvenating properties, and the town quickly acquired a reputation as a health resort.

BELOW: at the rodeo, Lightning Ridge.

conditions. Many of the 300,000 people who visit the baths each year are regulars who swear by the therapeutic effects of the water.

Moree is home to a large number of Kamilaroi, the local indigenous population, whose cultural traditions and contemporary artwork are well represented in the **Moree Plains Gallery** (Heber and Frome streets; tel: 6757 3320; Mon–Fri 10am–5pm, Sat 10am–2pm). Housed in a florid Italianate Victorian building that was a bank, the gallery displays the Robert Bleakley collection of Kamilaroi artefacts, a selection of local stone objects and two pairs of traditional "king" plates. In 19th-century Australia, these inscribed neck plates were given to high-ranking Aboriginal men, and sometimes to their wives, to denote status and recognition by the white community. Although individual plates are not uncommon, pairs are rare.

Near Warialda, east of Moree off the Gwydir Highway, is the **Myall Creek Memorial** (Whitlow Road, off the Delungra–Bingara Road), which marks the site of the Myall Creek Massacre of 1838. In an unprovoked attack, 28 Kamilaroi were hacked to death by stockmen seeking revenge for damage to their stock. What makes this event exceptional in Australian history was not the massacre itself but the outcome. Seven men were found guilty of murder and hanged – the only time that Europeans were punished for the murder of Aborigines.

Land of opal

Some distance west of Moree, off the Castlereagh Highway, is **Lightning Ridge** ⓭, which means just one thing – opals. And a very special kind of opal, too. This is one of the world's few reliable sources of black opal, a glossy, luminous gem with flecks of red, green and blue that make the stone radiate an inner fire.

The town takes its name from the ridge of brown ironstone on which it sits. The ironstone attracts lightning, and local legend has it that one luckless shepherd and 600 sheep were killed there during a storm.

Opal was first mined here in the early 1900s, when a miner, who was

Map on page 182

passing through from the opal mines at White Cliffs, was shown some stones by a boundary rider. He recognised what they were and set up a syndicate to mine for opals – although it took several years to convince dealers that the black opals were not completely worthless.

As recently as the 1960s, building materials were in short supply in Lightning Ridge. Bottles were not, however, and the walls of The **Bottle House Museum** (60 Opal Street; tel: 6829 0618; daily 9am–5pm; admission charge) were built entirely from bottles, cemented together with mortar. Originally a private dwelling, it's now a mineral and mining museum.

Some of the town's disused mines can be explored on guided tours underground. Among these is the **Walk in Mine** (Bald Hill; tel: 6829 0473; daily 9am–5pm; admission charge). The mine also has a fossicking site where you can search for opal, and an opal showroom for when you abandon the search.

The **Bore Baths** (Pandora Street; open 24 hours) is a pool fed by an artesian bore flowing at a constant 42°C (108°F). The potassium-enriched water is said to be especially effective for rheumatic and arthritic pains – but at the very least, it's a wonderful soak after a day of dust and digging.

Local artist **John Murray** (8 Opal Street; tel: 6829 1130; daily 9am–5pm) captures the foibles and follies of life, work and play at Lightning Ridge in his photo-realist paintings. Murray draws his inspiration from the birds, animals, vernacular architecture and surreal skyscapes of the Outback in his work, which includes limited edition prints, posters and gift cards as well as acrylic paintings.

Tourism is a major money-spinner for Lightning Ridge. Chances are you'll see more tourists than miners, and there are many home comforts.

Brewarrina

Known as "Bre" to the locals, **Brewarrina ⑭** is a small, sleepy town that owes its existence to the Barwon River. If you come during a dry spell, when the river level falls

Hard labour at Lightning Ridge, one of Australia's most profitable mining towns.

BELOW: cement trucks load up at Lightning Ridge.

Map
on page
182

*The uncluttered
graphic qualities of
much Aboriginal art
make it ideal for
murals on public
and commercial
buildings.*

BELOW: the Barwon
River at Brewarrina.

to a trickle, it seems impossible that
river steamers could once navigate
as far upstream as Brewarrina along
the Barwon River, which becomes
the Darling River southwest of the
town. Off Bathurst Street, the **Old
Bridge** on the Barwon, the town's
original road bridge, was built so
that it could be raised or lowered to
allow steamers to pass below.

In the 1870s this was an important
staging post for Cobb & Co., which
ran stagecoaches through here en
route to Bourke. This coincided with
a growth spurt in Brewarrina, when
a church, a court house and bank
were built. Today its historic buildings and the parks alongside the Barwon make it a pleasant diversion
from the bleached and featureless
landscape of the state's north – but
scarcely worth a long detour.

Brewarrina has a large Aboriginal
population, for whom the region has
special significance. The drystone
Fish Traps that they used for many
thousands of years on the bed of the
Barwon River are the largest of their
kind, and they indicate a sophisticated culture capable of executing

complex engineering works.
Stretching for about ½ km (⅓ mile)
along the river, the fish traps consist
of a series of drystone weirs and
ponds arranged to form a "net"
across the river. Fish swimming
upstream would enter the wide
opening of the pear-shaped pens,
which would then be sealed with
large rocks. The fish would be
forced to swim into the narrow, shallow end of the enclosure where they
could be easily caught.

During the fishing season, neighbouring tribes would come together
for initiation ceremonies and ex-
changes, and early settlers in the
region report several thousand Aborigines at these events. The **Brewarrina Aboriginal Cultural Museum**
(Bathurst and Darling streets; tel:
6839 2868; Mon–Fri 9am–5pm;
admission charge) relates the history
of the local Aboriginal people, from
stories of the creation period when
mythical beings sculpted the landscape, to an intriguing display of the
conditions when they were forced to
live on missions.

Bourke ⓯ is probably better
known for what it represents than
what it is. Few using the expression
"back of Bourke" to mean somewhere impossibly remote will actually have been there. And it's their
loss. This isolated town is another 96
km (60 miles) west of Brewarrina
and sits on the Murray River. The
river was for a long time the town's
lifeline, as paddle steamers under-
took the tortuous journey to the coast
bearing the wool that brought the
area prosperity. The wool now goes
by road, but one of the steamers
remains to provide pleasure cruises.
A major tourist attraction, the A$6
million **Back O' Bourke Exhibition
Centre**, dedicated to all things Outback, is on its way. When that opens,
Henry Lawson's quote may be even
more apposite: "If you know
Bourke, you know Australia." ❏

RESTAURANTS, CAFÉS & BARS

Restaurants

Bathurst

The Crowded House
1 Ribbon Gang Lane
Tel: 6334 2300
Open: B & L Mon-Sat; D Tues-Sat). **$**
www.crowdedhousecafe.com.au
In a converted church school with a lovely enclosed courtyard, the Crowded House claims its "modern Australian food is French based with a Mediterranean influence". Both food and ambience excel.

Bourke

Port o' Bourke Hotel
33 Mitchell Street
Tel: 6872 2544
Open: L & D Mon-Sat. **$**
Well-executed pub food in this friendly old hotel.

Cowra

Neila
5 Kendal Street
Tel: 6341 2188
www.alldaydining.com
Open: D Thur-Sat. **$$$**
A short menu of uncluttered dishes is devoted to local produce. The results are exquisite.

Dubbo

Sticks and Stones
215 Macquarie Street
Tel: 6885 4852
Open: D daily. **$**
Wood-fired pizzas and traditional Italian favourites of a high standard in family friendly environment.

Forbes

Cobb & Co Restaurant
Albion Hotel,
135 Lachlan Street
Tel: 6851 1881
Open: L & D Mon-Sat. **$**
Grab a spot on the balcony, order some dependable pub grub and settle in for the night.

Mudgee

Elton's Brasserie
81 Market Street
Tel: 6372 0772
www.eltons.com.au
Open: B & L daily, D Tues-Sat. **$$**
Elton's appears to have set out to feed Mudgee single-handedly so there are enticing breakfasts from 8am, some deft lunches and then in the evening a choice between simple but effective a la carte dining or pizza from the wood-fired oven. BYO.

Orange

Lolli Redini
48 Sale Street
Tel: 6361 7748
www.lolliredini.com.au
Open: L Fri, D Tues-Sat. **$$$**
The people of Orange are lucky. They can enjoy Mushroom and slow braise veal shin risotto with slivers of local cultivated truffle and parmesan cheese, or its equivalent, on a regular basis, and then finish with a daunting "chocolate nemesis". Superb. The rest of us have to dip in when we can. BYO.

Selkirks
179 Anson Street
Tel: 6361 1179
www.selkirks.com.au
Open: D Tues-Sat & long weekend Sundays. **$$$**
Firmly grounded in well-matched local food and wine, Selkirks serves up some inventive and sophisticated meals in this grand old Federation home.

Cafés and bars

Bathurst

Zieglers
52 Keppel Street
www.bathurstnsw.com/Zieglers
Tel: 6332 1565
Open: B, L & D daily. **$**

The coffee is freshly ground and Italian and Asian influences dominate in the food. BYO.

Lithgow

The Backyard Deli Café
128 Main Street
Tel: 6351 3300
Open: B & L Mon-Fri. **$**
Carefully sourced sumptuous goodies.

Parkes

Cedar Café & Art Gallery
Greenparkes Centre
Tel: 6862 6212
Open: B & L daily. **$**
In a small market, this café stands out for its fine food and service.

PRICE CATEGORIES

Prices for a three-course dinner per person with a half-bottle of house wine:
$ = under A$50
$$ = A$50–A$75
$$$ = over A$75
L = lunch, D = dinner, BYO = bring your own alcohol

RIGHT: into temptation in Bathurst.

CENTRAL COAST AND THE HUNTER VALLEY

North of Sydney you will find picturesque villages and historic industrial towns, beaches, protected forest areas, snow-capped mountains and fertile vineyards where some of the country's finest wines are produced

eginning just north of Sydney and extending 200 km (125 miles) further north, this giant region encompasses sensations as diverse as the boom and hiss of waves on sand, the heady bouquet of a late-harvest Semillon wine and the tinkling sound of a bellbird calling from the forest.

Although the Central Coast falls within Sydney's commuter zone, the region's beaches, National Parks and a straightforward approach from the capital still make it a favourite weekend escape for jaded urbanites.

In early colonial Australia, the rivers along the east coast provided relatively easy access to the interior. This was especially so of the Hunter River, which begins in the Barrington Tops National Park *(see page 209)* and enters the sea at Newcastle, flowing through plains that provided grazing and rich soil for wheat and other crops. Several towns grew up along the river in the 18th century.

The Hunter Valley is also the state's most prestigious wine-growing region, while the area's National Parks provide a treasury of sights, sounds and smells for nature-lovers.

Rising from the edge of the large sea inlet of Brisbane Water, the city of **Gosford ❶** is the bustling commercial heart of the Central Coast. If you stick to the main roads, it's easy to dismiss Gosford and its surroundings as nothing more than suburban sprawl and super-size shopping malls, yet the area also has several lovely beaches and large tracts of pristine forest.

Back to nature

A fine example of the area's natural attractions is **Rumbalara Reserve** (Dolly Avenue, off Springfield Road), which sprawls across the bush-clad hills to the east of Gosford, overlooking **Brisbane Water**.

Map on page 198

LEFT: harvesting grapes at a vineyard in Pokolbin.
BELOW: a man fishing off a jetty, Brisbane Water, Gosford.

The blue-tongued lizard is a type of skink. When cornered it will open its mouth and stick out its tongue to scare away the threat.

BELOW: pelicans at The Entrance.

Named after the indigenous word for "rainbow", the 53-hectare (130-acre) reserve has a number of walking trails, the longest of which is the 5-km (3-mile) walk to **Katandra** (Song of Birds) **Reserve**, which borders Rumbalara to the northeast. Blue-tongued lizards, tree snakes, brush-tailed possum and marsupial mice can be discovered here, and the bird life is prolific.

On the northern side of Gosford is the **Australian Rainforest Sanctuary** (Ourimbah Creek Road, Ourimbah; tel: 4362 1855; Wed–Sun and public holidays 10am–5pm; admission charge; www. australianrainforest.com.au), which sits in a valley surrounded by heavily forested slopes that provide a habitat for almost 200 species of rainforest flora and over 126 native bird species. The ringing sound of bell-birds calling from the forest canopy is particularly appealing.

The sanctuary is a popular attrac-tion, frequently visited by tour buses. However, events such as the bird feeding offer an opportunity for a close-up view of spectacular native bird species that are almost impossible to see any other way. The sanctuary has 5 km (3 miles) of forest trails that make it easy to escape the crowds. At the bottom of the valley is a grassy picnic area, and light refreshments are available.

The beaches

On the peninsula that curls an arm around the eastern shores of Brisbane Water, **Bouddi National Park** has several small, beautiful surf beaches cupped by forests and cliffs. Among the loveliest is Maitland Bay, which is the heart of a marine extension, where all sea life is protected. The trail leading to the beach is rather steep, however – especially when it's time to climb back to the top at the end of a day of lazing in the sun.

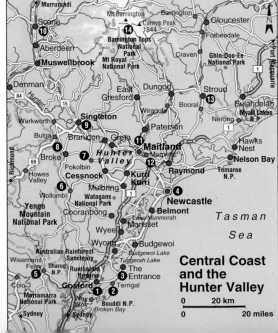

Central Coast and the Hunter Valley

0   20 km
0   20 miles

For an easier journey, you may like to try Little Beach, which is enclosed by a small, rocky bay, popular for surfing and picnics. To reach Bouddi, head east from Gosford towards Erina and turn right onto Avoca Drive. Continue to Kincumber and turn right to Empire Bay Drive. For Little Beach and Maitland Bay, turn left onto the Scenic Road about 300 metres (330 yards) along Empire Bay Drive.

North of Bouddi, at about the mid-point of the Central Coast area, is **Terrigal ❷**, a busy resort town, dominated by a large hotel complex. Terrigal Beach is the southern end of a 4-km (2½-mile) strip of sand that extends north as far as Wamberal, another patrolled beach that is popular with families.

Just over the hill from Terrigal's main shopping area, **The Skillion** is a prominent local landmark, a narrow section of a headland that rises sharply, jutting out into the sea. A ramp-like walking trail along the grassy top of the formation leads to a lookout, from where there are fine views along the coast.

A Central Coast highlight

North of Terrigal the coastline narrows to a strip of land that separates the ocean from **Tuggerah Lake**, a vast, shallow inlet. A natural channel allows water to flow between the lake and the ocean, and on the southern shore of this channel is **The Entrance ❸** (www.theen-trancetcm.com.au), the northern end of the Central Coast holiday towns.

The commercial nucleus of The Entrance is **The Waterfront**, which has open-air cafés and facilities for children. The area is best-known for its huge pelican population, and every day at 3.30pm, the pelicans assemble to be fed – one of the tourism highlights of a visit to the Central Coast. The birds also receive medical attention at these feeding sessions, since fishing hooks and lines are a common hazard. The pelican-feeding takes place at a special ramp known as **Pelican Plaza**, which lies just on the ocean side of the bridge.

Along with Lake Munmorah and Budgewoi Lake, Tuggerah Lake forms an 80-sq. km (30-sq. mile)

Map on page 198

BELOW: the beach with a swimming pool, Newcastle.

Whales and Dolphins

The coast of New South Wales is one of the best places to see whales and dolphins in the wild. Watching a pod of dolphins splashing just beyond the breakers turns a day at the beach into something very special, while the whales' winter migration takes them along the length of the state's coastline. Over the past few years, stray whales have spent several days in Sydney Harbour, to the delight of ferry passengers.

The most common whales are humpbacks, which travel north along the coast from about May, heading north into the warm waters off the Queensland coast and returning south between September and November. Other species that are sighted less frequently include southern right whales, false killer whales, orcas, minke and, very occasionally, blue whales, the biggest creatures on the planet.

All the major holiday towns along the coast offer whale- and dolphin-watch cruises. Whale tours at Eden, deep on the state's south coast, have a fascinating edge to them, a little like visiting the scene of a crime with the criminal who did the deed. Until the 1930s, this was a whaling station, and the various species of whales were hunted in a gruesome alliance between killer whales and whaling boats. Eden was one of the first towns in the state to develop a whale-watching industry, and its whaling history, the depth of knowledge that these operators bring to their task and their obvious affection for "their" whales make this more than just a wildlife tour.

A two-hour drive south of Sydney, Jervis Bay has a pod of resident dolphins, and the relatively placid waters of the bay make this a prime viewing spot. To the north of Sydney, Port Stephens, Coffs Harbour and Byron Bay all have whale- and dolphin-watch cruises.

Unlike the fast, acrobatic dolphins that never seem to idle for long, whales move slowly. On a whale-watch trip, the vessel will probably venture out into the open sea, where it will spend a good deal of time stopped and pitching in the waves while watching the whales. For anyone who suffers from motion sickness, this is not an ideal situation. If you start feeling queasy when you're out at sea, it's already too late to do much about it. If you are subject to seasickness, take medication before you set foot on the boat.

An excursion is a mixture of competitive anticipation, as children and adults alike vie to be the first to catch a glimpse of the quarry. Vessels are not allowed to approach a whale closer than 100 metres (330 ft). Whales are curious creatures and they will often swim closer to a stationary vessel, but you can't count on a close-up look, and larger vessels with an upper deck will usually give you a better vantage point. The best place to stand is usually forward of the bridge.

Much of the action takes place below the water, and out of sight if you're standing on the deck of a boat, but if the vessel is properly equipped you can tune in to what's happening below. Whales and dolphins communicate via high-pitched squeaks and whistles. Whales, in particular, are known for their "songs", and the humpback is one of the most vocal of all the whales. If your vessel has a hydrophone, an underwater microphone, you can listen to them "talking" over the public-address system. ❏

LEFT: two bottlenose dolphins leap out of the water.

inland waterway popular for fishing, boating sailing and sailboarding. Families prefer its beaches since the shallow, sheltered waters offer safe swimming for children, but they're often crowded, and the lake water is less bracing than the open sea.

An industrial centre

About an hour's drive north of Tuggerah is **Newcastle** ❹, the state's second-largest city and a brawny, no-nonsense place that has developed as a major industrial centre. Located around the mouth of the Hunter River, the city was founded to exploit the coal reserves that lay upriver.

Australia's first export was a load of Hunter River coal, sent to Bengal in 1799. In 1801 a convict camp was established at the mouth of the river, and this was soon expanded to harvest the timber found along the branching tributaries of the Hunter. The first school in Australia was built here, in 1816, followed by a gaol and a hospital, although none of the buildings survive from this early period.

Throughout the 19th century the city flourished as a coal producer, port and railhead. At the beginning of the 20th century, Newcastle added steelmaking to its industrial repertoire when BHP, as it was known at the time, opened a refinery. By the late 1990s, the company had begun to shut down its Newcastle operations, and today, the city's heady steel days are over. It remains an important coal port, however, as well as a manufacturing centre, due to the skills developed during its days as an industrial powerhouse.

The Sydney–Newcastle Freeway approaches Newcastle to the west and joins with the Pacific Highway to bypass the city. If you want to have a closer look around, take the Newcastle Link Road, which fuses with Hunter Street to take you along the waterfront, past the city centre and to **Fort Scratchley**, built on the headland that guards the southern jawbone of Newcastle Harbour.

The rocky knoll on which Fort Scratchley sits was handed to the military in 1843, but it was not until

Map on page 198

The centre of Newcastle is a mixture of distinguished civic buildings and more mundane commercial blocks.

BELOW: fishing in the Hunter River estuary, with Newcastle's industrial powerhouse in the background.

the 1880s that the site was fortified, prompted by fears of Russian expansionism. The fort had its finest hour in 1942, when the city came under attack from a Japanese submarine, and the guns of the fort answered with the only shots fired at an enemy vessel from Australia's mainland. By 1972 the fort was transformed into the **Newcastle Region Maritime and Military Museum** (tel: 4929 3066; noon–4pm weekends and holidays; admission charge).

From the foot of Fort Scratchley, a tapering finger juts out into the sea to end at the lighthouse on **Nobby's Head**. The promontory is man-made, but coal was originally mined here by convict labour, on what was then a small, rocky island. It is a pleasant walk along the promontory past the lighthouse and to the end of the breakwater, which has views along Stockton Beach, which disappears in the distance toward Port Stephens.

Not far from the northern break-water, visible just off the beach, is the wreck of the *Sygna*, which ran

The huge, ornate Kurri Kurri Hotel is testament to the town's affluence in the days when it was one of the biggest mining towns in the area. Kurri Kurri is 47 km (29 miles) inland from Newcastle.

BELOW: take a seat at Nobby's Beach.

aground here in 1974. Away from the ocean about ½ km (⅓ mile) along Hunter Street, **Queen's Wharf** has a marina ringed by restaurants, shops and a boutique brewery. This is a popular spot for an evening drink or a meal, especially on sunny weekends. From the ferry wharf you can make a short trip across the harbour to the northern suburb of Stockton.

The western route

If you are not taking the main route to Newcastle from the south, consider taking the winding, picturesque road through the sleepy village of **Wisemans Ferry 5**. It stands west of Gosford on the banks of the Hawkesbury River and takes its name from Solomon Wiseman, a convict settler who was granted land in this area.

Wiseman not only lived up to his name, he was shrewd as well. When the government decided to build a road north from Sydney, it was he who persuaded the surveyors that the best route was through his land. He also won the contract to supply

provisions to the convict gangs building the road, as well as the licence to operate the ferry. On a hillside overlooking his estate, Wiseman built a grand manor house, Cabham Hall, which survives as **Wisemans Inn Hotel**.

These days, it's a slightly tortuous route from Sydney to Wisemans Ferry, but worth considering if you're travelling to the Hunter Valley and looking for an alternative to the freeway. If you take the vehicular ferry north across the Hawkesbury, Wiseman's Ferry Road will lead you on a meandering journey through rugged bushland along the north bank of the river and then to Central Mangrove. From here you can simply rejoin the Sydney–Newcastle Freeway or continue to Wollombi.

At Bucketty, just south of Wollombi, this road joins with the old Great North Road, which was built by convict labour between 1825 and 1836. For many years, the 240-km (150-mile) track between Sydney and the Hunter Valley was the only road running north from Sydney. In several sections of the road, you can see good examples of convict-built walling underpinning the road.

Aboriginal meeting place

The Aboriginal word for "meeting of the waters" provides the name for the village of **Wollombi** ❻, the back door to the Hunter Valley. Located at the intersection of narrow, wooded valleys between the Hawkesbury and Hunter river systems, this was also a meeting place for local Aboriginal people, and more than 100 significant Aboriginal sites have been identified close to the village.

Towards the middle of the 18th century Wollombi became the centre of a farming community as well as a stop for coaches travelling from Sydney along the Great North Road, and a number of the town's buildings date from this period. When the village was bypassed by the more easterly highway, Wollombi fell into a slumber, and its inns, its blacksmith's shops and wheelwrights were left to succumb gently to the passage of time.

Today the village is at least half

Map on page 198

Newcastle's working-class roots have given it a great pub culture, and some of Australia's best-known rock bands have made their start in the pubs around town. (see page 281 for listings).

BELOW: a view over the Hawkesbury River and valley, near Wisemans Ferry.

awake most of the time, the focus of a small but passionate community composed largely of urban refugees who value the village's authentic character, and the isolation that the bush-covered hillsides provide. Wollombi's notable buildings include the school, the post office, St Michael's Catholic Church and the general store.

Buried in the cemetery opposite the school are several veterans of the Napoleonic Wars, who were granted 40-hectare (100-acre) lots here from about 1830 after they were discharged from New South Wales regiments. Social life revolves around the bar at the **Wollombi Tavern**, one of Australia's oldest country pubs and home of the well-known Doctor Jurd's Jungle Juice, which is perhaps an acquired taste.

The Hunter Valley

Further north, **Pokolbin** ❼ is the largest and most important of the six sub-regions that make up the Hunter Valley wine-growing area, and while the entire region accounts for less than 2 percent of Australia's total wine crush, the quality of its wines is beyond question.

This is one of the hottest of Australia's wine-growing regions, with high humidity and the likelihood of late summer rains at vintage time, yet the Hunter consistently produces white wines of remarkable finesse and longevity.

The Hunter's traditional strengths are Semillon and Shiraz wines, which sometimes carry a "hermitage" label. The region also produces excellent wines from Chardonnay grapes. This is the oldest wine-growing area in the country; by 1823, about 8 hectares (20 acres) of vineyards had been established on the north bank of the Hunter River. By 1840 that figure had increased to more than 200 hectares (500 acres), although it was not until the 1860s that wine grapes were grown in the Lower Hunter, in and around Pokolbin.

The Lower Hunter wineries are concentrated on low, gently rolling country that lies in the shadow of the Brokenback Mountain Range. Although this is referred to as the

BELOW: Hunter Valley wine country.

Map on page 198

Pokolbin area, in fact Pokolbin itself is little more than a tiny shopping centre rather than a true township.

How to taste wine

Any tour of the region should begin at the **Vintage Hunter Wine and Visitors Centre** (455 Wine Country Drive, Pokolbin; tel: 4990 0900; Mon Sat 9am–5pm, Sun 9am–4pm). This impressive facility includes a visitor information centre, The Hunter Valley Wine Society, The Wine Country Café and a Wine Interpretive Centre. This is a great place to pick up information and maps, and for anyone with limited time, the Wine Society showroom allows you to taste a few wines from one of the region's vineyards.

Although wine tasting might seem like a daunting business, with its sniffing and slurping and talk of passion-fruit aromas and vanilla flavours, all you really need is a set of taste buds.

When you visit a winery you'll be asked which wines you prefer and offered a sample, usually starting with the lighter wines followed by the more full-blooded styles. The idea is to approach the wine slowly and delicately with a sniff to get the aromas, then hold the wine in your mouth without swallowing to allow your palate to absorb the sensations.

Remember that a wine might taste quite different when paired with food – and it takes experience before you can successfully judge a wine from a stand up tasting room session, especially when you'll be sampling several. The sample is only a mouthful, but to avoid total inebriation, it's perfectly acceptable to taste and spit.

Some wineries charge a small fee to cover the cost of tasting, which is then refunded if you buy. If in doubt, take a wine tour and you'll get a few tips from an expert.

There are about 70 wineries in the Lower Hunter, and more than half of these are in the Pokolbin area, most of them open for cellar-door sales. While the prestige labels of the leading winemakers are essential to any tour of the region, no trip to Pokolbin is complete without visiting some of the smaller boutique winemakers.

In many cases, the limited-edition wines they produce are never seen on the shelves of shops. The only way to sample these wines is by visiting the winery, where you may purchase your bottle from the winemaker who has tended the vines, picked and crushed the grapes, fretted over the fermentation, inserted the corks and stuck the labels on the bottles.

On the tourist trail

Although it depends on wine for its living, the Pokolbin region is more a wine showcase than a serious producer. For many years now, it has gained more income from tourism than from the grape. However, this does not diminish the quality of the product, and it does mean

Most wineries now make a small charge for tasting sessions.

BELOW: no trip is complete without a visit to a winery.

that the area is superbly equipped with accommodation, dining and recreation options, from cycle wine tours to hot-air balloon flights.

Broke

The quaint village of **Broke** ❽ was settled as far back as 1824, and subsequently became an important staging point on the overland cattle route between the Hunter and Sydney. Located 30 km (20 miles) north of Wollombi on the eastern bank of the Wollombi Brook, Broke has become the hub of an emerging wine-growing area – the Broke–Fordwich sub-region. This is one of the few remaining areas within Hunter Valley suitable for vineyard estate expansion. The area planted to vines has increased since the early 1990s, and there are now about 50 vineyards producing grapes for about 30 wine labels, some 15 of which are open for cellar-door sales.

Tranquil, rusticated and set against the dramatic backdrop of the Yellow Rock escarpment, Broke attracts only a fraction of the numbers who visit the Pokolbin region. The township has several cafés and restaurants, and shops selling local produce.

Broke is also the centre of an industry that may eventually rival wine production in economic value. Since 2000, tens of thousands of olive trees have been planted in irrigated groves along Wollombi Brook. Wollombi Road, which joins Broke with Wollombi, is highly recommended for those people who prefer their journeys slow and scenic and don't mind a few bumps along the way.

Coal country

From Broke you need to head 24 km (15 miles) north to **Singleton** ❾, the heart of the Hunter Valley coal-mining region, which produces slightly less than half the state's coal. From whichever direction you approach the town, it's impossible to miss the huge, open-cut mines – some of the deepest mining pits in the country. Coal earns more for Australia than any other export. New South Wales and Queensland are the only significant coal produc-

BELOW: a train transports coal at sunset, Maitland.
RIGHT: the end of another shift on the coal face.

ers, and although NSW produces slightly less than its northern neighbour, it has much larger reserves.

This is also the state's largest export industry, as well as the major source of fuel for electricity generation. About three-quarters of the state's coal is shipped overseas from the port of Newcastle *(see page 201)*, mainly to Japan and China. Two large coal-fired power stations are located close to Singleton, easily identified by their chimneys and cooling towers.

The town sprang to life in the 1830s as the centre of a grazing and agricultural region dominated by large estates granted to men of substantial means who used convict labour to improve their properties. These days it's a brisk and businesslike town, underpinned by the mining industry.

Most of Singleton's historic buildings lie along George Street, but this is also the New England Highway, and the subtle delights of the **Royal Hotel** (1859), the **Caledonian Hotel** (1859) and the original **Post Office** (1878) are compromised by the semi-

trailers that thunder past. The town claims to have the world's largest sundial, as do Carefree in Arizona and Lloydminister in Alberta, but don't be deceived – it's Jaipur in India that gets the gold medal.

Horse capital

Travelling north along the highway for 73 km (45 miles) you will reach **Scone ⑩** (rhymes with cone). Set in a pretty valley enclosed by hills to the east and west, it subtitles itself "The Horse Capital of Australia", and the 65 well-tended horse studs that surround it give the town a faintly patrician flavour.

The region's thoroughbred industry is said to be second only to Kentucky, USA, in size and value, and several well-monied international racing syndicates maintain stables here, including some from the Middle East. The town of Scone itself is unremarkable; in fact it's the surroundings rather than the town that provide the appeal. However, if you happen to pass through in mid-May, during the 14-day Scone Horse Festival, a stop is worthwhile.

Map on page 198

BELOW: Segenhoe Stud Farm, Scone.

A broom maker at work in historic Morpeth village.

BELOW: Grossman House, Maitland.

Historic Maitland

You need to return now along the New England Highway to the historic city of **Maitland** . Early in the 19th century this was the commercial centre of the prosperous Hunter River agricultural area, and for a while, Australia's largest inland town. Later it was outpaced by Newcastle *(see page 201)*, but not before a number of fine sandstone buildings were erected.

Its main thoroughfare, **High Street**, was originally a bullock track. The buildings simply grew up alongside the track, and you'll notice the narrowness of the street if you drive along it. Several of the historic buildings in High Street are submerged beneath neon signs and unsympathetic commercial frontages, but the city still has an attractive historic quarter in Church Street.

Grossmann House (Church Street; tel: 4933 6452; Thur–Sun 10am–3pm; admission charge; www. nsw.nationaltrust.org.au) is one of a matched pair of Victorian Regency mansions that was built for prosperous business partners. The house is maintained by the National Trust in all its Victorian splendour, with an extensive collection of 19th-century costumes and textiles.

Diagonally opposite, the Victorian Gothic spire of **St Mary the Virgin Anglican Church** dominates the city's skyline, while the rectory next door is a fine example of Victorian Italianate architecture; the grounds are at their best when the roses are in bloom.

High Street becomes the Heritage Mall, a pedestrian plaza that runs through the heart of Maitland, but it offers no glimpses of the Hunter River, which flows a few metres away. Diagonally opposite the post office at the start of the mall, a passageway leads to the river, and a paved walkway has information panels that sketch the story of Maitland's river trade. Another walkway leads back to the mall, past Lavender's Riverside Café, which is shaded by an enormous camphor laurel tree.

Morpeth

Further upstream along the Hunter and just a short drive from Maitland,

the town of **Morpeth**  was once an important inland trading post for the Hunter River Steam Navigation Company. The river trade was effectively over by about 1890, but the town's comparative isolation meant that its historic shopfronts, wharves and even the hitching posts along the main street have survived intact.

Today Morpeth is no longer a backwater, but a town crammed with cafés and craft shops where you can purchase a quilt, handmade soap or even a set of Peruvian wind chimes. There are no outstanding buildings to speak of, but Morpeth's character can be easily absorbed in a stroll along the main street. Avoid the weekend crowds, if you can.

To the northeast on Bucketts Way is **Stroud**, a town whose appeal is almost indefinable, yet it's well worth detouring to visit this small and serene village marinated in the green fastness of the Karuah Valley.

The region was originally settled as part of a land grant of 200,000 hectares (500,000 acres) made to the Australian Agricultural Company (AAC), which was established to provide fine wool and crops to England using convict labour. The AAC, Australia's oldest agricultural company, exists to this day, and its landholding has swollen to a massive 7.9 million hectares (20 million acres) – one percent of Australia's land mass.

Classified in its entirety by the National Trust, the town has some fine examples of domestic colonial architecture. The local tourist information office (Stroud Newsagency, Cowper Street; tel: 4994 5117; daily 9am–5pm) has a brochure with a self-guided historic walking tour of 32 sites in the town.

Barrington Tops

Fifty km (31 miles) north of Stroud is the town of **Gloucester**, standing at the edge of **Barrington Tops National Park**, which is administered by the National Parks and Wildlife Service (59 Church Street, Gloucester; tel: 6558 1408; daily 9am–5pm). The park, best visited between October and April, comprises a vast, undulating, basalt-capped plateau that rises sharply

Map on page 198

BELOW: cascades in the rainforest, Barrington Tops National Park.

Park life

With more than 600 National Parks or nature reserves in the state under the aegis of the NSW National Parks and Wildlife Service, you won't find it difficult to find a patch of accessible nature. At just 44 of them you will have to pay a daily entry fee for your vehicle and, with five exceptions, that fee is in single figures. Everywhere else you're free to come and go as you please. Where there is a fee it's sometimes a matter of purchasing a "pay and display" ticket, so make sure you have plenty of coins on you. For full information on any or all of the parks, visit: www.national parks.nsw.gov.au.

from the surrounding valleys to a height of almost 1,600 metres (5,250 ft) – a world of gushing streams, waterfalls, frosted forests and soaring cliffs.

In stark contrast to the mild, Mediterranean climate of the coast a few kilometres away, "The Tops", as it is known, has a cool, wet climate. Winter snowfalls are common at higher altitudes, and annual rainfall is on average 140 cm (55 inches). This rain collects in peat bogs on the top of the plateau, providing a habitat for several species of waterfowl and a constant flow of water to feed the Manning, Hunter, Barrington and Gloucester rivers. Racing away from the plateau, these streams fall sharply – as much as 1,000 metres in 13 km (3,300 ft in 8 miles) – and to the south, east and west, the sides of the plateau are deeply indented with gorges, rapids and waterfalls.

This varied terrain also gives Barrington Tops a diverse plant and animal life, from alpine wild flowers that thrive on the wet, chilly heights to subtropical species found in the lowland gullies. The icon for the National Park is the moss-bearded Antarctic beech, often shrouded in a veil of mist, adding a moody atmosphere to the landscape.

In its higher altitudes Barrington Tops is dominated by snow gums interspersed with towering mountain gums. Extensive tracts of subtropical rainforest cover the lower regions, where thick vines snake down from the dense canopy that all but shuts out the light.

Rare species

The Tops is home to several plant species found nowhere else on the planet, such as the donkey orchid, which occurs abundantly at 1,500 metres (5,000 ft), and a species of native pepper tree which grows on the fringes of the high swamps.

More than 220 bird species have been recorded, while the list of mammals includes wombats, grey kangaroos, red-necked wallabies and dingoes, although the most abundant are the shy, nocturnal species (quolls, potoroos and pademelons) that are rarely seen by visitors.

"Posties" don't usually deliver to the door, so each property has its stand-alone mail box, some more extravagant than others.

BELOW: forest along the banks of Williams River, Barrington Tops.

Its unique topography, its diversity, its natural beauty and the presence of rare animal species endemic to the area have won the National Park a coveted place on UNESCO's World Heritage list.

Barrington Tops is perfectly equipped for invigorating outdoor pursuits. The chilly streams that gush down from the plateau offer excellent trout fishing, for which an inland fishing licence is required. Some of the park's most captivating scenery is accessible via its four-wheel-drive trails. Horse trekking is popular in the areas bordering the boundaries of the park, particularly in the magnificent countryside around Gloucester, but by far the main visitor activity is bush-walking.

Bush-walking territory

The two main areas for walking are on the southern and eastern flanks of the plateau, both accessible by road. From the south, the easiest approach is via Dungog and then along Salisbury Road, which climbs past Barrington Guest House into the southern outskirts of the park

and ends at the small Lagoon Pinch picnic area at an elevation of 700 metres (2,300 ft).

Access to the eastern side is via Gloucester Tops Road, which branches off Bucketts Way, the road linking Gloucester to Stroud, about 10 km (6 miles) south of Gloucester. Beyond the Gloucester River Camping Area, which is 30 km (20 miles) from the turn-off, a network of walking trails fan out towards the plateau.

The one-hour **Gloucester Falls** Walk leads through subalpine woodland and Antarctic beech to a lookout above the spectacular falls. The five-hour Barrington Tops Walk is the finest of the park's one-day walks, winding across a subalpine plateau through frost hollows, swamps, bogs and woodlands to the 1,544-metre (5,065-ft) summit of **Careys Peak**.

The Gloucester-Stroud region is home to several guesthouses and self-catering cottages, located in mellow, rolling countryside surrounded by some of the loveliest river valleys in the state. ❑

Map on page 198

In New South Wales many towns have a cinema with at least one screen showing the latest releases. Some are worth visiting for their heritage as well as entertainment value, with the National Trust launching a campaign in recent years to try to preserve them for future generations of cinema-goers. Included in its list was Dungog Cinema (6 Brown Street, Dungog; tel: 4992 1191).

BELOW: scenery on the Central Coast.

RESTAURANTS, CAFÉS, PUBS & BARS

Restaurants

The Entrance

Flair
Shop 1, 488 The Entrance
Road, Erina Heights
Tel: 4365 2777
Open: L Wed-Fri,
D Tues-Sat. **$$**
Seek this out and be
blown away by deft
Mod Oz juxtapostions of
premium local produce.
BYO.

Entrance Hotel LP
87 The Entrance Road
Tel: 4332 2001
Open: L &D daily. **$**
A beer garden and terrific
views over the channel
augment the usual range
of bistro dishes.

Gosford

Cafe Sicilian
131 Henry Parry Drive
Tel: 4322 0434
Open: B, L & D Tues-Sat. **$$**
A popular Italian restau-
rant with an especially
busy weekend trade and
live band. Gets noisy.
Even the owners sing
when the trade is particularly healthy. Book ahead.

PRICE CATEGORIES

Prices for a three-course
dinner per person with a
half-bottle of house wine:
$ = under A$50
$$ = A$50–A$75
$$$ = over A$75
L = lunch, D = dinner, BYO
= bring your own alcohol

Maitland

**The Old George and
Dragon**
48 Melbourne Street, East
Maitland
Tel: 4933 7272
www.oldgeorgeanddragon.com.au
Open: D Wed-Sat. **$$$**
The antidote to all the
architect-designed win-
ery restaurants, this is
where sumptuousness
Victorian furnishings and
hangings assert them-
selves. The menu pays
more than a nod to tradi-
tion as well with plenty of
rich sauces. High quality
wine list too.

Newcastle

The Brewery
The Boardwalk, 1 Honey-
suckle Drive
Tel: 4929 5792
Open: L daily, D Mon-Sat. **$$**
Down by the harbour in a
decidedly sleek modern
building, here you'll find
some of Newcastle's
sharpest cooking
matched with the
coolest local wines.

Café Supply
Corner Watt & King Streets
Tel: 4929 2222
Open: B & L daily,
D Tues-Sat. **$$**
A dowdy old bank has
been transformed
into an exciting contem-
porary meeting and eat-
ing place. From the
vanilla risotto at break-
fast, there's invention
and promise on the

menu. Fortunately the
chefs are up to it. BYO.

Longbench on Darby
161 Darby Street, Cooks Hill
Tel: 4927 8888
Open: B, L & D daily. **$$**
Busy right through the
day, and the mixture of
staples with more innov-
ative fare demonstrates
why. BYO.

Pokolbin

Esca Bimbadgen
790 Mc Donalds Road
Tel: 4998 4666
www.bimbadgen.com.au
Open: L daily. **$$$**
Another dramatic modern
dining room with vineyard
views. This one shows
off the work of
Bradley Teale, who excels
in the contemporary mix-
ing and matching of hith-
erto disparate elements.

Roberts
Halls Road
Tel: 4998 7330
www.robertsrestaurant.com
Open: L & D daily. **$$$**
Robert Molines' menu
changes daily and
makes the most of the
freshest regional ingredients. The outcome is
richly satisfying food with
a European slant.

Terroir
Hungerford Hill Winery,
1 Broke Road
Tel: 4990 0711
www.hungerfordhill.com.au
Open: L daily, D Wed-Sat.
$$$

Much more than just a
vehicle to promote the
wines, award-winning
Terroir is a destination
restaurant where chef
Darren Ho works with real
flair and invention. How
about lamb's brains
crumbed in panko and
black sesame seeds and
fried, served with rhubarb
and chinese black vinegar
relish.

Scone

Quince
109 Susan Street
Tel: 6545 2286
Open: B Sun, L Thur-Sun,
D Thur-Sat. **$$**
Gourmands should be
flocking to this old con-
verted cottage where the
food is finely detailed
and sophisticated.

Singleton

Henri's Brasserie
Level 1, 85 John Street
Tel: 6571 3566
www.henris.com.au
Open: D Mon-Sat. **$$**
A good reason to visit
Singleton is an evening
at Henri's enjoying
seared scallops with
crispy prosciutto and
pumpkin sauce or one
of the devastating
desserts.

Stroud

Stroud Central Hotel
52 Cowper Street
Tel: 4994 5197
Open: L & D daily. **$**
Standard bistro meals in
Stroud's social hub.

Terrigal

Dekk
3-5 Kurrawyba Avenue
Tel: 4385 3100
www.dekk.com.au
Open: L & D daily. **$$$**
Trendy ambience and
modern dining displaying
real attention to detail.

The Reef
The Haven
Tel: 4385 3222
www.reefrestaurant.com.au
Open: L daily, D Mon-Sat.
$$$
Relaxed, spacious
restaurant offering the
best view in the area and
food to match. Heavy
emphasis on fresh
seafood prepared with
imaginative contempo-
rary counterpoints.

Wisemans Ferry

Wisemans Ferry Inn
Old Northern Road
Tel: 4566 4301
Open: L & D daily. **$**
Basic bistro meals are
about all you can find in
this settlement.

Cafés, pubs & bars

Gloucester

Perenti Catering
69 Church Street
Tel: 6558 9219
Open: B & L daily. **$**
A whole range of home-
baked quiches and
cakes make this modern
cafe pretty special. BYO.

Gosford

Caffe Jam
Shop 4, 103 Victoria Street,

East Gosford
Tel: 4324 8708
Open: L daily. **$**
Light meals of real dis-
tinction and some rather
wonderful cakes, not to
mention the coffee,
justifiably make this a
favourite haunt among
locals.

Newcastle

Beach Hotel
Corner of Frederick and
Ridge Streets, Merewether
Tel: 4963 1574
Open: L & D daily. **$**
Choose between the
Aqua Bar and Grill or
Eats on the Beach, the
latter being a little more
informal although
there's not much in it.
Otherwise just down a
beer on the terrace over-
looking the sea.

Crown & Anchor
Corner of Hunter and
Perkins Streets
Tel: 4929 1027
Open: L & D daily. **$**
In this spruced up pub
there are the usual bars
and enclaves down-
stairs. Frostbites!
upstairs is a cocktail bar
for clubbers .

Harry's Cafe de Wheels
Wharf Road
Open: B, L & D daily. **$**
Essentially a cart, but in
their own words, "an
Australian icon serving
pies, pasties and hot
dogs to celebrities,
tourists and locals". In
our words, they are
rather good at it.

The Kent
59-61 Beaumont Street,
Hamilton
Tel: 4961 3303
Open: L & D daily. **$**
If our bars, a brasserie, a
beer garden and space
for live music all make
the Kent one of the most
popular pubs in town.

Lime
52 Glebe Road, The Junction
Tel: 4969 2060
Open: B, L & D daily. **$$**
It's all-day opening and
rewarding snacks place
Lime in the cafe section,
but some of the meals
being produced with
inspiring adventurous-
ness make it worthy of
promotion to the restau-
rant section.

Pokolbin

Beltree @ Margan
266 Hermitage Road
Tel: 6574 7216
www.margan.com.au/cafebeltree.htm

Open: L Fri-Mon, D Sat. **$**
Order a platter or two
and share it with friends,
or just make the most of
the deck with a coffee
and cake. BYO.

Toby's Coffee House
Rothbury Estate, Broke Road
Tel: 4998 7363
www.therothburyestate.com
Open: L daily. **$**
Coffees and cakes are
supplemented at
lunchtime by cheese and
meat platters to enjoy
with wines from the
Rothbury estate.

Scone

Kerv Espresso Bar
108 Liverpool Street
Tel: 6545 3111
Open: L daily. **$**
Buy your home and
kitchen wares as you
tuck into rather good
snacks and lunches in
this trendy café-cum-
shop.

RIGHT: choose one of the daily specials.

HUNTER VALLEY WINES

The Hunter Valley, while by no means the best wine-growing area in Australia, is the most popular with visitors

Were you searching for somewhere to start growing grapes for wine today, you would not choose the Hunter Valley. The soil is all wrong, and the climate is unpredictable, with the wrong combination of heat and rainfall. (The rainfall is there, it just comes during the wrong seasons.) And yet wines have been produced here since the mid 19th century. In the Upper Hunter Valley Chardonnay and Semillon thrive, while in the Lower Hunter it is the red varieties that do well. There are few out-and-out classics as yet but Rosemount is getting close in the Upper Hunter, and there are enough reliable and interesting wines being produced across the region to sustain a strong market in wine tourism. Indeed, tourism in the Lower Hunter Valley is as important to the local economy as anything produced by the viticulturalists. So do your bit to help and start ticking off the tasting rooms. In a crowded market you could do worse than take a look at Brokenwood, Pepper Tree, Tyrrell's, Tower Estate and Lake's Folly.

ABOVE: pretty commercial. While vineyards stretching out across rolling hills look attractive and draw the tourists, the vines still have to be productive and the grapes need to be processed on an industrial scale, preferably in buildings that aren't going to blight the landscape **(BELOW)**.

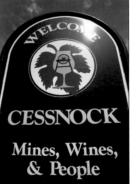

WELCOME

CESSNOCK

Mines, Wines, & People

BELOW: are predatory birds to be shocked by the larger than life figure, or the fact that it's rattling beer cans in an area supposedly devoted to the finer subtleties of wine making?

ABOVE: as mining has diminished as Cessnock's economic driving force, the town – the largest in the area – has hitched its wagon to wine tourism and offers itself as a cheaper base for exploration than some of the exclusive "boutique" (apparently another word for expensive) establishments that pepper the Hunter Valley.

OTHER NSW WINE AREAS

While the Hunter Valley has the highest profile of New South Wales' wine-growing areas, there is considerable activity elsewhere in the state, not least in the Riverina area in the south, on the plains to the west of the Great Dividing Range. Centred on Griffith, it's the biggest producing area by volume, with well over 100,000 tonnes of grapes picked annually. Here and further west in the Murray Darling basin, the river systems are used to irrigate vast areas of vines and traditionally the emphasis has been solely on quantity. However, as snobbery about irrigated wines has diminished and the wine makers have refined their techniques, the quality has risen markedly across all the area's varieties: Chardonnay, Cabernet Sauvignon, Shiraz and Merlot. Many of the big names, such as Rosemount, Lindemans, Jacob's Creek and Yellow Tail, produce reliable favourites here. De Bortoli, meanwhile, has been developing some fabulous sweet wines, or "stickies" as they are known to the locals.

BELOW: the Hunter Valley is within easy travelling distance of Sydney and Newcastle and has rapidly become a prime weekend destination, with many establishments pitched at the well-heeled, child-free, romantic couples in need of some pampering.

ABOVE: Pokolbin's claim to be the capital of Hunter Valley wine country is bolstered by the presence there of the Hunter Valley Wine Country Visitor Information Centre.

RIGHT: the difficulty is not getting there but knowing where to start the tasting.

NEW ENGLAND

Sheep and sapphires were the mainstays of New England's economy in the 19th century. Today, visitors enjoy the untamed beauty, and the lovingly preserved historic towns. Country music fans think it's worth a visit for the Tamworth Festival

Sydney

L ying west of the Great Dividing Range in the state's north, New England is a high, undulating plateau that makes its living from some of Australia's richest sheep and cattle country. Settlement began in the 1830s, relatively soon after European incursion, and although gold provided some of the impetus for development, it was the well-watered pasturelands that became its mainstay. Scots were prominent among the early settlers, and the region honours its Celtic roots with place names, festivals and a fondness for bagpipes.

At the eastern end of the region, spreading across the ranges that form the edge of the escarpment, is a mosaic of National Parks that are part of the Central Eastern Rainforest Reserves, one of Australia's World Heritage areas. Tracks that wind through spongy rainforests, towering granite tors, wilderness views and the highest waterfalls in the state are all good reasons to put on walking shoes.

Gemstones are another speciality of the region. New England is the world's major source of sapphires, and anyone is welcome to search for the blue gems by panning in the creek and river beds. There is even a touring route, The Fossickers' Way, devoted to this fiery stone. It

begins at Nundle, southeast of Tamworth, runs north to Warialda and turns east to Glen Innes.

New England Highway

The main route through the region is the New England Highway, which has its southern end on the outskirts of Newcastle, linking with the Sydney–Newcastle Freeway. Between Sydney and Brisbane, the New England Highway is just 30 km (18 miles) longer than the Pacific Highway, which makes it a viable

Map on page 218

LEFT: Bald Rock at sunrise.
BELOW: historic hotel in Armidale.

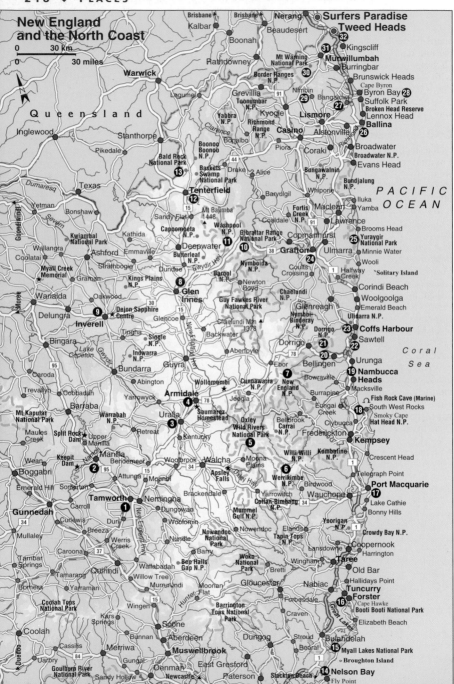

New England and the North Coast

Queensland

PACIFIC OCEAN

Coral Sea

0   30 km
0   30 miles

Brisbane · Brisbane · Nerang · Surfers Paradise Tweed Heads
Kalbar · Beaudesert · ③②
Boonah · ③① Kingscliff
Rathdowney · Mt Warning National Park · Murwillumbah · Burringbar
Warwick · Border Ranges N.P. · ③⓪ · Brunswick Heads
Legume · Grevillia · Nimbin · ②⑨ Bangalow · Cape Byron · Byron Bay ②⑧
Toonumbar N.P. · Yabbra N.P. · Kyogle · ②⑦ · Suffolk Park
Stanthorpe · Richmond Range N.P. · Lismore · Broken Head Reserve · Lennox Head
Inglewood · Bonalbo · Casino · Alstonville · Ballina ②⑥
Pikedale · Bald Rock National Park · ⑬ · Piora · Coraki · Broadwater
Texas · Baskets Swamp National Park · Drake · Alice · Bungawalnin N.P. · Broadwater N.P. · Evans Head
Dumaresq · Bonshaw · ⑫ Tenterfield · Baryulgil · Whiporie · Bundjalung N.P. · Iluka
Yetman · Mt Balimba 1448 · Washpool N.P. · Coaldale · Fortis Creek N.P. · Maclean · Yamba
Sandy Flat · Capoompeta N.P. · ⑪ · Gibraltar Range National Park · Copmanhurst · Lawrence · Brooms Head
Kwiambal National Park · Kathida · Deepwater · ⑩ · ②⑤ Yuraygir National Park
Ashford · Emmaville · Butterleaf N.P. · ③⑧ Grafton · Ulmarra · Minnie Water
Wallangra · Strathbogie · Dundee · Gwydir Hwy · Barool N.P. · Nymboida N.P. · ②④ · Wooli · Solitary Island
Coolatai · Graman · Newton Boyd · Coutts Crossing · Halfway Creek · Corindi Beach
Myall Creek Memorial · Kings Plains N.P. · ⑧ Glen Innes · Guy Fawkes River National Park · Chaelundi N.P. · Glenreagh · Woolgoolga · Emerald Beach
Warialda · Oakwood · Glencoe · Chaelundi Mtn 1378 · Nymboi-Binderay N.P. · Ulidarra N.P.
Delungra · ⑨ Dejon Sapphire Centre · Backwater · Dorrigo N.P. · ②③ Coffs Harbour
Inverell · Tingha · Aberfoyle · ②① · Sawtell
Bingara · Single N.P. · Guyra · Ebor · Dorrigo · ②⓪ · Urunga · ②②
Caroda · Indwarra N.P. · ⑦ New England N.P. · Bellingen · ⑲ Nambucca Heads
Trevallyn · Abington · Cunnawarra N.P. · Bowraville · Macksville · Fish Rock Cave (Marine)
Cobbadah · Yarrowyck · Jeogla · Burrapine · Eungai Creek · South West Rocks
Mt Kaputar National Park · Warrabah N.P. · Armidale · ④ · Saumarez Homestead · Oxley Wild Rivers National Park · Bellbrook · Clybucca · Smoky Cape · Hat Head N.P.
Maules Creek · Uralla · ③ · Kentucky · Carrai N.P. · Frederickton · ⑱
Split Rock Dam · Upper Manilla · Retreat · ⑤ · Willi Willi N.P. · Kempsey
Wean · Keepit Dam · Manilla · Woolbrook · Walcha · Moona Plains · Kumbatine N.P. · Crescent Head
Boggabri · ② · Bendemeer · Oxley Hwy · Werrikimbe N.P. · ⑥ · Birdwood · Telegraph Point
Emerald Hill · Somerton · Attunga · Moonbi · Apsley Falls · Yarrowitch · Port Macquarie ⑰
Gunnedah · Nemingha · Brackendale · Cottan-Bimbang N.P. · Wauchope · Lake Cathie
Carroll · Tamworth ① · Dungowan · Mummel Gulf N.P. · Elands · Bonny Hills
Curlewis · Duri · Woolomin · Nowendoc National Park · Nowendoc · Tapin Tops N.P. · Yoorigan N.P. · Crowdy Bay N.P.
Mullaley · Breeza · Nundle · Lansdowne · Coopernook
Caroona · Werris Creek · Barry · Woko National Park · Wingham · Harrington
Tambar Springs · Tamarang · Quirindi · Wallabadah · Ben Halls Gap N.P. · Bretti · Gloucester · Nabiac · Taree · Old Bar
Bomera · Yarraman · Willow Tree · Murrurundi · Moonan Flat · Barrington Tops National Park · Forbesdale · Halladays Point · Tuncurry Forster ⑯
Coolah Tops National Park · Wingen · Kars Springs · Craven · Cape Hawke · Booti Booti National Park
Coolah · Cassilis · Scone · Bunnan · Dungog · Stroud · Bulahdelah ⑮ · Elizabeth Beach
Dunedoo · Uarby · Merriwa · Aberdeen · Denman · East Gresford · Booral · Myall Lakes National Park · Broughton Island
Gungal · Muswellbrook · Sandy Hollow · Newcastle · Paterson · Stockton Beach ⑭ Nelson Bay
Goulburn River National Park · Fly Point

alternative. Although there are fewer passing lanes on the New England Highway – and the route is popular with semi-trailers (articulated lorries) – it's usually a faster trip during the summer months, when the Highway is clogged with holiday traffic.

Country music capital

At the southern gateway to the New England region, **Tamworth ❶** wears its heart on its rhinestone sleeve. The city proudly bears the title "Country Music Capital of Australia", and trumpets its affection with a huge roadside guitar, a guitar-shaped swimming pool in the Alandale Motor Inn and what is claimed to be the world's biggest festival of Country and Western music.

This elevated status came about almost by accident. When the advent of television in the mid-1960s caused a decline in radio audiences, local station 2TM fought back with a series of special-interest programmes, one of which was *Hoedown*, which featured Country and Western music. The show took off, management decided to capitalise on its

popularity, and in 1973 the station staged the first Country Music Awards, which later became the Golden Guitar Awards, and ensured the city's eminence in the world of Country music.

The Country Music Festival, which grew up in support of the awards, is the highlight of Tamworth's year. It takes place over 10 days in late January, a celebration of twanging guitars, crooning and yodelling, denim and Tex-Mex food. Virtually the whole city becomes a performance venue, with events in pubs, parks, schools, churches and sports grounds.

The ultimate prize of Australian Country music, the Golden Guitar Awards, are held during the festival, and the winners chosen on the basis of material they have produced over the preceding year.

For most of the year, Tamworth is a bustling mini-metropolis, as befits its status as the largest city in the New England region. While true Country music devotes will find much to savour in Tamworth, most visitors to the city will have their

Map on page 218

One artist is added to the Australasian Country Music Roll of Renown each year.

BELOW: the world's longest line dance in Tamworth.

Captain Thunderbolt had racked up more than 80 hold-ups and robberies before he was killed in 1870. The proceeds of his robberies amounted to close to £20,000.

desires sated by a visit to the **Big Golden Guitar Tourism Centre** (2 Ringers Road; tel: 6765 2688; daily 9am–5pm; admission charge; www. biggoldenguitar.com.au). Easily spotted by the 12-metre (40-ft) golden guitar at the front, the centre has a **Gallery of Stars Wax Museum**, with Slim Dusty, Jimmy Little, John Williamson and other stars. There's also a café and a music shop.

Built for Philip Gidley King, the first mayor of Tamworth, **Calala Cottage Museum** (142 Denison Street; tel: 6765 7492; Tues–Fri 2–4pm, Sat–Sun 10am–4pm; admission charge) has been diligently restored by the local historical society to offer an authentic look at the domestic life of early settlers. Several other buildings have been relocated to the cottage grounds, such as a slab hut, stables and a blacksmith's shop, all typical of the buildings that would have stood here in King's time.

Captain Thunderbolt

Almost encircled by a loop in the Namoi River, **Manilla ❷** is at the centre of a mixed-farming area, with the emphasis on wool, wheat and cattle. Close to the town, **Split Rock Dam** and **Keepit Dam** provide irrigation water for the cotton farms, and aquatic recreation areas that are hugely popular with local residents. These reservoirs also attract wildlife, and the area is well known for wading birds in particular.

The town of **Uralla ❸** began in the mid-19th century when Samuel McCrossin built the Travellers' Rest Inn, but it was the discovery of gold in the Rocky River near by just a few years later that brought it to life. At the peak of mining activity there were about 4,000 miners on the goldfields, many of them Chinese, which caused considerable resentment. When mining activity slumped, agriculture filled the gap, and so it remains, a quietly slumbering town built around a broad main street.

In the local **Cemetery** is the grave of Frederick Ward, also known as Captain Thunderbolt, one of the most famous bushrangers. Born in the mid-1830s at Wilberforce near Sydney, Ward was an itinerant horse breaker and an

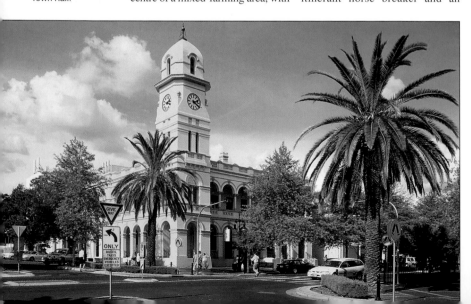

excellent horseman – the source of his nickname – who drifted into a life of crime. From 1865 until 1870 he held up mail coaches and shops, stole horses, waylaid travellers and generally terrorised the New England district. He was also a courteous and gentlemanly bandit, who never wounded anyone in the course of his robberies, preferring to trust to speedy horses rather than his revolver when cornered by police.

He was eventually shot by the police in 1870, although his family disputes whether it was actually Ward and not his half-brother, Harry, who was killed and buried in Uralla. Ward is the bronze figure on horseback at the junction of the New England Highway and the Walcha Road.

Inside what was once the town's original wheat mill, **McCrossin's Mill Museum** (31 Salisbury Street; tel: 6778 3022; Mon–Fri noon–5pm, Sat–Sun 10am–5pm; admission charge; www.uralla.com) is the home of the Uralla Historical Society. The museum mines the rich vein of local history to mount thoughtful exhibitions that delve into gold mining in

the district, Chinese society on the goldfields, and Captain Thunderbolt.

Cool, calm Armidale

Set in a hollow surrounded by green hills, **Armidale** ❹ conveys an immediate impression of calm and grace. The city is dominated by church spires rising from green pillows of chestnut and maple trees that were planted extensively in the city's streets and parks, and which gild the city in autumn.

At an altitude of around 1,000 metres (3,300 ft), Armidale has four distinct seasons and even an occasional winter snowfall, and the cool climate contributes to the appeal of its gardens.

Grazing properties were established in the district in the 1830s, but it was the discovery of gold in the area that galvanised Armidale, financing the construction of many fine public buildings, hotels, banks and emporia. At the end of the 19th century, the city established a reputation as an educational centre, with a number of boarding schools that derive their architecture as well

Map on page 218

TIP

Follow Scenic Drive 19 for about 11 km (7 miles) east out of Uralla, until you reach the privately owned village of Gostwyck. Beautiful little Gostwyck Chapel, set on the banks of a willow-edged stream, is covered with trailing vines that blaze red around April.

BELOW: the old courthouse in Armidale.

BELOW: St Mary's and St Joseph's Roman Catholic Cathedral.

as their playing fields from the English public-school model. Far more than most regional centres, Armidale has cherished its heritage, and the city has a fine array of 19th-century buildings.

The city is the seat of the University of New England, the oldest regional university in the country, and its population of about 4,000 students – almost 20 percent of the city's total – adds noticeably to its buoyant spirit, especially when the pubs close on Friday night. It's also a compact place. A walking tour of the city that takes in Dangar Street, The Mall and Faulkner Street will show you the best that Armidale has to offer in the way of parks, historic hotels, churches and public buildings – with several cafés along the way for rest and refreshment.

The **Visitor Information Centre** (82 Marsh Street; tel: 1800-627 736; Mon–Fri 9am–5pm, Sat 9am–4pm, Sun 10am–4pm) has a brochure on self-guided heritage walks. A two-hour bus tour of the city departs daily at 10am from the centre. The trip is free, but booking is essential.

Architecture and art

The most prominent of the churches in the city centre is **St Mary's and St Joseph's Roman Catholic Cathedral** (corner Dangar and Barney streets), considered a fine example of the Gothic Revival style, notable for its polychrome brickwork and the lantern tower, with turrets and needle spire. Diagonally opposite in Central Park, **St Peter's** (corner Rusden and Dangar streets), is the cathedral church of the Anglican diocese of Armidale. This is a far more austere building, but – for connoisseurs of the mason's trade – the brickwork is said to be exceptional.

Armidale has an outstanding art gallery, the **New England Regional Art Museum** (corner Kentucky and Marsh streets; tel: 6772 5255; Tues–Sun 10.30am–5pm; admission charge; www.neram.com.au). The museum began as the private collection of Howard Hinton, who migrated from England to Sydney and rose through the ranks of the shipping industry, and who began collecting art at the beginning of the

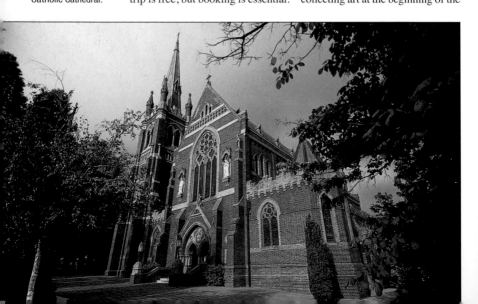

20th century. Hinton lived alone – in a 3 x 4-metre (10 x13-ft) room in a boarding house in the northern Sydney suburb of Cremorne. The room was not big enough to house his growing art collection, so Hinton sent it to what was then the Armidale Teachers' College. In 1933, he determined to create the best collection of art in any regional gallery in the country, and over the next 15 years, until his death, he sent more than 1,000 works of art to their new home.

The museum's Hinton Collection includes most of the great names of Australian painting from the late 19th and 20th centuries, such as William Dobell, Hans Heysen, Margaret Preston, Thea Proctor, Tom Roberts, Arthur Streeton and Norman Lindsay. The museum also has a fine body of paintings and sculpture representing some of the best of Australian contemporary art.

A patrician homestead

About 6 km (4 miles) south of Armidale, **Saumarez Homestead** (Saumarez Road; tel: 6772 3616; Sept–mid-Jun: daily 10am–4pm;

admission charge) is a 30-room Edwardian mansion and a prime example of the patrician homesteads that flourished on the rich grazing lands of the New England highlands. This was the site of the first grazing run in the Armidale district, established in 1835, although the homestead itself was built between 1888 and 1906.

The original landholder was Henry Dumaresq, who had served as a staff officer at the Battle of Waterloo, where he was severely wounded. The property takes its name from his family's estate at Jersey in the Channel Islands.

Surrounding the house are another 15 farm buildings, including stables, poultry houses and a slaughterhouse, each with collections of agricultural equipment. The grounds are open daily from 10am, but the interior of the house can only be visited on a guided tour, which takes place daily at 10.30am and 2pm, with additional tours at weekends at 3pm and 4pm.

If you're looking for small, atmospheric lodgings, a number of

Map on page 218

Armidale's Court House in Beardy Street was built in 1860 but had several later additions.

BELOW: the dry rural landscape of Glen Innes, New England.

Sturt's desert pea is an iconic Australian flower found mostly in arid areas. It was named after explorer Charles Sturt, who saw many examples of the flower when exploring the centre of the country in 1844.

BELOW: New England drovers.

Armidale's fine houses close to the city centre have been converted to offer bed-and-breakfast accommodation. The city also makes a good base for exploring some of the National Parks that lie on the ranges to the east of Armidale.

Waterfalls and wilderness

Spreading over the heights of the Great Dividing Range, southeast of Armidale, **Oxley Wild Rivers National Park ❺** (tel: 6776 0000) is a 1,200-sq. km (450-sq. mile) wilderness, into which the fast-flowing streams of the Macleay River system have carved deep gorges.

Rugged bush-walks, untamed rivers, dry rainforest and waterfalls are the park's distinguishing features. Among them is **Wollomombi**, the highest waterfall in the state, falling in two separate drops over a total height of 480 metres (1,580 ft), the larger of which measures 335 metres (1,100 ft), although the flow varies considerably depending on rainfall. The park is accessible from the Waterfall Way, which runs east of Armidale towards Dorrigo.

There are some spectacular walks around **Apsley Falls**, but this is in the southern section of the park, close to the town of Walcha on the Oxley Highway, which is one of the less practical routes between New England and the coast – unless you're planing an extensive bush-walking trip in the National Park. The park office is located in Armidale.

Just south of Oxley Wild Rivers, **Werrikimbe National Park ❻** (tel: 6586 8300) is another untamed beauty that spreads across the hills that form the catchment of the Hastings River. Cascading streams and forests of Antarctic beech and snow gum (a type of eucalyptus also known as White Sallee) are among the highlights of the park, which has a number of moderate and easy walking trails. Werrikimbe is also accessible from the Oxley Highway, between Walcha and Wauchope. However, the 40-km (25-mile) unsealed road leading off the highway into the park is narrow and tortuous. The information office for the park is in Port Macquarie.

Extending eastwards from the rim

of the New England plateau and into the valleys at its feet, **New England National Park ⑦** (tel: 6657 2309) is full of rewards for wilderness lovers of all inclinations – from those who demand nothing more than a fine panorama from a viewing platform close to a car park, to bush-walkers with a passion for wild and remote places.

Massive lava flows that bubbled to the surface about 500 million years ago lie along the crust of the escarpment within the park, while erosion has exposed ancient sedimentary rocks at lower altitudes.

The diversity of soils, elevations and rainfall has created a diversity of plant and animal life, from snow gums to subtropical rainforest, from swamp wallabies to whip birds (named for their distinctive whip crack call). Most of the park's walking trails are located on the plateau, offering views over the valleys where the Bellinger River rises. Access to the park is from Waterfall Way, 85 km (50 miles) east of Armidale. The park's information office is at Dorrigo.

Land of the Beardies

Glen Innes ⑧ revels in its Celtic roots. A bagpiper plays at midday in the town square on Friday, and the dominant landmark is **The Standing Stones**, a circle of upright granite boulders based on the Ring of Brodgar, a megalithic stone circle in the Orkney Islands – or possibly the Stones of Callanish on the Isle of Lewis, since sources disagree.

As you travel around the town, you'll often come across the name "Land of the Beardies". The "Beardies" were Duval and Chambers, two exuberantly hairy convict stockmen who worked for Henry Dumaresq, and whose knowledge of the area was vital for early pioneers. The town takes its name from Major Archibald Clunes Innes, who was instrumental in building a road between New England and Port Macquarie, which was pivotal for the economic success of the region.

Housed in what was once the town's hospital, the **Land of Beardies Museum** (corner West Avenue and Ferguson Street; tel: 6732 1035; Mon–Fri 10am–noon and 1–4pm,

Every May, Glen Innes plays host to the Australian Celtic Festival, a celebration of Celtic culture which draws national groups and clans, artists and performers from far and wide. Rise at dawn to hear the skirl of the bagpipes weave their magic across the Standing Stones (www.australian celticfestival.com)

BELOW: the view over Glen Innes from Martins Lookout.

BELOW: New South Wales is one of the world's biggest sapphire centres.

Sat–Sun 1–4pm; admission charge; www.beardieshistory house.info) is a folk museum with a vast collection that details just about everything that has happened in Glen Innes since the mid-1800s. Forestry, bee-keeping, horse carriages, the original Glen Innes telephone exchange, hats, furniture, letters of congratulation from the Girl Guides Association – nothing has escaped the attention of this historical hold-all.

While the sheer volume of material on display might leave you with a spinning head, if you've ever wondered what a badly warped wooden tennis racquet looks like, this is the place to find out.

Sapphire country

Inverell ❾ exists primarily as a service centre for the mixed-farming district that surrounds it, but the town is also the heart of a major gemstone region.

About three-quarters of the world's sapphires come from Australia, the vast majority from New South Wales, and the alluvial and volcanic deposits around Inverell

are the centre of the action. Sapphires and diamonds are mined commercially, but anyone can go fossicking – looking for gemstones in rivers or dry gravel beds.

There are several designated fossicking areas within the district, but you need either plastic buckets to wash away the river gravel in the creeks or a pick and shovel in the dry fossicking areas – as well as some expertise. For those without any of the above, the best bet is one of the privately owned fossicking areas close to Inverell, some of which offer equipment for hire as well as expert advice.

These private operations include **Poolbrook Gems Fossicking Park** (Nullamanna Road; tel: 6722 2781; Fri–Wed 9am–5pm, Thur noon– 5pm), **7 Oaks Fossicking Property** (Frazer Creek; tel: 6752 1582; daily 9am–5pm) and **Billabong Blue Fossicking Park** (204 Glen Innes Road; tel: 6728 8161; Wed–Sun 10am– 4pm). An admission charge is payable at all three.

For a look at the finished product, visit the **Gem Centre** (108 Byron Street; tel: 6722 1290; daily 9am– 5pm), a gallery where the stones are polished, cut and set. East of Inverell, the **Dejon Sapphire Centre** (Gwydir Highway; tel: 6723 2222; daily 9am–5pm) is a sapphire plant where you can watch stones being cut and polished direct from a mine on the site. If inspired to try their hand, visitors can also hire equipment for do-it-yourself fossicking.

National park treasures

Extending over 250 sq. km (100 sq. miles), **Gibraltar Range National Park** ❿ is relatively small, but it's easily accessible as the Gwydir Highway cuts through its midriff. The park is known for its wild flowers, including waratahs, the crimson flower that is the state emblem, and which is at its best in spring.

Map on page 218

The many streams that are born on this high granite plateau, and which feed the Clarence River, have gnawed deep, sheer-sided gorges from the escarpment, frequently plummeting from the heights in spectacular cascades. The main visitor area in the park is the Mulligans Hut Rest Area, which is just 9 km (5 miles) off the highway. Five easy walking trails begin at the rest area, and the 5-km (3-mile) **Dandahra Falls** Walk, which passes rosewood and cedar trees and walking-stick palms en route to the 240-metre (790-ft) cascades, is especially worthwhile. A fee is payable at the park entrance.

Washpool National Park ⑪ lies just to the north of the Gwydir Highway, forming a continual band of wilderness together with its southern neighbour, Gibraltar Range National Park. The name comes from the large pool lower down on one of the park's creeks, where sheep were washed on what was once Yulgibar Station.

The park's crowning jewel is its 3,000 hectares (7,400 acres) of warm temperate rainforest, the world's largest forest of the coachwood tree, used for cabinet work, woodcarving and veneers, as well as spars and masts for boats.

The park's soaring volcanic ridges are deeply pleated by creeks that find their way into the **Clarence River**, but so rugged is this region that walking trails barely penetrate the park. Those that do begin at the Coombadjha Creek Rest Area, where the short and spectacular Coombadjha Nature Walk winds through forest to **Coachwood Pool**.

In the same area, the 10-km (6-mile) Washpool Walk winds through rainforest and into up a majestic blue-gum forest. The picnic area is just a few kilometres along Coombadjha Road, which turns north off the Gwydir Highway.

A historic speech

It's fairly easy to speed through **Tenterfield** ⑫ without giving it a second glance, but the town has an outstanding museum in the **Sir Henry Parkes Memorial School of Arts**, which is concise, uncluttered and devotes itself to a single moment in Australia's history. The museum subtitles itself "Birthplace of Our Nation", and this is no exaggeration. So important was the speech made at a dinner here in 1889 by Sir Henry Parkes, the state's premier, that both Parkes and the building are held dear not only in the hearts but also in the pockets of the nation – depicted on the Federation $5 note, which has been in circulation since 2001.

The speech that Parkes made that night in what became known as the Tenterfield Oration was a persuasive and passionate argument for a unified Australia. At that time, each of the states had a separate government, which levied its own taxes and pursued its own interests – often at the expense of the common good. Most famously, New South Wales,

Tourists can explore Ghost Gully, a dry creek bed in Tenterfield.

BELOW: The Needles, Gibraltar Range National Park.

Map
on page
218

*For over a century,
the New England
region has
periodically sought
to secede from New
South Wales and from
its own state. The
movement reached its
peak in the 1960s,
partly in response to
the growing pre-
eminence of Sydney
at the time.*

BELOW: admiring the
view at Bald Rock.

Victoria and Queensland had each
adopted a different railway gauge,
which meant that passengers and
freight had to be unloaded from one
train to another each time they
crossed a state border.

The year following Parkes'
speech, state representatives sat
down to discuss the issue at an inter-
colonial conference in Melbourne.
A year later, Parkes presided over
the first federal convention held in
Sydney – leading ultimately to Federation on 1 January 1900.

Around the walls of the **Banquet
Room** where he made the speech
are political cartoons and newspapers with contemporary reactions to
the speech, varying from amusement to naked contempt. The importance of the event was summed up
by a report in Melbourne's *Age*
newspaper: "What Sir Henry Parkes
said that night had set rolling a ball
the future size and weight of which
no one could estimate."

The museum also has a collection
of memorabilia from Parkes' life,
including walking sticks and photographs. Parkes was an intriguing

character. Born in England in 1815,
he emigrated to Australia at 24 and
was elected to the New South Wales
Parliament in 1854. During his political career – which included five
periods as premier of New South
Wales – he became increasingly con-
vinced of the need for a united federal government for Australia.

He married three times, the final
time to Julia Lynch in 1895, when
he was 80 and she was 24. During
his two previous marriages he
fathered 17 children. He died in
1896, before his dream of Federation was realised.

Another Australian hero of a very
different order, Peter Allen, the song-
writer/showman, was born in Tenterfield in 1944. One of his best-known
songs is *The Tenterfield Saddler*,
which he wrote about his beloved
grandfather George, who ran the
local saddlery. The song has probably ensured the eternal success of the
Tenterfield Saddler's shop, which
can be found at 123 High Street, just
off the New England Highway.

Bald Rock

Bald Rock National Park ⓭ is
devoted to a single dramatic feature –
a huge chunk of granite that soars
200 metres (650 ft) above the surrounding forest. This enormous
dome measures 750 metres (2,500
ft) from end to end and 500 metres
(1,650 ft) across. The run-off from
the rock nourishes a forest of wet
eucalypt species at its base, which
are noticeably different from the
trees of the more remote forest.

Take care – the 1-km (½-mile)
walking track from the parking area
to the top of the rock is slippery in
wet weather, but the view is spectacular, extending as far as the
ranges along the Queensland border.

Bald Rock is 30 km (18 miles)
north of Tenterfield, off the Mount
Lindesay Road. A fee is payable at
the park entrance. ❏

RESTAURANTS, CAFÉS & BARS

Restaurants

Armidale

Imperial Hotel
Faulkner Street
Tel: 6772 2405
Open: D daily. **$**
Excellent, popular bistro
covers all the bases in
this homely town centre
hotel.

Lindsay House
128 Faulkner Street
Tel: 6771 4554
www.lindsayhouse.com.au
Open: D Wed-Sat. **$$**
Sandy Phillips is the chef
preparing what's
regarded as the best
food in Armidale. Local
ingredients are put
through their paces to
emerge transformed into
gourmet delights.

Restaurant Q
Girraween Shopping Centre,
Queen Elizabeth Drive
Tel: 6771 1038
Open: L & D Thur-Mon. **$$**
Stylish decor belies the
shopping centre loca-
tion, and the cooking in
contemporary Oz style
does its best to trans-
port you as well. BYO.

Squires Cottage
Country Comfort Motor Inn,
86 Barney Street
Tel: 6772 8511
Open: D Mon-Sat. **$$**
A lovingly restored 19th-
century dwelling plays
host to cooking that

mixes adventure with
tradition.

Glen Innes

Hereford Steakhouse
Rest Point Motor Inn, New
England Highway
Tel: 6732 2255
Open: D daily. **$$**
Steaks cooked
simply and well. Diners
who manage to chomp
their way through "The
Beast" rump steak get
their name put on the
"Wall of Fame" and a
free bottle of wine. It
takes an hour to cook
the thing.

Inverell

**Sapphire Chinese
Restaurant**
23 Byron Street
Tel: 6722 2266
Open: D daily. **$**
A clear cut above the
average country town
Chinese.

Tamworth

Café Eataliano
251 Peel Street
Tel: 6761 2993
Open: D daily. **$**
Award-winning pizzas
with other Italian dishes
in supporting roles.

Longyard Hotel
New England Highway
Tel: 6765 3411
Open: L & D daily. **$**
Standard pub food but
done well and in huge
portions.

Uralla

Stokers
Bushranger Motor Inn, 37
Bridge Street
Tel: 6778 3777
Open: D Mon-Sat. **$**
Open fires in a
comfortable dining
room and accomplished
food.

Cafés and bars

Armidale

Fusion
Suite 8/9, Hanna's Arcade
Tel: 6772 6266
Open: B & L Mon-Sat,
D Thur-Sat. **$**
The fusion is of Asian,
Mediterranean and mod-
ern Australian styles.
Day and night menus,
and all-day breakfasts
keep staff on their
toes.

Tamworth

Cafe 2340
15b White Street
Tel: 6766 9466
Open: B & L daily. **$**
Fresh ingredients in satis-
fying combinations.

Uralla

White Rose Café
82 Bridge Street
Tel: 6778 4052
Open: B & L daily. **$**
A pies and fries café
with some interesting
twists.

RIGHT: burgers with bite and bounce.

MUSIC FESTIVALS

New South Wales celebrates its multicultural heritage with a vivid and varied calendar of music festivals

With selfless dedication to hedonism, the state's promoters seem to have a music festival lined up for every weekend of the year. There are the high-profile international events, and then there are the idiosyncratic local affairs. Take the Bellingen Local Carnival. Although it doesn't feature any major stars, it has evolved into one of the funkiest of all music festivals. The carnival blends classical, contemporary and electronic music in a package that is intended to reflect Australia's multicultural heritage. World music in all its multifarious forms is its natural diet, and past carnivals have featured Quebecois vocalists, Japanese drummers and flautists, Bengali singers, jazz, ska, reggae and tribal song and dance groups from West Papua. Wearing its alternative heart proudly on its sleeve, the carnival reflects the spirit and the aspirations of the Bellingen community. The Carnival takes place between Friday and Sunday at the end of September. While few other festivals incorporate quite such an eclectic mix, it's worth sniffing around to see what's happening in an area, if only to get a handle on what makes the locals tick.

BELOW: the 10 days and 2,000 events of the Tamworth Country Music Festival make it the biggest event of its kind outside Nashville. It takes place at the end of January.

ABOVE: bands such as Wolfmother can create a stir on the pub and club scene but see their careers transformed overnight by a successful spot in a festival such as Homebake.

RIGHT: the Big Day Out comes round every January when a circus of big-name international and local bands plays in the capital cities of the big states. In Sydney the venue of choice is the Showgrounds.

BEAT ROOTS

Fans of folk and roots music are well served by festivals across the state. Byron Bay puts on its best beads and tie-dyes for the East Coast Blues and Roots Music Festival, Australia's largest international event of its kind. Beginning on a Thursday and spread across five days over the Easter weekend, the festival's four stages offer a non-stop diet of African, rap, jazz, Cuban and world music. Easter is one of the wettest times in the subtropical north, and soggy footwear goes with the festival like lingering deafness, but it still sells out months in advance. The Blue Mountains Music Festival of Folk, Roots and Blues in Katoomba has the virtue of smallness while pulling in some big-time performers. Held over a March weekend, the festival is strategically timed and geographically placed to fall between the much bigger festivals at Port Fairy in Victoria and Byron Bay, thereby attracting some of the international acts en route between the two. Canberra in its autumn glory is the backdrop for the capital's National Folk Festival, when several hundred musicians perform in a non-stop 5-day flow of entertainment in more than 20 venues.

ABOVE: Splendour in the Grass takes place over a weekend in July at Belongil Fields in Byron Bay and features a strong bill of international and local acts with an indie bent.

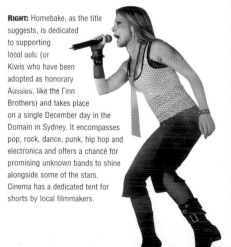

RIGHT: Homebake, as the title suggests, is dedicated to supporting local acts (or Kiwis who have been adopted as honorary Aussies, like the Finn Brothers) and takes place on a single December day in the Domain in Sydney. It encompasses pop, rock, dance, punk, hip hop and electronica and offers a chance for promising unknown bands to shine alongside some of the stars. Cinema has a dedicated tent for shorts by local filmmakers.

ABOVE: it goes without saying that at both of the festivals in Byron Bay you can get high very quickly.

BELOW: adopt this stance and with perseverance and practice you can apply mascara to both eyes at once.

THE NORTH COAST

Sand and surf, resorts like family-friendly Coffs Harbour and right-on Byron Bay – these are the acclaimed highlights of the north coast. But it also has National Parks and lakes, a wealth of wildlife, some historic towns, and the counter-culture capital of Australia

Sydney

Map on page 218

Unfurling from Port Stephens, just north of Newcastle, as far as the Queensland border, the north coast is the state's holiday playground. For the most part the coastline is a succession of sandy crescents separated by sculpted headlands, and by almost any measure – size, isolation, the warmth of the sea, the general disposition of rocks and trees – these are some of the finest beaches in the country.

Tourism and tradition

Tourism has been a boom industry for many north coast towns over the past couple of decades, and a number have thrown themselves wholeheartedly into the business, creating theme parks and adventure sports to enhance their visitors' experience. Even at the peak of summer, and even in the busiest of these coastal resorts, such as Nelson Bay and Coffs Harbour, it's relatively easy to find a beach with an acre of sand to call your own.

There are still some towns that rely on the traditional pursuits of agriculture and fishing, and many of these have a depth of character that complements that of their barefoot, beachy cousins.

Travelling north, you'll notice a distinct change in the landscape and its products as you push into warmer climates, from cattle to bananas, sugar cane and macadamia nut plantations. Seduced by the possibility of a life lived mainly outdoors and by the abundance of subtropical rainforests and rare frog species in need of salvation, many communities of people looking for alternative lifestyles have established themselves in the rich coastal river valleys. A visit to some of their towns, galleries and craft markets can bring another memorable dimension to your journey.

LEFT: the north coast is a major surfing centre. **BELOW:** Byron Baywatch. A lifeguard at work.

Broughton Island is 12 km (7 miles) north of Port Stephens. A protected nature reserve it is the nesting and breeding site of rare bird species, as well as a popular diving spot.

Running parallel to the coast, the Great Dividing Range is another world, often tangled with subtropical rainforests and slashed by streams that leap from cliffs and disappear into the trees below. So rugged are these ranges in many parts that they have defied the plough, and nature has been left to run riot in National Parks.

If possible, avoid travelling along the coast in January, when holiday traffic snarls the Pacific Highway.

Nelson Bay

Nelson Bay is one of the state's major holiday playgrounds, teeming with visitors from Newcastle, Sydney and the inland towns of the Hunter Valley throughout the summer months. In particular, the region has developed a broad array of attractions to cater to families, who make up the bulk of its visitors.

Its appeal lies in its position. Situated on the southeastern shores of Port Stephens, the town is the gateway to an aquatic paradise. On the town's doorstep within the sheltered arms of the bay there are safe, calm beaches that are ideal for small children, while the coastal beaches just a five-minute drive away are washed by booming waves.

Port Stephens lays claim to the title "Dolphin Capital of Australia". The bay is home to around 150 bottlenose dolphins, and there are several tour operators in Nelson Bay which offer dolphin-watching trips. These aquatic acrobats seem to relish the attention, often riding the bow wave just a couple of metres from the vessel.

Between May and June humpback whales cruise past the town on their northern migration, returning south between September and November, and these huge mammals are often encountered on the dolphin cruises.

To the south of Nelson Bay, **Stockton Beach** has the country's largest coastal dune system, stretching for more than 30 km (18 miles) to the northern outskirts of Newcastle. Several adventure operators offer various trips among the dunes, from dune-buggie trips to quad-bike safaris, horse-riding, camel treks and dune tobogganing.

BELOW: Relaxing in the bow net on a dolphin-watching expedition.

Below the waves, the action is just as thrilling. To the east of Nelson Bay, **Little Beach** ends at a tiny promontory, Fly Point. So prolific is the marine life here that the area has been declared an aquatic reserve.

The main feature of the **Fly Point-Halifax Park Aquatic Reserve** is a 100-metre (330-ft) sponge-covered ledge at a depth of 10–15 metres (30–45 ft), with schools of bream, nannigai and blue grouper, some of which can be hand-fed. It is also accessible. Walk to the end of Nelson Bay, step off the beach and you're there.

Divers have another superb site just off the coast at **Broughton Island**, with such outstanding features as the "Looking Glass", a split that runs through the middle of the island, crowded with marine life.

The lakes

Spilling across an area of almost 500 sq. km (200 sq. miles) to the north of Port Stephens, **Myall Lakes National Park** ⑮ is a vast system of shallow saltwater lakes connected by rivers and channels. Fringed by paperbarks and casuarinas, the lakes provide a habitat for pelicans, sea eagles, kangaroos and koalas – and a natural playground for fishermen, canoeists, and anyone else who enjoys messing about in boats.

Although the lakes are stained brown from the ti trees that leach tannin into their waters, they are perfectly safe for swimming. There are several campsites and bush-walking trails in the National Park, but Myall Lakes reveals its secrets only to those who are prepared to tackle it from the waterline. By far the best way to explore the lakes in leisurely style is by houseboat. The main base for houseboat operations is the town of Bulahdelah, on the Pacific Highway, which has access to the lakes via the Myall River. The boats can accommodate between two and 12 people.

Set on opposing sides of the inlet where Wallis Lake flows into the Pacific Ocean, **Forster** ⑯ and its hyphenated twin, **Tuncurry**, form the epicentre of Great Lakes, a region dominated by watersports. Dolphin cruises, fishing, sailboarding and

Map on page 218

Some men go to extraordinary lengths to persuade their loved ones that they're on the beach rather than in the local bar.

BELOW: the beach at Shoal Bay in Port Stephens.

In order to minimise the impact of walkers on the environment, National Parks in New South Wales have well-maintained paths, including boardwalks over fragile terrain. This example is in Dorrigo NP.

BELOW: South West Rocks rocks. Or so it seems in summer.

scuba diving are among the activities that attract large numbers of visitors to the town, and the ocean-front beach at the front of the town is majestic. There are few places in the state that offer such a superb choice of fishing – deep-sea, lake, rock, river or beach. Meanwhile, the oysters that are farmed in Wallis Lake are a local speciality.

Covering the narrow isthmus just south of Forster, **Booti Booti National Park** incorporates a marvellous stretch of coastline between Cape Hawke and Seagull Point. The 223-metre (730-ft) summit of Cape Hawke offers majestic coastal views, but it's a steep climb to the top.

Port Macquarie

Although it has fine beaches and several large resort hotels, **Port Macquarie ⑰** has been overshadowed as a tourist area by Coffs Harbour, a one-hour drive further north. The town has none of the glitz of its northern neighbour, but it does have a rip-roaring history.

Port Macquarie began life as a satellite penal settlement for con-

victs who had reoffended in New South Wales. Beginning in 1820, convicts cleared the land and established farms, built a stockade, a hospital and a church, but it was quickly realised that the area had potential as a free settlement, and from about 1830 its importance as a convict settlement had begun to decline.

Later it became the business centre for the agricultural region of the Hastings Valley and, later still, a holiday town and major retirement centre. Built by convict labour between 1824 and 1826, **St Thomas' Anglican Church** (Hay and William streets; Mon–Fri 9.30am–noon and 2–4pm) is Australia's fifth-oldest church still in use, its sturdy walls constructed with hand-made bricks cemented together with crushed oyster shells burned to extract the lime. Look closely at the bricks and you might be able to see a fingerprint, thought to be a tally mark, since each convict was required to produce a certain number of bricks per day. Inside, the pulpit, altar and box pews are all made from local cedar. Beneath the

front pew is the grave of Captain Rolland, the commander of the Port Macquarie garrison, who died of sunstroke and was buried a month before the church's foundation stone was laid.

South West Rocks

South West Rocks **⑱** is the very incarnation of a sleepy coastal town at its barefoot best. There's not much to it apart from a glorious beach, a fish-and-chip shop, an oyster barn and the golf course, but those who go there year after year treasure its unpretentious ways.

Two km (1¼ miles) offshore, **Fish Rock Cave** is a local divers' delight and one of the best cave dives in the country, a 125-metre (410-ft) passage through the centre of a small island, with an amazing variety of marine life, including grey nurse sharks.

Just to the east of South West Rocks is a place that sheds light on a fascinating chapter of Australia's history. Set in a commanding position on cliffs high above the sea, **Trial Bay Gaol** (Arakoon State Recreation Area; tel: 6566 6168; daily 9am–4.30pm; admission charge) was built in the 1880s to house low-security prisoners who were deemed to be capable of reform. For several years the prisoners worked to build a breakwater around the bay below, but the project was abandoned when it was only partially completed.

The prison was closed in 1903, but it was reopened in World War I as an internment camp for men of German and Austrian origin resident in Australia, even though some were second- or third-generation Australians. To fill in the day, the 550 internees fished, swam, played cards and tennis and staged more than 50 theatrical performances. The gaol even had its own symphony orchestra and newspaper.

Nambucca Heads ⑲ is one of the prettiest towns on the coast, where surf and river-scapes, hills and long, flat stretches of bush and sand dunes combine to glorious effect. Its popularity as a holiday destination is celebrated in the **Vee Wall**, a breakwater on which visitors have recorded their impressions with colourful and often irreverent wit.

Turn inland from the Pacific Highway, just north of Urunga, and you will find yourself on a quiet road that winds through one of the prettiest river valleys in New South Wales. This is the **Bellinger Valley**, named after the river that runs to your right, more or less parallel to the road.

Bellingen

Slinking through green pastures that rise towards forested slopes, the road approaches **Bellingen ⑳**. Even before you reach the town, you can get an inkling of what it's all about if you tune to 2BBB, at 93.3 and 107.3 on the FM dial. This is the voice of Bellingen, which has firm opinions on logging, big business,

The views from the lookout tower at Cape Hawke in Booti Booti National Park (www. nationalparks.nsw.gov. au) are spectacular. You can see south to the foot of Barrington Tops. The park has walking trails, a picnic area and camping facilities but only Elizabeth Beach is patrolled by volunteer lifesavers during the swimming season.

BELOW: Trial Bay Gaol.

*The Hammond &
Wheatley Emporium
in Bellingen was
built in 1909,
restored 70 years
later, and is a
superlative example
of an early colonial
department store.*

BELOW: inside the
Emporium.

disposable nappies, nuclear power, red meat and most other things.

Originally founded to exploit the rich cedar forests and later a centre for the local dairy industry, Bellingen has taken on a surprisingly green tinge these days. During the 1970s and 1980s, the town and the undulating subtropical country surrounding it became a favourite refuge for urban escapees seeking a more mellow existence, and the signs of cosmic consciousness are everywhere, from the advertisements for reiki and yoga classes to the organically grown produce in the wholefoods shop.

The influx has given Bellingen a new lease of life. In particular, the sensitive New Age types who make up much of its population have been careful to preserve its historic character, and the town itself has an undeniable appeal, which you can easily absorb in a stroll along Hyde Street, the main thoroughfare.

A number of writers, artists and performers have made their home here at various times, including author Peter Carey, who was inspired to write his Booker Prize-winning novel, *Oscar and Lucinda*, based on his time here. It was along the Bellinger that the Revd Oscar Hopkins floated his glass church in the last chapters of the novel. Among the current notable residents of the district is the pianist David Helfgott, the subject of the film *Shine*.

Dorrigo National Park

From Bellingen, the road to Dorrigo follows the river upstream with the hills closing in on either side, then sprints up the face of the escarpment and into the subtropical rainforest of **Dorrigo National Park ㉑**.

The name Dorrigo comes from an Aboriginal word meaning stringy bark (*dundurriga*), although there are still some local people who will swear that it was named after a Spanish general who fought in the Napoleonic Wars – and whom, Spanish military archives have confirmed, never existed.

The park rises to more than 800 metres (2,600 ft), and covers a rugged chunk of the coastal escarpment, a remnant of the Dorrigo

Scrub that was once heavily logged for its cedar trees. Here the many streams that are born on the New England plateau to the west tumble over the cliffs and disappear into the valleys to the east. Dorrigo's bird life includes bowerbirds, pittas and lyrebirds, the mimics of the bush.

There are several easy walks within the National Park, as well as a number of long and difficult bush-walks. The Walk with the Birds includes an elevated section that takes you up high into the forest canopy. The two-hour Wonga Walk penetrates deep into the rainforest, where the buttress roots of the yellow carabeen trees stretch their claws across the forest floor.

Just south of Coffs Harbour, **Sawtell** ㉒ awoke from its seaside slumber at the start of the new millennium to find that the houses overlooking its waterfront were being snapped up by savvy city slickers who realised that the price was an all-time bargain.

Apart from its beaches, which are about par for this part of the world, the most distinctive feature of

Sawtell is the main street, which is divided by a median strip planted with enormous fig trees that now provide shade for the chic cafés and designer stores that have taken root there. Today Sawtell is smart and relaxed, and far removed from the bustle of Coffs Harbour, even at the peak of summer.

Coffs Harbour

Coffs Harbour ㉓ is the holiday capital of north coast tourism, packed with family-friendly attractions and crowded with traffic in the summer months. The city of 65,000 has it all – beaches, watersports, adventure sports, indoor attractions, restaurants and cafés – in fact, something for just about every taste, with the possible exception of those looking for quiet and isolation.

Coffs also has a huge choice of accommodation, from motels to resorts with all the trimmings, to small, exclusive boutique retreats. Apart from the peak summer months, prices are keen.

This is also the state's "Banana Republic". The hillsides around the

Map on page 218

BELOW LEFT: Dangar Falls at Dorrigo.
BELOW: the Dorrigo Hotel.

town are smothered with banana palms, and the icon for the city is the **Big Banana** (351 Pacific Highway; tel: 6652 4355; daily 9am–5pm; admission charge; www.bigbanana.com), one of the most photographed backdrops in the country. The Big Banana is the prelude to a multi-faceted experience that incorporates audiovisual presentations, shops, a toboggan run and an ice-skating rink, as well as telling you everything you might want to know about banana cultivation.

Near the port, the **Pet Porpoise Pool Oceanarium** (Orlando Street; tel: 6652 2164; daily 9am–5pm; admission charge; www.petporpoisepool.com) has daily seal and dolphin shows at 10am and 2pm. Arrive early for the seal kisses and dolphin handshakes that take place before every show. The Oceanarium also has sharks, reef fish and turtles.

Follow the signs to the jetty for an evening stroll to one Coffs Harbour attraction that won't cost a cent. A footpath along the breakwater that forms the northern arm of the harbour leads to dome-shaped **Mutton-**

bird Island. Every evening between November and April, muttonbirds return to their hillside burrows on the island after spending the day fishing out at sea. For all their grace on the wing over the waves, however, the birds are less agile when it comes to landing, and you have to be careful not to be struck by an incoming bird.

After dodging the birds, the **Coffs Harbour Yacht Club** (30 Marina Drive; tel: 6652 4390) is a fine place for an evening drink. A little further along Orlando Street is a small group of restaurants with varied menus and outside tables. The best beaches – and most of the resorts – are on the north side of the city.

Grafton

The centre of the Clarence Valley sugar cane and dairying district, **Grafton** ❷ sits on the banks of the broad Clarence River, which is the largest river system on the state's north coast.

For almost 100 years, commencing in the mid-19th century, the river was an important artery for timber and agricultural produce, but these days its wharves are disused. Weatherboard and wrought lace are the preferred building materials, and these elastic materials, combined with Grafton's twining subtropical vegetation, give the city its languid, gracious character.

Grafton is known for its jacarandas, a feathery, deciduous native of Brazil that erupts in mauve blossoms in spring, which were originally planted in the 1870s by a local seed merchant by the name of Volkers. The city puts its best foot forward for the Jacaranda Festival, which begins on the last Saturday in October, coinciding with the massed flowering of the trees. The city's geography is a little confusing, however, and it's worth stopping off for directions and a map at the **Visitor Centre** (Pacific Highway, South Grafton; tel: 6642 4677;

BELOW: jacaranda trees in bloom, Grafton.

daily 9am–5pm), which is signposted on the western side of the highway.

Cross the bridge and follow Fitzroy Street, which lies directly ahead on the other side. The street has some fine examples of local domestic architecture. The Federation-style **Schaeffer House** (190 Fitzroy Street; tel: 6642 5212; Tues and Sun 10am–4pm; admission charge), the headquarters of the Clarence River Historical Society, has a collection of furniture, china and glassware.

Just a few doors away, the **Grafton Regional Gallery** (158 Fitzroy Street; tel: 6642 3177; Tues–Sun 10am–4pm; admission charge; www.graftongallery.nsw.gov.au) does an excellent job of showcasing some of the talented local artists. The gallery has a distinguished collection of photographs of Aboriginal inhabitants of the Clarence River Valley, made on a large-format camera by John William Lindt in the 1870s. The gallery displays the Lindt collection from time to time. The courtyard of the gallery is home to one of the best of the local café/restaurants, **Georgie's** (tel: 6642 6996).

Located to the east of Grafton, **Yuraygir National Park ㉕** is an unbridled strip of coast with pristine beaches, high dunes, paperbark lagoons, wildlife galore, freshwater creeks that spill into the sea and some of the best coastal walking tracks in the state. Emus are fairly common, and several species of exotic birds, such as brolgas, jabirus and black-necked storks, are found in the estuarine waterways. Access to the park is not easy, but the effort is more than justified in order to see what the coast looked like in its pristine state. From Grafton, head south on the Pacific Highway for 10 km (6 miles) to the Wooli and Minnie Water turn-off. Follow the signs to Minnie Water and then to the Illaroo Camping Area, where there are walking tracks.

Bustling Ballina

At the mouth of the Richmond River, **Ballina ㉖** is another bustling holiday town, although it is no competition for its neighbour, Byron Bay, in the glamour stakes. Until the 1930s, Ballina was a busy port for

Map on page 218

Shell sell. Sharp-eyed young entrepreneurs pile up their wares in attempt to raise some ice-cream money.

BELOW: rugged coastline south of Byron Bay.

Wisdom of Oz. There are plenty of opportunities to pick up souvenirs that seem like a good idea at the time.

BELOW: Mad Dog Surf Shop at Byron Bay.

cargoes of timber from the interior. The town has a fascinating attraction in the **Ballina Naval and Maritime Museum** (Regatta Avenue; tel: 6681 1002; daily 9am–4pm; admission charge), which lies next to the visitors' centre. Begun by sailors who served in the Royal Australian Navy in World War II, most of the museum is dedicated to ships and armaments of that period. Dominating the museum is the raft *Aztlan*, the sole remnant of the La Balsa Expedition, which sailed from Ecuador and arrived off the coast of Ballina in 1973. Made solely from balsa-wood logs lashed together, and propelled by a square sail, the vessel covered 15,500 km (9,000 miles) in 178 days.

Like Thor Heyerdahl's Kon-Tiki Expedition of 1947, the La Balsa Expedition set out to prove that the islands of Polynesia might have been colonised by people sailing from South America. In fact, this theory has now been discounted. Genetic and other evidence now clearly indicates Asia as the origin of the Polynesian people – but the voyage of the *Aztlan* was a brave journey nevertheless. Heading north, it's well worth abandoning the Pacific Highway at Ballina in favour of the coast road to Byron Bay, signposted "Tourist Drive 30". Although it's a dawdler, the road winds past some lovely beaches and stretches of coastal bushland.

Bangalow

While the pub and the attractive verandas that shade the main street of **Bangalow** ㉗ suggest a sleepy country town, nothing could be further from the truth. In fact, Bangalow has very sophisticated tastes, as a stroll past the cafés, produce shops, furniture shops and therapists in the main street will confirm. There's not much to the town, but it's simple and refreshing, and a quiet change for anyone looking for an alternative to nearby Byron Bay.

One of the town's minor treasures is the walking track that winds along the edge of Byron Creek. Within a few paces you're swallowed up in a forest of strangler vines and huge, mottled trees that shut out the

sunshine, while water monitors scuttle away from the path and into the brown creek alongside. A five-minute stroll will deliver you to a shady park with neat garden beds and arbours covered with rioting greenery – the perfect spot for a picnic if you've brought along supplies from one of the shops along the main street.

Byron Bay

If you're looking for cool, a sense of style and a perfectly frothed cappuccino to go with your beach escape, **Byron Bay** ㉘ is the place. Dominating the town, the **Lighthouse** on the headland at Cape Byron is the easternmost point of the Australian mainland. This is the brightest of any lighthouse in the country, and as its spotlight suggests, Byron Bay has star quality.

Among its natural credentials are a glorious array of beaches, dolphins that ride the breaking waves below the lighthouse, and storms that hang rainbows on the ranges to the west. It's also at the cutting edge of Generation Y chic. A sarong, a tattoo, a pierced eyebrow and something tribal around your neck is the way to go in Byron Bay, and the town has become a major party zone for Anka, Bjorn and the rest of the international backpacker brigade on the east-coast circuit.

A sleepy coastal town until it was discovered by surfers in the 1970s, Byron Bay has also become a refuge for urban escapees, and especially those with artistic inclinations. Architects, designers, writers, craft-workers and software designers have set up shop, grafting their talents and energy onto this small, relaxed coastal village. Consequently, today Byron Bay is a seaside town with superb beaches, deep pockets and heaps of flair. The intermingling has given Byron a style all its own, especially in the shopping department, where whole-foods, handicrafts and back-to-nature prevail.

However, this eco-friendly and socially aware community has also kept at bay some of the forces that would seek to capitalise on the area's tourism appeal, and plans for

Map on page 218

BELOW: light of Byron.

Alternative Culture

Warmth, a reasonably tolerant society, an abundance of cheap rural land and a fair number of disaffected youths have created ideal conditions for the rise of alternative cultures in New South Wales. While there are alternative communities scattered throughout coastal regions of the state – typically in moist river valleys on the eastern side of the Great Dividing Range – alternative-lifers tend to concentrate in a couple of areas in the north. At their best, these communities embody much that is laudable, such as concern for the environment and one's fellow creatures, a noble spirit of self-reliance and the ability to recycle and reuse. However, the process of re-engineering a society is an experimental one, and it doesn't always work out.

The village of Nimbin is the most visible symbol of alternative culture, and it causes the temperatures of middle Australia to rise. Its drug subculture is all too apparent, and although the town has been the incubator for some innovative ventures, such as the Rainbow Power Company, which designs and manufactures renewable-energy generators based on solar, wind, hydro and biomass energy

sources, there are other elements that provide plenty of ammunition for detractors. The Big Joint acts as a light-hearted focus for a serious cannabis legalisation campaign; it even has its own website (www.bigjoint.org). However, Nimbin's reputation also attracts hardcore drug users, some of them with serious dependency, and crime levels reflect the desperation of some to get the wherewithal for the next fix.

A more appealing departure from conventional lifestyles is evident in the town of Bellingen, which sits in a serene river valley against a backdrop of rainforests and blue-toned ranges. Bellingen is a country classic, its faded weatherboard façades peering out from the verandas that line the main street. Its New Age tinge is obvious in the whimsical architecture that owes its inspiration as much to The Hobbit as it does to Country Style magazine. On the outskirts of the town, the Old Butter Factory Co-Op is a studio and gallery for local craftworkers – well worth a look for anyone searching for distinctive, one-off souvenirs.

Festivals are a good place to get a glimpse of the sunnier side of alternative culture, and musical shin-digs feature prominently in the north coast calendar. Country markets offer another intriguing insight into these cultures. Byron Bay Market is but one of several local weekend markets that rotate from one week to the next through local villages. Bellingen Community Market, held on the third Saturday of each month, is another celebration of all things New Age.

Byron Bay itself reflects the paradox of what was once alternative becoming mainstream. It may have been the hippy drop-out destination in the 1970s, but now it also attracts some seriously moneyed individuals looking for an idyllic retreat without the overdevelopment that has blighted other parts of the coast – the green-tinged local council has made sure of that. All the New Age retail outlets and service providers are there, but they are selling hard in what has become a cutthroat market. They've got high rents to pay, so if you want to be part of their take on alternative culture, you've got to be prepared to pay for it.   ❏

LEFT: New Age van hire.

a Club Med and McDonalds have been fought and scuttled.

The beaches are the focus of the action at Byron Bay – Main, Watego's and the great sweep of Tallow. Watego's has one of the best right-hand breaks of any beach in the state, which is a big attraction if you're a surfer, and some of the most expensive coastal real estate outside Sydney.

Held on the first Sunday of each month, the **Byron Bay Market** (Butler Street Reserve; 8am–4pm) is part country fair, part rock festival and part macrobiotic/alternative-energy trade fair. Healing, health and hemp in all its legal forms are prominent at the market, which attracts lots of families, as well as some of the exotic tribes who live in the hinterland.

If the relentless grooviness of Byron Bay's beaches gets a bit too much, head south along the road to Ballina and turn off where a sign points to the Broken Head Caravan Park. At the bottom of this road, turn right onto a gravel road, identified by the sign "Broken Head Reserve". For 5 km (3 miles) this road twists through the woodland at the back of **Broken Head**.

At several points there are trails that disappear over the brow of the hill and into the banksia forest on the seaward side of the headland. Almost any one of them will deliver you to a majestic stretch of coast. At some there are pure, golden sweeps of sand that are practically deserted for all but the peak months of summer; at others, the trails ends on cliffs where the sea hurls itself against jagged basalt vertebrae.

Counter-culture capital

Set in a luscious green valley where limestone spires erupt from green forests, the village of **Nimbin** ㉙ is the counter-culture capital of Australia. In the early 1970s, what was

once a sleepy dairy-producing village was catapulted into the Woodstock era when Australia's universities held their combined Aquarius arts festival on the green slopes around the town. Some of those who attended could not help but notice that the demise of the dairy industry meant that local land was available and cheap, and Nimbin became the incubator for a communal society that aimed to get back to grass-roots living, reinvigorate the human psyche and generally save the planet.

The experiment curdled somewhat when drug pushers and various other social misfits took advantage of the anything-goes mentality and moved in. Consequently, Nimbin – population 400 – is the only town of this size in the state that finds it necessary to install security cameras in the main street.

A great deal of what is good about Nimbin goes on out of sight in the hills around the town, where individual communes have forged a meaningful and creative lifestyle in surroundings of undeniable beauty.

Map on page 218

Acute local awareness of the harmful effects of the sun means that most children wear body-suits on the beach.

BELOW: Hitting the shops on Jonson Street.

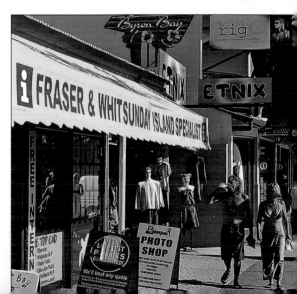

The town still wears its hair, its bells and its slightly outrageous manners with pride, and it's not for the faint-hearted. A short while after you arrive in Cullen Street, the main thoroughfare, chances are you'll be identified as an outsider, and tempted with a range of agricultural substances that you won't find in any fruit-and-vegetable shop, with no attempt at discretion. If this offends you, walk the length of Cullen Street breathing deeply and you'll probably feel something close to empathy by the time you reach the post office.

As well as its multicoloured cafés and organic-produce shops, Nimbin has a number of galleries that display the work of the many artists who live in the region.

Mount Warning Park

Named after the rhino-horn spike that dominates the north coast landscape, **Mount Warning National Park** ⓷⓪ is the first point on the Australian mainland to feel the glow of the rising sun. The mountain is actually the plug of the Tweed Volcano,

the lava that solidified in the cone of the ancient volcano.

About 23 million years ago, the Tweed Volcano began oozing lava. This was no Krakatoa, but when it had finished its business three million years later, layers of lava and ash had spewed over a huge area. What remains today is the extinct crater of that volcano, a vast bowl-shaped caldera some 40 km (25 miles) across, and the cradle for a biological wonderland. Over the aeons, the lava laid down by the volcano has broken down to a lush, red soil that has been colonised by sub-tropical rainforests so rich with life that the region is home to three National Parks that now have World Heritage listing.

For all its serene beauty, at ground level this is a landscape with teeth, as you will discover if you take the 4-km (2½-mile) hiking trail from Breakfast Creek to the 1,157-metre (3,795-ft) summit of Mount Warning. Start early if you can, allow five hours for the hike there and back, and take plenty of drinking water. Access to the park is via

BELOW: camping on the Hawkesbury River.

the Murwillumbah Road, which cuts diagonally across the floor of the caldera, parallel to the Tweed River as it unspools through a landscape of surreal beauty. Pillars of bare rock rise from subtropical forests, and in the morning, the peaks float on a fleece of clouds.

Where the forest has been cleared there are dairy farms and banana plantations, and sugar cane farms on the valley floor. Towering in the background, the steep blue hills of the northern rim of the caldera form the border with Queensland.

Murwillumbah ㉛ is a sprawling sugar town on the banks of the Tweed River, but it has an unusual place in the art world. The town's **Tweed River Regional Art Gallery** (5 Tumbulgum Road; tel: 6670 2790; Wed–Sun 10am–5pm; admission charge) is the home of the Doug Moran Portrait Prize, the world's richest prize for portraiture. Awarded in even-numbered years, the prize is worth A$100,000 to the winner. Entry conditions require that both the painters and their subjects be Australian citizens.

Tweed Heads

Hard against the Queensland border, **Tweed Heads** ㉜ is the last town on the coast of New South Wales, although it's often twinned with its northern neighbour, Coolangatta, since the two cities run seamlessly together. Tweed Heads has become a major retirement centre, known particularly for its enormous clubs, the **Twin Towns Services Club** and the **South Tweed Bowling Club**. Poker-machine gambling was legalised in New South Wales-registered clubs in 1956, but it was not until 1990 that Queensland legalised poker machines, and these Tweed Heads clubs used the anomaly to seduce many would-be gamblers from the nearby Gold Coast, which had been a burgeoning holiday mecca since the 1960s.

On the vast profits that poured from their poker machines, they were able to finance their clubs' lavish facilities. These days, it's live entertainment and low-priced meals that attract the crowds to these clubs as much as the chance to lose money on the one-armed bandits. ❏

Map on page 218

In Hollywood, movie stars are honoured with pavement plaques. In Tweed Heads it's a horse – albeit a triple Melbourne Cup winner.

BELOW LEFT: Tweed Heads statues. **BELOW:** Twin Towns Club.

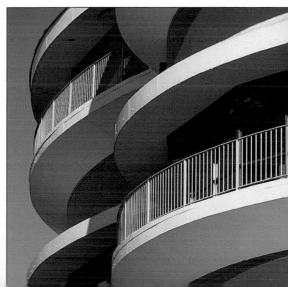

RESTAURANTS, CAFÉS & BARS

Restaurants

Ballina

Spinnakers
Ballina RSL Club,
River Street
Tel: 6686 2544
www.ballinarsl.com.au
Open: D Wed-Sat. **$$**
Mediterranean leanings
in this freshly renovated
eatery that sets new
standards for social club
cooking.

Bangalow

Bang Thai
2/43 Byron Street
Tel: 6687 2000
www.bangthai.com.au
Open: D daily. **$$**
Top of the range Thai
eating in this stylish and
deservedly popular Thai
restaurant where the
chefs are not afraid to
experiment in full view of
the diners. BYO.

Utopia
13 Byron Street
Tel: 6687 2088
Open: B & L Tues-Sun,
D Fri-Sat. **$$**
A welcoming space
where ingredients are
kept simple but there's
always a twist to keep

you interested, from
breakfast through to
dinner. BYO.

Bellingen

No. 2 Oak Street
2 Oak Street
Tel: 6655 9000
Open: D Tues-Sat. **$$**
The beautifully converted
cottage has been witness
to superlative Mod Oz
cooking for over 10 years
now and there's no sign
of any decline from the
highest standards. BYO.

Byron Bay

Beach Hotel
Bay Street, Byron Bay
Tel: 6685 6402
www.beachhotel.com.au
Open: L & D daily. **$**
There seems to be a by-
law that every visitor has
to pass through here at
least once and be
rewarded with bistro
food a cut above the
average.

Boomerang
Shop 5, 2 Fletcher Street
Tel: 6685 5264
Open: L Thur-Sun, D daily.
$$$
Select your capacity -
from two to five courses -
and wallow in the range
and ambition of this
renowned shrine to
fusion cooking.

Dish
Shop 4, corner of Jonson
and Marvell Streets
Tel: 6685 7320
Open: D daily. **$$$**

Attractive wood and white
space for the inspired
Euro-flavoured cooking of
Luke Southwood.

Fins
The Beach Hotel, corner of
Jonson and Bay Streets
Tel: 6685 5029
www.fins.com.au
Open: D daily. **$$$**
Cosmopolitan fine dining
in Byron with styles from
around the globe applied
to fresh, mostly line-
caught fish and the odd
meat or vegetarian dish.

Coffs harbour

Tide & Pilot Brasserie
Marina Drive
Tel: 6651 6888
Open: L & D daily. **$$**
With its view-filled spot
at the Marina, it's no sur-
prise that the emphasis
here is on fish – and very
well handled it is too.
BYO.

Dorrigo

Hotel Dorrigo
Corner of Hickory and Cudgery Streets
Tel: 6657 2016
www.hotelmoteldorrigo.com.au
Open: L & D daily. **$**
Good old-fashioned hotel
with a family bistro
which, while it won't win
any awards, more than
meets expectations.
Great steaks.

Forster

Forster Bowling Club
Strand Street
Tel: 6554 6155

www.forsterbowl.com.au
Open: L & D daily. **$**
There are two venues
to choose from:
Danny's Family Restau-
rant, which has all-you-
can-eat buffets, and
Alley's Restaurant and
Bar for the marginally
more dressy crowd. The
emphasis in both is on
value for money.

Grafton

Georgie's at the Gallery
Grafton Regional Gallery,
158 Fitzroy Street
Tel: 6642 6996
Open: L Tues-Sun,
D Tues-Sat. **$$**
Confident, flavour-filled
dishes display a creativ-
ity that aspires to match
the works in the gallery.
It all makes for a refresh-
ing change.

Nambucca Heads

Bluewater Brasserie
White Albatross Holiday
Centre, Wellington Drive
Tel: 6568 6468
Open: L & D daily. **$**
Great views over the har-
bour and reliable,
straightforward dishes
for all the family.

Nirvana Sawadee
4 Pacific Highway
Tel: 6568 9622
Open: L & D daily. **$**
Traditional Thai eatery
not far from the Visitor
Centre, serving the
usual array of dishes
made with fresh local
ingredients.

Nelson Bay

The Point
Sunset Boulevard,
Soldiers Point
Tel: 4984 7111
www.thepointrestaurant.com.au
Open: L & D daily. $$$
There aren't many
places on the East Coast
where you can watch the
sun setting over the
water. This is one, and it
can be done over some
rather excellent cooking,
with an emphasis on
seafood. BYO.

Rock Lobster LP
D'Albora Marina, 6 Teramby
Road
Tel: 4981 1813
Open: L & D daily. $$
Right on the beach and
packed full of fresh
seafood, this is perfect
holiday eating.

Zest
16 Stockton Street
Tel: 4984 2211
Open: D Tues-Sat $$
Every item on the menu
in this culinary haven
deserves a detailed
description. For
instance, the... No,
go along and see for
yourself.

Port Macquarie

Ca Marche
Cassegrain Winery, 764
Fernbank Creek Road
Tel: 6582 8320
www.camarche.com.au
Open: L daily, D Fri only. $$
Picture windows
overlook the sprawling
vineyards or you can hit
the deck and enjoy well

presented contemporary
food that shows off the
wine.

Portabellos
Shop 6, 124 Horton Street
Tel: 6584 1171
Open: B & L Tues-Sat, D
Wed-Sat. $$
Sound, sometimes
arresting contemporary
food combined with
friendly and attentive
service. BYO.

South West Rocks

The Rocks
Rockpool Motor Inn, 45
McIntyre Street
Tel: 6566 7755
www.rockpoolmotorinn.com.au
Open: D daily. $$
Seasonal menu with a
few ever-presents like
steak or oysters, and a
modern Australian bent
that makes the most of
local produce while dip-
ping its toe into SE Asia.

Tweed Heads

Twin Towns RSL Club
Wharf Street
Tel: 5536 2277
www.twintowns.com.au
Open: B, L & D daily. $$
Seven dining options in
this enormous club
range from basic cafete-
ria fare to rather good
swanky dining.

Cafés and bars

Bellingen

Lodge 241 Gallery Café
117-121 Hyde Street
Tel: 6655 2470
Open: B & L daily. $
Reverberating weather-

board former Masonic
Lodge at the top of Hyde
Street with solid range of
snacks and goodies. Art
on the walls and more
upstairs in the gallery.

Nambucca Heads

The Pub with No Beer
Taylors Arms Road,
Taylors Arms
Tel: 6564 2100
www.pubwithnobeer.com.au
Open: L & D daily. $
Iconic brewery pub
immortalised in one of
Australia's most famous
songs. Worth a visit.

Nimbin

Nimbin Oasis Cafe
80 Cullen Street
Tel: 6689 0199
Open: B & L daily. $
"Come and enjoy the joint
with friends", they say.
There's good coffee and
snacks as well. Not for
the conservatively
minded.

Rainbow Cafe
64 Cullen Street
Tel: 6689 1997
Open: B & L daily. $
Co-operative-run and
packed with vegetarian
offerings, although
not exclusively, this
is archetypal Nimbin.

Port Macquarie

Cafe Rio
74 Clarence Street
Tel: 6583 3933
Open: B, L & D daily. $
Full a la carte selections
or just an excellent
coffee at this busy
venue.

Signatures Bar Steak and Seafood
72 Clarence Street
Tel: 6584 6144
Open: L & D daily. $$
The name says it all.
Settle on the deck over
good plain food, or show
off your pool skills in the
bustling bar.

RIGHT: traditional fish and chips.

BIG THINGS

It's big, it's sometimes clever, and it's the ultimate way for a town to put itself on the map when it really doesn't have much else going for it

The first Big Thing in Australia was in New South Wales. It was at Coffs Harbour on the north coast that the Big Banana was erected in 1964 as a way of attracting custom to a plantation on the Pacific Highway. It was ludicrous, it was tacky and it immediately struck a chord with passers by. It became a destination in itself, and once that happened every desperate or mediocre enterprise that had no other distinguishing feature considered adopting the idea.

New South Wales was fertile ground for big things and many a small company or local council has jumped on the bandwagon. At the last count there were close to 40 of the things around the state, some being quite distinguished feats of engineering and construction, some more simple but still alluring, and some, frankly, rubbish. Originality doesn't count for much either; there are two sheep, two chickens and three bottles. Still, keep your eyes open and look out for that serendipitous moment when the Big Potato looms over the horizon.

Trident Fish
Fresh Prawns &
Seafood Packs

LEFT: Big Gold Panner Man towers over the Western Highway on the eastern outskirts of Bathurst. According to *Big Things*, the bible for aficionados by David Clark, he is repainted in the colours of one of the racing teams for the Bathurst 1000.

ABOVE: Ballina's Big Prawn displays an attention to detail that sets it apart from some of its more slapdash rivals.

LEFT: the Big Golden Guitar in Tamworth pays its way by reminding visitors of the Country Music Festival for the 11 months of the year when the place isn't swamped by musicians in cowboy hats.

BIG THINGS AS ART FORMS

While it could be argued that they go against the ethos of the Big Thing as the epitome of tackiness, there are a couple of examples of big things which have been put together by serious artists. Pro Hart was probably the most famous of the Broken Hill

artists and it was he who constructed the Big Ant in 1982. It is now on a high plinth that resembles a winding tower over a mine shaft, situated in Lions Park opposite the Visitor Information Centre in Broken Hill. The other artist is Brett Whitely who was responsible for *Almost Once,* the pretentious name for what ought to be dubbed the Big Matchsticks. There are two of them, one pristine, the other the charcoal remains of a spent match; both are several metres high. You can find them in Sydney on the Domain Sculpture Walk behind the Art Gallery of New South Wales.

ABOVE: the famous Big Merino on the outskirts of Goulburn has hit a spot of bother. It used to be on the Hume Highway and attracted a lot of passing trade to its shop and museum complex. However, a by-pass has been built around the town and business is slow. The solution is to move it a few hundred metres down the road so that it's visible from the highway again. Pleasant as it is to contemplate a Big Sheepdog being brought in to shoo it on its way, the reality is more prosaic: it will be taken apart, trucked down the road and then bolted back together again. Visitors can go inside the structure, climb some steps and look out of the eyes.

ABOVE: it all began with the Big Banana on the Pacific Highway just outside the resort of Coffs Harbour, and it must still be one of the most visited of all the big things with claims that millions have passed through it in the 40+ years since it was built. There's a cafe and a shop selling absolutely everything that could possibly carry the banana insignia. You can see the real, smaller, things on a monorail trip around the plantation.

LEFT: Wauchope is a small town a few kilometres inland from Port Macquarie on the Oxley Highway. It's no doubt a pleasant place but wasn't going to feature in this book. But it's got the Big Bull and now it does. See, works a treat.

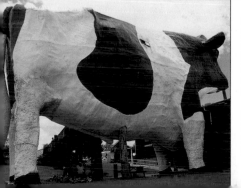

LORD HOWE ISLAND

Lord Howe Island is a UNESCO World Heritage Site, and in this small patch of land there is an abundance of bird life, rare vegetation, breathtaking beaches, coral reefs, forests and mountains. Visitors can dive, snorkel, walk, or simply kick back and admire glorious views

Sydney

L ord Howe Island, one of Australia's quiet surprises, barely registers with the wider world, and there are plenty of Australians who prefer it that way. Pitched into the Pacific Ocean some 550 km (345 miles) adrift from the nearest point of the New South Wales coast, Lord Howe Island measures just 11 km (7 miles) long and is less than 3 km (2 miles) across at its widest point, yet its natural wonders far outstrip its modest dimensions.

UNESCO treasure

This is an island of extremes, roaring vertiginously from the sea at one moment and stroking your arms the next with soft forests of kentia palms (*Howea forsteriana*, named after the island). Huge, regal banyan trees shade the interior, while the island is fringed with crashing surf, white-sand beaches, the world's most southerly coral reefs and giant rock pools the size of backyard swimming pools, each one a window on a captive world of squirming sea life. The southern end is dominated by two leaping volcanic peaks, which typically hide their heads in a fleecy halo of cloud.

Due to its superlative beauty and rare plant and animal species, the island was included on UNESCO's World Heritage List in 1982.

The sea life is quite phenomenal. In the surrounding waters, warm and cool currents collide, spawning a wealth of marine creatures including giant clams, sea turtles, clownfish, lionfish, tuna, butterfly fish and a wrasse known as the double-header, a species that is unique to the island's waters.

A biological ark

The island is also a biological ark, a remote perch for exotic species of seabirds on migratory journeys that

Map on page 254

LEFT: Lord Howe Island's fabulous scenery.
BELOW: fisherman with yellowfin tuna.

A round of golf takes you through palm forest and along the edge of the ocean.

BELOW: Old Settlement Beach.

might take them as far north as Siberia and south to New Zealand. Boobies nest along the windy cliffs, white terns drift like snowflakes among the kentia palms and ternlets nest along the base of the cliffs. Lord Howe is the only place on earth where providence petrels breed. The red-tailed tropic bird can be sighted along the island's northern cliffs, and so prolific are the shearwaters that stepping into one of the bird's sandy burrows and twisting an ankle is a local hazard.

Lord Howe Island's natural bounty is hugely invigorating. Everyone swims, snorkels, hikes, fishes, bicycles, takes up birdwatching or plays golf for the sheer pleasure of whacking a ball around the glorious course. The island also has an excellent network of hiking trails, and the local tourism office has leaflets with maps for the do-it-yourself explorer. There are good

reasons to take a tour with a local guide, since it takes a resident expert to decipher the island's rich botany and bird life. Especially recommended are the tours with naturalist Ian Hutton, a fluent and authoritative voice on the birds, geology, botany and history of the island (Nature Tours; tel: 9232 5733; www. lordhowe-tours.com.au).

Despite the abundance of wildlife, poisonous snakes are absent, as are sand-flies – a real bonus for the tourism industry.

The north

Lagoon Road, the island's "highway", reaches its northern terminus at **Old Settlement Beach ❶**. This was the site of the original settlement of 1833, when the population consisted of a small group of New Zealanders who traded provisions with the crews of whaling ships. From the road's end a walking track wanders across the paddock behind

Lord Howe Island

Map on page 254

the beach towards the northern end of the island.

A slight diversion from this track to the upper end of the paddock leads to the mangled wings, tail fin and engines of an RAAF Catalina flying boat which crashed here in 1948 when it overshot its landing in the lagoon, killing seven of the nine-man crew. Until the airstrip was built in the 1970s, Catalinas provided the only air service between the island and the Australian mainland.

At the far side of the paddock, the track winds through a dense and lush forest of native kentia palms, the mainstay of the island's economy before tourism. The leaves were traditionally used for thatching roofs, but it became valuable as a decorative plant, and the seeds were exported around the world.

Kentia palms are cultivated at the Lord Howe Nursery in Middle Beach Road, where you can take a one-hour guided tour (reservations essential at the Visitor Centre, free-phone tel: 1800-240 937 or 6563 2114; every Friday and Tuesday in peak season 10.30am).

After clearing the forest, the track leads to the 147-metre (480-ft) summit of **Mount Eliza** ❷, which offers one of the island's picture postcard views, with North Beach in the foreground and the opal blue of the lagoon against the hulking peaks of Lidgbird and Gower. Sooty terns nest at the summit between October and January, often swooping low over walkers and shrieking violently in defence of their young.

Another lovely viewpoint is the grassy crown of **Signal Point** ❸, which is at its photogenic best at sunrise and sunset.

The collection of shops and cafés at the junction of Lagoon Road and Neds Beach Road is the not-so-bustling island **Township** ❹. This is the place to sign up for guided tours; they often book out several days in advance, so it's wise to get your name down for fishing, diving, sightseeing, hiking, snorkelling and glass-bottomed boat trips.

Sweeping south from Signal Point, the crescent of **Lagoon Beach** ❺ is the island's most popular stretch of sand, especially

TIP

There are daily flights to Lord Howe Island from Sydney and less frequent flights from Coffs Harbour and Brisbane. Flight time is less than two hours.

BELOW: feeding the fish.

The water's inviting, and visitors can make the most of it with swimming, diving, snorkelling, kayaking, sailing, fish feeding and fishing. The last two may be concurrent.

BELOW: coastal scenery and Mount Lidgbird.

enjoyed by families. The mottled colours of the lagoon promise an abundance of corals and other marine life, and if you strap on a mask, snorkel and fins (or flippers) you won't be disappointed. The rocky headland at the northern end offers shelter from the wind, and a day without breezes is rare on beautiful Lord Howe.

Fish, books and banyans

Neds Beach ❻ is a marine reserve, with an abundance of corals and fish that make it a rewarding place for snorkelling. The marine life here is not usually known for its aggression, yet late in the afternoon, when Clive Wilson wades into the water to feed the fish, it's time to head for the beach. While Clive heaves fish scraps collected from the island's restaurants into the sea, the water around him boils with sand mullet, Australian salmon and kingfish. So frenzied is the feeding that it's not uncommon for spectators standing in knee-deep water to be whacked hard by a muscular tail, or even knocked off their feet.

In words, pictures and videos, the **Lord Howe Island Museum ❼** (Tel: 6563 2114; Sun–Fri 9am– 3pm) charts the island's history, geology, and plant and animal life. The museum also has the best collection of books on the island, sells postcards and maps, provides a booking service for local tours and houses the island's Visitor Information Centre.

At the end of Anderson Road, a walking trail crosses a paddock to the **Valley of the Shadows ❽**, where the massive branches of the giant banyan are propped up by aerial roots, enabling them to span an area of more than 100 sq. metres (1,100 sq. ft). Continue to Clear Place to catch your breath on the bench seat conveniently placed there, and enjoy a breathtaking view over the cliffs.

The south

Set on the brow of a hill against the soaring green backdrop of Mount Lidgbird, **Capella Lodge ❾** has the finest view of any accommodation on the island. Non-guests can share

the spectacular vistas from the lodge's deck for the price of a sunset cocktail.

South of the lodge, Lagoon Road dives downhill across moist pastures towards **Lovers Bay** ⑩, and ends at a palm-lined track that curls along the beach, skirting the base of the southern peaks. Woodhen can often be seen along this track.

Despite the abundance of exotic winged creatures, the brown, flightless Lord Howe Island woodhen is possibly the most fetching of all the island's birds. About the size of a large pigeon, it responds to unusual noises by popping out of the undergrowth for a look around. This made it a favourite menu item for early settlers, who must have considered the woodhen the ultimate in self-delivery meals.

By the mid-19th century – just 15 years after the first settlers arrived – the woodhen was to be found only on the higher slopes of the two southern mountains. By 1973, when only about 30 birds remained on the summit of Mount Gower, two adult pairs were removed to begin a captive breeding programme. A decade later, 85 captive-bred birds were re-introduced to the wild, and thanks to strict controls over domestic cats, dogs and rats, there are now about 300 of them living in their natural environment.

Scaling Mount Gower

The trail continues to a beach, at the end of which is the path to the summit of **Mount Gower** ⑪, the most challenging of all the island's walking trails. Visitors are only permitted to follow it with the services of a guide, and the full-day trek is not for the faint-hearted. After hopping across a beach of ankle-turning rocks, hikers must scramble up a trail that disappears vertically into the forest on the lower slopes of Mount Lidgbird. The next task is to skirt the exposed southwest scarp of the mountain by creeping along a narrow ledge, face to the cliff and clinging to a rope with a sheer drop at your back. After that, the climb through dripping vegetation to the 875-metre (2,870-ft) summit of Mount Gower is a doddle.   ❑

There's no public transport, but cycling is easy and there are plenty of places to hire bikes.

RESTAURANTS & BARS

Restaurants

Arajilla
Old Settlement Beach
Tel: 6563 2002
www.arajilla.com.au
Open: D daily. **$$$**
While guests may breakfast and lunch here, the restaurant is only open to others for dinner, where the menu is firmly in the contemporary Australian vein.

Capella Lodge
Lagoon Road
Tel: 6563 2008
www.lordhowe.com
Open: D daily. **$$$**
The menu changes daily with the highest quality ingredients combined Mod Oz style. Great views out over the sea. As you might expect, seafood features prominently. The Lodge provides other meals for guests.

Beachouse on the Moon
Milky Way Villas,
Old Settlement Beach
Tel: 6563 2106
www.milkyway.net.au
Open: D Mon, Wed & Fri. **$$**
A good place for casual dining without pretention or fuss.

Cafés and bars

Blue Peter
Lagoon Road
Tel: 6563 2002
Open: D Mon, Wed & Fri. **$$**
Seafood dominates; cooked plainly but well.

Palm Sugar
Skyline Drive
Tel: 6563 2120
Open: L & D daily. **$$**
Home made cakes and reliably good meals.

The Bowling Club
Lagoon Beach
Tel: 6563 2106
Open: D daily. **$**
Good bistro food, or you can just drop in for a drink.

● ● ● ● ● ● ● ● ● ● ●
Prices for a three-course dinner per person with a half-bottle of house wine.
$ = under A$50
$$ = A$50–A$75
$$$ = over A$75
L=lunch, D=dinner, BYO = bring your own alcohol.

TRANSPORT

GETTING THERE AND GETTING AROUND

GETTING THERE

By Air

About 50 international airlines fly into Sydney Kingsford Smith Airport. Qantas is the main Australian carrier, with the most flights to the largest number of destinations, and an extensive domestic network as well. Other major players include British Airways, Singapore Airlines, Air Canada and United Airlines.

Flights between Australia and Europe take about 22 hours, although with stopovers and delays the journey could take more like 30 hours. A stopover in an Asian capital (or on the Pacific coast or Hawaii if travelling from Canada or the US) is worth considering.

The peak season for travel is around December. Apex fares will reduce the flat economy fare by about 30–40 percent during the less busy periods. If you are flexible and can fly at short notice, check with discount flight centres for fares on unsold tickets. Many of the heavily discounted fares, refunds and changes in flight times are generally ruled out.

By Sea

Up until the 1960s, arriving in and departing from Australia by boat was a common and reasonably inexpensive practice, but in these days of cheap air fares, sailing Down Under has become something of a luxury activity. That said, if time and money permits, there is no better introduction to Sydney than arriving by boat.

Ocean liners berth at the Overseas Passenger Terminal at Circular Quay and the Darling Harbour Terminal. Passengers are required to pass through customs on arrival.

The following companies include Sydney as a destination or stopover on their itineraries: **Carnival Australia** handles bookings for many of the cruise liners to visit Sydney, tel: 13 24 69 (in Australia); www.carnivalaustralia.com. **Cunard Line**, tel: 0845 071 0300 (UK); www.cunard.com **P&O**, tel: 0845 355 5333 (UK); www.pocruises.com **Princess Cruises**, tel: 1800-PRINCESS (US); www.princess.com

GETTING AROUND

Regional Air Services

Australia has three major domestic carriers, Qantas, its budget subsidiary Jetstar, and its rival budget carrier Virgin Blue. Each of these airlines flies from Sydney's domestic airport to other capital cities and tourist locations outside New South Wales.

AIRLINES

Major airlines flying to Sydney:
British Airways:
Tel: 1300 767 177 (Sydney)
Tel: 0870 850 9850 (UK)
Tel: 1 800 403 0882 (N. America)
www.britishairways.com
Qantas:
Tel: 13 13 13 (Australia)
Tel: 0845 774 7767 (UK)
Tel: 1 800 227 4500 (N. America)
www.qantas.com.au
United Airlines:
Tel: 13 17 77 (Australia)

Tel: 0845 844 4777 (UK)
Tel: 1 800 864 8331 (N. America)
www.united.com
Air Canada:
Tel: 1300 655 767 (Sydney)
Tel: 08712 201 111 (UK)
Tel: 1 888 247 2262 (N. America)
www.aircanada.com
Singapore Airlines:
Tel: 13 10 11 (Sydney)
Tel: 0844 800 2380 (UK)
Tel: 1 800 742 3333 (N. America)
www.singaporeair.com

Within NSW Jetstar and Virgin Blue cater to passengers wanting to cut the travel time between Sydney and the laid-back town of Byron Bay on the far north coast. Both fly to the Ballina Byron Gateway Airport, and from there it is another 30 km (19 miles) to Byron Bay. Virgin Blue also flies regularly to Coffs Harbour on the mid-north coast.

To fly to other destinations in New South Wales you will need to contact one of the regional airlines QantasLink or Regional Express. QantasLink flies from Sydney to coastal locations such as Newcastle, Port Macquarie and Coffs Harbour, country music capital Tamworth, and regional centres such as Dubbo and Armidale, as well as Lord Howe Island.

Regional Express covers major centres near and far, including Cooma near the Snowy Mountains, Broken Hill and Lightning Ridge in the Outback, and Bathurst, Mudgee, Orange, Dubbo and Armidale.

Canberra is well served by flights from other Australian cities.

Qantas/QantasLink, tel: 13 13 13; www.qantas.com.au
Jetstar, tel: 13 15 38; www.jetstar.com.au
Virgin Blue, tel: 13 67 89; www.virginblue.com.au
Regional Express, tel: 13 17 13 www.rex.com.au

From Sydney Airport

Sydney International Airport is also Australia's main international airport. Officially called Kingsford Smith International Airport, it is 10 km (6 miles) south of the city, and known to many Sydneysiders as "Mascot Airport", after the nearby suburb. The domestic airport is a further 2 km (1 mile) away: passengers in transit should use the shuttle buses provided by the appropriate airlines.

The efficient Airport Link train (built for the 2000 Olympics) is the fastest and most convenient way to reach the centre of Sydney. There are rail stations in both the domestic and the international terminals. Trains run every 10 minutes from 5.09am to 11.45pm, and the journey into the city takes only 13 minutes. A single ticket from the airport to the city costs A$12 from the domestic terminal and A$12.60 from the international terminal.

A taxi from the airport to the city centre will cost around A$25 one-way plus a A$2 airport toll, and should take around 20 minutes in light traffic. Each terminal has its own sheltered taxi rank, with supervisors on hand in peak hours. All the major car-hire (rental) companies have offices at the airport terminals.

Depending on your destination in Sydney it may be possible to catch a public bus from the airport. For instance, there are buses that travel to Sydney's eastern suburbs, including Bondi Junction.

For those arriving at the Ballina Byron Gateway Airport the Ballina Taxi Service (tel: 02-6686 9999) meets all flights. There are also a number of transfer services covering the 30-km (18-mile) journey to Byron Bay.

The Coffs Harbour airport is just 3 km (2 miles) from the city centre. To take a cab into the centre contact Coffs District Taxi Cab Network (tel: 13 10 08) or Nambucca Radio Cabs (tel: 02-6568 6855).

From Canberra Airport

Canberra Airport is only 15 minutes drive from the city, with a typical taxi fare of around A$15. Airport buses (A$7 one-way) operate to/from the city at 30-minute intervals.

Public Transport in and around Sydney

Suburban Trains

Sydney's safe and reasonably comprehensive railway system, **CityRail**, is a great way to get to suburban destinations, as well as providing an excellent inner-city service. The City Circle connects the city stations of St James, Museum, Circular Quay, Wynyard, Town Hall and Central. Travel out to Bondi Junction on the Eastern Suburbs line. Trains for all suburban lines can be caught at Town Hall and Central Station, which is also Sydney's main country terminal. Trains run until midnight.

It's worth noting that after peak hours in the evenings, stations and trains are sparsely staffed; passengers are advised to use the "Nightsafe" section of the platform and to travel in the train guard's carriage, marked by a blue light. Ring the Transport Info Line for further information. From midnight to 4.30am "Nightride" buses replace trains on key routes in Sydney.

Buses

In Sydney, government-run buses operate from the city, ferry wharves and railway stations. The main bus termini are in Wynyard Park on George Street, at Circular Quay and at Railway Square near Broadway and Central Station. Free maps are available from outlets at the airport, Circular Quay, Wynyard Bus Station and Queen Victoria Building.

In some cases buses are the only way to access a particular area of Sydney. For instance, there is no train service to Sydney's northern beaches. Anyone who wants to travel further north than Manly (which can be accessed by ferry from Circular Quay) will have to take a bus or a taxi.

For sightseeing, catch the **Sydney Explorer**. It travels in a 28-km (17-mile) circuit around 26 of the city's major tourist attractions. A one-day ticket (A$36) allows you any number of journeys on the circular route. The buses run from 8.40am, with the last departing at 5.22pm.

The **Bondi Explorer** travels a 30-km (18-mile) circuit around the eastern harbourside bays and coastal beaches. There are

TRANSPORT

ACCOMMODATION

ACTIVITIES

A – Z

recorded commentaries on board, and passengers can get on and off as they please using the same ticket. The Bondi Explorer departs from Circular Quay every 30 minutes from 9.15am to 4.15pm. A Bondi Explorer ticket (A$36) also allows you free travel on all regular Sydney buses within the Bondi Explorer circular route up to midnight on the same day.

A two-day combined Explorer ticket (including Sydney and Bondi Explorers) costs $A62.

The **Blue Mountains Explorer Bus** (tel: 4782 4807; www.explorer bus.com.au) is a similar service run by a private operator, taking in 30 stops from Katoomba to Leura. Adult tickets are $A25, and include unlimited travel for a day and a guide book.

Ferries

Sydney is a harbour city, and ferries have been part of its transport scene since the arrival of the First Fleet in 1788. Today, ferries provide an efficient commuter service to many of the harbourside areas, with all services beginning and ending at Circular Quay.

Some of the city's tourist attractions, including Taronga Zoo, Manly and Darling Harbour, are best reached by ferry. A fleet includes high-speed JetCats, the grand old Manly ferries and the RiverCats that run along Parramatta River. Plan your itinerary around at least a couple of rides.

Sydney Ferries run harbour cruises (with commentary) morning, evening and night, which take between one and 2½ hours and are not expensive. There are also a number of private operators, including Captain Cook Cruises and Matilda Cruises, leaving from Circular Quay and Darling Harbour. Trips on offer include everything from a one-hour whiz around the top sights to a full dinner afloat. A very special trip is to be had aboard the HMAV *Bounty*, a replica of Captain Bligh's 18th-century tall sailing ship.

Sydney Ferries, tel: 13 15 00; www.sydneyferries.info
Captain Cook Cruises, tel: 9206 1122; www.captaincook.com.au
Matilda Cruises, tel: 9264 7377; www.matilda.com.au
Bounty Cruises, tel: 9247 1789; www.thebounty.com

Taxis

Sydney's taxis can be hired in the street if they are showing the "Vacant" sign or if the light on top of the cab is lit. Passengers may need to phone for a taxi during busy times or outside city locations. There is an additional charge of A$1.40 on the fare for phone bookings. Taxis use meters, and tipping is not necessary as a rule. A short trip will cost A$6–7. Toll fees, of which there are now several in Sydney, are all added to the bill. It is often possible to pay by credit card, for which there is a surcharge.

All taxi drivers are required to display an official photo ID licence on their car's dashboard or sun visor. Complaints should be made to the individual taxi company involved (displayed on the side of the vehicle) or to the NSW Taxi Council (tel: 9332 1266).

If you are travelling with a child under 12 months of age and you don't have a suitable restraint, you must ask for one when booking a cab. It is compulsory for all passengers to wear seat belts.

ABC Taxis, tel: 13 25 22
Legion Cabs, tel: 13 14 51
Premier, tel: 13 10 17
RSL Taxis, tel: 9581 1111
Silver Service Taxis, tel: 13 31 00
Taxis Combined Services, tel: 8332 8888

MONEY-SAVING TICKETS

Travel by public transport can be expensive if you purchase individual tickets as you go. There are a range of day tickets and passes available to cut the cost.

TravelPass
This ticket allows you unlimited seven-day travel on buses, trams and ferries, provided you stay within set zones, or you can buy a bus-only pass.

TravelTen
This gives you 10 bus or ferry trips for nearly half the cost of paying for each trip separately. More than one person can use this ticket; simply validate the ticket the appropriate number of times at the machines that are found on board buses and at the ferry wharves.

SydneyPass
If you intend to use public transport extensively, the best value of all has to be the SydneyPass. Available for three, five or seven days, it offers unlimited hop-on, hop-off travel on all regular Sydney Buses and Sydney Ferries services, plus the Sydney Explorer and Bondi Explorer, three Harboursights Cruises, return transfers on AirportLink trains, and free travel on all regular CityRail trains within the Red TravelPass zone.

Public Transport around New South Wales and Canberra

Visitors should contact the State Transit Authority for information on bus, train and ferry routes, ticket prices and timetables. Its **Transport Infoline** (tel: 13 15 00) and website (www.131500.com.au) provide information on transport options in the areas bounded by Port Stephens in the north, Scone and Dungog in the Hunter Valley, Bathurst in the west, Goulburn in the Southern Highlands, Bomaderry in the south and Sydney in the east.

TRAVEL INFORMATION

Transport Infoline (State Transit Authority) tel: 13 15 00, daily 6am–10pm; www.131500.com.au
Countrylink Rail and Coach Reservations, tel: 13 22 32; www.countrylink.info

Buses

Canberra

In **Canberra**, the government operates the ACTION bus service (tel: 13 17 10 or 6207 7611, www.action.act.gov.au). Daily, weekly and monthly tickets are available (purchased from newsagents and kiosks); standard tickets are purchased from the driver.

Other places in NSW

Newcastle is the only city in New South Wales apart from Sydney with a government-run bus system. Obtain timetable information by phoning the customer service centre (tel: 4974 1600) or from www.newcastlebuses.info. The fare system is time-charged rather than based on distance. **Newcastle Bus Depot** (corner Denison Street and Gordon Avenue, Hamilton) can also provide timetables and maps.

Elsewhere in New South Wales travellers will be dependent on private buses. Services tend to be limited, or sometimes non-existent in the evenings and at weekends.

Armidale Edwards Coaches, tel: 6772 3116; www.edwards coaches.com.au
Bathurst/Lithgow Bathurst Coaches, tel: 6352 3888; www.jonesbros.com.au and Selwood's Coaches, tel: 6362 7963
Bega/Eden Deanes Buslines, tel: 6496 1422; www.deanesbus lines.com.au
Blue Mountains Blue Mountains Bus Co, tel: 4751 1077; www.mountainlink.com.au
Byron Bay Blanch Coaches, tel: 6686 2144
Central Coast Busways, tel:

4368 2277 (Gosford) or 4392 6666 (Wyong); www.busways.com.au and Red Bus Services, tel: 4332 8655; www.redbus.com.au
Coffs Harbour Busways, tel: 6652 2744 (Coffs Harbour) or 1300-555 611; www.busways.com.au
Cooma Cooma Coaches, tel: 6452 1259
Dubbo Dubbo Buslines, tel: 6882 2900; www.dubbobuslines.com.au
Forster/Tuncurry Busways, tel: 4997 4788 (Bulahdelah); www.busways.com.au
Grafton/Yamba Busways, tel: 6642 2954 (Grafton) or 1300-555 611; www.busways.com.au
Hunter Valley/Newcastle Rover Coaches, tel: 4990 1699; www.rovercoaches.com.au
Illawarra Dion's Bus Service, tel: 4228 9855; www.dions.com.au Greens Northern Coaches, tel: 4267 3884; www.greensnorthern coaches.com.au and Premier Illawarra, tel: 4271 1322; www.premierillawarra.com.au
Orange Orange Buslines, tel: 6362 3197; www.orangebuslines. com.au and Selwood's Coaches, tel: 6362 7963
Port Macquarie Busways, tel: 6583 2499 or 1300-555 611; www.busways.com.au
Port Stephens/Nelsons Bay Port Stephens Coaches, tel: 4982 2940; www.pscoaches.com.au
South Coast Stuart's Coaches, tel: 4421 0332; www.stuartscoaches. com.au
Southern Highlands Berrima Buslines, tel: 4871 3211; www.berrimabuslines.com.au

Long-Distance Coaches

New South Wales has a fairly extensive rail network, but there are areas where the only alternative for people without access to a vehicle will be to travel by coach. For instance, travelling to coastal areas any further south than Bomaderry (Nowra) will require an alternative to train travel.

Greyhound Australia is Australia's only national coach company. It stops at the major

centres on routes between Sydney and Melbourne (stops include Canberra, Gundagai, Wagga Wagga and Albury); Sydney and Adelaide (stops include Canberra, Gundagai, Wagga Wagga, Leeton and Griffith); Sydney and Brisbane via both the Pacific Highway (stops include Newcastle, Forster, Taree, Port Macquarie, Coffs Harbour, Byron Bay and Murwillumbah) and the inland route along the New England Highway (stops include Newcastle, Singleton, Muswellbrook, Scone, Tamworth, Armidale and Tenterfield). Its main terminus is at the **Sydney Coach Terminal** (tel: 9281 9366), in Eddy Avenue near Central Station, but in most cases it also picks up at the domestic and international terminals at Sydney Airport.

A range of different operators service other localities in New South Wales, and travelling from town to town can be difficult unless you are starting or ending in major centres such as Sydney, Dubbo, Newcastle or Canberra. If you want to travel to a particular area it pays to check whether the local bus or coach service has a long-distance service to the area. For instance, **Busways** operates coaches from Sydney to Forster and Sydney to Taree, and **Rover Coaches** does trips from Sydney to the Hunter Valley.

Travel to points further west than Dubbo, including Broken Hill and Bourke, is covered by **Frasers Coaches** (tel: 6884 3101), and in the north of the state around Lismore, **Kirklands** (tel: 6622 1499) is a good name to know. For Sydney to south coast locations contact **Priors Bus Service** (tel: 4472 4040) or pick up a coach to Eden in Canberra.

The Transport Infoline website has excellent information on other options in the Country Transport section of its website (www.131500.com.au).

Greyhound Australia, tel: 13 14 99 (in Australia) or 07-4690 9950 (international); www.greyhound.com.au. Sydney to Canberra in 3½ hours, Sydney to Melbourne in 12 hours, Sydney to Brisbane in 17 hours.
Firefly Express, tel: 1300-730 740 (in Australia) or 03-8318 0318 (international); www.fireflyexpress.com.au (Sydney to Melbourne in 12 hours).
Premier Motor Service, tel: 13 34 10 (in Australia); www.premierms.com.au (runs Sydney to Melbourne and Sydney to Brisbane).

Inter-City Trains

Country and interstate rail travel is the domain of the government service, **Countrylink**. The XPTs (short for express passenger train) are the fastest way to travel longer distances. Intercity trains run regularly from Sydney (Central Station) to Canberra (3–4 daily, 4½ hours); between Sydney and Melbourne (via Wagga Wagga; 2 daily, 11–12 hours); Sydney and Brisbane (via Grafton and Casino; 1 daily, 14 hours); and Sydney and Dubbo, making limited stops. The network extends as far as Moree and Armidale in the north, Broken Hill in the west, Griffith and Albury in the south. Often there will be Countrylink coaches or local coaches to continue beyond the point where the rail line stops. For instance, to reach Lightning Ridge you have to take a train to Dubbo and then transfer to a coach service.

Tickets that are booked and paid for more than 24 hours in advance may qualify for a discount. If booking online, select the "best available" option.

There are also a number of money-saving travel passes for people expecting to do extensive train travel within Australia.

There are Countrylink Travel Centres at Sydney's Central and Wynyard stations.

Sydney's **CityRail** network extends far beyond the city into the Blue Mountains and Lithgow, Goulburn and the Southern Highlands, the south coast (Nowra Bomaderry) and beyond the central coast to Newcastle. There is also a regional service linking Scone and Dungog in the upper Hunter Valley with Newcastle. As with other trains in the CityRail network, there are no seat reservations or on-board dining options on these services.

Transport Infoline, tel: 13 15 00; www.131500.com
Countrylink, tel: 13 22 32 or 02-8202 2000; www.countrylink.info

Ferries

A ferry service makes frequent crossings of the Hunter River connecting Newcastle's Queens Wharf with the beaches and town of Stockton and a private ferry operator runs between Iluka and Yamba on the Clarence River in the north of the state.
Newcastle Ferries, tel: 13 15 00; www.newcastlebuses.info
Clarence River Ferries, tel: 6646 6423

Taxis

Most towns have at least one taxi service. The Transport Infoline website has contact details in its Country Transport section. Otherwise ask at the local pub or visitor's centre. They are often posted in public telephone booths.

Canberra, tel: 13 22 27

Albury, tel: 6025 3631
Armidale, tel: 6771 1455
Bathurst, tel: 6331 1511
Bega, tel: 4476 4476
Broken Hill, tel: 08-8087 4279
Byron Bay, tel: 6685 6290

Cessnock, tel: 4990 1111
Coffs Harbour, tel: 6658 9999
Cooma, tel: 6452 7777
Dubbo, tel: 6882 1911
Forster, tel: 6555 3031
Goulburn, tel: 4821 2222
Inverell, tel: 6722 3533
Jindabyne, tel: 6457 2444
Kiama, tel: 4237 7505
Lightning Ridge, tel: 6829 0833
Newcastle, tel: 4979 3000
Orange, tel: 6362 1333
Parkes, tel: 6862 2222
Port Macquarie, tel: 6581 0081
Tamworth, tel: 6766 1111
Wollongong, tel: 4229 9311

Driving

Visiting overseas drivers are not required to obtain a NSW driver's licence or an International Driving Permit, provided they have an up-to-date driving licence from their home country. If the licence is not in English, it is a good idea to carry a translation.

Most of NSW's road rules are based upon international rules, and it is simply a matter of following the signs, sticking to specified speed limits and so on. But there are a few points that drivers should be aware of:
• Drivers should equip themselves with a complete up-to-date road directory, available at your car hire outlet.
• Drivers must give way to the right, unless otherwise indicated, to pedestrians (keep an eye out for zebra crossings), and to all emergency vehicles.
• The speed limit in most built-up city and suburban areas is 50 kph (30 mph) unless otherwise indicated. Look out for 40 kph (25 mph) zones near schools and in areas of high pedestrian use.
• Parking can be a problem in and around city and town centres, particularly in Sydney. Carry change for meters and read the signs carefully, keeping a lookout for the areas that change into clearways during peak periods (cars are automatically towed away if found in these spots). A sign saying "2P" means that

there is a limit of two hours parking and, if there is a charge, it will direct you to a meter or machine. You should always park in the same direction as the traffic.
• It is the responsibility of the driver to ensure restraints (including for children and babies under 12 months old) are used by passengers at all time.
• There is a 0.05 percent blood alcohol limit for drivers, which is widely enforced by the use of random breath tests carried out by the police.

Car Hire

Car-rental companies have offices located throughout the Sydney area, including the airport as well as at airports and major centres throughout the state and in Canberra. Car hire provides the flexibility to discover the NSW countryside, and offers many opportunities to take detours from main roads and highways in order to explore small towns. It is also possible to hire camper vans. If you have not already organised car hire as part of a package, you should shop around for the best deal: the smaller independent operators tend to be cheaper.

An important point to consider is insurance. Many companies have an excess charge of

CAR HIRE COMPANIES

Apollo Motorhome Holidays (camper vans) tel: 9556 3550
Avis, tel: 13 63 33; www.avis.com.au
Britz Campervan Rentals, tel: 9667 0402 or freecall 1800 331 454 (in Australia); www.britz.com
Budget, tel: 13 27 27; www.budget.com.au
Dollar Rent A Car, tel: 9955 3970
Hertz, tel: 13 30 39 or freecall 1800-550 067; www.hertz.com.au
Thrifty, tel: 1300-367 227; www.thrifty.com.au

A$700–2,500, which means that you pay that amount in the case of an accident. It is wise to pay a little bit extra per day to reduce the figure. When you are getting a quote from the company, ask for the full amount including insurance and charges for items such as baby restraints. Many car hire companies do not insure normal vehicles for off-road travel, which means that the driver is liable.

For disabled drivers, all the major hire companies have a small number of cars with hand controls. To be sure of availability, you should contact them well in advance.

Breakdown Services

The NRMA (National Roads and Motorists Association) provides roadside service to members, and has reciprocal arrangements with motoring organisations overseas. Most car-hire outlets arrange their own roadside service, but the NRMA is a good point of contact for all sorts of motoring advice.

The Road and Traffic Authority can provide information about road rules and conditions.
NRMA, tel: 13 11 11 for roadside assistance, or 13 11 22 for travel, touring and general enquiries.
Roads and Traffic Authority, tel: 13 22 13.

Cycling

Sydney now has continuous cycle paths stretching from as far west as Penrith, through Windsor,

Dural and Riverstone all the way to Botany Bay and the North Shore. For free maps and a complete list of Sydney's cycling tracks, contact the Roads and Traffic Authority (tel: 13 22 13).

For an excellent run with wonderful views, take a ride along the track from Tempe to Homebush along the Cooks River, or Botany Bay waterfront to Brighton, or Glebe to Parramatta along the Parramatta River.

Visitors who prefer to cycle in the picturesque surroundings of Centennial Park may have to share the dedicated cycle lanes with horses, in-line skaters and recreational runners, but do not let this deter you. The park was used as part of the cycle road race at the 2000 Olympics, as its open plan allows riders to reach impressive speeds.

Further afield, the **Blue Mountains** offer challenging cycling for those who like hills, and a bike is a great way to see some of the wineries in the Hunter Valley and Mudgee wine regions. **Canberra** offers the ultimate in flat cycling along designated cycle routes and tracks.

For further information for cyclists, call the **Bicycle Insitute of New South Wales** (commonly known as Bicycle NSW), tel: 9218 5400; its website www.bicyclensw. org.au has information on Bugs (Bicycle User Groups) in the various parts of New South Wales and their social ride programmes.

TRANSPORT

ACCOMMODATION

ACTIVITIES

A – Z

A CCOMMODATION

SOME THINGS TO CONSIDER BEFORE YOU BOOK THE ROOM

OVERVIEW

For most overseas visitors, the first night's accommodation will be in Sydney, where there is a range in quality and price similar to any international city. And, likewise, once you leave, you realise what a premium you've had to pay. However, that burgeoning market sector, the "boutique" hotel, is muddying the waters. A weekend break in one of these in the Blue Mountains, the Hunter Valley or Byron Bay can cost a fortune. But the level of pampering is second to none.

Conventional resort hotels operate in the main holiday centres. And then there are the ubiquitous motels. Wherever you go in the state, there will be roadside motor inns preferring middle-of-the-road, decent-but-dull accommodation. A traveller may encounter proud new motel owners – refugees who have retired from city life with an amorphous dream of life in the bush and a determination to reintroduce design standards from their youth. At the moment the favoured period seems to be the late 1970s.

The other omnipresent is the "hotel", in the Australian sense

of the word. This is closer to an inn in other cultures: a pub with acccommodation. As with inns, some of them will have evolved to be just drinking dens, so it's quite possible to find "hotels" with no rooms to let. Those that do provide accommodation are often in older buildings, unrenovated for years, and the rooms will be cheap because the facilities are down the hall. Some have "motel" (with en-suite) units, usually in a separate building or adjunct.

Bed-and-breakfast operations tend to have a few bedrooms within a largish house, and breakfast, sometimes cooked, is in a communal dining room. However, "bed and breakfast" can also mean a few provisions left in the room along with a kettle and a toaster. Tea and coffee is provided in accommodation of all levels, usually in the bedroom; if not, try the communal room(s).

The backpacker scene still thrives. Campsites are generally well maintained and spacious, and, almost without exception, have cabins to rent.

Visitor Information Centres can offer advice on all levels of accommodation, and some will make bookings for you.

Many hotels offer lower rates

outside peak seasons (which relate to factors like school holidays). Watch out for "schoolies' week" in November, when kids who've finished their exams take over whole resorts and discover that if you drink a lot, you fall over (see www.schoolies.org.au).

Listings below include websites. It is an easy way of checking availability, tariffs and offers. There are also brokers who clear unsold rooms at hefty discounts, especially in the cities and main tourist centres. See:

www.wotif.com
www.flightcentre.com.au
www.okjack.com.au

TRANSPORT

SYDNEY

Hotels are listed alphabetically within price categories

City Centre

Sir Stamford at Circular Quay
93 Macquarie St
Tel: 9252 4600 or
1300-301 391
Fax: 9252 4286
www.stamford.com.au
Classical French furnishings and beautiful paintings create a distinguished ambience. Located in the business district, this is a clubby place, popular with business people. The excellent restaurant is the place to close a deal. **$$$$**

Astor Martin Place
1 Hosking Place
Tel: 9292 5016
Contains 100 studio and one-bedroom apartments in the heart of the city. The complex also includes a swimming pool for cooling off after a hard day's sightseeing. **$$$**

InterContinental Sydney
117 Macquarie St
Tel: 9253 9000
www.sydney.intercontinental.com
Soaring out of the shell of the historic Treasury building, this 31-storey, 498-room hotel combines old-world style with modern facilities. Many rooms have classic harbour views. Located in the Circular Quay area, within minutes of the Opera House and harbour. Four restaurants. **$$$**

Merchant Court
68 Market St
Tel: 9238 8888

emailus.sydney@swissotel.com
In the very centre of the city, atop the Sydney Central Plaza building. 361 rooms, furnished in Australian maple, with great views. In-house spa and sauna. **$$$**

Oaks Hyde Park Plaza
38 College St
Tel: 9331 6933
www.theoaksgroup.com.au
Overlooking Hyde Park in the centre of the business district, large apartment-style rooms including full kitchen facilities. Functional design. **$$$**

Sheraton on the Park
161 Elizabeth St
Tel: 9286 6000
Fax: 9286 6686
www.sheraton.com/sydney
Huge rooms with dramatic city and park views. **$$$**

Sydney Marriott
36 College St
Tel: 9361 8400
www.marriott.com
Facing Hyde Park, this 241 room hotel enjoys a fine reputation for the quality of its rooms and service. Amenities include rooftop pool and spa, and modern-Australian cuisine in the Windows on the Park restaurant. **$$$**

Capital Square Hotel
corner of Campbell, George & Day streets
Tel: 9211 8633
Good-value boutique hotel in the heart of Sydney's entertainment district. Korean, Thai and Japanese restaurants. 94 rooms. **$$**

Park Regis
27 Park St
Tel: 9267 6511
www.parkregiosydney.com.au
Occupies the top 15 floors of a 45-storey building, well placed in the central business district, near the Town Hall. 120 rooms, of no great character, but light, airy, efficient and good value. **$$**

Travelodge Sydney
33 Wentworth Ave
Tel: 8224 9400
www.travelodge.com.au
Modern, efficient, no-frills but reasonably priced accommodation just one block south of Hyde Park. 406 rooms on 18 floors. **$$**

The Maze Backpackers/ CB Hotel
417 Pitt St
Tel: 9211 5115
www.mazebackpackers.com
A 200-room hostel in the heart of the city, with TV lounges, jukebox, games room, etc. Dorms, doubles, twins and singles, no ensuites. Cheap and cheerful. **$**

Nomads Backpackers
Head Office: Suite 704, Charles Building, 89 York St
Tel: 9299 7710 or 1800 819 883
www.nomadsworld.com
Hostel franchise with city-centre and beach suburbs accommodation available. **$**

Sydney Central YHA
11 Rawson Place, Haymarket
Tel: 9281 9111
sydcentral@yhansw.org.au
Technically a youth

Sydney

hostel, but it's also an excellent, centrally-located hotel in a heritage building opposite Central Station. Less than A$100 for an en-suite double/twin, with special rates for YHA members. **$**

The Rocks

Bed and Breakfast Sydney Harbour
140–142 Cumberland St
Tel: 9247 1130
fax: 9247 1148
www.bedandbreakfastsydney.com
This restored early 20th-century mansion is located around the corner from the busiest part of The Rocks. The rooms, some with harbour views, are nicely fitted out with period furniture, and most have their own bathroom. The cooked breakfasts have been highly praised. 9 rooms. **$$$$**

PRICE CATEGORIES

Price categories are for a double room without breakfast:
$ = under A$80
$$ = A$80–A$130
$$$ =A$130–A$200
$$$$ = over A$200

ACCOMMODATION

ACTIVITIES

A – Z

Four Seasons
199 George St
Tel: 9238 0000
www.fourseasons.com/sydney
Formerly The Regent Sydney, this hotel has claims to be Australia's finest. In a wonderful location at Circular Quay; impressive atrium foyer, 620 rooms and suites on 34 floors and every possible facility, including a luxurious new spa. **$$$$**

Observatory
89–113 Kent St,
Millers Point
Tel: 9256 2222
www.observatoryhotel.com.au
Designed by prominent Sydney architect Phillip

Cox, this beautiful establishment offers absolute luxury in the heart of The Rocks precinct. With opulent yet intimate ambience, it features Sydney's most sumptuous suites. Stunning star-ceilinged 20-metre indoor pool. 77 rooms, 23 suites. Special rates for internet reservations. **$$$$**

Park Hyatt
7 Hickson Rd
Tel: 9241 1234
www.sydney.park.hyatt.com
Possibly Sydney's most luxurious hotel, opened in 1990 and completely

renovated in 1998. Clinging to the best spot on the inner city's harbour shore, in a low gracious building within a few minutes' walk of the city centre. Spacious, supremely comfortable rooms have privileged water-level views of the harbour; wake up, open the curtains with a switch and watch the Opera House appear. Great views from the harbour kitchen restaurant and bar too. 158 rooms. **$$$$**

Quay West Sydney
98 Gloucester St
Tel: 9240 6000
or 1800-805 031
Fax: 9240 6060
www.mirvac.com.au
Another of the modern towers that front Sydney Harbour, but this one has self-contained luxury apartments, as well as executive penthouses. There's also a Roman bath-style swimming pool. For a different view – looking back towards the Harbour Bridge from near the Opera House – Mirvac also owns a similar luxury apartment development called Quay Grand. **$$$$**

The Russell
143a George St
Tel: 9241 3543
www.therussell.com.au
A charming boutique hotel in The Rocks district. Friendly, intimate surroundings, and convenient. 29 rooms (some with shared bathroom facilities). **$$$$**

Australian Hotel
100 Cumberland St
Tel: 9247 2229
Fax: 9241 3262
www.australianheritagehotel.com

A lovely old pub built in 1913 with very comfortable rooms offering an inexpensive accommodation option in The Rocks. Bathrooms are shared. The roof terrace has views of the Harbour Bridge and Opera House. Price includes breakfast. 18 rooms. **$$$**

Shangri-La
176 Cumberland St
Tel: 9250 6000
www.shangri-la.com
Quintessential harbour views can be had from every room of this award-winning, 563-room modern tower hotel with a lot of style. The Horizons Bar is one of the city's best, and the Japanese restaurant is excellent too. **$$$**

Lord Nelson Brewery Hotel
19 Kent St
Tel: 9251 4044
www.lordnelson.com.au
The best value for money in Sydney, this historic pub provides cheap, comfortable rooms in the city's liveliest district. **$$**

Around Darling Harbour

Grand Mercure Apartments
50 Murray St, Pyrmont
Tel: 9563 6666
Stylish two- and three-bedroom apartments with private balconies, full kitchens and laundry, plus hotel services and facilities including 50-metre indoor rooftop pool, spa, gym and sauna. **$$$$**

Crowne Plaza Darling Harbour
150 Day St,
Darling Harbour
Tel: 9261 1188

http://darlingharbour.crowneplaza.com
Formerly the Park Royal at Darling Harbour, this 12-storey hotel with 349 rooms has a boutique feel, while providing all the facilities expected of an international business hotel. Great location near the Darling Harbour waterside. **$$$**

Four Points by Sheraton
161 Sussex St,
Darling Harbour
Tel: 9290 4000
www.starwood.com/fourpoints
One of Sydney's largest hotels (631 rooms on 15 floors), although its elegant, curved design facing Darling Harbour belies its size. Award-winning Corn Exchange restaurant and pleasant Dundee Arms pub. **$$$**

Novotel Sydney on Darling Harbour
100 Murray St, Pyrmont
Tel: 9934 0000
www.novotel.com
A large, comfortable hotel geared towards business travellers, with gym, tennis court and sauna. 525 rooms. **$$$**

Aarons Hotel
37 Ultimo Rd, Haymarket
Tel: 9281 5555
www.aaronshotel.com.au
Good standard motel-style accommodation located right in the middle of the city. The restaurant, Café Nine, has cabaret Thur–Sun. 94 rooms. **$$**

Goldspear Hotel
corner of Campbell and George streets, Haymarket
Tel: 9211 8633
www.goldspear.com.au
A newish boutique hotel adjacent to the Capitol Theatre and on the fringe of Chinatown. **$$**

Hotel Ibis Darling Harbour

70 Murray St, Pyrmont
Tel: 9563 0888
www.accorhotels.com.au
A modern (1995) three-star hotel on the west side of Darling Harbour. Standard rooms are not large, but comfortable enough. Good value for its location. Fine views across the harbour, especially from the Skyline restaurant and bar, with outdoor terrace. 256 rooms. **$$**

Mercure Hotel Lawson

383 Bulwara Rd, Ultimo
Tel: 9211 1499
Friendly, efficient service in this 96-room modern hotel located behind Darling Harbour. **$$**

Darlinghurst, Surry Hills & other inner Sydney suburbs

Harbourside Apartments

2A Henry Lawson Ave, McMahons Point
Tel: 9963 4300
www.harboursideapartments.com.au
Terrific harbour views of the Opera House underneath the Sydney Harbour Bridge. Compact but comfortable – and the city ferry is right on the doorstep. **$$$**

Medina on Crown Executive

359 Crown St, Surry Hills
Tel: 8302 1000
www.medinaapartments.com.au
Surry Hills is an attractive terrace-house suburb not far from the city centre, with a concentration of galleries, antique shops and restaurants. These are serviced apartments. **$$$**

Morgan's of Sydney

304 Victoria St, Darlinghurst
Tel: 9360 7955
www.morganshotel.com.au
One of the "boutique" hotels fashionably located in the area. Aimed at successful young business people, Morgan's is stylish and comfortable; the downstairs bar is a scene for the "beautiful" people. Paid parking only. **$$$**

Regents Court

18 Springfield Ave, Potts Point
Tel: 9358 1533
www.regentscourt.com.au
Converted in the early 1990s to become Sydney's first true designer hotel, in a quiet cul-de-sac. Rooftop garden with barbecue. 30 studio apartments. **$$$**

Sebel of Sydney

23 Elizabeth Bay Rd, Kings Cross
Tel: 9358 3244
Sydney's oldest five-star hotel, tucked away in Elizabeth Bay, the best part of Kings Cross. Popular with celebrities, who love its discreet, club-like atmosphere. 143 rooms, 23 suites. **$$$**

Simpsons of Potts Point

8 Challis Ave, Potts Point
Tel: 9356 2199
www.simpsonspottspoint.com.au
Simpsons is an elegant boutique hotel (14 rooms) in a historic 1892 family home. It is within walking distance of the city, and minutes from Macleay Street's restaurants. **$$$**

Vibe North Sydney

88 Alfred St, Milsons Point

Tel: 9955 1111
www.vibehotels.com.au
Long a favourite with corporate travellers, this hotel (formerly the Duxton) looks across, from a North Shore perspective, to the Harbour Bridge and Opera House. 165 rooms, including executive suites. **$$$**

The Waldorf Apartment Hotel

57 Liverpool St
Tel: 9261 5355
www.warldorf.com.au
Glitzy tower containing one- and two-bedroom apartments with good views over the city centre and Darling Harbour. At the high end of this price range. **$$$**

All Seasons on Crown

302–308 Crown St, Darlinghurst
Tel: 9360 1133
An elegant boutique hotel in the city's restaurant district. The hotel has its own popular Crown Café. 93 rooms, some with harbour views. **$$**

The Grantham

1 Challis St, Potts Point
Tel: 9357 2377
www.thegrantham.com.au
Many of these apartments have great views across the city skyline to the Botanic Gardens and Sydney Harbour. Functionally designed, with all the facilities you need, the rooms are good value for money. **$$**

Kirketon Hotel

229 Darlinghurst Rd, Darlinghurst
Tel: 9332 2011
www.kirketon.com.au
A well-run boutique hotel the epicentre of hip Darlinghurst. Stylish design – enough to get it voted one of 21 hip

hotels for the 21st century. Remarkably good value. **$$**

L'Otel

114 Darlinghurst Rd, Darlinghurst
Tel: 9360 6868
This luxury "European-style boutique hotel" has 16 all-white rooms, described as a fusion of French chic and hi-tech. **$$**

Glebe Point YHA

262 Glebe Point Rd
Tel: 9692 8418
A bright, comfortable hostel with friendly staff who organise BBQs and backpackers' activities. Great city views from roof recreation area. **$**

Wattle House

44 Hereford St, Glebe
Tel: 9552 4997
www.warldorf.com.au
A budget guesthouse which is much more sedate than the sometimes boisterous backpacker accommodation to be found in this part of the city. Friendly operators, a free breakfast and some of the keenest prices make this a favourite. **$**

Y Hotel Hyde Park

5–11 Wentworth Ave, Darlinghurst
Tel: 9264 2451
www.yhotel.com.au
This terrific value-for-money hostel offers everything from dorm-style accommodation to en-suite rooms. All rooms are clean and comfortable. **$**

PRICE CATEGORIES

Price categories are for a double room without breakfast:
$ = under A$80
$$ = A$80–A$130
$$$ = A$130–A$200
$$$$ = over A$200

THE SYDNEY SUBURBS

Bondi

Ravesi's on Bondi Beach
corner of Campbell Parade and Hall St, Bondi Beach
Tel: 9365 4422
www.ravesis.com.au
This is a great place to combine a beachside holiday with a trip to a busy metropolis. Great beach views and an intimate atmosphere. **$$$**

Lamrock Hostel
7 Lamrock Ave,
Bondi Beach
Tel: 9365 0221
A "boutique" hostel, this place deserves a special mention for its great location just up from the beach and its friendly and intimate atmosphere. **$**

Coogee

Coogee Bay Boutique Hotel
9 Vicar St, Coogee
Tel: 9315 6055
www.coogeebayhotel.com.au
Heritage-style seaside pub, nicely renovated. Located opposite picturesque Coogee Beach, with ocean views from the front rooms. Bus to city takes about 40 mins, taxi 15 mins. **$$$**

Double Bay

Sir Stamford Double Bay
22 Knox St, Double Bay
Tel: 9302 4100
www.stamford.com.au
Fastidious interior decoration, with valuable original artworks. Each room has a carefully designed theme – there's even a Manhattan loft-style room. Double Bay is a wealthy suburb close to the city, known primarily for its shopping. **$$$$**

Ritz Carlton
33 Cross St,
Double Bay
Tel: 9362 4455
If you want luxury away from the city, then this is one of your best bets. Designed with a Mediterranean theme, it provides a discreet retreat in one of Sydney's prettiest suburbs. **$$$**

Manly

Manly Pacific Parkroyal
55 North Steyne, Manly
Tel: 9977 766

Situated right on the beach, this large hotel has a lively, resort-style atmosphere. **$$$**

Radisson Kestrel Hotel
8–13 South Steyne, Manly
Tel: 9977 8866
Beachside hotel with 83 comfortable rooms and a restaurant with balcony and views. **$$$**

Periwinkle Guesthouse
19 East Esplanade, Manly
Tel: 9977 4668
Friendly family-style accommodation on the sea at Manly. Bathrooms are shared. **$**

Palm Beach

Barrenjoey House
1108 Barrenjoey Rd,
Palm Beach
Tel: 9974 4001
www.barrenjoeyhouse.com.au
Lovely traditional-style guesthouse. **$$$**

Parramatta

Courtyard by Marriott
18-40 Anderson St
Tel: 9891 1277
Modern, high-standard business hotel with a choice of rooms or suites. **$$$**

Richmond

Best Western Colonial Motel
161 March St
Tel: 4578 1166
www.colonialmotel.com.au
Reasonable rooms in this workaday motel. **$$**

University Motel
Hawkesbury Conference Centre, University of Western Sydney, Hawkesbury
Tel: 4570 1202
Single or twin shares; clean, bright, simple rooms on part of the university campus. **$$**

Windsor

Windsor Terrace Motel
47 George Street
Tel: 4577 5999
www.windsorterracemotel.com
Comfy modern motel with views across the Hawkesbury River and to the Blue Mountains. **$$**

THE BLUE MOUNTAINS

Blackheath

Federation Gardens Lodge
185 Evans Lookout Rd
Tel: 4787 7767
www.federationgardens.com
Family cottages with a comprehensive range of entertainment distractions for kids and adults. **$$$**

Jemby Rinjah Lodge
336 Evans Lookout Rd
Tel: 4787 7622
www.jembyrinjahlodge.com.au
Simple timber cabins or four-bedroom lodges. **$$$**

Katoomba

Echoes Boutique Hotel
3 Lilianfels Ave,

Tel: 4782 1966
www.echoeshotel.com.au
Modern luxury and old-fashioned atmosphere in this immaculately renovated boutique hotel with tremendous views. **$$$$**

Lilianfels
Lilianfels Ave, Echo Point,
Katoomba
Tel: 4780 1200

A five-star resort with a renowned restaurant on

the edge of the Jamison Valley. **$$$$**

Blue Mountains YHA
207 Katoomba St
Tel: 4782 1416
www.yha.com.au
Bright, well appointed hostel in 1930s art-deco building. **$**

The Clarendon Guest-house
68 Lurline St
Tel: 4782 1322
www.clarendonguesthouse.com.au
A choice of budget and smarter rooms in this small hotel. Also houses a working theatre. **$**

Leura

Peppers Fairmont Resort
1 Sublime Point Rd
Tel: 4784 4144
www.peppers.com.au
A luxury resort built in the 1980s when the area was revived as a holiday escape. More than 200 rooms are surrounded by gardens with views across the Blue Mountains. Good family deals. **$$$$**

Old Leura Dairy
61 Kings Rd

Tel: 4782 0700
www.oldleuradairy.com
"The milking shed had everything we needed and more", is an unusual endorsement but fully deserved here. Old dairy buildings have been turned into luxurious cottages. **$$$**

Medlow Bath

Mercure Grand Hydro Majestic
Great Western Hwy
Tel: 4788 1002
www.hydromajestic.com.au
Perched above the Megalong and Kanimbla Valleys, the views alone make a visit to the Grand Hydro worthwhile. Add in the glorious building, originally begun in 1891 and substantially rebuilt in art-nouveau style in the 1930s, and there's no excuse for not dropping by, if only to drink. **$$$**

Mount Victoria

The Manor House
Montgomery St
Tel: 4787 1389
www.themanorhouse.com.au
Atmospheric old guest-house with fine period fittings and a good restaurant. **$$$**

The Imperial Hotel
1 Station St
Tel: 4787 2786
www.hotelimperial.com.au
A spread of options are available in this substantial old pub, ranging from luxury suites to four-bed backpacker rooms. **$$**

The Victoria and Albert Guesthouse
19 Station St
Tel: 4787 1241
The splendid façade has changed little in the last 100 years. Inside, however, there have been some unfortunate "upgrades" over the years and some of the atmosphere has been lost. **$$**

THE SOUTH COAST

Batemans Bay

Bay Waters Inn
corner Princes Hwy and Canberra Rd
Tel: 4472 6333
The rooms may be uninspiring, but there are extensive grounds, complete with a pool and other facilities. **$$**

Easts Riverside Holiday Park
Wharf Rd
Tel: 4472 4048
There's a range of well-equipped cabins along with powered and "en-suite" sites. Well sited overlooking the town – the centre is just five minutes walk away. **$$**

Berry

Berry Village Boutique Motel
72 Queen St
Tel: 4464 3570
www.berrymotel.com.au
Modern, well-designed motel with lots of wood and minimalism. There is a heated salt-water pool. **$$$**

Bunyip Inn
122 Queen St, Berry
Tel: 4464 2064
Cosy, historic accommodation in this pretty converted bank building on Berry's main street. Nine rooms with four more in converted stables. **$$$**

Central Tilba

Dromedary Hotel
Bate St
Tel: 4473 7223
Atmospheric old wooden pub with simple rooms, named after the local mountain – the highest point on the south coast. **$**

Eden

Eagle Heights Holiday Units
12 Yule St
Tel: 6496 1971
www.eagleheights.info
Ten self-contained quiet, comfortable units staggered down to the

edge of the cliffs above Twofold Bay. **$$**

PRICE CATEGORIES

Price categories are for a double room without breakfast:
$ = under A$80
$$ = A$80–A$130
$$$ = A$130–A$200
$$$$ = over A$200

STAY WITH US AT 'THE DROM.'
ACCOMMODATION
BED & BREAKFAST

Jervis Bay

Paper Bark Camp
605 Woollamia Rd
Tel:4441 6066
www.paperbarkcamp.com.au
An eco-resort with permanent tents complete with en suites. Delightful bush setting and loads of activities, such as canoes for fishing in the creek. Great restaurant – The Gunyah – elevated on stilts. $$$$

Kiama

Kiama Harbour Cabins– Blowhole Point
Lighthouse Rd
Tel: 4232 2707
Right down on the spit leading to the blowhole, there are good cabins with one, two or three bedrooms. $$$
Kiama Ocean View Motor Inn
9 Bong Bong St
Tel: 4232 1966
Just a short hop from the waterfront, this well-equipped motel is notable for the helpfulness of the owners. $$

Merimbula

Cetacea Luxury Apartments
46 Fishpen Rd
Tel: 6495 1818
www.cetaceaapartments.com
Modern, bright apartments facing onto the river. $$$
Sapphire Valley Caravan Park
29 Sapphire Coast Drive
Tel: 6495 1746
sapphirevalleycaravanpark.com.au
Well-designed cabins and 114 camping and caravan sites. $

Narooma

Amooran Court
30 Montague St
Tel: 4476 2198
www.amoorancourt.com.au
A selection of apartments and studios make this an ideal place for a family holiday. Golf packages are available as well. $$$
Forsters Bay Lodge
55 Forsters Bay Rd
Tel: 4476 2319
Comfortable clean rooms in a quiet area with views across the water. Good value. $$

Southern Highlands

Peppers Manor House
Kater Rd, Sutton Forest
Tel: 4868 2355
www.peppers.com.au
A luxurious retreat in an old country house, complete with baronial great hall. It has a gourmet restaurant, "Katers", attached. $$$$

Links House
7 Links Rd, Bowral
Tel: 4861 1977
www.linkshouse.com.au
A golf course on the doorstep provides some distraction, but otherwise there's no reason to abandon this comfortable home. $$$
Solar Springs Health Retreat
96 Osborn Ave, Bundanoon
Tel: 4883 6027
The place to come for a spot of holistic rejuvenation combined with a decent dollop of pampering. $$$
Tree Tops Guest House
101 Railway Ave,
Bundanoon
Tel: 4883 6372
www.treetopsguesthouse.com.au
An early 20th-century country guesthouse which offers, amongst the usual facilities, "Super Sleuth" murder-mystery packages. $$$
Twin Falls Bush Cottages
Throsby Rd, Fitzroy Falls
Tel: 4887 7333
www.fitzroyfalls.com
A modest bush retreat in the region's escarpment country, backing onto Moreton National Park. $$$
Berrima Bakehouse Motel
corner Wingecarribee St and Old Hume Hwy, Berrima
Tel: 4877 1381

www.highlandsnsw.com.au/berrimabakehouse
Standard motel scores with terrific location right in the heart of the village. $$
Ranelagh House
Illawarra Hwy, Robertson
Tel: 4885 1111
An imposing old mansion in a historic Southern Highlands town. The exotic grounds are populated with exotic birds and other wildlife. $$

Ulladulla

Ulladulla House
39 Burrill St
Tel: 4455 1796
www.treetopsguesthouse.com.au
Five-star, slightly over-upholstered guesthouse with an art gallery attached, a restaurant and pretty gardens. $$$

Wollongong

Rydges Wollongong
112 Burelli St
Tel: 4229 7444
www.rydges.com
Modern four-star hotel that provides all the facilities demanded by its mainly business clientele, and is handy for the centre. $$$
Boat Harbour Motel
7 Wilson St
Tel: 4226 4878
www.boatharbourmotel.com.au
Perfectly adequate motel which offers some rooms with balconies and ocean views. $$
Keiraview
75–79 Keira St
Tel: 4229 1132
Accommodation complex which includes the YHA. The larger rooms are a good option for families. $

CANBERRA

Centre

Hyatt
Commonwealth Ave
Tel: 6270 1234
www.ichotelsgroup.com
This is the five-star offering in town, close to Parliament and the lake. Unlike most of the business hotels in town, it is architecturally distinguished, too. Built in 1924 and Heritage-listed, it retains many attractive art-deco features **$$$$**

Crowne Plaza
1 Binara St
Tel: 6247 8999
www.ichotelsgroup.com
All the features of a good upmarket hotel and handily placed in the centre. **$$$**

Olims
corner Ainslie and Limestone Ave
Tel: 6243 0000
www.olimshotel.com
Built in 1927 and listed by the National Trust, Olims has an attractive courtyard garden and plenty of character.

Rooms are spacious and reasonable value. There is, though, a danger that areas looking well-worn now will soon be full-on tatty. **$$$**

Canberra City Accommodation
7 Akuna St
Tel: 6257 3955
www.yha.com.au
Very central position for this large hostel offering a mix of rooms – some with en suites – and dorms. Lots of facilities like a pool, sauna, internet café, and a bar with live music. **$**

Acton

University House
1 Balmain Crescent
Tel: 6125 5211
Located within the Australian National University, there are 143 rooms available, including 36 suites, in a quiet setting within easy distance of the city centre or Lake Burley Griffin. Pretty good value. **$$**

Ainslie

Best Western Tall Trees Motel
21 Stephen St
Tel: 6247 9200
talltrees.bestwestern.com.au
A four-star spotless motel away from the hurly-burly. Popular, so book ahead. **$$$**

Kingston

The York
31 Giles St
Tel: 6295 2333
www.yorkcanberra.com.au
Twenty-five sleek modern suites in this boutique. **$$$$**

Kingston Terrace Serviced Apartments
18 Eyre St
Tel: 6239 9499
www.kingstonterrace.com.au
One of several options in the serviced apartment sector (all the peripatetic politicians and civil servants have to stay somewhere), these are as good as any, with excellent facilities and inoffensive

décor. The operators also have a block in Manuka. **$$$**

Victor Lodge
29 Dawes St
Tel: 6295 7777
www.victorlodge.com.au
Family-run budget guesthouse that gives a free all-you-can-eat breakfast. A range of options includes dorms, and it's justifiably popular. **$**

Symonston

Canberra South Motor Park
Canberra Ave
Tel: 6280 6176
www.csmp.net.au
Cabins, motel rooms, caravan and campsites, 4 km south of the city centre. **$$$**

THE SOUTHEAST

Albury

Elizabeth's Manor
531 Lyne St
Tel: 6040 4412
www.elizabethsmanor.com.au

PRICE CATEGORIES

Price categories are for a double room without breakfast:
$ = under A$80
$$ = A$80–A$130
$$$ = A$130–A$200
$$$$ = over A$200

Bizarre mock-Tudor manor, complete with four-poster beds and suits of armour, providing five-star B&B. The traditional English-style food (and the breakfast) is well-prepared. **$$$**

Albury Backpackers
452 David St
Tel: 6041 1822
Set up in an old house, there are the usual facilities, as well as bike and canoe hire. **$**

Cooma

Snowtels Caravan Park
Snowy Mountains Hwy
Tel: 6452 1828
www.snowtels.com.au
The usual mix of accommodation options and on-site facilities including mini golf, tennis and a kids' playground. **$**

White Manor Motel
252 Sharp St
Tel: 6452 1152
www.whitemanor.com

Well refurbished buildings, attention to detail and a friendly reception raise this motel above the average. **$**

Goulburn

Alpine Heritage Motel
248 Sloane St
Tel: 4821 2930
www.argylecounty.com.au/alpine
Imposing Heritage-listed building with spacious high-ceilinged rooms in the front and slightly more recent motel rooms at the back. Look out for the idiosyncratic wallpaper murals. Good value. $–$$

Griffith

Best Western Kidman Wayside Inn
58–72 Jondaryan Ave
Tel: 6964 5666
Old homestead with 80 units in well-maintained landscaped gardens. Features a highly-rated restaurant. $$

Gundagai

Poets Recall Motel
West and Punch streets
Tel: 6944 1777
www.poetsrecall.com.au
Incorporating part of an old 1875 hotel, this is now a dependable place to stay, complete with pool and restaurant. $$

Jindabyne

Banjo Paterson Inn
1 Kosciusko Rd
Tel: 6456 2372
www.banjopatersoninn.com.au
Unusually tasteful pub, with a wide range of rooms, some with lake-view balconies. $$$

Quality Resort Horizons
Kosciusko Rd
Tel: 6456 2562
www.horizonsresort.com.au
Over 100 luxury apart-
ments. Views over lake and mountains. $$$

Thredbo

Thredbo Alpine Hotel
Friday Drive
Tel: 6459 4200
www.rydges.com
In the middle of the village and metres from a ski lift Prices double in peak season. $$$$

Alpenhorn Lodge
Buckwong Place
Tel: 6457 6223
www.alphorn.com.au
Stylishly spruced up, with its own bar and restaurant, handy for the ski slopes. $$$

Tumut

Ribbonwood Cottages
116 Lacmalac Rd
Tel: 6947 2527
www.ribbonwoodcottages.com.au
Riverside two-bed cottages just out of town. Good value. $$

Wagga Wagga

Carlyle Motel
148 Tarcutta St
Tel: 6931 0968
Roomy and comfortable accommodation in an old Victorian building. $$

The Manor
38 Morrow St
Tel: 6921 5962
www.themanor.com.au
Beautifully appointed old Federation house. $$

Romano's Hotel
corner Sturt and Fitzmaurice streets
Tel: 6921 2013
www.romanoshotel.com.au
Iconic pub has 46 rooms with some nice period touches. $

FAR WEST OUTBACK

Broken Hill

The Astra
393 Argent St
Tel: 08-8087 5428
An absolute fortune has been spent on renovating this massive hotel – and the evidence is in the rooms. $$$

The Imperial
88 Oxide St
Tel: 08-8087 7044
www.imperialfine
accommodation.com
Magnificent old hotel converted into a sumptuous guesthouse. Huge bedrooms, DVD library, billiards room and a garden. $$$

Mario's Palace Hotel
corner Argent and Sulphide streets
Tel: 08-8088 1699
Remarkable old Victorian pile made distinc-
tive by the prolific mural artist who has covered even the most inaccessible surface with daubs of Outback scenes, quotes from classic paintings and whatever else sprang to mind. The rooms are basic but cheap. $$$

Royal Exchange Hotel
320 Argent St
Tel: 08-8087 2308
www.royalexchangehotel.com
Pristine art-deco building with lots of original features in the public areas. Sadly the rooms, though comfortable, are entirely bereft of these features. $$$

Caledonian Bed & Breakfast
140 Chloride St
Tel: 08-8087 1945
www.caledonianbnb.com.au
Another listed former
hotel but smaller in scale, with splendid homely rooms and lounge which make the most of old features. Impeccable hosts who do as much or as little as guests require. This reviewer, incognito, was invited to dinner. $

Hay

Saltbush Motor Inn
193 Lachlan St
Tel: 6993 4555
www.saltbushmotorinn.com.au
New (2005) motel has a pool, broadband internet access to all rooms but little style. $$

Menindee

Burke & Wills Menindee Motel
Yartla St

Tel: 08-8091 4313
Perfectly adequate for the night, but cross the road to Maidens Hotel for atmosphere. $

Mungo NP

Mungo Lodge
Arumpo Rd
Tel: 03-5029 7297
www.mungolodge.com.au
Comfortable cabins, along with a bar and restaurant, make a good base for exploring the National Park. $$

Tibooburra

The Family Hotel
Briscoe St
Tel: 08-8091 3314
www.outbacknsw.com.au/family_hotel
Hotel rooms or motel cabins across the road are the options at this historic pub, famed for its murals. **$**

Tibooburra Hotel
Briscoe St
Tel: 08-8091 3310
www.outbacknsw.com.au/

tibooburra
The other hotel in town, this one with two storeys. Simple rooms, good food and a load of moth-eaten hats pinned to the walls of the bar. **$**

Wentworth

Willow Bend Caravan Park
Darling St
Tel: 03-5027 3213
Delightful site right on

the Darling River, and river cabins have boat moorings. There are also on-site vans, powered sites and squads of possums **$**

White Cliffs

PJ's Underground Bed and Breakfast
Dugout 72, Turley's Hill
Tel: 08-8091 6626
babs.com.au/pj
Five well-appointed rooms under, as they

put it, a 64-million-year-old roof. **$$**

White Cliffs Underground Dug-Out Motel
Smith's Hill
Tel: 08-8091 6677
www.undergroundmotel.com.au
Expediency in the face of searing summer heat means living underground in a comfortable year-round 22 degrees. Each room has its own ventilation shaft. There's a bar, bistro and restaurant. **$$**

CENTRAL OUTBACK

Bathurst

Country Comfort Bathurst
corner Brilliant and Stewart streets
Tel: 6332 1800
www.constellationhotels.com
Well-managed four-star operation just outside the centre. **$$$**

Royal Apartments
108 William St
Tel: 6332 4920
www.bathurstheritage.com.au
Exceptional place to stay in the old Royal Hotel. Also rooms in The Mews and some furnished cottages as well. **$$$**

Bourke

Bourke Riverside Motel
3 Mitchell St

Tel: 6872 2539
www.bourkeriversidemotel.com
Renovated historic hotel with award-winning rose gardens. **$$**

Comeroo Station
Tel: 6874 7735
www.comeroo.com
Stay on a working Outback camel station. **$**

Cowra

Vineyard Motel
Chardonnay Rd
Tel: 6342 3461
www.vineyardmotel.com.au
Set amongst vineyards in pleasant gardens, it's one of very few motels where sitting on the veranda's a pleasure. Meals available. **$$**

Dubbo

Zoofari Lodge
Western Plains Zoo
Tel: 6881 1488
www.zoofari.com.au
All-in deal includes dinner, breakfast and two days' zoo admission. **$$$$**

Cattleman's Motel
8 Whylandra St
Tel: 6884 5299
www.cattlemans.com.au

Big, central motel and apartment complex with heaps of facilities. **$$**

Forbes

Apex Riverside Tourist Park
88 Reymond St
Tel: 6851 1929
www.touristpark.com.au
Lovely setting in woodland by the river along from a historic iron bridge. Two-bedroom villas, smaller cabins and a camping ground. **$**

Gilgandra

Cooee Motel
corner Newell Hky and Hargraves Lane
Tel: 6847 2981
www.goldenchain.com.au
Sound, reliable motel with meals available. **$**

Lightning Ridge

Lightning Ridge Hotel
Onyx St
Tel: 6829 0304
Log cabins, a pub, a restaurant and a caravan park on 10 acres. **$**

Lithgow

Zig Zag Motel
Bells Line of Road
Tel: 6352 2477
www.zigzagmotel.com.au
Coventional but high-standard motel with pleasant gardens and a pool. **$$**

Lithgow Tourist and Van Park
58 Cooerwull Rd
Tel: 6351 4350
www.lithgowcaravanpark.com.au
Cabins of three different standards, plus camping and van sites. **$**

PRICE CATEGORIES

Price categories are for a double room without breakfast:
$ – under A$80
$$ = A$80–A$130
$$$ =A$130–A$200
$$$$ = over A$200

Moree

Sundowner
2 Webb Ave
Tel: 6752 2466
www.sundownermotorinns.com.au
Features include a thermal artesian spa. **$$**

Mudgee

Evanslea
146 Market St
Tel: 6372 4116
www.evanslea.com

Four luxurious cottages on 9 acres running down to the river, Evanslea is proudly the only five-star property in town. **$$$$**

Lawson Park Hotel
corner Short and Church streets
Tel: 6372 2183
www.pubboy.com.au
Historic pub with reasonable rooms, good guest lounge and fabulous views. **$$**

Narrabri

Big Sky Caravan Park
Tibbereena St
Tel: 6792 1294
Quiet, central riverside site has all the standard amenities. **$**

Orange

Duntryleague Guesthouse
Woodward Ave
Tel: 6362 3822

www.duntryleague.com
Immaculately maintained Victorian mansion with 14 guest rooms. **$$$**

Parkes

Coachman Motel
Welcome St
Tel: 6862 2622
www.coachman.com.au
Standard and executive rooms. Good bar and food. **$**

CENTRAL COAST

The Entrance

Kims
16 Charlton St, Toowoon Bay
Tel: 4332 1566
www.kims.com.au
Ultra-luxurious bungalows dotted along a beautiful bay. **$$$$**

Gloucester

Great Escape Lofts
40 Hume St
Tel: 6558 9166
www.greatescape.com.au
A handful of self-contained apartments with the bedroom in the loft. A generously proportioned pool as well. **$$**

Maitland

The Old George and Dragon Guesthouse
50 Melbourne St
Tel: 4934 6080
www.oldgeorgedragonguesthouse.com.au
Individually decorated sites are stuffed with antiques in this paean to pampering. **$$$**

Morpeth

Bronte Guest House
147 Swan St

Tel: 4934 6080
www.bronteguesthouse.com.au
Six suites, two lounges and lashings of comfort in historic Morpeth. **$$$**

Newcastle

Clarendon Hotel
347 Hunter St
Tel: 4927 0966
www.clarendonhotel.com.au
A superb example of 1930s art-deco styling, the Clarendon has been turned into a very chic boutique hotel upstairs, while retaining its drinking clientele with a cool bar renovation. **$$$**

Grand Hotel
corner Bolton and Church streets
Tel: 4929 3489
Good value standard accommodation with friendly service, handy for the beach and centre of town. **$**

Newcastle Beach YHA
30 Pacific St
Tel: 4925 3544
www.yha.com.au
Not many hostels boast chandeliers and panelled walls, or a ballroom. But not many are in such historic buildings. **$**

Pokolbin

Peppers Convent
Halls Rd
Tel: 4998 7764
www.peppers.com.au
Seventeen guest rooms in a beautiful old convent surrounded by vineyards. **$$$$**

Hunter Valley Gardens
Broke Rd
Tel: 4998 4000
www.hvg.com.au
A kind of garden theme park over 300 ha (740 acres), there are three different places to stay ranging from three- to four-star. **$$$**

The Hunter Valley Wine Country Tourism Centre
Main Rd
Tel: 4991 7396
www.winecountry.com.au
There are so many places to stay in the area that your best bet is to start here.

Terrigal

Crowne Plaza
Pine Tree Lane
Tel: 4384 5798
www.terrigal.crowneplaza.com
Massive 196-room resort dominates the shore. Every possible

amenity on offer. **$$$$**

Salty Rose Boutique B&B
31 Surf Rider Ave, North Avoca
Tel: 4384 6098
Intimate retreat on this beautiful coastline. **$$**

Terrigal Beach Lodge
12 Campbell Crescent
Tel: 4385.3330
www.yha.com.au
Just off the beach, this friendly place is strong on activities and even offers free use of surf- and bodyboards. **$**

Wisemans Ferry

Wisemans Inn Hotel
Old Northern Rd
Tel: 4566 4301
www.wisemansinnhotel.com.au
Full of character, this old hotel incorporates part of an 1826 home and is full of old features. Basic rooms in the pub or motel units. **$**

NEW ENGLAND, NORTH COAST & LORD HOWE ISLAND

Armidale

Lindsay House
128 Faulkner St
Tel: 6771 4554
www.lindsayhouse.com.au
Big old mock-Tudor mansion which has been painstakingly turned into a fine B&B. Restaurant Wed–Sat. **$$$**

Bellingen

Bellingen Backpackers
2 Short St
Tel: 6655 1116
www.bellingenyha.com.au
YHA hostel housed in a gorgeous old timber house encircled by spacious verandas. If the copious facilities within pall, seek refuge in the tree house. **$**

Byron Bay

Byron Bay Accommodation
Tel: 6680 8666
www.byronbayaccom.ne
There are hundreds of private holiday houses and apartments in the area, and this is the main clearing house. Prices soar around Christmas/New Year and during the festivals.
Beach Hotel
Bay St
Tel: 6685 6402
www.beachhotel.com.au
Luxury beachfront

PRICE CATEGORIES

Price categories are for a double room without breakfast:
$ = under A$80
$$ = A$80–A$130
$$$ =A$130–$200
$$$$ = over A$200

rooms and suites right on top of Byron Bay's main meeting, drinking and eating place. **$$$$**

Coffs Harbour

Opal Cove Resort
Pacific Hwy
Tel: 6651 0510
www.opalcove.com.au
One of several large resorts, this one has its own golf course to go with the pools, restaurants and beach. **$$$**

Dorrigo

Hotel Motel Dorrigo
corner Hickory and Cudgery streets
Tel: 6566 6160
www.hotelmoteldorrigo.com.au
Bedrooms are on the uninspiring side but the hotel itself is full of character and there's a reasonable bistro. **$**

Glen Innes

King Plains Castle
King Plains Rd
Tel: 6733 6808
www.kingsplainscastle.gleninnes.biz
Built in 1908 to echo Scottish baronial castles, now guests live it up as the laird. **$$$**

Nelson Bay

Peninsula Motor Inn
52 Shoal Bay Rd
Tel: 4981 3666
Four-star motel rooms, suites or excellent apartments make this a good choice for an extended beach holiday. **$$**
Samurai Beach Bungalows
Corner Frost Road & Robert Connell Close
Tel: 4982 1921

www.samuraiportstephens.com
A backpackers which also runs to deluxe doubles Great bush setting for wildlife. **$**

South West Rocks

Trial Bay Eco Tourist Park
161 Phillip Drive
Tel: 6566 6142
www.trialbay.com.au
Four-star deluxe cabins and cottages or every kind of camping provision in this exceptionally well resourced park. Quiet setting behind the beach which is a 10-minute walk away. **$$**
Arakoon State Conservation Area
Cardwell St
Tel: 6566 6168
www.nationalparks.nsw.gov.au
Basic campground with minimal facilities, but it's set just above a stunning beach and just below Trial Bay Gaol. **$$**

Tamworth

Quality Hotel Powerhouse
Armidale Rd
Tel: 6766 7000
www.qualityhotelpowerhouse.com.au
Glitzy modern hotel with 61 rooms and 20 five-star apartments. **$$$**

Sydney

Tenterfield

Tenterfield Lodge Caravan Park
2 Manners St
Tel: 6736 1477
www.tenterfieldbiz.com/tenterfieldlodge
Backpacker accommodation in the heritage-listed Lodge, plus a campsite with a range of cabins. **$**

Lord Howe Island

Mary Challis Cottages
Tel: 6563 2076
www.lordhoweisland.info/stay/mary
Two one-bedroom cottages in garden setting, away from the sea. This explains the price. **$$**
Capella Lodge and Apartments
Lagoon Rd
Tel: 6563 2008
www.lordhowe.com
Hard to beat this intimate retreat for service, comfort, setting or food. **$$**

A CTIVITIES

THE ARTS, NIGHTLIFE, SHOPPING, SPORTS AND FESTIVALS

THE ARTS

Art Galleries

Art-lovers will find an exciting smorgasbord of galleries in Sydney and Canberra. The regional galleries of New South Wales also have plenty to offer, with the artistically inclined congregating in areas such as the Blue Mountains, the Southern Highlands, Newcastle, Hill End and Sofala and Byron Bay. Visitors also shouldn't miss the Outback art scene in the state's far west.

The best way to get in touch with what's on is to buy a copy of *Art Almanac*, a monthly pocket-sized booklet that lists galleries and their current exhibitions. It costs A\$3 and is available at good bookshops and galleries.

Sydney

Art Gallery of New South Wales
Art Gallery Road, The Domain
Tel: 9225 1744;
www.artgallery.nsw.gov.au
The leading museum of art in the state, and one of Australia's foremost cultural institutions. Open daily 10am–5pm, Wed to 9pm.
Australian Galleries
15 Roylston Street, Paddington
Tel: 9360 5177
Features established contem-

porary Australian artists including Jeffrey Smart. Open Mon–Sat 10am–6pm.
Hogarth Galleries
Aboriginal Art Centre, 7 Walker Lane, Paddington
Tel: 9360 6839
Australia's oldest established Aboriginal fine-art gallery, presenting works by established and emerging artists. Open Tues–Sat 10am–5pm.
Mori Gallery
168 Day Street, Darling Harbour
Tel: 9283 2903;
www.morigallery.com.au
Showing both established and new contemporary artists. Open Wed–Sat 11am–6pm.
Museum of Contemporary Art
Circular Quay West, The Rocks
Tel: 9245 2456; www.mca.com.au
Contains several unique art collections, including work by Australia's finest contemporary artists. Open daily 10am–5pm.
Ray Hughes Gallery
270 Devonshire Street, Surry Hills. Tel: 9698 3200
Emphasis on vibrant Australian works and more unusual overseas works. Open Tues–Sat 10am–6pm.
Roslyn Oxley 9 Gallery
Soudan Lane, 27 Hampden Street, Paddington
Tel: 9360 4484
Features new work in a range of media, from painting and sculp-

ture to photography, performance, installation, video and other electronic media. Open Tues–Fri 10am–6pm, Sat 11am–6pm.
Sherman Galleries
16–18 Goodhope Street, Paddington. Tel: 9331 1112
Exhibits contemporary Australian painters and sculptors, and occasional exhibitions of international artists. Open Tues–Fri 10am–6pm, Sat 11am–6pm.
Utopia Art Sydney
2 Danks Street, Waterloo
Tel: 9699 2900
Specialises in Aboriginal work. Open Tues–Sat 10am–5pm.

Around NSW

Outside of Sydney there are excellent regional galleries in **Newcastle** (Laman Street; tel: 4974 5105; www.ncc.nsw.gov.au. Open Tues–Sat 10am–5pm), **Bathurst** (70–78 Keppel Street; tel: 6331 6066. Open Tues–Sat 10am–5pm, Sun 11am–2pm) and **Orange** (Civic Square; tel: 6393 8136; www.org.gov.au. Open Tues–Sat 10am–5pm, Sun 12pm–4pm). The **New England Regional Art Museum** in Armidale (Kentucky Street; tel: 6772 5255; www.neram.com.au. Open Tues–Fri 10am–5pm, Sat–Sun 9am–4pm) houses a collection that includes well-known Australian artists such as William

Dobell, Tom Roberts, Margaret Preston, Brett Whitley and Arthur Streeton, and the **Wollongong City Gallery** (corner of Kembla and Bureilli streets; tel: 4228 7500; www.wollongongcitygallery.com. Open Tues–Fri 10am–5pm, weekends 12pm–4pm) is one of the largest regional galleries in Australia. Wagga Wagga's Civic Centre houses the **Wagga Wagga Art Gallery** (Baylis Street, Wagga Wagga; tel: 6926 9660. Open Tues–Sat 10am–5pm, Sun 12pm–4pm) and **Community Gallery**, as well as the **National Art Glass Gallery** (tel: 6926 9700). In the Blue Mountains visitors to the **Norman Lindsay Gallery and Museum** at Faulconbridge (14 Norman Lindsay Crescent; tel: 4751 1067. Open daily 10am–4pm) can see the voluptuous nudes of one of Australia's best-known artists. At **Wangi Wangi**, near Newcastle, is the house of 1940s and 50s portrait painter William Dobell (47 Dobell Drive; tel: 4975 4115. Open weekends 1pm–4pm), and south of Sydney is **Bundanon**, with works by four generations of the Boyd family (Illaroo Road, West Cambewarra; tel: 4423 5999; www.bundanon.com.au. Open Sun 10.30am–4pm). **Broken Hill** has a thriving artistic community, and includes the oldest regional gallery in the state, The **Broken Hill Regional Art Gallery** (corner of Blende and Chloride streets; tel: 08-8088 5491. Open daily 10am–5pm), **Pro Hart's Gallery** (108 Wyman Street; tel: 08-8088 2992; www.prohart.com.au. Open Mon–Sat 9am–5pm, Sun 1.30pm–5pm) and the **Living Desert Reserve and Sculpture Symposium**, 12 sculptures created out of Wilcannia sandstone boulders by artists from around the world in 1993.

Canberra

Beaver Galleries
81 Denison Street, Deakin
Tel: 6282 5294
Canberra's largest privately owned gallery, with four exhibi-

tion spaces and a sculpture garden featuring contemporary Australian artists.
Open daily 10am–5pm.
National Gallery of Australia
Parkes Place
Tel: 6240 6502; www.nga.gov.au
More than 100,000 works, with collections of Australian, aboriginal and international art.
Open daily 10am–5pm.
National Portrait Gallery
Old Parliament House, King George Terrace, Parkes Place
Tel: 6270 8236; www.portrait.gov.au
(also at Commonwealth Place)
The national portrait collection is housed in two locations, with all media represented at Old Parliament House (open daily 9am–5pm) and an emphasis on photography at the Commonwealth Place site (open Wed–Sun 10am–5pm).
Nolan Gallery
Tharwa Drive, Tharwa
Tel: 6235 5688
Contains work by Sidney Nolan of the Ned Kelly series fame and other renowned Australian artists.
Open Tues–Sun 10am–4pm.

Concerts

The major names in the classical arena in New South Wales belong to the **Sydney Symphony Orchestra** (SSO) and the **Australian Chamber Orchestra** (ACO) and in the national capital to the **Canberra Symphony Orchestra** (CSO).
The SSO, established in 1932, performs around 180 concerts a year. Its home ground is the Concert Hall in the Sydney Opera House, but its biggest gig is Symphony under the Stars, a free summer evening concert in Sydney's Domain.
The ACO performs at both the Concert Hall and the City Recital Hall in Sydney and Llewellyn Hall at the Australian National University School of Music in Canberra, and takes performances to the regional centres listed below.
The CSO performs four concerts a year at Llewellyn Hall as well as an annual end-of-summer

Proms in the picturesque setting of Government House at Yarralumla in February.

Sydney
Australian Chamber Orchestra
Sydney Opera House
Tel: 9250 7777 (box office)
This young orchestra plays about 24 concerts at the Concert Hall each year.
Musica Viva
Tel: 8394 6666
This large chamber-music association organises tours of national and international music groups. Concerts are held in the City Recital Hall Angel Place in Sydney, Llewellyn Hall in Canberra and the Concert Hall at the Newcastle University Conservatorium.
Sydney Symphony Orchestra
Sydney Opera House
Tel: 9250 7777 (box office)
The largest orchestra in Australia plays about 100 concerts a year at the Opera House Concert Hall.

Canberra
Canberra Symphony Orchestra
Level 8, 15 London Circuit.
Tel: 6247 9191
Llewellyn Hall
Childers Street, Acton. Tel: 6125 4993

Around NSW
Newcastle
Newcastle City Hall
290 King Street. Tel: 4974 2996

Wollongong
Wollongong Town Hall
Corner of Crown and Kembla streets. Tel: 4225 2633

Theatre

Theatre goers with a taste for something beyond the big-budget musicals and tried and tested classics will find the New South Wales theatre scene offers some tantalising fare. Although Sydney is the natural epicentre for such activity, many of the regional centres have theatres and playhouses, where touring companies appear alongside local troupes on the annual billing.

For the latest in new work try to catch some of the performances at the Sydney Festival in January *(see page 289).*

Sydney

Bell Shakespeare Company
88 George Street, The Rocks
Tel: 9241 2722
Stages unusual productions of Shakespeare, touring extensively in regional New South Wales.
Belvoir Street Theatre
25 Belvoir Street, Surry Hills
Tel: 9699 3444
The place to see alternative, well-crafted work. Australia's most critically acclaimed company.
Capitol
13 Campbell Street, Haymarket
Tel: 1300-136 166
Built in the 1920s to a design inspired by the grand palaces of Italy, this 2,000-seat theatre hosts major musicals and large concerts.
The Old Fitzroy Hotel
129 Dowling Street
Woolloomooloo
Tel: 9294 4296
Atmospheric pub with a tradition of showing the latest new talent.
Stables Theatre
10 Nimrod Street, Kings Cross
Tel: 9361 3817
Home to the Griffin Theatre Company, which performs new Australian works in this very challenging small venue.
State Theatre
49 Market Street, City
Tel: 9373 6861
A 2,000-seat theatre built in 1929 in Cinema Baroque style. Hosts the Sydney Film Festival and a variety of other events.
Sydney Theatre Company
The Wharf Theatre, Pier 4, Hickson Road, Millers Point
Tel: 9250 1777
Sydney's main company performs Australian, foreign and classic works. It is housed in the magnificent Wharf complex in Walsh Bay and also performs at the Sydney Theatre opposite, and at the Opera House. Each year it takes the Wharf Revue, its serv-

BUYING TICKETS

Performance venues often sell tickets through ticket agencies such as Ticketek and Ticketmaster, and in the ACT through Canberra Ticketing. Names and numbers of venues are published in all listings of what's on.

Some companies also sell unsold tickets cheaply a half-hour before the performance starts, direct from the venue.
Ticketek 195 Elizabeth Street, inside Myer Sydney department store (corner of George and Market streets), Theatre Royal, MLC Centre, 106 King Street, and other outlets in Sydney. Outside Sydney there are agencies in Albury, Bathurst, Goulburn, Lismore, Newcastle, Nowra, Orange, Wagga Wagga and Wollongong.
Tel: 13 28 49
www.ticketek.com.au
Ticketmaster
Shop 2C Channel 7 Complex
52 Martin Place
Sydney
Tel: 13 61 00
Other locations in Sydney as well as Albury, Cessnock, Gosford, Lismore, Lithgow, Newcastle, Penrith and Port Macquarie.
www.ticketmaster.com.au
Canberra Ticketing
Civic Square,
London Circuit
Canberra
Tel: 6275 2700 or 1800-802 025 (if calling from elsewhere in Australia).

ing of satire, on the road to regional centres around NSW.
Sydney Theatre
22 Hickson Road, Walsh Bay
Tel: 9250 1999
Theatre Royal
MLC Centre, 108 King Street, City
Tel: 13 28 49
Host to large-scale musicals.

Canberra

Canberra Theatre Centre
Civic Square
Tel: 6275 2700 (box office)
The hub of the performing arts in the national capital.
The Street Theatre
Corner of Childers Street and University Avenue. Tel: 6247 1519
Stages experimental works as well as more traditional pantomimes and musicals.

Arts Centres around NSW and Canberra

Many towns around the state have a major venue where large-scale concerts, dance and other performances are held, as well as those of touring companies from Sydney and interstate.
Albury Performing Arts Centre
Swift Street, Albury

Tel: 6051 3051
Bathurst Memorial Entertainment Centre
105 William Street, Bathurst
Tel: 6333 6161
Dubbo Civic Theatre
Tel: 6684 8599
Laycock Street Theatre
Laycock Street, Gosford
Tel: 4323 3233
Griffith Regional Theatre
Neville Place, Griffith
Tel: 6961 8388
Newcastle Civic Theatre
375 Hunter Street
Tel: 4929 1977
Hosts plays, musicals, dance and comedy events in a 1920s theatre.
Newcastle Entertainment Centre
Brown Road, Broadmeadow
Tel: 4921 2121
The largest entertainment venue in Australia's sixth-largest city.
Orange Civic Theatre
Byng Street. Tel: 6393 8112
Tamworth Regional Entertainment Centre, Greg Norman Drive
Tel: 6762 5971
Wagga Wagga Civic Theatre
Burns Way. Tel: 6926 9688
Win Sports and Entertainment Centre

Corner of Crown and Harbour streets, Wollongong
Tel: 4220 2828
Illawarra Performing Arts Centre
32 Burelli Street, Wollongong
Tel: 4226 3366

Dance

The **Australian Ballet**, the main classical dance company, has two seasons each year in Sydney's Opera Theatre, performing both old classical favourites and new works. The company also caters to the appetites of dance-lovers in the national capital by including the Canberra Theatre Centre in its annual regional tour.

The **Sydney Dance Company**, based at the Wharf, is the state's main contemporary dance company.

The **Bangarra Dance Theatre** is a mostly Aboriginal company drawing both on traditional indigenous and contemporary.

All three dance companies have at least one regional tour each year performing in centres such as Newcastle, Wollongong and Albury – and in Bangarra's case the tour includes locations such as Griffith, Lismore and Wagga Wagga.

Sydney
Australian Ballet
Sydney Opera House
Tel: 9250 7777 (box office)
National ballet company with two seasons at the Opera House:
Mar–Apr and Nov–Dec.
Bangarra Dance Theatre
The Wharf Theatre, Pier 4, Hickson Road, Millers Point
Tel: 9251 5333
Combines Aboriginal, Western and other dance traditions.
Sydney Dance Company
The Wharf Theatre (as above)
Tel: 9211 4811
Performs at the Wharf and the Opera Theatre.

Gambling

New South Wales has only one legal venue for gambling: the Star

City Casino. Located near Darling Harbour in Sydney, it offers acres of gambling tables set within massive gaming rooms. There are also shops, cafés, bars, live shows and a 352-room hotel. In Canberra the place to indulge in blackjack or roulette is the richly-refurbished Casino Canberra near the National Convention Centre.
Star City Casino
355 Bulwara Road, Ultimo, Sydney; tel: 9777 9000 or 1800-700 700 (toll-free).
Casino Canberra
21 Binara Street, Canberra; tel: 6257 7074

NIGHTLIFE

Bars

Sydney
Bambini Wine Room
185 Elizabeth Street
Tel: 9283 7098
Expect elegance and intimacy and a stellar wine list from this tiny bar opposite Hyde Park.
Bondi Icebergs
1 Knotts Avenue, South Bondi
Tel: 9130 3120
Enjoy a beer while soaking up one of the best views in Sydney. Live music Fri–Sun nights.
Blu Horizons Bar
Shangri-La Hotel, 176 Cumberland Street, The Rocks
Tel: 9250 6013
The classy atmosphere and sensational harbour views here lend themselves to enjoying a glass or two of native Australian wine.
Opera Bar
Sydney Opera House
Lower Concourse Level
Tel: 9247 1666
Enjoy the buzz of Sydneysiders of all ages getting together for a drink at this funky bar with fabulous views of the Harbour Bridge. Regular live music.
Orbit
Level 47, Australia Square
264 George Street
Tel: 9247 9777

Once Sydney's tallest building, its revolving floor makes this a popular place to have a drink and watch the city go by.
Slip Inn
111 Sussex Street, City
Tel: 8295 9999
This complex of five bars, a restaurant and a nightclub is popular with Sydney's young city types.
The Soho Lounge
171 Victoria Street, Kings Cross
Tel: 9358 6511
The young and fashionable of Kings Cross cram into this lounge bar in the Piccadilly Hotel.

Byron Bay
The Balcony Restaurant and Bar
7/3 Lawson Street
Tel: 6680 9666
Dine on cocktails at this upstairs corner restaurant and bar with an L shaped balcony.
La La Land
6 Lawson Street
Tel: 6680 7070
Plush lounges and mood lighting create a cosy atmosphere.

Canberra
Antigo Café and Bar
131 London Circuit
Tel: 6249 8080
A funky little bar that is a popular spot for a tipple for people coming and going from the Canberra Theatre.
ANU Bar
Australian National University, Acton
Tel: 6125 3660
Hobnob with university students at this bar that often has gigs by touring Australian bands.
Benchmark Wine Bar
65 Northbourne Avenue
Tel: 6262 6522
Join public servants and businesspeople at this wine bar with 100 labels available by the glass.
Hippo Lounge Bar
17 Garema Place
Tel: 6257 9090
This bar above Garema Place cultivates a laid-back yet sophisticated air. Live jazz Wed, DJs and eclectic

TRANSPORT

ACCOMMODATION

ACTIVITIES

A – Z

sounds on Thur, Fri and Sat.

The Julep Lounge
8 Franklin Street, Manuka
Tel: 6239 5060
Named after a cocktail from the 1700s, this Canberra hideaway does both classic and contemporary well.

Newcastle

Silo Lounge Bar
18/1 Honeysuckle Drive
Tel: 4926 2828
One of the stylish bars contained in the Honeysuckle precinct.

Terminal One
Harbour Square
1 Honeysuckle Drive
Newcastle
Tel: 4927 1722
A great place to sip cocktails and take in the harbour views to Nobbys Headland.

Wollongong

Five Islands Brewing Company
Corner of Crown and Harbour streets
Tel: 4220 2854
Sip freshly-brewed beer on the terrace near the beach.

Novotel Northbeach
2-14 Cliff Road
Tel: 4224 3111
Set on the hill in North Wollongong, this hotel has several bars overlooking the beach.

Traditional Pubs

Sydney

Customs House Bar
Sydney Renaissance Hotel,
Macquarie Place, City
Tel: 9259 7316
Drinking spot for office workers.

Hero of Waterloo
81 Lower Fort, Millers Point
Tel: 9252 4553
Historic ambience in what is reputedly the oldest pub in Sydney.

Hotel Bondi
178 Campbell Parade, Bondi
Tel: 9130 3271
This is the real Bondi – loud, friendly, sun-and-sea-soaked.

Lord Nelson Brewery Hotel
19 Kent Street, The Rocks
Tel: 9251 4044
Charming historic atmosphere.

Royal Hotel
Five Ways, Paddington
Tel: 9331 2604
Ornate Victorian architecture and great food.

Canberra

The Phoenix
21 East Row, Civic
Tel: 6247 1606
A Canberra mainstay known for its Guinness.

Wig and Pen Tavern and Brewery
Canberra House Arcade
Alinga Street
Tel: 6248 0171
An old English-style pub in the heart of the city which has its own brewery on the premises.

Gay Bars

Sydney

Beauchamp Hotel
267 Oxford Street, Darlinghurst
Tel: 9331 2575
For mature gays.

Colombian Hotel
117–123 Oxford Street
Tel: 9360 2151
This bar's prime position makes it the perfect place to watch Oxford Street's passing parade.

Lizard Lounge
Exchange Hotel, 34 Oxford Street, Darlinghurst
Tel: 9331 6245
Popular lesbian bar.

Midnight Shift
85 Oxford Street, Darlinghurst
Tel: 9360 4463
Quirky and extravagant nightclub.

Newtown Hotel
174 King Street, Newtown
Tel: 9557 1329
Dim, smoky interior, noted for kitschy drag shows with camp humour.

Stonewall Hotel
175 Oxford Street, Darlinghurst
Tel: 9360 1963
Sweaty atmosphere and ultra-modern décor hidden inside an old-fashioned, colonial building.

Canberra

Cube Nightclub
33 Petrie Plaza, Civic
Tel: 6257 1110
Canberra's gay and lesbian nightclub does karaoke on Thur, drag shows on Fri and theme nights on Saturdays.

Live Music Venues

Sydney

Annandale Hotel
17 Parramatta Road, Annandale
Tel: 9550 1078
The place for indie and rock fans.

The Basement
29 Reiby Place, Circular Quay
Tel: 9251 2797
One of Sydney's best jazz venues. Mostly international acts, but also local bands.

Excelsior Hotel
64 Foveaux Street, Surry Hills
Tel: (freecall) 1800-000 549
A venue for R&B and indie rock enthusiasts.

Hopetoun Hotel
416 Bourke Street, Surry Hills
Tel: 9361 5257
Rock, hard blues and ska.

The Metro
624 George Street, City
Tel: 9287 2000
International and local acts at the city's main rock venue.

The Vanguard
42 King Street, Newtown
Tel: 9557 7992
An intimate venue which draws big name jazz, blues and contemporary music acts.

Sandringham Hotel
387 King Street, Newtown
Tel: 9557 1254
Spacious venue with live music most nights of the week.

Selina's
Coogee Bay Hotel, corner Coogee Bay Road & and Arden Street, Coogee
Tel: 9665 0000
Well-known suburban rock venue on the Coogee beachfront.

Woollahra Hotel
corner Queen and Moncur streets, Woollahra
Tel: 9363 2782

Presents contemporary jazz on Sunday evenings.

Byron Bay

Beach Hotel
Jonson Street
Tel: 6685 6402
This open-air bar opposite the beach throngs with crowds enjoying live rock and DJs in the evenings, and has a relaxed atmosphere during the day.

Buddha Bar and Restaurant
Skinners Shoot Road
Tel: 6685 5833
A more eclectic alternative to the pubs in the centre of town. DJs, latino music, electronica, world music and acoustic can be found here.

Hotel Great Northern
Jonson Street
Tel: 6685 6454
This grand Australian hotel draws national and international touring bands to its Backroom.

Railway Friendly Bar
Jonson Street
Tel: 6685 7662
Another of Byron's live music stalwarts.

Canberra

Tilley's Devine Café Gallery
Unit 8, 54 Brigalow Street, Lyneham
Tel: 6247 9712
A focal point for live music and the arts in Canberra.

Newcastle

The Cambridge
789 Hunter Street
Tel: 4962 2459
Australian bands on tour find their way to this pub in Newcastle West.

The Delaney
134 Darby Street
Tel: 4929 1627
The live music options at the Del range from acoustic to rock, with gigs on Wed–Sun.

Queens Wharf Brewery Hotel
150 Wharf Road
Tel: 4929 6333
Beers are brewed on the premises, and there is live entertainment from DJs to cover

bands and original acts Wed–Sun.

Wollongong

Heritage Hotel
240 Princes Highway, Bulli
Tel: 4284 5884
The place to go in the Illawarra to see blues, roots and jazz.

Oxford Tavern
47 Crown Street
Tel: 4228 3892
The Gong's longest-running live music venue has bands Wed–Sun.

Cinema

Australia's mainstream cinemas are Hoyts (www.hoyts.com.au), Greater Union/Birch Carroll and Coyle (www.greaterunion.com.au) and Reading Cinemas (www.readingcinemas.com.au). This is where you'll find all the big blockbuster movies and latest releases. Check the daily papers for cinema listings, and the weekend papers for the best film reviews.

To see an arthouse or foreign-language film some of the best bets are the **Palace** (www.palace.net.au) or **Dendy** cinemas (www.dendy.com.au) in Sydney, **Byron Cinemas** or **Pighouse Flicks** in Byron Bay, the **Belgrave Twin** in Armidale and **Showcase** Cinema in Newcastle, and the **Electric Shadows Cinema** in Canberra (set to open a new nine-screen complex with Dendy in late 2006 in the Section 84 development on Bunda Street).

Belgrave Twin
137 Dumaresq Street, Armidale. Tel: 6773 3833
www.belgravecinema.com.au

Byron Cinemas
108 Jonson Street, Byron Bay. Tel: 6680 8555
www.byroncinemas.com

Dendy Cinemas
261–263 King Street, Newtown, Sydney. Tel: 9550 5699
www.dendy.com.au
Varied cinema programmes, just to the left of mainstream. Also at

Circular Quay.

The Edge Cinema
225–237 Great Western Hwy, Katoomba. Tel: 4782 8900
www.edgecinema.com.au
Shows the Blue Mountains wilderness and latest feature films on a six-storey high screen.

Electric Shadows Cinema
Akuna Street, Canberra (new location from late 2006 Section 84 on Bunda Street, Canberra)
Tel: 6247 5060
An arthouse institution.
www.electricshadows.com.au

Greater Union/ Birch Carroll and Coyle
505 George Street, Sydney City
Tel: 9273 7431
www.greaterunion.com.au
Multi-cinema mainstream. Also at other locations, including Coffs Harbour, Lismore, Newcastle, Tuggerah and Wollongong.

Hoyts
The Entertainment Quarter, Bent Street, Moore Park, Sydney
Tel: 9332 1300
Broadway Shopping Centre, Broadway, Sydney
Tel: 9211 1911
www.hoyts.com.au
Multi-cinema mainstream. Also at other locations in Sydney and beyond, including the central coast and Charlestown.

IMAX Theatre
Southern Promenade, Darling Harbour, Sydney. Tel: 9281 3300
Mega-movies on a giant screen.

Metro Cinema
144 Piper Street, Bathurst
Tel: 6331 8000
www.metrocinemas.com.au

Palace Academy Twin
3a Oxford Street, Paddington, Sydney. Tel: 9361 4453
Long-established non-mainstream release cinema.

Palace Verona
17 Oxford Street, Paddington, Sydney. Tel: 9360 6099
Part arthouse, part-Hollywood showing "cross-over" product.

Pighouse Flicks
Skinners Shoot Road, Byron Bay. Tel: 6685 5828

Reading Cinema
Market City Shopping Centre

Level 3/9–13 Hay Street
Haymarket, Sydney.
Tel: 9280 1202
www.readingcinemas.com.au
Multi-cinema mainstream plus
some foreign films. Also in
Dubbo and Maitland.
Showcase Cinemas
31 Wolfe Street,
Newcastle. Tel: 4929 5019

Comedy

Sydney has several dedicated
comedy venues as well as pubs
where stand-up comedians enter-
tain the punters on a particular
night of the week. Outside the
Sydney metropolitan area the
town's main entertainment
venue is usually the place to
check for comedians on tour.

Fringe Bar
106 Oxford Street (corner
Hopewell Street), Paddington,
Sydney
Tel: 9360 3554
Monday is comedy night at this
inner-city bar.
Laugh Garage Comedy Club
Corner Church and Phillip
streets, Parramatta, Sydney
Tel: 8883 1111
The main comedy venue in
Parramatta.
The Old Manly Boatshed
40 The Corso, Manly, Sydney
Tel: 9977 4443
Monday-night comedy and dinner.
Sydney Comedy Store
Bent Street, Moore Park, Sydney
Tel: 9357 1419
www.comedystore.com.au
Australia's best-known acts and
international names as well as
open-mic nights.

Kids' Entertainment

Sydney

There are many ways to keep
even the most demanding
children happy while holidaying.
Conveniently, two of Sydney's
leading attractions are located in
Darling Harbour: the **Monorail**
(kids love it) and **Tumbalong**

Park, with a free playground and
a stage for free concerts.
The "Search and Discover"
section on the second floor of the
Australian Museum lets children
get their hands on all sorts of
exciting exhibits that most museums would keep out of bounds.
The **Powerhouse Museum** has
stimulating Kids Interactive Discovery Spaces (KIDS), designed
to involve younger children in
hands-on activities related to the
themes in the museum's exhibitions. They explore subjects such
as music, machines, life in the
home, film and television.
The **Opera House** runs children's events such as the Babies
Proms, which allows toddlers to
get close to the musical instru-
ments (tel: 9250 7111). The **Art
Gallery of New South Wales**
holds special family events on
Sundays, such as renditions of
Aboriginal Dreamtime stories (tel:
9225 1700).

Around NSW

Close to the Blue Mountains,
Jenolan Caves (tel: 6359 3911)
makes a wonderful introduction
to the amazing world of stalag-
mites and stalactites. The Lucas,
Chifley and Imperial are three of
the show caves, with the Imperial
cave the easiest to negotiate,
taking just one hour for a tour.
Jamberoo Recreation Park
(tel: 6359 3911) near Kiama
thrills kids with its combination of
waterslides, wave pools, chair-
lifts and toboggan rides. Open
September to April.
**Timbertown Heritage Theme
Park** (Oxley Highway, Wauchope;
tel: 6586 1940) is a re-creation
of an 1800s village complete
with heritage steam train,
sawmill and blacksmith while the
Pet Porpoise Pool in Coffs Harbour (Orlando Street; tel: 6652
2164) gives kids the chance to
see dolphins and seals close-up.
In central New South Wales
pay a visit to the **Western Plains
Zoo** (Obley Road, off the Newell
Highway; tel: 6882 5888) and
the old gaol in the Dubbo area.

Canberra

Two major attractions with appeal
to kids are the **National Zoo and
Aquarium** (tel: 6287 8400) and
the **National Museum of
Australia** (tel: 6208 5000), with
its KSpace FutureWorld gallery.
Kids also love the **Questacon
(National Science and Technology Centre)** (tel: 6270 2800).

SHOPPING

What to Buy

Aboriginal Art

Aboriginal artists sell their work
in art centres, specialist galleries
and craft retailers and through
agents. Each traditional artist
owns the rights to his or her particular stories, motifs and
tokens. Indigenous fabric
designs by artists such as Jimmy
Pike are eagerly sought. Bark
paintings are the most common
form of Koori (Aboriginal) art, but
look out for contemporary works
on board, boomerangs and
didgeridoos.

Antiques

Sydney's Paddington and Woollahra district is full of antique
shops. Worthy pieces to seek out
include clocks, jewellery, porce-
lain, silverware, glassware,
books and maps. Start your
search in Queen Street, off
Oxford Street.

Clothing

Australian merino sheep produce
fine fleece ideally suited for spinning. All sorts of knitwear, from
vivid children's clothing to Jum-
buk brand greasy wool sweaters
(which retain the sheep's natural
water resistance), are available
throughout the city.

Food and Drink

Local delicacies include macadamia nuts, bush honey, royal jelly,
chocolates and the inevitable
Vegemite, a savoury spread.

CONSUMER RIGHTS

If you have a complaint or query concerning shopping, contact the NSW Department of Fair Trading (tel: 13 32 20) to find out what your rights are. If the goods purchased are defective in any way, customers are entitled to a full refund, but be prepared to accept a credit note or exchange.

Larger stores generally offer greater consumer protection. Ask to speak to a manager or customer service officer if you are unhappy with the service.

Australian wines can be bought at any pub or bottle shop, with fair quality wines starting at A$10 a bottle.

Gemstones

Australia is the source of about 95 per cent of the world's opals. Sapphires are also mined, and creative Australian jewellery designers work wonders with them. The jewellery shops in Sydney's central shopping district, particularly in Pitt and Castlereagh streets and around The Rocks, are good places to buy.

Where to Shop

The city of Sydney is the retail heartland, with all the major retail chains represented. The neighbouring Rocks and Darling Harbour precincts provide a good range of shops offering products with an Australian theme. The inner-city "villages" of Paddington, Newtown, Surry Hills, Glebe, Balmain and Double Bay are great spots to do some browsing for a more eclectic, unusual range of products.

In Canberra check the shops around Garema Place in the city for souvenirs, and Kingston and Fyshwick for antiques.

Further afield there are plenty of browsing opportunities in the Southern Highlands and the Blue Mountains for antiques, arts and crafts or books. Byron Bay is good for handicrafts and artworks.

Australiana

Sydney
Australian Wine Centre
Shop 3, 1 Alfred Street, Circular Quay. Tel: 9247 2755
A great gift can be made of Australia's excellent-quality, reasonably priced wine.
Australian Geographic Shop
Shop C15A Centrepoint, Market Street, Sydney City
Tel: 9231 5055
(also at Shop DF18, Canberra Centre, Bunda Street, Canberra. Tel: 6257 3035)
www.australiangeographic.com.au
Many excellent Australian products to do with the great outdoors. Also in Erina, Tuggerah, Charlestown and Coffs Harbour.
Flame Opals
119 George Street, The Rocks
Tel: 9247 3446
One of Sydney's many opal jewellers.
Gavala Aboriginal Cultural Centre
Shop 32, Harbourside, Darling Harbour. Tel: 9212 7232
Aboriginal art and crafts.
Done Art and Design
123–125 George Street, The Rocks, Sydney
Tel: 9251 6099 (and other stores)
Popular Australian artist Ken Done makes his work up into a wide range of fashion items.
Ken Duncan Gallery
Shop 14, Hunter Valley Gardens Village, Broke Road, Pokolbin
Tel: 4998 6711
The place to find books and prints by well-known Australian landscape photographer Ken Duncan.

Canberra
Aboriginal Dreamings Gallery
19 O'Hanlon Place, Gold Creek Village, Nicholls. Tel: 6230 2922
Australian Choice
Shop DG33, Canberra Civic Centre. Tel: 6257 5315

Australian clothes, boomerangs and the usual souvenirs.
R.M. Williams
7 Garema Court, City Walk
Tel: 6257 6668
www.rmwilliams.com.au
Suppliers of bush gear including riding boots, Akubras and oilskin bushman's coats. Also in other locations.
Vangeli
Ground Floor, Bank House
Shop 2, Woden Town Square
Tel: 6282 9235
Manufacturing jeweller specialising in Australian opals, Argyle diamonds and South Sea pearls.

Around NSW
The Opal Cave
51 Morilla Street, Lightning Ridge. Tel: 6829 0333
One of the opal retailers in Lightning Ridge, home to Australia's black opal.
Vintage Hunter Wine and Visitors Centre
455 Wine Country Drive, Pokolbin Hunter Valley. Tel: 4990 0900
Pick up visitors' guides and maps of the area's vineyards so you can try and buy some of Australia's best wines at their source.
DeJon Sapphire Centre
Glen Innes Highway, Elsmore. Tel: 6723 2222
A place where you can learn about sapphires and buy some quality specimens.
Mudgee Honey Haven
Hill End Road, Mudgee
Tel: 6372 4478
Sells a variety of seasonal and creamed honeys, with tasting allowed before purchase.

Australian Designers

Many of Australia's best-known fashion designers make their base in Sydney's Paddington and Woollahra, so visitors wanting to pick up some Australian or international designer wear should do their shopping before they leave the capital.
Akira Isogawa
12a Queen Street, Woollahra, Sydney.
Tel: 9361 5221

Bettina Liano
440 Oxford Street
Paddington, Sydney
Tel: 9380 5771
Carla Zampatti
20 Furneaux Street
Manuka, Canberra
Tel: 6295 6955. Also in the Canberra Centre in the city.
Collette Dinnigan
33 William Street
Paddington, Sydney
Tel: 9360 6691
Lisa Ho
2a–6a Queen Street
Woollahra
Tel: 9360 2345
Maggie Shepherd Studio and Head Office
Unit 2, 151 Newcastle Street
Fyshwick, Canberra
Tel: 6280 8555
Scanlan & Theodore
122 Oxford Street
Paddington, Sydney
Tel: 9380 9388

International Brands

Sydney has a respectable collection of big-name international designer stores. Castlereagh Street is the city's most exclusive retail colony.

Cartier
43 Castlereagh Street, City
Tel: 9235 1322
Chanel
70 Castlereagh Street, City
Tel: 9233 4800
Giorgio Armani
Level 1, 4 Martin Place, City
Tel: 8233 5800
Hermès
Shop C21, Skygarden, 77 Castlereagh Street, City
Tel: 9223 4007
Louis Vuitton
63 Castlereagh Street, City
Tel: 9236 9624
Prada
44 Martin Place, City
Tel: 9231 3929
Tiffany & Co.
28 Castlereagh Street, City
Tel: 9235 1777
Versace
128 Castlereagh Street, City
Tel: 9267 3232

Canberra
Millers of Manuka
18 Franklin Street
Manuka
Tel: 6295 9784
Momento Dezigns
Manuka Court, Bougainville Street, Manuka
Tel: 6295 1146

Books

Australia's major chains of bookshops are **Angus and Robertson** (www.angusrobertson.com.au) and **Dymocks** (www.dymocks.com.au). Another to look out for is the ABC Shops. They have an excellent range of current Australian literature, biographies and travel. The list below includes the major chains, some specialist booksellers, second-hand bookshops and a few independents.

Sydney
Abbey's
131 York Street. Tel: 9264 3111
Arguably Australia's biggest range of crime fiction, plus most other genres.
ABC Shop
Shop 48, Level 1, Queen Victoria Building. Tel: 6247 2941
Also in other locations in Sydney, Canberra, Erina and Newcastle.
Angus & Robertson
Imperial Arcade, 168–174 Pitt Street. Tel: 9253 1188.
Also at many other locations in Sydney, Canberra and NSW.
Ariel
42 Oxford Street, Paddington.
Tel: 9332 4581
Excellent range of cinema, travel, food, design, architecture and current fiction.
Berkelouw Books
19 Oxford Street, Paddington.
Tel: 9360 3200
www.berkelouw.com.au
New books downstairs, antiquarian and rare upstairs, second-hand further up again. First-floor café. Also at Berrima in the Southern Highlands is the Berkelouw Book Barn (Old Hume

Highway, Berrima; tel: 4877 1370), a converted barn that houses about 300,000 second-hand books.
Better Read Than Dead
265 King Street, Newtown
Tel: 9557 8700
Blue Mountains Books
92 Katoomba Street, Katoomba
Tel: 4782 6700
New and pre-loved books on Katoomba's main street.
The Bookshop
207 Oxford Street, Darlinghurst
Tel: 9331 4140
Specialises in gay and lesbian publications.
Borders
77 Castlereagh Street, City
Tel: 9235 2433
The US-giant has several shops in the Sydney metropolitan area as well as one in Tuggerah.
Dymocks
424–426 George Street
Tel: 9235 0155
www.dymocks.com.au
Also at other locations in Sydney and Canberra, Albury, Armidale, Coffs Harbour, Erina, Lismore, Nowra and Wollongong.
Gleebooks
49 Glebe Point Road, Glebe
Tel: 9660 2333
Some 35,000 titles, including academic texts; strong on popular culture and sci-fi. Second shop at No. 191 sells children's and second-hand books.
Horden House
77 Victoria Street, Potts Point
Tel: 9356 4411
Rare books, manuscripts, prints, maps. Specialises in Australiana and Pacificana.
Kinokuniya Bookstore
The Galleries Victoria, Level 2, 500 George Street
Tel: 9262 7996
State Library of NSW Bookshop
Macquarie Street, City
Tel: 9320 1611
Great collection of Australian publications.

Around NSW
Browzers Bookshop
345 Argent Street

Broken Hill
Tel: 8088 7221
Byron Books
Shop 3, 1 Marvel Street
Byron Bay
Tel: 6680 9717
Coffee Table Bookshop
2/3 Railway Parade Kiama
Tel: 4233 1060
Independent bookseller with a
cosy café.
MacLean's Booksellers
69 Beaumont Street
Hamilton, Newcastle
Tel: 4969 2525
An independent bookseller in
busy Beaumont Street.
Percy's Books
175 Keira Street
Wollongong
Tel: 4226 9966
Second-hand bookseller open
until 10pm daily.
Readers Companion
151 Beardy Street
Armidale
Tel: 6771 2544

Canberra
Electric Shadows Bookshop
City Walk, off Akuna Street
Tel: 6248 8352
An independent bookseller
specialising in film/media, art,
photography and Australian and
Aboriginal literature.
Paperchain Bookstore
34 Franklin Street Manuka,
Tel: 6295 6723

Shopping Centres and Arcades

For the largest shopping centres in
New South Wales look for the
Westfield banner (www.westfield.com).
They are usually home to department stores such as Myer and
David Jones, as well as many of
the well-known retail chains and a
food court.
   Stockland shopping centres
(www.stockland.com.au) are the place
to find major supermarkets such
as Woolworths, Coles and Aldi
along with speciality retailers and
banks. Centro shopping centres
have a similar mix on a smaller
scale.

Department Stores

The main department stores in
New South Wales are **Myer** (formerly Grace Bros; www.myer.com)
at Centrepoint (100 Market
Street, City) and **David Jones**.
They offer an extensive range of
goods from food to fashion, hardware to homeware. The David
Jones Elizabeth Street Store in
Sydney has extraordinary flower
displays in spring. Target
(www.target.com.au) and Kmart
(www.kmart.com.au) are variety
stores at the lower end of the
price spectrum.

Markets

While some produce markets are
open throughout the week, other
"community" markets open only
at weekends or on certain days
of the month. Most stallholders
handle cash only, and it can
sometimes be worth bargaining
over the cost of your purchase.
Some of Sydney's permanent
markets are listed. Elsewhere
there are farmers' markets and
community markets in towns
both large and small throughout
New South Wales. These can be
interesting to visit. Ask at the
local visitors' centre for the dates
and times.

Sydney
Fish Markets
Blackwattle Bay, Pyrmont
An amazing choice of seafood,
delis, sushi bars and fresh pro-
duce. Open 7am–4pm daily.
Glebe Markets
Glebe Public School, 193 Glebe
Point Road, Glebe
Community-style market of
around 200 outdoor stalls.
Crafts, jewellery and second-
hand clothes. Open 10am–5pm
Sat.
Paddy's Markets
9 Hay Street, Haymarket
Sydney's oldest market, with
1,000 stalls. Huge range, from
fresh produce to appliances and
clothing. Open 9am–4.30pm
Sat–Sun.

Paddington Bazaar
Uniting Church, corner of Oxford
and Newcombe streets,
Paddington.
Trendy market with works by local
artisans. Open 10am–5pm Sat.
The Rocks Markets
George Street, The Rocks
Hundreds of stalls sell
antiques, paintings, homeware.
Weekend street performances
feature the best of Australian
buskers. Open 10am–5pm
Sat–Sun.

Around NSW
Berry Country Fair Markets
Berry Showground
Alexandra/Victoria streets, Berry
Tel: 4468 1476
Held on the first Sunday of the
month, with stalls featuring craft,
fashion and produce.
Byron Bay Markets
Butler Street Reserve
Arts and crafts market on the
first Sunday of the month
Tel: 6680 9703
Coffs Harbour Jetty Market
Every Sunday, 8am–2pm.
Gipps Street Markets
98 Gipps Street, Wollongong
Tel: 4295 4237
Jewellery, clothing, souvenirs and
gifts, Thursdays and Saturdays.
Honeysuckle Markets
Corner Workshop Way and
Right Lane, Newcastle
Tel: 4927 5330

Canberra
Old Bus Depot Markets
21 Wentworth Avenue, Kingston
Tel: 6239 5306
Contemporary art and crafts,
organic produce, jewellery are
sold from about 200 stalls in this
former bus depot. Open Sun
10am–4pm.
**Gorman House Arts Centre
Markets**
Ainslie Avenue, Braddon
Tel: 6247 3202
A historic 1920s house provides
the backdrop for these weekly
markets selling everything
from leatherwork to locally-
made earrings. Saturdays
10am–4pm.

TRANSPORT
ACCOMMODATION
ACTIVITIES
A – Z

SPORT

Spectator Sports

It's well known that Australians are obsessed with sport. If you are keen to see one of the big football or cricket games, you'd be well advised to ask your travel agent to find out about tickets prior to arrival. The ticket agency, **Ticketek** (tel: 9266 4800), handles ticketing for most of the big spectator games in Sydney.

Venues in Sydney

Sydney Cricket Ground
Moore Park
Tel: 9360 6601/0055 63132 (match information).
Hosts all the major cricket matches and Australian Rules Football.

Aussie Stadium
Moore Park
Tel: 9360 6601
Hosts all major rugby league and union games (bar the finals, which are at Telstra Stadium).

Telstra Stadium
Olympic Park
Tel: 8765 2000
Sydney's largest stadium, hosting all the most important rugby league and union, Australian Rules and soccer matches.

Sydney to Hobart Yacht Race
The ultimate spectator yacht race; sets off from Sydney Harbour on Boxing Day.

Sydney Flying Yacht Squadron
McDougall Street, Milsons Point
Tel: 9955 8350
Departure point for spectators of 18-footer yacht races.

Venues around NSW

Central Coast Stadium
Corner of the Pacific Highway and Dane Drive, Gosford
Tel: 4337 2500
Home to the A-League's Central Coast Mariners.

EnergyAustralia Stadium
Turton Road, Lambton, Newcastle
Home to the Newcastle Knights National Rugby League and New-castle United Jets A-League teams.

WIN Stadium
Corner of Crown and Harbour streets, Wollongong
Tel: 4220 2800
Home to St George Illawarra Rugby League Club.

Venues in Canberra

Canberra Stadium
Battye Street, Bruce
Tel: 6256 6700
Home to the NRL's Canberra Raiders team and the ACT Brumbies Rugby Club.

Horse Racing

Melbourne may play host to Australia's premier horse-racing event, stopping the nation for at least 15 minutes each year on the first Tuesday in November. But New South Wales racetracks also draw a colourful mix of racing enthusiasts and people who just like the opportunity to head out in a hat. The spring and autumn racing seasons are particularly popular, but other events are held throughout the year. Racing NSW (tel: 7551 7500; www.racingnsw.com.au) can supply information on racing throughout the state.

In Sydney the Australian Jockey Club (tel: 9663 8400) races at Royal Randwick and Warwick Farm racecourses while the Sydney Turf Club (tel: 9930 4000) races at Rosehill Gardens and Canterbury Park. In Canberra races are held at Canberra Racecourse (Tel: 6241 3888). The area surrounding Sydney has five provincial clubs: Gosford, Hawkesbury, Illawarra, Newcastle and Wyong; see below for their corresponding racetracks.

Sydney
Canterbury Park Racecourse
King Street, Canterbury
Tel: 9930 4000
Royal Randwick Racecourse
Alison Street, Randwick
Tel: 9663 8400
Rosehill Gardens Racecourse
76 McDougall Street, Milsons Point
Tel: 9955 8350

Warwick Farm Racecourse
Hume Highway, Warwick Farm
Tel: 9602 6199

Around NSW
Broadmeadow Racecourse
(Newcastle), Darling Street, Broadmeadow
Tel: 4961 1573
Gosford Racetrack
Racecourse Road, West Gosford
Tel: 4325 0461
Hawkesbury Racecourse
Racecourse Road, Clarendon
Tel: 4577 2263
Kembla Grange Racecourse
(Illawarra)
Princes Highway, Kembla Grange
Tel: 4261 7211
Wyong Racecourse
Howarth Street, Wyong
Tel: 4352 1083

Participant Sports

Boating and Rafting

Boating enthusiasts will want to spend at least some time out on the water in Sydney Harbour. As well as organised tours there are various places where craft of all types can be hired. **Yachting NSW** (tel: 9660 1266; www.yachtingnsw.com.au) has information.

Most charters in **Sydney** are for a full or half-day rather than overnight. Some of the best places to hire yachts and motorboats in Sydney are Rushcutters Bay, Rose Bay or The Spit at Mosman, north of the Harbour Bridge.

Visitors to **Canberra** will find there are ample opportunities to see the city from a boat on **Lake Burley Griffin**, the lake at the geographic heart of the city.

For a houseboat holiday on the **Hawkesbury River** try Brooklyn near Sydney, with many of the more luxurious houseboats. Often all you have to provide is groceries, fishing and swimming gear. Outside of Sydney **Myall Lakes**, near Port Stephens and Lake Macquarie are favoured destinations for sailors as well as canoeing and kayaking enthusiasts. The **Nymboida River** in the New England area is popular for both canoeing and white-water rafting, a 50-km (31-mile) stretch of river has grade 3, 4 and some grade 5 rapids.

NSW Maritime Authority Centre
Level 6, 207 Kent Street, Sydney
Tel: 9241 6307 or 13 12 56
www.maritime.nsw.gov.au
Open Mon–Fri 8.30am–4.30pm
Lake Burley Griffin Boat Hire
Acton Ferry Terminal
Tel: 6249 6861
Canberra Yacht Club Hire
Coronation Drive,
Yarralumla, Canberra
Tel: 6273 7177
www.canberrayachtclub.com.au

Bush-walking

Two sensational **Sydney** hikes are Bondi to Clovelly Cliff and Spit Bridge to Manly through harbour-side bushland. The Royal National Park in the city's south is the world's second-oldest national park and has a 26-km (16-mile) walk that takes in a variety of terrains from coastal scrub to rainforest.

Outside of Sydney there are more than 600 **National Parks** and reserves, with large tracts of bushland, hiking and camping opportunities and Heritage sites. The **Blue Mountains National Park**, located west of Sydney, has 140 walking tracks, including the **Grand Canyon Track** at Blackheath, which takes you on a strenuous walk to the valley floor and back again. The **Warrumbungle National Park** near Coonabarabran in central NSW is another highlight for walkers, with its dramatic volcanic remnants visible on the Grand High Tops track.

The NSW **National Parks and Wildlife Service** website (www.nationalparks.nsw.gov.au; tel: 1300-361 967 in Australia or 9995 5000) has detailed information on the parks, walks, campgrounds and Aboriginal Heritage sites.

The Department of Lands website (www.lands.nsw.gov.au) has

information on longer walks: The Great North Walk, a 250-km (155-mile) trail from Sydney to Newcastle and Pokolbin in the Hunter Valley; the Hume and Hovell walk from Yass to Albury, a 440-km (270-mile) walk following the route taken by explorers Hamilton Hume and William Hovell for their expedition to Port Phillip in 1824; and the Six Foot Track, a 45-km (28-mile) walk following the original horse track from Katoomba to the Jenolan Caves in 1884.

Centennial Park and Moore Park Trust
Grand Drive, Centennial Park
Tel: 9339 6699
City to Surf Fun Run
Tel: 9282 2747 or 1800 555 514
Lands Map Shop
Ground Floor,
Department of Lands,
1 Prince Albert Road, Sydney
Tel: 9236 7720

Diving

It may be overshadowed by the wonders of the Great Barrier Reef in Queensland, but the New South Wales coastline offers plenty of opportunities, too. In Sydney some of the best diving spots are at Gordons Bay near Coogee and Clovelly. In the Port Stephens area, dive trips centre on sites such as Broughton Island and Cabbage Tree Island as well as various wrecks. Experienced divers can tackle the SS *Satara*, the largest diveable wreck in

Australia, from a base in the Forster-Tuncurry area. Divers head to Byron Bay to visit the Julian Rocks Marine Reserve.

Pro Dive Sydney
478 George Street,
Sydney City. Tel: 9264 6177.
Also in Coogee, Cronulla and Manly.

Outside Sydney
Jervis Bay Sea Sports
47 Owen Street,
Huskisson. Tel: 4441 5012
Pro Dive The Entrance
96 The Entrance Road,
The Entrance, central coast
Tel: 4334 1559
Pro Dive Nelson Bay
D'Albora Marina,
Teramby Road,
Nelson Bay. Tel: 4981 4331

Golf

New South Wales caters well for the holidaying golfer, with 100 courses in Sydney alone. There are many inexpensive, well-equipped and scenic courses as well as golf resorts. Ask at your own golf club before leaving home about reciprocal membership arrangements with **NSW** clubs. The **NSW Golf Association** (tel: 9505 9105; www.nswga.com.au) is a good starting point for golf players from abroad looking for a round. Its website carries contact details of golf clubs listed alphabetically and by district.

The following courses have been recognised for their quality. Some are resorts

and some are private, so whether you get a round or not may depend on reciprocal membership rights.

Sydney
The Australian
Bannerman Crescent, Rosebery
Tel: 9663 2273
Long Reef Golf Course
Anzac Avenue, Collaroy
Tel: 9971 8113
The Lakes
corner of King and Vernon Avenue, Eastlakes
Tel: 9669 1311
Moore Park Golf Club
corner of Cleveland Street and Anzac Parade, Moore Park
Tel: 9663 3877
NSW Golf Course
Henry Head, off Anzac Parade, La Perouse
Tel: 9661 4455
Royal Sydney Golf Club
Kent Road, Rose Bay, Sydney
Tel: 9371 4333

Around NSW
Bonville International Golf Resort and Country Club
North Bonville Road, Bonville (near Coffs Harbour)
Tel: 6653 4002
Cypress Lakes
Corner McDonald and Thompson roads, Pokolbin, Hunter Valley
Tel: 4993 1555
Horizons Golf Resort
Salamander Way, Salamander Bay, Port Stephens
Tel: 4982 0502
Narooma Golf Club
Ballingalla Street, Narooma
Tel: 4476 2522
The Vintage Golf Club
Vintage Drive off McDonald Road, Rothbury, Hunter Valley
Tel: 4998 6789

Canberra
Royal Canberra Golf Club
Westbourne Woods, Yarralumla
Tel: 6281 3882
Yowani Country Club
Northbourne Avenue, Lyneham
Tel: 6241 3377

Skiing
Visitors travelling in Australia's winter may have the opportunity to experience another aspect of its landscape. The major ski resorts in the Snowy Mountains include Thredbo (home to several black diamond ski runs), Perisher Blue and Mount Selwyn (best suited to beginner to intermediate skiers). The ski season starts in June, but the best chance of snow is from mid-July to early September. People used to skiing in Europe or North America may find the long runs in the Australian resorts relatively easy and the harder ones short. Cross-country skiing is a popular alternative to downhill runs. Perisher Blue has more than 100 km (62 miles) of marked trails for cross-country skiing.

Anyone who plans to ski while in New South Wales should begin booking accommodation and equipment if needed, as early as possible. The limited season means the most popular months are booked well in advance.

Cooma Visitor Information Centre
119 Sharp Street, Cooma
Tel: 6450 1742
Perisher Blue Ski Resort
Perisher Valley
Tel: 6459 4495
www.perisherblue.com.au
Selwyn Snowfields
Kings Cross Road
Mount Selwyn
Tel: 6454 9488
www.selwynsnow.com.au
Thredbo Resort Centre
Friday Drive, Thredbo Village
Tel: 6459 4100 or 1300-020 589 (central reservations in Australia) or 6459 4294 (reservations from overseas)
www.thredbo.com.au

Swimming
Swimming is the best way to deal with Australia's summer heat. Many of the major hotels have their own pools, but serious lappers (a *lap* is equivalent to a length outside Australia) might find that these are a bit short for a good

workout. Many of the chlorinated swimming pools have salt water, and some are heated in winter.

A good alternative to chlorine is a swim in one of the sea baths that dot the coastline.
Sydney
Andrew (Boy) Charlton Pool
Mrs Macquarie's Road, Domain, Sydney. Tel: 9358 6686
Coogee Women's Baths
Beach Street, Coogee, Sydney
Cook + Phillip Park
Corner of College and William streets, Sydney. Tel: 9326 0444
North Sydney Olympic Pool
Alfred Street, Milsons Point, Sydney. Tel 9955 2309
Wiley's Baths
Southern end of Coogee Beach
Tel: 9665 2838

Around NSW
Ballina Olympic Pool and Waterslide
River Street, Ballina
Tel: 6686 3771
Coffs Harbour War Memorial
Coff Street, Coffs Harbour
Tel: 6652 1779
Katoomba Sports and Aquatic Centre
Farnells Road, Katoomba
Tel: 4782 1748
Moree Olympic Pool and Spa Baths
Anne Street, Moree
Tel: 6752 7480
Nowra Olympic Pool
Scenic Drive, Nowra
Tel: 4421 2093
Oasis Regional Aquatic Centre
Morgan Street, Wagga Wagga
Tel: 6937 3737
Orange Olympic Pool
Migrant Officer Hill Street, Orange. Tel: 6393 8690

Canberra
Canberra Olympic Pool
Corner of Constitution Avenue and Allara Street.
Tel: 6248 6799

Tennis
Play in the early morning and/or late afternoon to avoid the sun. Ask about equipment hire when ringing to book a court. A good

stop for information is **Tennis NSW** (tel: 9763 7644; www.tennisnsw.com.au). It also has links to a website for tennis clubs in regional and country New South Wales.

EVENTS AND FESTIVALS

Sydney hosts many of Australia's biggest events, and visitors to the city should try to time their stay to coincide with one of the big "party" days on the calendar, such as the magnificent spectacle of the Sydney to Hobart Yacht Race, which leaves from Sydney Harbour on Boxing Day each year, or the annual Mardi Gras. In New South Wales most towns hold an annual jazz festival, many have food festivals and, of course, in the rural areas there are agricultural shows and rodeos.

The following is a rundown of some of the state's events, with some useful contact numbers provided.

Spring (Sep–Nov)

Floriade, mid-Sept to mid-Oct, Canberra. Australia's premier celebration of Spring. Tel: 6205 0666
Wagga Wagga Jazz Festival, Sept.
Royal Botanic Gardens Spring Festival, Sept. Spectacular seasonal displays, complete with brass bands, art shows and food stalls. Tel: 9231 8111
Japanese Cherry Blossom Festival, Sept. Held in Cowra.
Spring Racing Carnival, Sept. Sydney's top racing event, culminating in the Sydney Cup. Tel: 9663 8400
Illawarra Folk Festival, Sept. Tel: 1300-887 034.
Australian Rugby League Grand Final, late Sept. Tel: 9339 8500
Grafton Bridge to Bridge Ski Classic, Oct. A popular water-skiing event.
Hay Rodeo, Oct.
Jacaranda Festival, Oct–Nov, A celebration of the lilac-coloured

blossoms in Grafton. Tel: 6642 3959
Land of the Beardies Festival, Nov. Glen Innes celebrates its Celtic heritage. Tel: 6732 2397

Summer (Dec–Feb)

Cherry Festival, Dec. Young marks its status as cherry capital of Australia.
Carols in The Domain, Dec. Sydney celebrates Christmas with carol-singing. Tel: 9596 8199
Sydney to Hobart Yacht Race, 26 Dec. Thousands watch the start in Sydney Harbour.
Concerts in The Domain, Jan. Free night-time performances by Opera Australia and the Sydney Symphony Orchestra.
The Sydney Festival, Jan. A three-week festival of local and imported music and theatre. Tel: 8248 6500
Australasian Country Music Festival, Jan. A 10-day festival held in Tamworth.
Parkes Elvis Festival, mid-Jan.
Australia Day, 26 Jan. Ceremonies are held all over New South Wales on this holiday.
Gay and Lesbian Mardi Gras, Feb/Mar. A hugely popular parade and street party in Sydney. Tel: 9568 8600
Chinese New Year, mid-Feb festival featuring food, firecrackers, lion and sword dancing. Tel: 9368 7277
National Multicultural Festival, Feb, An annual celebration of Australia's multicultural community takes place in Canberra. Tel: 13 22 81

Autumn (Mar–May)

Golden Slipper Festival, Mar. Popular horse-racing event in Sydney. Tel: 9930 4000
Sydney Royal Easter Show. The country comes to town: woodchopping, cattle contests, sideshows. Tel: 9704 1111
Food of Orange Week, Mar–Apr. A week of dinners, wine tasting and showcasing the produce of Orange.
National Folk Festival, Mar–Apr. Thousands gather for traditional

folk and world music performances, dance and poetry on the Easter weekend in Canberra. Tel: 6249 7755
Archibald, Wynne and Sulman exhibitions, Mar–Apr. Popular art event at the New South Wales Art Gallery. Tel: 9225 1700
St Patrick's Day Parade, mid-Mar. Tel: 9211 3410
St Patrick's Day Races, Mar. Broken Hill parties for four days at this annual race meeting.
Thirroul Seaside and Arts Festival, early Apr. Performing artists, exhibitions and workshops, north of Wollongong. Tel: 4267 4700
Canberra Balloon Fiesta, Apr. An annual spectacle as hot air balloons take to the skies from the lawn of Old Parliament House.
Bluesfest, mid-Apr. An annual international blues and roots festival held in Byron Bay. Tel; 6685 8310; www.bluesfest.com.au
Sydney Writers Festival, late May. Book readings, public lectures and special literary events. Tel: 9252 7729
National Rugby League State of Origin Series, May–June. Annual series between NSW and Queensland. Tel: 9339 8500

Winter (Jun–Aug)

Yulefest, June–Aug. The annual celebration of Christmas northern hemisphere style in the Blue Mountains.
Lismore Lantern Parade, mid-June. A parade featuring giant lanterns, a party and street fair.
Sydney Film Festival, mid-June. About 250 screenings in two weeks, many in the grand old State Theatre. Tel: 9280 0511
NAIDOC Week, early July. Celebrates indigenous culture.
Splendour in the Grass, July. An annual rock music festival draws crowds to Byron Bay.
Biennale of Sydney, mid-July (even-numbered years). International arts festival. Tel: 9368 1411
City to Surf Race, early Aug. Thousands of runners join the race from the City to Bondi. Tel: 9282 2747

AN ALPHABETICAL SUMMARY OF PRACTICAL INFORMATION

A dmission Charges

Several of Sydney's cultural sites are administered by the Historic Houses Trust (tel: 8239 2442; www.hht.net.au). Admission to a few of its properties – The Mint and Government House – is free. Charges for entry to the Museum of Sydney, Elizabeth Bay House, Hyde Park Barracks and Vaucluse House range from A$8–10 for adults and A$4–5 for children.

General admission to the National Maritime Museum, the Art Gallery of New South Wales and the Museum of Contemporary Art in Sydney and the National Gallery of Australia in Canberra is also free, but they all charge for temporary exhibitions. Both the Australian Museum and the Powerhouse

Museum charge $10 for adults and $5 for children.

In Canberra it is free to visit Parliament House but $2 for adults and $1 for children to gain entry to Old Parliament House. The prices for some attractions are relatively high: Questacon, the national science and technology centre in Canberra, charges $15.50 for adults and $9 for children, Sydney Aquarium $27 for adults and $14 for children, the Australian Reptile Park on the central coast is $20 for adults and $10 for children, the Pet Porpoise Pool in Coffs Harbour is $25 for adults and $12.50 for children, and Western Plains Zoo in Dubbo $32 for adults and $17.50 for children. Families can save by opting for family tickets.

B udgeting for Your Trip

Australia has low inflation, and the basics – food, accommodation, admission charges – are still comparatively inexpensive. A plate of noodles or pasta in an average restaurant costs about A$10. A bottle of Australian wine from a liquor store starts at about A$8, a 260ml glass of beer (about ½ pint) costs from A$2.50, and a cup of coffee or tea about the same.

Hiring a small car costs from $50 per day and petrol (gasoline) costs around $1.20 per litre. A half-day coach sightseeing tour is $50–150 per person.

A room at a backpacker hostel can be as little as $20 a night, and a room in a five-star hotel $250 and upwards. Sydney has a

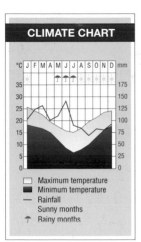

CLIMATE CHART

- ☐ Maximum temperature
- ■ Minimum temperature
- — Rainfall
- ☂ Sunny months
- ☂ Rainy months

full range of accommodation in between *(see pages 265–8)*. There are not significant differences in the cost of travelling to other parts of the state – a meal or a coffee will cost the same in most places – although petrol is more expensive when you leave the city behind.

Business Hours

Banks generally open 9.30am–4pm Monday to Thursday, and 9.30am–5pm on Friday. Some banks also open on Saturday mornings. Currency-exchange facilities at Sydney Airport are open all hours. Most **shops** are open 9am–5.30pm Monday to Friday and to 4pm Saturday. In Sydney and the larger centres shops open all day Sunday as well, although often with slightly shorter hours (generally 10am–4pm). Thursday night is late-night shopping, when some shops stay open until 8 or 9pm. However, visitors will find plenty of late-night shops operating all week in Sydney, including chemists, gift stores and bookshops, particularly around the main tourist centres. Major **supermarkets** will stay open until midnight six days a week in some areas. Canberra has late-night

shopping on Fridays and banks open 9am–4pm on Fridays.

C limate

The varied geography of New South Wales means it has one of the most mixed climates in Australia. Sydney is usually mild and sunny with beautifully warm (though often quite humid) summer days, cooled in the evenings by southerly breezes. The wettest months are March and June *(see chart, left)*.

Visitors during the winter months may encounter snow in the Blue Mountains and further west in areas such as Bathurst, Lithgow and Orange, with temperatures in both winter and summer likely to be considerably cooler than in Sydney. In Bathurst temperatures range from about 13 to 27°C (56 to 82°F) in summer and 1 to 12°C (34 to 53°F) in winter. Canberra is at a relatively high altitude, and can be frosty at night in winter. Days are usually several degrees cooler than those on the coast.

In the Outback the average maximum temperature in summer is 32°C (90°F) and it can reach 45°C (113°F) at the height of summer. In the north Byron Bay rarely dips below 20°C (68°F) in summer and its mild winters see daytime temperatures of 20°C plus in July and August.

Crime & Safety

Common-sense rules apply when visiting New South Wales. Sydney attracts the most visitors, and crimes against tourists have become something of an issue. Most often, these offences are in the order of petty thefts in popular visitor locations. Keep wallets out of sight, do not leave valuables visible in the car or luggage unattended.

Kings Cross has a fairly unsavoury reputation, but unless you get involved in something you shouldn't, the crime there is not likely to affect you directly. In fact,

Kings Cross, with its constant urban buzz, is probably a lot safer than the average suburban street come midnight. It's best to avoid Hyde Park after dark, particularly if you're on your own.

Many city and suburban train stations are either unstaffed or run with a skeleton staff during off-peak periods. Some stations have "night safe" areas on the platforms, with security cameras and an intercom for contacting staff, and trains have a blue light on one of the front carriages, indicating that there is a guard travelling in the carriage. Generally, travel on public transport is safe at any time in the inner-city area. Avoid longer, quieter trips after 10pm.

Canberra is generally a safe place to visit, with statistics showing it is well below the national average in violent crime.

Outside urban areas it still pays to protect yourself and your possessions. Don't leave valuables on the beach when you are having a swim, be wary of accepting drinks from strangers, and exercise caution when using ATMs at night.

The emergency number for police is 000.

Customs

Australia has extremely strict regulations about what can and cannot be brought into the country. Before disembarking from the plane, visitors are asked to fill in an Incoming Passenger Card. Australian customs officers check the information on the cards when passengers disembark, and may initiate a baggage search. There are heavy fines for false or inaccurate claims. It is always best to declare an item if in doubt.

Strict quarantine laws apply in Australia to protect the agricultural industries and native Australian flora and fauna from introduced diseases. Animals, plants and their derivatives must be declared on arrival. All food products, no matter how well processed and packaged, must be declared on arrival.

All weapons are prohibited, unless accompanied by an international permit. This includes guns, ammunition, knives and replica items.

Medicinal products must be declared. These include drugs that are illegal in Australia (narcotics, performance-enhancers, amphetamines); legally prescribed drugs (carry your doctor's prescription with you); non-prescription drugs (painkillers and so on); and vitamins, diet supplements and traditional preparations.

Customs Information Centre tel: 1300-363 263 (in Australia); +61 2-6275 6666 (outside Australia); www.customs.gov.au

Duty-free Allowances

Anyone over the age of 18 is allowed to bring into Australia A$900-worth of goods not including alcohol or tobacco; 2.25 litres (about 4 pints) of alcohol (wine, beer or spirits); 250 cigarettes, or 250 grams of cigars or tobacco products other than cigarettes. Members of the same family who are travelling together may combine their individual duty/tax-free allowances.

D isabled Travellers

New South Wales caters reasonably well for people with disabilities, but you would be wise to start making enquiries and arrangements before leaving home. A good place to begin is with the **National Information Communication Awareness Network (NICAN)**, a national organisation that keeps a database of facilities and services with disabled access, including accommodation and tourist sights. They also keep track of the range of publications on the subject.

A website which has comprehensive information about accessible accommodation, tourist sights and transport in Sydney and New South Wales is www.accessibility.com.au.

Spinal Cord Injuries Australia publishes Access Sydney, which lists a wide variety of places with disabled access, as well as various services.

The **State Library of NSW** offers a good telephone service, where operators deal promptly with queries on topics such as equipment hire and access to medical and other services. You can also make a request via its website.

Spinal Cord Injuries Australia PO Box 397, Matraville, NSW 2036; tel: 9661 8855; www.scia.org.au **NICAN** PO Box 407 Curtain, ACT 2605; tel: 6285 3713 or 1800-806 769; www.nican.com.au **State Library of NSW Disability Service**, tel: 9273 1583; www.sl.nsw.gov.au

E lectricity

The current is 240/250v, 50Hz. Most good hotels have universal outlets for 110v shavers and small appliances. For larger appliances you will need a converter and a flat three-pin adaptor.

Embassies & Consulates

In Sydney

British Consulate General Level 16, 1 Macquarie Place; tel: 9247 7521; www.britaus.net **Canadian Consulate General** Level 5, 111 Harrington Street; tel: 9364 3000; www.canada.org.au **Consulate General of Ireland** Level 30, 400 George Street; tel: 9231 6999 **US Consulate General** MLC Centre, 19–29 Martin Place; tel: 9373 9200; after-hours emergencies, tel: 4422 2201

Embassies in Canberra

Canada Commonwealth Avenue; tel: 6270 4000. **Ireland** 20 Arkana Street, Yarralumla; tel: 6273 3022 **United Kingdom** Commonwealth Avenue, Yarralumla; tel: 6270 6666. **USA** Moonah Place, Yarralumla; tel: 6214 5600.

Overseas Missions

Canada Australian High Commission, Suite 710, 50 O'Connor Street, Ottawa, Ontario K1P 6L2; tel: (613) 236 0841 (plus consulates in Toronto and Vancouver) **Ireland** Australian Embassy, Fitzwilton House, Wilton Terrace, Dublin 2; tel: (01) 664 5300; email: austremb.dublin@dfat.gov.au **United Kingdom** Australian High Commission, Australia House, The Strand, London WC2B 4LA; tel: (020) 7379 4334; www.australia.org.uk **United States** Australian Embassy, 1601 Massachusetts Avenue, Washington DC NW 20036-2273; tel: (202) 797 3000; email: library.washington@dfat.gov.au (plus Consulates in New York, Los Angeles, San Francisco, Miami, Detroit, Atlanta, etc)

Entry Requirements

Visitors to Australia must have a passport valid for the entire period of their stay. All non-Australian citizens also require a visa – except for New Zealand citizens, who are issued with a visa on arrival in Australia.

ETA visas The Electronic Transfer Authority (ETA) enables visitors to obtain a visa on the spot from their travel agent or airline office. The system is in place in over 30 countries, including the US and the UK. ETA visas are generally valid over a 12-month period; single stays must not exceed three months, but return visits within the 12-month period are allowed. ETAS are issued free, or you can purchase one online for A$20 from www.eta.immi.gov.au.

Tourist visas These are available for continuous stays longer than three months, but must be obtained from an Australian visa office, such as an Embassy or Consulate. A$20 fee applies. Those travelling on tourist visas and ETAs are not permitted to work while in Australia. Travellers are asked on their applications to prove they have an adequate source of funding while in Australia (around A$1,000 a month).

Temporary residence Those seeking temporary residence must apply to an Australian visa office, and in many cases must be sponsored by an appropriate organisation or employer. Study visas are available for people who want to undertake registered courses on a full-time basis. Working-holiday visas are available to young people from the UK, Ireland, Japan, the Netherlands, Canada, Malta and Korea who want to work as they travel. **Department of Immigration and Multicultural Affairs**, tel: 13 18 81 or the nearest mission outside Australia; www.immi.gov.au

G ay & Lesbian Visitors

Sydney is awash with facilities and attractions for gay and lesbian travellers, and the old discriminatory attitudes are rarely seen these days. However, random violence towards gays is not unknown, particularly in the area around the gay heartland of Oxford Street. The best way to avoid trouble is to stick to the main streets, and walk with friends at night.

One of Sydney's premier events is the Sydney Gay and Lesbian Mardi Gras, which is accompanied by a major cultural and arts festival, held in February/March each year. The free *Sydney Star Observer* is the city's most popular gay and lesbian paper for news, gossip and what's on; overseas subscriptions can be arranged for forward planning.

To make travel plans outside of Sydney, consult the **International Gay and Lesbian Travel Association**, a professional body for people involved with gay tourism. Visitors can ring to be put in touch with providers of different travel services. A similar organisation within Australia is **GALTA** (Gay and Lesbian Tourism Australia). It will put you in touch with gay and gay-friendly accommodation, shopping and travel agents.

International Gay and Lesbian Travel Association, tel: 9818 6669; www.iglta.com
Gay and Lesbian Tourism Australia, www.galta.com.au
Sydney Gay and Lesbian Mardi Gras, tel: 9568 8600; www.mardi gras.org.au
Sydney Star Observer, tel: 8263 0500; www.ssonet.com.au

Guides & Tours

Tour companies offer a broad choice of excursions, from half-days in Sydney to long-haul journeys into the Outback. In Sydney, harbour cruises range from a general sightseeing tour to specialised visits to historic Fort Denison. There are also local walking tours – around The Rocks, for instance. Many tour operators cater to visitors wanting to indulge their special interests or for those wanting to pick up a new skill, with tours for cyclists, wildlife-lovers, surfers and motorcycle enthusiasts.

H ealth & Medical Care

Australia has excellent medical services. For medical attention

out of working hours, go to the casualty department in one of the large hospitals or, if the matter is less urgent, visit one of the 24-hour medical clinics around the city and suburbs. Look under "Medical Centres" in the Yellow Pages, or ask at your hotel.

No vaccinations are required for entry to Australia. As in most countries, HIV and AIDS is a continuing problem, despite efforts to control its spread. Heterosexual and homosexual visitors alike should wear condoms if engaging in sexual activity.

Emergency medical assistance, tel: 000

Pharmacies

"Chemist shops" are a great place to go for advice on minor ailments such as bites, scratches and stomach trouble. They also stock a wide range of useful products such as sun block, nappies (diapers) and non-prescription drugs.

If you have a prescription from your doctor, and you want to take it to a pharmacist in Australia, you will need to have it endorsed by a local medical practitioner.

Local Health Hazards

The biggest danger for travellers in Australia is the sun. Even on mild, cloudy days it has the potential to burn. Wear a broad-brimmed hat and, if you are planning on being out for a while, a long-sleeved shirt made from a light fabric. Wear SPF 15+ sunblock at all times, even under a hat. Avoid sunbathing between 11am and 3pm.

Care should be taken while swimming at the beach. Rip tides resulting in dangerous conditions are fairly common along New South Wales beaches, but it is not always obvious to those unfamiliar with the coastline. The best advice is to swim only at beaches that are patrolled, and to swim between the yellow and red flags. Never swim at night after a few drinks.

The shark bells do ring from

time to time along the beaches, but it is usually a false alarm. Some of Sydney's harbour beaches have shark nets, so if you are nervous, swim there.

Snakes and Spiders

New South Wales is home to two dangerous spiders, the funnel-web and the redback. Because you will not necessarily be able to identify these creatures, seek medical help for any spider bite. Dangerous snakes are also part of the landscape, but most will not attack unless directly provoked. Avoid trouble by wearing covered shoes when walking in the bush, and checking areas such as rock platforms and rock crevices before making yourself comfortable. Again, seek medical advice for any bite.

Holidays

Banks, post offices, offices and most shops close on the following public holidays:
1 January New Year's Day
26 January Australia Day
March/April Good Friday, Holy Saturday, Easter Monday
March Canberra Day (only observed in Canberra and the ACT)
25 April Anzac Day
June (2nd Mon) Queen's Birthday
August (1st Mon) Bank Holiday
October (1st Mon) Labour Day
25 December Christmas Day
26 December Boxing Day

There are four school holidays a year: mid-December to the end of January, two weeks over Easter, two weeks in July and two weeks at the end of September. It can be difficult to get discounted air fares and accommodation during these peak periods.

I nternet Cafés

It is rarely a problem finding an internet café when you are travelling in New South Wales. In places where there are no internet cafés, check the local public library. Access is generally free, although booking may be

required. For a list of public libraries in NSW see www.nswnet.net.

L eft Luggage

The lockers and left-luggage facilities at Sydney's Central Station have been closed as a result of increased security measures. There is a storeroom at the Sydney Coach Terminal but it closes at 7pm and luggage cannot be left overnight. At Sydney Airport, Smarte Carte Baggage Storage (tel: 9667 0926) offers a left luggage service on arrivals level 1 of T1 International Terminal and there is also a baggage storage area in the domestic terminal. Elsewhere, the best options are generally to ask at the hostel or hotel where you are staying.

Lost Property

You should report loss or theft of valuables to the police immediately, as most insurance policies insist on a police report. The Police Assistance Line is manned 24 hours a day for the reporting of non-urgent crime and incidents; tel: 13 14 44.

Property left on Sydney Buses is kept at the depot from which the bus operates. Property left on harbour ferries is kept at Sydney Ferries offices at Wharf 3, Circular Quay, tel: 9207 3101. For items lost at the airport, call Sydney Airports Lost Property on 9667 9583 or go to level 3 of T1 International Terminal. If left at the domestic terminal, tel: 9352 7450. Property left at Countrylink offices and stations will be held there for seven days and then sent to the Sydney Lost Property Office at Central Station, Lee Street (tel: 9379 3341), which is open from 8.30am to 4.20pm Mon–Fri. Any property left on Cityrail and Countrylink trains is sent there immediately. Once there it costs $4.40 to retrieve an item.

To find out about lost property left on Action buses in the ACT call its enquiries line (tel: 13 17

10 or 6207 7611) or phone 6275 2225 for anything left at Canberra International Airport.

M edia

Publications

Sydney has two daily newspapers, *The Sydney Morning Herald* and the *Daily Telegraph*. The first is a well-respected broadsheet with good national and international coverage and the second is an energetic tabloid, with plenty of local news and gossip, always good for entertainment value. Other regions of New South Wales have their own daily newspapers. In the Wollongong area, south of Sydney, it is the *Illawarra Mercury*, and in the Newcastle area, the *Newcastle Herald*.

The *Canberra Times* is the daily newspaper in the Australian Capital Territory, but many of the capital's public servants choose to read Australia's national paper, *The Australian*. Both *The Australian* and the other national paper, the *Financial Review*, are excellent publications at the serious end of the scale. The weekly *Bulletin* is a long-running magazine with good news analysis and there is also a weekly Australian edition of *Time* magazine.

Foreign newspapers and magazines are available at news agencies in Sydney and other tourist centres, usually within a couple of days of publication.

Radio and Television

The Australian Broadcasting Commission (ABC) runs a national television channel as well as an extensive network of radio stations. ABC Television is broadcast on Channel 2 and offers excellent news and current affairs, as well as local and imported drama, comedy, sports and cultural programmes. The commercial TV stations, Channels 7, 9 and 10, offer news, drama, soaps, infotainment, travel shows and, between them, coverage of all the major international sporting events. Many hotels provide access to a large number of cable television stations.

The radio stations include Triple J-FM (105.7), rock and comment for the twenty-somethings; Classic FM (92.9), continuous classical music; and Radio National AM (576), excellent national news and events coverage. Commercial radio stations include 2UE AM (954), for continuous talkback and unadulterated opinion; and Triple M FM (104.9), for popular local and international rock.

Of particular interest to overseas travellers is Australia's ethnic/multicultural broadcaster, SBS. The organisation's television channel offers many foreign-language films and documentaries, and Australia's best coverage of world news. SBS Radio 2 FM (97.7) and SBS Radio 1 AM (1107) offer programmes in a large variety of languages.

Keep an eye out for the information on local radio stations as you enter towns when you're on the road, as they often have visitor information on the area.

Money

Currency

The local currency is the Australian dollar (abbreviated as A$ or simply $), made up of 100 cents. Coins come in 5, 10, 20 and 50 cent units and 1 and 2 dollar units. Notes come in 5, 10, 20, 50 and 100 dollar units. Single cents still apply to many prices, and in these cases the amount will be rounded down or up to the nearest 5c amount. Carry smaller notes for tipping, taxis and payment in small shops and cafés.

There is no limit to the amount of foreign or Australian currency that you can bring into or out of the country, but cash amounts of more than A$10,000 (or its equivalent) must be declared to customs on arrival and departure.

Banks

The four big banks in Australia are the National, the Commonwealth, Westpac and ANZ. Trading hours are generally 9.30am–4pm Monday to Thursday and 9am–5pm on Friday or 9am–4pm Friday in Canberra. A few of the smaller banks and credit unions open on Saturday mornings. Most banks will have an internal board or a window display advertising exchange rates; if not, ask a teller.

Credit Cards and ATMs

Carrying a recognised credit or debit card such as Visa, Master-Card, American Express or Diners Club, is always a good idea when travelling. A credit card should provide access to EFTPOS (electronic funds transfer at point of sale), which is the easiest and often the cheapest way to exchange money – amounts are automatically debited from the selected account. Many Australian businesses are connected to EFTPOS. Be aware that many service providers such as airlines and petrol stations now charge a surcharge for people choosing to pay by credit card.

There are literally hundreds of Automatic Teller Machines (ATMs) in New South Wales, allowing for easy withdrawal of cash, and again a linked credit card will provide access to both credit and other bank accounts.

Many small businesses are still cash only.

Exchange

Most foreign currencies can be cashed at the airport, with major exchange outlets operating to fit in with flight arrival times. There are many bureaux de change in the city and some in major centres, which generally open 9.30am–5pm, but you'll usually get a better rate at one of the big banks.

Travellers' Cheques

All well-known travellers' cheques can be cashed at airports, banks, hotels and similar establishments, and are as good as cash with many of the larger retail outlets and the shops in major tourist areas. Smaller restaurants and shops may be reluctant to cash cheques, so you should also carry cards or cash.

Banks offer the best exchange rates on cheques in foreign currencies; most banks charge a fee for cashing cheques. Travellers' cheques can also be purchased at one of the large banks.

LOST CHEQUES & CARDS

If you lose your travellers' cheques or want replacement cheques, contact the following:
American Express, tel: 1800-688 022
MasterCard Travellers' Cheques, tel: 1800-120 113 (for international visitors)
Visa, tel: 1800 127 477
If you lose your credit card, call:
American Express, tel: 1300-132 639
Diners Club, tel: 1300-360 060
MasterCard, tel: 1800-120 113 (for international visitors)
Visa, tel: 1800-450 346

P ostal Services

Post offices are generally open from 9am to 5pm Monday to Friday. The General Post Office in Pitt Street in Sydney is open from

TRANSPORT

ACCOMMODATION

ACTIVITIES

A – Z

8.15am–5.30pm, Monday to Friday and 10am–2pm Saturday. The Canberra GPO is at 53–73 Alinga Street.

Domestic Post

Posting a standard letter to anywhere in Australia costs 50 cents. The letter will reach a same-city destination overnight, but may take up to a week if it is being sent to a remote part of the country.

Yellow Express Post bags can be used to send parcels and letters overnight from Sydney to other Australian capital cities or between towns within New South Wales. The cost ranges from $4 to $9.70 and represents very good value for money when compared to courier costs. **Postal enquiries and information**, tel: 13 13 18

Overseas Post

The cost of overseas mail depends on the weight and size of the item. Postcards cost $1.20 by airmail to the UK and the US. Standard overseas mail takes about four to six working days to most destinations.

Express Post International (EPI) will arrive in the UK within four to five working days and is priced according to weight and size. **EPI**, tel: 13 13 18

Faxes

There are many places from which you can fax documents, including hotels, video stores, newsagents, a variety of small businesses, and also post offices, where the rates are very reasonable.

elephones

Local calls in Australia are untimed, and cost 25c from private phones and 50c from public phones. Instead of making expensive calls from hotel rooms, use public phones. Having a phonecard will make this much easier. These are widely available from newsagents and other outlets displaying the Telstra logo. There are four cards ranging in price from $5 to $50.

Most interstate (STD) and international (ISD) calls can be made using phonecards. These calls are timed, and can be expensive, but cheaper rates are available after 6pm and at weekends. Most overseas numbers can be dialled direct without the need for operator assistance.

To find business or residential phone numbers listed in alphabetical order, consult the White Pages telephone directory. It also contains contact numbers for government departments and a complete listing of services in the area. To find commercial phone numbers listed under sub-

TOURIST INFORMATION CENTRES

Armidale
82 Marsh Street
Tel: 1800-627 736
Bathurst
1 Kendall Avenue
Tel: 6332 1444
Blue Mountains Tourism Authority
Echo Point, Katoomba and Great Western Highway, Glenbrook
Tel: 1 800-641 227 (toll-free) or 4739 6266
Broken Hill
Corner Blende and Bromide streets
Tel: 8088 9700
Byron Bay
80 Jonson Street
Tel: 6685 8050
Canberra
330 Northbourne Avenue
Tel: 6205 0044
Coffs Harbour
Corner Pacific Highway and McLean Street
Tel: 6652 1522 or 1300-369 070

Dubbo
Corner Newell Highway and Macquarie Street
Tel: 6801 4450 or 1800-674 443
Forster
2 Little Street
Tel: 6554 8799
Hunter Valley
455 Wine Country Drive, Pokolbin
Tel: 4990 0900
Kiama
Blowhole Point Road
Tel: 4232 3322
Merimbula
1 Beach Street
Tel: 6497 4900
Newcastle
361 Hunter Street
Tel: 4974 2999
Parkes
Corner Newell Highway and Thomas Street
Tel: 6863 8860
Port Macquarie
Corner Gordon and Gore streets
Tel: 6581 8000 or 1300-303 155

Port Stephens
Victoria Parade, Nelson Bay
Tel: 4980 6900
Snowy Region
Kosciuszko Road, Jindabyne
Tel: 6450 5600
Southern Highlands
Hume Highway, Mittagong
Tel: 4871 2888
Sydney
Palm Grove, between Cockle Bay and Tumbalong Park, Darling Harbour
Tel: 9240 8788
Corner Argyle and Playfair streets, The Rocks
Tel: 9240 8788
Tamworth
Corner Peel and Murray streets
Tel: 6767 5300
Wagga Wagga
Tarcutta Street
Tel: 6926 9621
Wollongong
93 Crown Street, Wollongong
Tel: 4227 5545 or (toll-free) 1800-240 737

ject headings you'll need to turn to the Yellow Pages.

Calls made from Sydney to other parts of NSW or from one region to another are charged at STD rates, although it is no longer necessary to dial an area code first. However, you do have to dial an area code to call interstate in Australia. The New South Wales area code is generally 02 (as is Canberra), with a few exceptions. Broken Hill is 08 and Tweed Heads 07. If you are calling from overseas, drop the 0.

1800 numbers are toll-free. Numbers beginning with 13 are charged at a local rate, even if the call is made STD.
Directory enquiries: 1223
Overseas assistance: 1225
Information on costs: 12552
International calls: 0011, followed by the national code of the country you are calling.

Mobile Phones

Most of the large urban areas and major rural centres are covered by a telecoms "net". Smaller towns and remote regions are not covered, which means that mobiles have virtually no use as a safety communications device when travelling in the Outback.

Contact your service provider before leaving home for information on bringing your phone with you. To hire a phone during your stay, look under "Mobile Telephones" in the Yellow Pages, and shop around for the best deal – this is a very competitive market.

Time Zone

New South Wales is generally on Eastern Australian Standard Time (EST), which is 10 hours ahead of Greenwich Mean Time, 15 hours ahead of New York and 18 hours ahead of California. The only differences are Broken Hill (9½ hours ahead of Greenwich Mean Time) and Lord Howe Island (10½ hours ahead of GMT). Daylight saving (one hour forward) operates from the last weekend in October to the last

weekend in March. GMT is something of a notional concept, so, once respective daylight savings are taken into consideration, real time differences with the UK are either 9 hours (late March-late October) or 11 hours.

Tipping

Tipping is not obligatory but a small gratuity for good service is appreciated. It is not customary to tip taxi drivers, hairdressers or porters at airports. Porters have set charges at railway terminals, but not at hotels. Restaurants do not automatically include service charges, but it is customary to tip waiters up to 10 percent of the bill for good service.

Toilets

Australians manage without euphemisms for "toilet". "Dunny" or "Thunder Box" is the Outback slang, but "washroom", "restroom", "Ladies" and "Gents" are all understandable. Public toilets are often locked after certain hours, but you can generally use the facilities in any pub or cinema without making a purchase. Toilets are generally clean, even in the Outback. For those who like to plan their rest stops, the government has produced the Toilet Map, available at www.toiletmap.gov.au, with details of the various public toilets in each of Australia's states.

Tourist Information

Each of the major regions has its own tourist information centre (see panel opposite), and these are always a good first stop when travelling out of town. Most tourist centres open seven days a week. Tourism New South Wales (tel: 13 20 77; www.visitnsw.com.au) can put you in touch with the relevant tourist authorities in Sydney and around the state. For information on Canberra and the Australian Capital Territory contact the

Canberra and Region Visitors' Centre (330 Northbourne Avenue, Dickson; tel: 6205 0044; www.visitcanberra.com.au) or the Australian Capital Tourism Corporation (tel: 1300 554 114).

In the excellent tourist centres/ kiosks dotted around Sydney (see panel opposite), you will find maps, accommodation guides, brochures and well-informed staff to help with all your traveller's queries, including information about composite tickets to many of the attractions.

W eights & Measures

Australia uses the metric system of weights, measures and temperatures.
1 metre = approx 39 ins
1 kilometre (km) = 1,093 yards or approx 0.6 mile
16 km = approx 10 miles
1 kilogram (kg) = approx 2.2 lb
1 litre = 1.75 pints
40 litres = approx 9 imperial gallons or 10 US gallons
20°C = 68°F
30°C = 86°F

What to Wear

Whatever the season, forget an overcoat. A sweater may come in handy, even in summer, when, after a hot day in the sun, the evening breeze off the harbour may feel chilly. A light raincoat will serve in any season, and if you are planning to head to the Blue Mountains or to the NSW central west or Canberra in winter or autumn months you may need a heavy jacket as well as sweaters. Anywhere you go, you'll need comfortable walking shoes.

Most Australians dress casually when not at work – shorts, a short-sleeved shirt or T-shirt and trainers or sandals are fine. Even in Sydney most restaurants have dropped the requirement for men to wear jacket and tie, but some establishments may refuse customers wearing T-shirts, tank tops, thongs (or flip-flops) or ripped jeans.

TRANSPORT

ACCOMMODATION

ACTIVITIES

A – Z

FURTHER READING

Of the making of books about Australia, there is no end. Those mentioned below are mostly of general interest. The majority are still in print, and the rest are likely to be found in Sydney's many second-hand bookshops and markets.

Aboriginal Australia

Archaeology of the Dreaming, J Flood
Dreamings: The Art of Aboriginal Australia, ed. P Sutton
The Whispering in Our Hearts, H Reynolds

Art & Architecture

The Art of Australia, R Hughes
Art in Australia: From Colonialization to Postmodernism, C Allen
Opera House Act One, D Messent
Sydney Architecture, G Jahn
Sydney: A Guide to Recent Architecture, F Morrison

Biography

Fishing in the Styx, by Ruth Park
Greer: Untamed Shrew, C Wallace
Patrick White: A Life, D Marr
Unreliable Memoirs, C James
A Fortunate Life, A.B. Facey
My Life as Me, B Humphries

Fiction

The Bodysurfers, R Drewe
Cliff Hardy series (various titles), P Corris
Eucalyptus, M Bail
For Love Alone, C Stead
Foveaux, K Tennant
A Harp in the South, R Park
Illywhacker, P Carey
Jonah, L Stone

Oscar and Lucinda, P Carey
The Service of the Clouds, Delia Falconer
The Great World, D Malouf
Seven Poor Men of Sydney, C Stead
The Vivisector, P White

Food & Wine

Sydney Eats (Universal Magazines), ed. J Newton & K Boyne
The Penguin Good Australian Wine Guide, H Hooke
The SBS Eating Guide to Sydney, J Savill
The Sydney Morning Herald Good Food Guide, ed. M Evans &

FEEDBACK

We do our best to ensure the information in our books is as accurate and up-to-date as possible. The books are updated on a regular basis, using local contacts, who painstakingly add, amend and correct as required. However, some mistakes and omissions are inevitable and we are ultimately reliant on our readers to put us in the picture.
We would welcome your feedback on any details related to your experiences using the book "on the road", and will acknowledge all contributions. We'll offer an Insight Guide to the best letters received.

Please write to us at:
Insight Guides
PO Box 7910
London SE1 1WE
United Kingdom
Or send e-mail to:
insight@apaguide.co.uk

S Thomsen
Tucker Track – A Curious History of Food in Australia, J Collerson

History

The Fatal Shore, R Hughes
The Future Eaters, T Flannery
The Birth of Sydney, T Flannery
The Great Shame, T Keneally
Manning Clark's History of Australia, M Clark
1788, W Tench

Other Insight Guides

Titles which highlight destinations in this part of the world include:

Insight Guide: Australia, a superbly illustrated guide to all the best that Down Under has to offer.

Insight Guide: Tasmania, a detailed look at the wide ranging attractions of Australia's smallest state.

Insight Guide: Queensland, a comprehensive guide to the sunshine state.

Insight Pocket Guide: Melbourne, a series of itineraries written by a local author guides you to the best of what has been described as the world's most liveable city.

ART & PHOTO CREDITS

All photography by Jerry Dennis except:
Tony Bee/Photolibrary.com 223
Walter Bibikow/Photolibrary.com 90
Paul Blackmore/Tourism New South Wales 203
Torsten Blackwood/AFP/Getty Images 54
David Burton/Alamy 1
Claver Carroll/ Photolibrary.com 163, 199, 219, 219T,
Claver Carroll/ Pictures Colour Library 38, 205
Coo-ee Picture Library 17, 18L, 18R, 19, 20, 21, 23, 26, 27, 183
Trevor Creighton/Tourism New South Wales 160T
David Curl/Anca 46
F W Flood/Coo-ee Picture Library 44
Michael Gebicki 3B, 41, 32, 39R, 41L, 41R, 48, 56/57, 68T, 123, 163T, 208, 211, 222, 241, 242, 252, 253, 254, 254T, 255, 256, 256T, 257, 275
Glyn Genin/APA 9TR, 30, 66, 67, 75, 80T, 94, 95T, 99, 100, 100T, 103, 249
Graeme Gillies/Photolibrary.com 201T
Nick Green/Photolibrary.com 72, 86, 105, 216
George Hall/Photolibrary.com 68
Terry Harris 77
John Van Hasselt/Corbis 53
Phillip Hayson/Photolibrary.com 47, 180
Geoff Higgins/Photolibrary.com 102, 209, 220T, 225, 227, 227T
Mark Higgins/Alamy 10/11
Holli Hollitzer/AFP/Getty Images 78
JTB Photo/Photolibrary.com 91
Catherine Karnow 8T, 33, 44, 87
Warwick Kent/Photolibrary.com 187
Lansdowne Picture Library 22, 198T
Jean-Marc La Roque/Auscape 31
Wayne Lawler/Auscape 188, 189T, 201
Lawrence Lawry/Getty Images 226
Tom LeBas 9C, 205T

James Lemass/Photolibrary.com 95
Charles & Josette Lenars/Corbis 25
D Lundt/Corbis 84
R. Ian Lloyd/Masterfile 206I
Mary Evans Picture Library 97T
Sally Mayman/Tourism New South Wales 204, 284
Grahame McConnell/Photolibrary.com 190, 192, 193, 193T
David McGonigal 131
David Messent/Photolibrary.com 49, 97, 98, 98T, 101T, 220
Graham Monro/Photolibrary.com 89, 96
National Library of Australia 4C
Robbi Newman 266
Orange City Council/Tourism New South Wales 39L
Christine Osborne Pictures/Alamy 196
Doug Perrine/NaturePL 200
Tony Perrottet 36, 40, 42, 70, 246
Photolibrary.com 194, 228, 240
Photo Simons 155
Nick Rains/Tourism New South Wales 159
Riverina Regional Tourism Organisation/Tourism New South Wales 162T
Chris Sattlberger 185
Robin Smith/Photolibrary.com 92T, 93, 210
Laurie Strachan/Alamy 202
Oliver Strewe/Wave Productions 224
Topham Picturepoint 24
Tourism New South Wales 6B, 81, 120T, 183T, 185T, 186, 187T, 189, 190, 198, 202T, 207, 208T
Trip/Australian Photo Library 103T
Grenville Turner/Wildlight/Tourism New South Wales 197
Wagga Art Gallery 162
D. H Webster/Photolibrary.com 28/29
Wildlight/Tom Keating 14, 191
Wildlight/Mark Lang 58/59
Wildlight/Shane Pedersen 190T
Wildlight/Philip Quirk 160/161
WorldFoto/Alamy 206R
Dave Young/Planet Earth 229

PICTURE SPREADS

Pages 106/107: Al Bello/Getty Images 106/107; Hamish Blair/Getty Images 107CL; Jerry Dennis 106BR; Harness Racing NSW 107TR; Nick Laham/ALL-SPORT/Getty Images 106CR; Chris McGrath/Getty Images 106BL; Nick Wilson/ALL-SPORT/Getty Images 107BR
Pages 150/151: Jerry Dennis 150BL, 150BR, 151TR, 151C, 151BL, 151BR; Mark Nolan/Getty Images 150CL; Tourism New South Wales 150/151, 150CR
Pages 214/215: Cephas Picture Library/Alamy 214BL; Grahame McConnell/Photolibrary.com 214/215; Anna Mockford & Nick Bonetti/APA 215TR; Charles O'Rear/Corbis 215CL; Pictures Colour Library 214CR, 215BL, 215BR; Mick Rock/Cephas Picture Library 214BR
Pages 230/231: Paul McConnell/Getty Images 231BL; Chris McGrath/Getty Images 231CR; Photolibrary.com/Claver Carroll 230BL; Wildlight/AAP 230/231, 230CR, 230BR, 231BR
Pages 250/251: Christine Osborne Pictures/Alamy 250CR; Jerry Dennis 250BL, 251TR, 251CR; Photolibrary.com/Claver Carroll 250BR; Wildlight/AAP 251BL; Wildlight/Philip Quirk 250/251

Cartographic Editor: Zoë Goodwin

Map section reproduced with kind permission of UBD, ©Universal Publishers Ltd DG 02/06

Cartography by: Stephen Ramsey, Mike Adams, James Macdonald ©2006 Apa Publications GmbH & Co Verlag KG Singapore Branch

Book Production: Linton Donaldson

GENERAL INDEX